USED ON ROUTE 66 RO
MAY 1ST - MAY 5th
ED KLEIN / BILL CONK

THE EZ66 GUIDE ™
FOR TRAVELERS
3RD EDITION

Written and illustrated by
JERRY McCLANAHAN

Published by

NATIONAL HISTORIC
ROUTE 66 FEDERATION

Cover paintings by Jerry McClanahan.

ISBN 978-0-9709951-9-3

WELCOME TO THE THIRD EDITION

Presenting the THIRD EDITION of the *EZ 66 GUIDE*! What a great trip it has been since 2005, when the first edition first hit the road. Through this humble book I have had the fortune to meet many friendly and fascinating people from around this globe we call Mother Earth…all joined by our abiding interest in the good old Mother Road.

Far from being a dead highway, Route 66 is still growing and changing daily. This edition represents months of work updating, revising and improving. You'll find the same features that have made the *EZ 66 GUIDE* a widely acclaimed success since 2005: detailed, west AND eastbound directions, area and detail maps, attractions, points of interest, Route 66 Icons, classic Mom and Pop motels and eateries, GIANT ALERTS, scavenger hunts, car games, advisories, and so on.

Since opening *McJerry's Route 66 Gallery* in Chandler, Ok, I have been able to meet with hundreds of travelers using the EZ Guide. Their enthusiastic input and advice is incorporated into this new edition. Many readers have reported to me their observations of changes along the road, or made suggestions about great places to stop along the way. Along with their valued input I have added personal research from many recent trips along the highway.

I have made a considerable effort to improve the functioning of the directions and transitions between pages and options. Certain routings, such as in St Louis and Oklahoma City, have been revised to make the tour EZer. However, due to its being chopped to pieces and disguised under many different names, following the true old Route 66 will never be completely simple. This book will make it as EZ as possible. New (by popular request) in Edition Three are more mileage points between turns and towns.

For full enjoyment of the *EZ 66 GUIDE*, please read the following text pages, which outline the "philosophy" of the book and how to use the directions and maps, especially the cautions and safety warnings. Your author and publisher have made an effort to produce the best, most accurate guide we can, but you are responsible for your own safety and well-being while using the *EZ 66 GUIDE*.

A pleasurable aspect of these revisions and updates has been adding newly restored Route 66 Icons, such as Cuba Missouri's Wagon Wheel Motel, or Oklahoma City's Lake Overholser Bridge, along with new museums, attractions and other businesses. It is heartening that so many people are investing new life into the old road. It is YOU fans from all over the world that are keeping Route 66 alive.

On the flip side of the 2-lane, the forces of nature, change and "progress" have removed some former faces and places from along the route. The Mother Road giveth, and it taketh away. So, take YOUR trip soon, and PLEASE go to www.mcjerry66.com to check the FREE UPDATES to the EZ 66 Guide before you leave. Also, do check out how to join the *National Historic Route 66 Federation* on the inside back cover-it's a road-worthy organization. I hope you can stop by my place in Chandler, Ok and visit me on your trip. I enjoy meeting fellow roadies, and will be happy to sign your copy of this book!

SEE YOU ON 66!

CONTENTS

Pages are divided into TEXT pages in the front and back, and STATE pages in the middle of the guide.

FOR FREE UPDATES to the *EZ66 GUIDE For Travelers* go to mcjerry66.com or the link at www.national66.org

AUTHOR'S INTRODUCTION

Route 66 consists of a community of friends, fans and fanatics from virtually every corner of the civilized world. It spans eight states (IL, MO, KS, OK, TX, NM, AZ and CA) and over 2,000 miles. Fueled by nostalgia and fired by preservation-minded folk, Route 66 is a magical cross section of the nation; from the massive skyscrapers of Chicago, over the green hills of the Ozarks, the grassy plains, the awesome deserts and mountains, then down into the fascinating mosaic of the Los Angeles basin. There's something for everyone here - the embodiment of freedom, the legendary emblem of 20th century roadside America.

Born in 1926, US 66 was pieced together from an existing network of promoted trails and unnamed roads, most of which were ornery dirt paths at the time. Despite the inexorable invasion of the interstates, at least 85 percent of old 66, in one guise or another, remains to be easily explored.

The road gained national attention in 1946 with the Bobby Troup song; "Get Your Kicks on Route 66," a timeless tune that captured the heart of the country, then was covered by hundreds of artists over the decades. Also enhancing the road's popularity was the TV series of the 1960s, "Route 66," wherein Todd and Buzz traveled the country in a Corvette, seeking adventure (in reality, almost never on '66).

Change has always been a part of the Mother Road. The late 1920s and 1930s watched "Dirt 66" rapidly transform into a paved, all weather highway by 1938. Dirt roads gave way to narrow, twisty 2-lanes, which in turn were straightened and widened, some becoming 4-lane superhighways before the Interstate Highway System began taking over in the late 1950's. Much of old 66 hung on during the 1960s as the Interstate began to usurp the route's path across the country, digging up old pavement and stranding towns with cruel bypasses.

Finally, 1984 brought the final bypass in Williams, AZ. The next year, Route 66 was decertified. No longer an "official" US Hwy, authorities and commentators expected the old road to fade into history like the Oregon Trail, the Chisolm Trail and so many other once famous byways.

Widely eulogized in the press, Route 66 began a surprising comeback, sparked by volunteers who formed state associations. Before long, positive books and articles were published about '66, and people began traveling the old road, hoping to find what was left of the glory days. Books, videos, merchandise, magazines and films all point to the continuing, grass roots resurgence. Route 66 marked about 59 years as a US Hwy, but over 8 decades as an American icon, and it is still going strong.

As you explore the Mother Road with the EZ66 GUIDE, take the time to stop and visit with the people you'll encounter. They are the greatest resource the highway has to offer, a treasure to be shared with the world.

THE EZ66 GUIDE PHILOSOPHY

I'm known in Route 66 circles for articles covering EVERY abandoned and obliterated fragment and dead end of Route 66, in exacting detail. Fortunately, the EZ66 GUIDE won't subject you to that level of obsession. Instead, you'll find a fun, EZ to follow tour that will take you down Route 66 with as few problems as possible, in a friendly, informal fashion.

To make it EZ for you to follow and enjoy Route 66, the EZ66 Guide includes DETAIL MAPS of most Route 66 towns (or tricky areas), along with larger-area SECTION MAPS.

The TOUR ROUTE given in the DIRECTION BOXES (distilled from the many versions of US 66) was selected to route you on as much vintage, quality 66 as possible without the bother of dead ends, dirt roads or very rough conditions. As always, conditions may change due to road construction, street changes, etc. Be prepared to navigate around any such obstacles.

I have not gone into the history of most towns and areas (for that, see the books listed in the reference section). This is a guide to Route 66 as it is TODAY (with the caveat that it is always changing).

HOW TO FOLLOW THE EZ66 TOUR

The book switches to a horizontal format for the actual TOUR GUIDE section to better showcase the mostly horizontal maps (the spiral binding makes it EZ to flip thru the pages in your car).

Read the boxed WB (westbound) and EB (eastbound) directions to follow the MAIN TOUR ROUTE. The WB and EB directions are on the SAME page, along with DETAIL MAPS where needed. The route is divided by STATE, and each state is broken up into SECTIONS. At the beginning of each state is an INTRO page, and at the start of each section is a SECTION MAP. Each state has its own page number sequence (ex: AZ Page-1 thru AZ page-25).

WESTBOUND drivers (those headed in the direction of the LA area): read thru the book as normal, following the directions in the WB direction boxes at the TOP of each page. Flip BACK to refer to section maps.

EASTBOUND drivers (headed towards Chicago): begin at the BACK of the book (or of the section you are traveling) following the EB direction boxes on the

BOTTOM of each page. Follow the page-number cues (below the EB directions on certain pages) to flip FORWARD to the SECTION MAPS and STATE INTRO (read the latter FIRST when entering a new state).

In the directions and text, I also refer to the compass points (east, north, etc.) when a specific direction of travel is indicated.

The informative TEXT for the towns and attractions on each page is located in between the direction boxes (separated so you don't have to wade thru the text to find your next turn). This text is generally arranged from west to east, reading down. EB drivers, look thru each page's info text to see what is ahead, noting that the lowest items will generally be encountered first (there is an unavoidable WB bias, but I've tried to soften this whenever possible).

Use the frequent DETAIL MAPS to help navigate thru towns and junctions and refer to the SECTION MAPS to get a picture of upcoming towns and turns. It's a good idea to read ahead a section or two for long-range planning, highlighting items of interest. When following the directions, street signs will sometimes be absent. In that case, refer to the detail maps (note: street grids are shown only to indicate the town area, use a local map to navigate off '66). This edition features many more mileage cues between intersections and towns. The mileage figures should be taken as approximate, unless underlined (due to odometer errors and the like). Most points are between the main intersection in town, the last turn, or other features. Others are not so precise, and are included to let you know when you can take your head out of the book and relax awhile.

On the section maps, the mileage between main points is given in a box at the bottom. In addition, interstate highway exit numbers correspond to mileage from the state line, so it's EZ to figure your mileage to towns anywhere along the route (remember that the mileage resets at state lines and on different roads).

"HISTORIC 66" SIGNS: Many of the eight states (and communities) have done a nice job of marking the old alignments with "Historic 66" signs. The problem is that these signs tend to "disappear" (except for those painted on the road) and a few mislead or lead to a section that is NOT a part of the EZ66 TOUR. Since you can't count on having a "Historic 66" sign before every turn, use the signs when they appear to reassure you, but follow the directions in your EZ66 GUIDE.

USING THE MAPS

The BOLDEST lines mark the OFFICIAL TOUR ROUTE, as described in the direction boxes. The NEXT BOLDEST lines are OPTIONS or SIDE TRIPS. Thinner lines are NON-66 roads, while sections of interstates or some divided roads that are NOT a part of the TOUR are shown with thin parallel lines. The width of line does not indicate the width of road. In other words, a narrow 2-lane section of Route 66 will appear BOLDER than a 4-lane NON-66 street.

The scale of the maps is exaggerated/modified to show detail. Some maps have been stretched or condensed to fit the page. The general scale of the section maps is mostly consistent within states (except where noted). The detail map scales vary depending on the area that needed to be shown. You can tell by the comparative size of roads and details. To fit the page efficiently, I have tilted the North-South orientation slightly on many section maps (as noted on the compass rose).

ABOUT THE DIRECTIONS

You'll encounter the following terms in the direction boxes:

• **BL 15, BL 40, etc. equals:** Business Loop. These are loops from one exit to another thru the business district of bypassed towns, usually along 66, but not always. So don't follow them blindly, use the EZ directions to know when to deviate from the business loops.

• **HWY (shown on the maps as circles or ovals):** Used to indicate any designated highway other than US highways or Interstates. Example: HWY 3. Those state highways numbered "66" are referred to as MO 66, KS 66, OK 66 and CA 66.

• **JCT:** Junction or intersection.

• **"Y":** A JCT shaped like a Y where two roads diverge.

• **"T":** A JCT like a T, where one road ends at a crossroad.

• **SLANT, VEER or ANGLE:** Describe variations of turns that are not 90 degrees.

• **BEAR LEFT or RIGHT:** Usually at a "Y" junction.

• **CURVE LEFT or RIGHT:** Used for curved transitions at corners.

• **QUICK LEFT / RIGHT or QUICK EXIT:** Means an "immediate" turn.

• **JOG LEFT or RIGHT:** Used in cases where the route turns off one road, then quickly turns again onto a parallel road (or similar quick change in direction).

• **CONTINUE or STAY AHEAD:** Do not turn off the road you are traveling. Usually used at junctions, intersections, underpasses and exits.

• **MERGE AHEAD:** As above, but indicates you are joining another highway number or street name.

NOTE: No matter how EZ you try to make it, some parts of Route 66 are unavoidably complex (think St Louis, OKC or LA). If you get confused, stop and look over the maps and text again (skimming ahead to study a city beforehand helps a lot).

ABOUT THE TEXT:

• **OPTIONS:** You can have a great trip by sticking ONLY to the MAIN TOUR, but the EZ66 GUIDE also has plenty of alternate OPTIONAL ROUTES to explore.

These are detailed in the text or detail maps, not the direction boxes. In some cases the OPTIONS are more interesting than the tour route, but were handled separately, due to complexity. These OPTIONS are especially recommended in the text. In a few cases, like west of ST Louis or the Santa Fe Loop, the Main Tour Route breaks into TWO OPTIONS. Read the text to choose which you prefer.

• **SIDE TRIP:** These either lead to cool places on sections of Old 66 or are non-66 local attractions. Generally, an OPTION can replace the MAIN TOUR, while a SIDE TRIP is suggested as "in addition to."

• **DIRT 66 OPTIONS:** Early 66 was mostly dirt road (some paved sections have devolved to dirt). I have selected some of those prime "Dirt 66" sections as options (if you don't mind a rock chip or two). AVOID these roads when they are muddy (or if rain threatens). Drive slowly and watch for oncoming vehicles (dust and gravel) and be careful of soft shoulders or ruts. DON'T drive into standing or running water!

• **NON-RECOMMENDED SECTIONS:** Some abandoned or extremely ROUGH (huge potholes, washouts, cross-ditches, broken pavement, etc) sections of old 66 are presented in the text or on the maps (as dashed lines) purely for historic information. These are NOT part of the EZ TOUR. If you decide to drive any of these rough sections, do so AT YOU OWN RISK. DO NOT TRESPASS.

ALERTS SPOTLIGHTING FUN STUFF

• **GIANT ALERTS:** Old 66 is full of larger than life people, animals and things (ignore inflated purple gorillas) such as Illinois' famous Muffler Men triplets.

• **PHOTO OP:** An especially cool or touristy thing to photograph or pose by. Historic 66 signs, state line markers and "Dip in Road" signs are all photo ops!

• **GIFT SHOP ALERTS:** Gift shops are everywhere, of course. But these highlight gift shops that have really cool stuff, or that are especially deserving of business, such as museums. Try to buy from the small guy when possible. You may wish to ship your new-bought treasures home at intervals, to save room!

• **FOLK ART ALERTS:** Interesting roadside assemblages or sculptures.

• **SCAVENGER HUNTS:** To encourage taking your time while driving old 66, try to find the answers to these questions. I tried to pick things that have some permanence (like the plaques on old bridges). The answers will be found on the Federation's web site *www.national66.org* (for FUN only, folks!). CAUTION: you may have to pull off and walk on the roadside to find some answers, so please BE CAREFUL!

• **MUSEUMS AND ATTRACTIONS:** Fun, interesting or historic places in towns along the road. Hours vary with season, holidays, etc. (and space was often limited in the text) so I have included phone numbers or web sites of most of the listed museums or attractions. Call ahead to check on hours of operation and price of admission, if any (some are open during the week, others only one day a week or by appt). There are many more museums along '66 than I could include, and you won't be able to see them all. Do try some of the small town history museums, for the flavor of America, but make sure to visit ALL the museums dedicated to Route 66!

• **CAR GAMES:** To encourage your kids to get their heads out of the video games, scattered thru the book are simple little games requiring observation of features along '66 (don't blame ME for arguments over who won!). Feel free to make up your own rules. Encourage your kids to make a trip scrapbook with photos (let them take some), business cards, postcards, flyers, drawings, notes, and leaves. Perhaps they could "interview" some of the living legends of '66.

• **SPOT OLD 66:** I do point out many sections of abandoned road, but keep your eyes open for more. Lines of old poles or fences, old bridges, swaths of different soil or vegetation, rows of trees, old fences and roads running straight from curves all can be clues to an old alignment of 66. If you want to explore every bit of old 66, check out the fine books in the resources section.

• **ROUTE 66 ETIQUETTE:** PLEASE respect the road and its treasures. Take only photographs, leave only tire tracks. There are plenty of souvenirs to be bought along the route, so please leave those tempting signs along the way for others to see. Don't trash the route, and the ONLY place you should leave your name is in guest books, or on the unofficial "Public Art Corridor" between Essex and Amboy, CA.

Business owners along the route are delighted to have you stop by, and most are friendly and happy to chat. Many have sunk much love and money into their corner of Route 66, so whenever possible, please PATRONIZE those businesses that are preserving the history of the Mother Road. By the way, it is a good idea to ask first before taking very many photos at an active business. It is polite, and most owners are happy to let you snap away (and you might make a new friend!).

• **CAUTIONS:** Your author and publisher have made a conscientious effort to produce an accurate guide, but we cannot be held responsible for any accidents, casualties or incidents resulting while using this book. Don't read this guide while driving. Appoint a navigator, or pull over and read ahead. Obey the speed limit (especially in small towns and school zones). Laws and streets change, so if a traffic sign is in opposition to the directions in this guide, OBEY the SIGN!

This guide is as accurate as possible at the date of publication. Conditions along 66 are in constant flux. Road conditions may change for the worse. Roads may close or be widened, streets may change name or become One-Way, and businesses may close or change management. Look for specific cautions and advisories in the text.

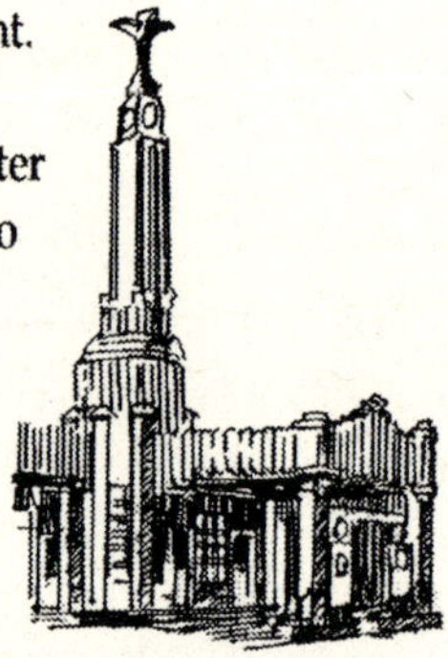

• **URBAN AREAS:** Avoid driving in questionable areas after dark. If a neighborhood gives you a bad feeling, drive on to the next area. Use the freeways as needed to bypass city traffic or neighborhoods. Tune to local radio for traffic bulletins. Hide cameras and other valuables from sight in your vehicle, and don't leave valuables in motel rooms. If a motel's neighborhood bothers you (bars, X-rated book stores, transients), move on.

• **DESERTS AND MOUNTAINS:** Carry some bottled water and a cell phone (AAA or other such membership is helpful). Stay with your car if it breaks down. Slow down on steep grades, and use a lower gear downhill to save on brakes. Don't crowd the centerline on blind curves. Avoid driving thru running water in flash flood-prone areas.

• **ADVISORIES:** Some sections of '66 are a bit rough (especially those with asphalt patches). I note many of them in the text (muscle car owners take note).

• **RV ALERTS:** My experience with RV's is limited to VW Campers, but I have noted in the text some areas on '66 that may prove problematic to big RVs. Much of Old 66 is narrow, so use care.

DON'T let all of the above scare you off Route 66. Its just common sense.

TRIP PREP

It's YOUR trip, so plan it the way you want. Some like to plan everything in advance, some just take off and hope for the best with very little forethought. I recommend taking the middle road. Allow for serendipity but put together a plan to visit the things you want to enjoy (phone numbers or websites are provided for most attractions along the way, please call ahead for hours of operation and fees). Make your motel reservations well in advance, or call ahead from the road a day or two ahead (or even that afternoon if you feel lucky!). It's up to you.

HOW LONG WILL IT TAKE?

Two weeks, one way, is rushing it if you want to see very much of what 66 has to offer. A good idea, if time is short, is to pick a section to explore, then hit another area next time (you WILL be back!). Or, use the guide to plan ahead, and skip and choose what sections you drive (expect your well-made plans to be changed by unexpected enjoyment).

WHEN TO TRAVEL 66

The traditional travel season is April/May thru September (give or take). Too early in the spring risks ice and snow (especially in higher elevations). Spring is also prime time for thunderstorms (keep an ear out for local weather reports). The snow-threat resumes in late fall. Usually the main roads clear quickly, but you may have to wait out a heavy snowfall. Summer is vacation time, but expect heat (and humidity in the east). Winter is the off-season. There's less tourists, but many museums and business have limited (or no) winter hours. You're driving a great distance across a continent, from a northerly region of the Midwest down into the desert southwest, so conditions may range from one extreme to another. Higher elevations bring cooler weather (even in summer).

FOOD AND LODGING

While this is not primarily a guide to dining and lodging, (I recommend the Federation's *Route 66 Dining & Lodging Guide*), I have indicated some places to eat or sleep in towns that are noteworthy. These may be famous road icons or places that I have enjoyed. Since one person cannot stop at every place, I also mention some that trusty sources have recommended. None of this constitutes an endorsement. I haven't been paid by anyone, and omission does not necessarily mean disapproval. Some sections of Route 66 have a wealth of suitable vintage motels, others none. A few have gotten mixed reviews, so in those cases, I do not include a phone, and suggest that you check them out in person. Other motels I mention for their nice signs or history, with no recommendations one way or the other. When in doubt, ask nicely to check out the room FIRST (a proud owner won't refuse). If you must stay at a chain, I've found Super 8 Motels to be quite inexpensive and good, as well as the newer, 3-story Motel 6 properties (like the fine one in Springfield, IL). If you would like to step up a few notches, consider Hampton Inns. They have contibuted to the preservation of the route.

Now that you've prepared for your dream trip along Route 66, what are you waiting for? The road starts on the next page!

ROUTE 66 ACROSS ILLINOIS

CHICAGO, **ILLINOIS** is the **Eastern Terminus** of fabled **Route 66**. Whether you **begin** or **end** your journey of roadside discovery here, the great state of **ILLINOIS** has a bounteous harvest to offer, from the hustle and bustle of downtown Chi-town, to the peace and quiet of an old concrete slab road zigzagging across the prairie. Roadside icons abound along the almost **300 miles** of **ILLINOIS Mother Road**: Odell Station and Soulsby's Shell, friendly giants at **WILMINGTON, ATLANTA** and **SPRINGFIELD**, historic **Abraham Lincoln** sites, big cities and small towns, farmland and prairie and woods, Funks Sirip and Cozy Dogs.

Illinois's Route 66 was blessed with pavement early on. A major change occurred in the route when the "temporary" official routing along Illinois 4 south from **SPRINGFIELD** to **STAUNTON** was bypassed in favor of the direct route thru **LITCHFIELD** (alongside current 1-55) in 1930. Another change in the '30s was the bypassing of **JOLIET** for the route along and near current I-55 thru **PLAINFIELD**. The **Joliet** route became "Alt 66" and is the traditional tour route today.

Beginning in the 1940s, **4-Lane 66** bypassed the earlier 2-lane road thru towns. So, by the mid fifties, many sections of early **Route 66** lost their traffic, and their roadside businesses. Those road-icons that remain are cherished gems. Today, long stretches of the ultimate 4-lane 66 have lost their extra lanes, devolving back to 2-lane status. Along these extensive 2 and 4-Lane remnants are **friendly towns** filled with the history of the Midwest and the lure of the **open road**.

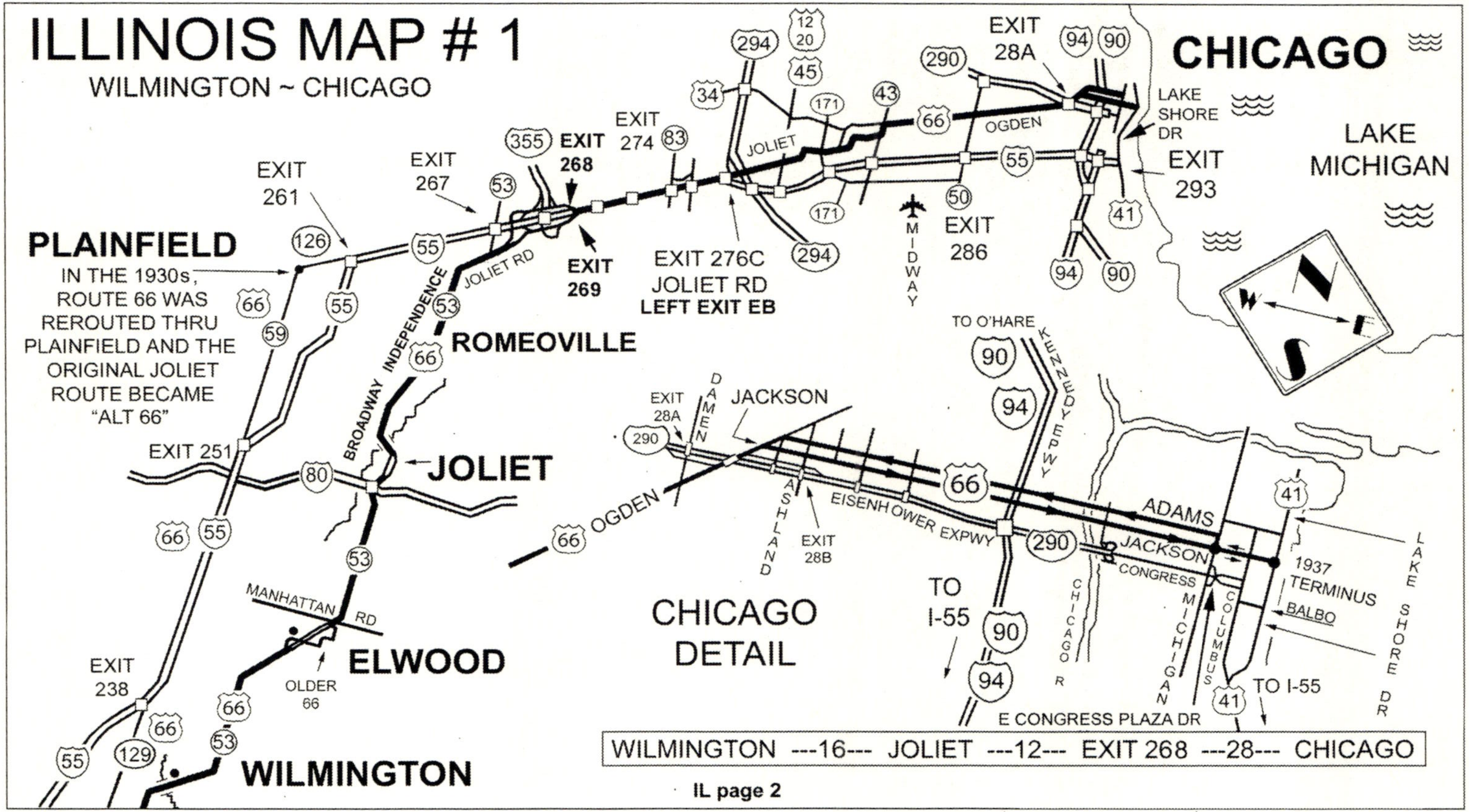
ILLINOIS MAP # 1
WILMINGTON ~ CHICAGO
PLAINFIELD
IN THE 1930s, ROUTE 66 WAS REROUTED THRU PLAINFIELD AND THE ORIGINAL JOLIET ROUTE BECAME "ALT 66"
EXIT 261
EXIT 267
EXIT 268
EXIT 269
EXIT 274
EXIT 276C JOLIET RD LEFT EXIT EB
EXIT 28A
EXIT 286
EXIT 293
EXIT 251
EXIT 238
CHICAGO
LAKE SHORE DR
LAKE MICHIGAN
OGDEN
JOLIET
JOLIET RD
MIDWAY
ROMEOVILLE
BROADWAY
INDEPENDENCE
JOLIET
MANHATTAN RD
ELWOOD
OLDER 66
WILMINGTON
TO O'HARE
KENNEDY EXPWY
EXIT 28A
DAMEN
JACKSON
OGDEN
ASHLAND
EXIT 28B
EISENHOWER EXPWY
ADAMS
JACKSON
CONGRESS
CHICAGO R
MICHIGAN
COLUMBUS
1937 TERMINUS
BALBO
LAKE SHORE DR
TO I-55
TO I-55
E CONGRESS PLAZA DR
CHICAGO DETAIL
WILMINGTON ---16--- JOLIET ---12--- EXIT 268 ---28--- CHICAGO

WB: From **Michigan Ave** in **CHICAGO,** take **Adams St** (One-Way WB) thru downtown. Cross the Chicago River and then cross I-90/94. Go 1 mi further, cross Ashland, then prepare for a **LEFT TURN** onto **Ogden Ave**. Cross I-290, and **continue** on **Ogden Ave**.

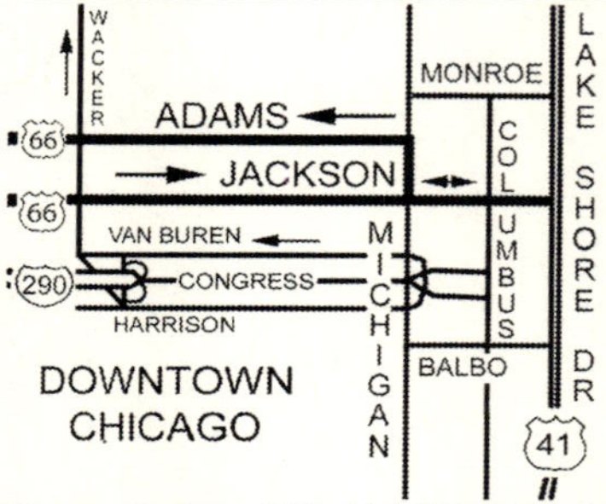

RV ALERT: downtown is crowded. **TRAFFIC ALERT**!

WB: To START in CHICAGO: To reach **Adams and Michigan Ave** from the north **(O'Hare Airport)**, follow **I-90** (Kennedy Expy), and continue past the JCT with **I-94** to the **I-290** JCT near downtown **CHICAGO**. Follow **I-290** (Eisenhower Expy) **EAST** to its end, and continue ahead on **Congress** to Michigan Ave (**NO** left turn). Cross, then quick **LEFT** on **E Congress Plaza Dr**, and bear **RIGHT** on **Michigan Ave**. Pass Jackson, then **LEFT** on **Adams** (**WB**).

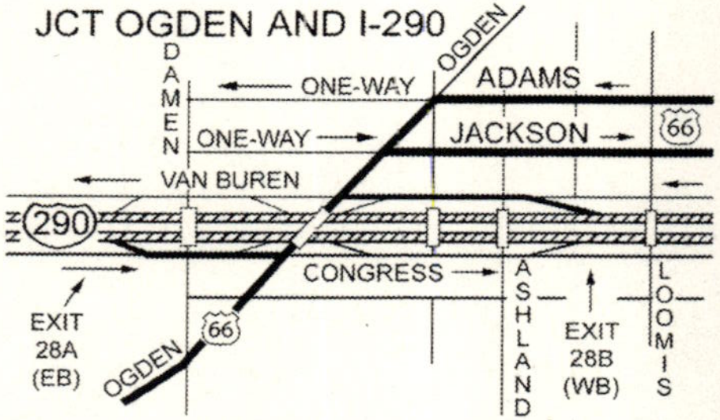

OR: from the south (**Midway Airport**): follow **I-55** (Stevenson Expy) east from the I-90/94 JCT, to its end at **Lake Shore Drive** (US 41 NORTH). EXIT **LEFT** (no trucks), and go about 2 mi to **Jackson Blvd** (Jackson at Lake Shore is the 1937 terminus!). Turn **LEFT** on **Jackson**, go 2 blocks and then **RIGHT** on **Michigan** and **LEFT** on **Adams. (See WB directions** to continue)

OPTION: Since **Jackson** (US 66 before the 1950s addition of Adams) is now **ONE-WAY EB** west of Michigan Ave, consider this "loop" route: Take **I-290 WEST** from the JCT with I-90/94. Take **EXIT 28B**, merge onto **Van Buren** and follow it west to **OGDEN**. Turn **RIGHT**, then **RIGHT** on **Jackson**. Follow **Jackson** east thru downtown to **Michigan Ave**. Turn **LEFT**, then **RIGHT** on **Adams St** (WB).

EB Drivers: Congratulations on being a true **Route 66 Road-Warrior**! After finishing your trip at **Jackson Blvd** and **Michigan**, (unless you wish to loop back on **Adams**) continue on to **Lake Shore Dr** (the **1937** end), then head south to I-55, to reach **Midway Airport** or to make connections to I-90/94. I-90 will take you north to I-190 and **O'Hare**. **Thanks for driving Route 66**, and come back again, real soon!

EB: Just past I-290, cross Van Buren, then next **RIGHT** onto **Jackson** (One-Way EB). Go 2.4 mi (across I-90/94 & the Chicago River) thru downtown **CHICAGO** to the original end at **Michigan Ave** (or continue ahead to **Lake Shore Dr** to reach the **1937 end**).

THINGS to SEE and DO in CHICAGO: Whether your trip begins or ends in **CHICAGO**, there's plenty to explore. So much so, you could spend days here. Since there are miles of Route 66 waiting, here's a sampling of some of the sites on or near the Mother Road, from **Grant Park** thru the downtown "canyons" of the "Loop" and under the 'EL." **Chicagoland Chamber of Commerce**: www.chicagolandchamber.org or (312) 494-6700. As usual in big cities use caution and stay in tourist friendly areas.

Jackson Blvd, the original US 66 thru downtown, has been **ONE-WAY** eastbound since the 1950s, when **Adams St** took over the westbound chores. The current "**END 66**" sign at Jackson and Michigan is only partially correct. Route 66 first began/ended there, but in 1937, the terminus moved out to **Lake Shore Drive**. Anchoring the eastern end of '66 is **Grant Park**, home since 1927 to **Buckingham Fountain** (between Columbus and Lake Shore, south of Jackson). Watch for the daily water show from April thru November, with lights and music at night. Try meter parking on Columbus, or the underground **Grant Park South Parking Garage** (pay) off Michigan, south of Jackson.

SCAVENGER HUNT! What fierce creatures guard the **Art Institute** just north of Jackson on Michigan Ave?

You'll need to crane your neck to see all of the former **Sears Tower**, the **tallest building on US 66** (once tallest in the world!) A public observation deck is reached from the Jackson Blvd entrance. If the skyscrapers of downtown intrigue you, then check with the **Architecture Foundation** (www.architecture.org) (312) 922-3432, which offers excellent narrated tours from their tour center in the **Railway Exchange Building**, on Jackson just before Michigan (a "**Santa Fe**" sign on the roof was a harbinger of the close association that US 66 had with that railroad much further west). Or go to **windycityroadwarrior.com** for info on walking and driving tours offered by Chicago expert **Dave Clark**.

Hungry? For breakfast or lunch try **Lou Mitchells** restaurant, at 565 W Jackson (near Jefferson St), which began on this same block in 1923. Or try the **Berghoff** on Adams St, with their great neon sign, or the many restaurants of "**Greektown**," west of the Kennedy Expwy. West of downtown, between Ashland and Laflin, is the **Jackson Blvd Historic District**. There's much more on **CHICAGO**'s 66.

WB: From I-290, take **Ogden Ave** for 7.5 mi (thru **CICERO** and **BERWYN**). At **Harlem Ave** (Hwy 43), turn **LEFT**. After 0.4 mi, curve **RIGHT** at **41st St/Joilet Rd**. Follow the boulevard as it curves thru **LYONS**, and past Hwy 171. Cross the RR tracks, then turn **RIGHT** on **55th St** (a detour). Turn **LEFT** on **East Ave**, go 1 mi, then **RIGHT** back onto **Joliet Rd**. Continue 2.5 mi (thru **COUNTRYSIDE** and **INDIAN HEAD PARK**). Cross under I-294 (**avoid "right-turn only"**), then merge **AHEAD** onto **SOUTH I-55**.

Ogden Ave cuts a wide swath thru a partly industrial, partly "economically disadvantaged" section of **CHICAGO**. **Lulu's Hot Dogs** at Taylor Street looks (and reviews) interesting. Keep an eye out on the south at 3801 for the defunct **Castle Car Wash** with its unique architecture. Across IL Hwy 50 in **CICERO** are more roadside goodies including **Henry's Drive In** ("It's a Meal in itself") with its **GIANT HOT DOG** sign. Neighboring **BERWYN** honors '66 with a small US 66 museum at 7003 W Ogden. (708) 484-9349 berwynrt66museum.org.

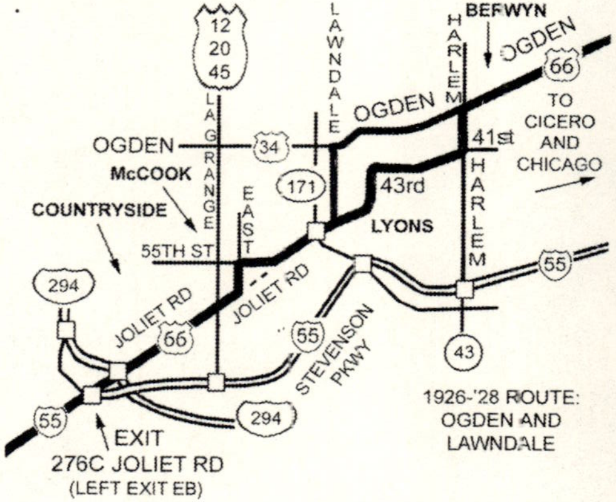

OPTION: ALT Route: Until **1928**, older US 66 followed **Ogden** (US34) into **LYONS,** instead of turning south on Harlem. Before then, there was no road thru what once was marshland, home to Gypsies. Then the early route turned south on **Lawndale**. To the north on "Joliet Ave" (NOT Joliet Rd) from Ogden is the **Hoffman Tower**, a castle-like structure built in 1908.

The current route is forced into a **DETOUR** because of a rock quarry that dug too close to the skirts of the Mother Road! Back on the true path, continue thru **McCOOK**, **COUNTRYSIDE** and **INDIAN HEAD PARK** towards a forced join-up with **I-55**.

EB: From **EXIT 276C** follow **Joliet Rd** under I-294 into **INDIAN HEAD PARK**. Continue 2.5 mi (thru **COUNTRYSIDE** and across La Grange Rd). Turn **LEFT** on **East Ave** (a detour), then **RIGHT** on **55th St** for 1 mi, then **LEFT** back onto **Joliet Rd** in **McCOOK**. Cross Hwy 171 and continue 2.3 mi, following the main blvd as it bends thru **LYONS**. Curve **LEFT** at the light onto **Harlem Ave** (Hwy 43). Go 0.4 mi, then turn **RIGHT** onto **Ogden Rd** and continue for 7.5 mi (thru **BERWYN** and **CICERO**) to cross I-290 in **CHICAGO**. (see **IL page-3** to continue)

WB: Follow **SOUTH I-55** from **EXIT 276**. Take **EXIT 268** (S Joliet Rd). **Follow** the "**Joliet Rd**" signs (do NOT rejoin I-55) and curve under I-55 onto **Joliet Rd.** In **ROMEOVILLE** continue (no turn) to join **HWY 53**/Independence Blvd, for 9.5 mi (en route becomes **Broadway St)**. Be in the left lane for the **Ruby St** stoplight, and turn **LEFT** with **Hwy 53** across the **Des Plaines River** into **JOLIET**.

SIDE TRIP: In **WILLOWBROOK**, take **EXIT 274** to visit **Dell Rhea's Chicken Basket**, a great roadfood stop since 1946, often featuring live music (2 of my paintings hang inside). Join **Kingery Rd** (Hwy 83) north, then first **RIGHT** on **Midway Drive**, and quick **RIGHT** to follow the frontage road curve **LEFT** to **Joliet Rd** (a cut off section of old 66) to the 'Basket and its super **neon sign**.

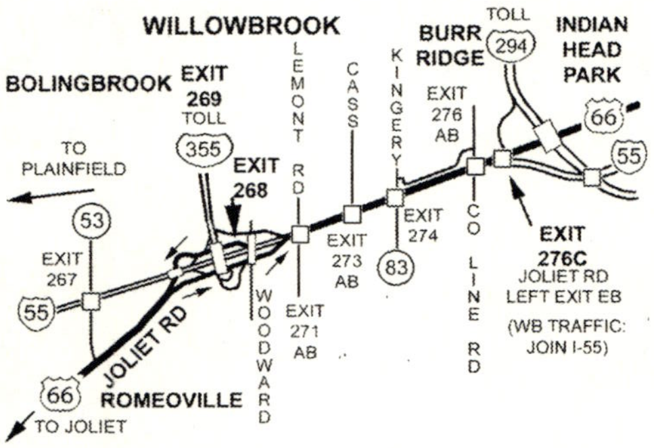

On the main route south from EXIT 268, notice **Montana Charlie's Little America Flea Market**, open from April thru October on weekends. Also look for the rooster sign and fence that mark **White Fence Farms**, which not only offers food, but antique cars and machines, rides and games. **Scavenger Hunt!** The **Illinois State Police Headquarters** building on Hwy 53 is vintage. What **DISTRICT** does it serve?___

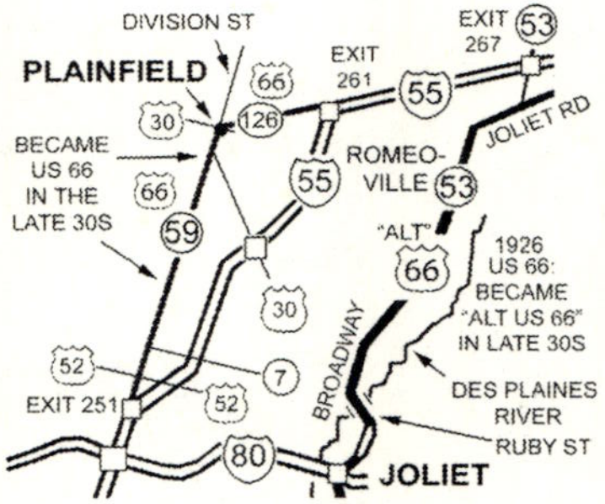

SIDE TRIP: In the 1930's, US 66 was re-routed thru **PLAINFIELD**, while Joliet Rd became "Alt 66." Our tour covers the **JOLIET** route, because the newer alignment was largely replaced by I-55, but use the detail map to visit **PLAINFIELD** if you wish. The brief section of **Hwy 59** that is co-signed as **US 30**, south of town, was at one time both the **Lincoln Highway AND US 66**. At I-55 EXIT 248/Channahon Rd (US 6) you might check out the Route 66 era **Manor Motel**. www.manor-motel.com

EB: From **JOLIET**, turn **RIGHT** at the light onto **Broadway (Hwy 53)** and continue (becomes **Independence**) 9.5 mi to **ROMEOVILLE**. When Hwy 53 turns, continue (no turn) with **Joliet Rd**. Nearing **I-55**, follow the signs "**To Chicago**" and merge onto **NORTH I-55**. Nearing EXIT 276AB, move to the **LEFT LANE**. At **EXIT 276C**, take the **LEFT EXIT** onto **Joliet Rd.**

WB: From **Broadway**, cross the **Des Plaines River** on **Ruby**, then curve **RIGHT** onto **Chicago St**. Stay with **Hwy 53** as it angles right onto **Ottawa** (becomes one-way SB). Follow **Ottawa/Hwy 53** south past downtown **JOLIET**. Stay with **Hwy 53** as it veers from Ottawa to rejoin the other lanes as **MLK Blvd**, then stay south on **Hwy 53** past I-80. Go 15.5 mi (passing **ELWOOD**) to **WILMINGTON**.

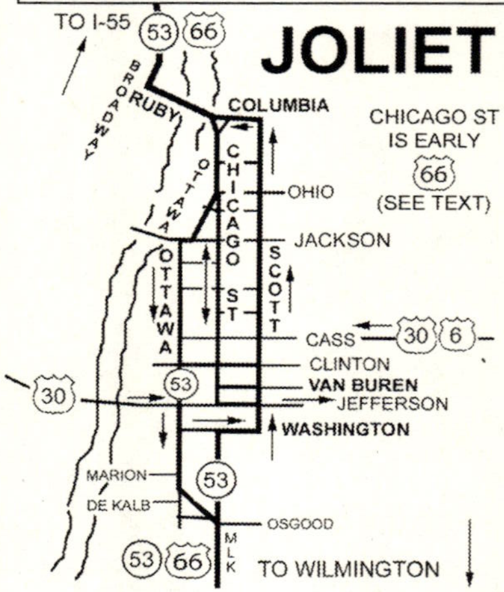

The "**Blues Bros**" dance atop **Rich and Creamy** at 920 N Bdwy at "**Kicks on 66**" park, overlooking ancient **Joliet Prison** (from the movie!). South of the **Des Plaines River** drawbridge (not in movie) sits **JOLIET**. The **Joliet Museum** (204 N Ottawa) has a **Route 66 Welcome Center** and **Gift Shop** (815) 723-5201. **ART ALERT**! See my big **ROUTE 66 MURAL**! Get a "Community Public Art Tour" brochure (look for replica gas pumps).

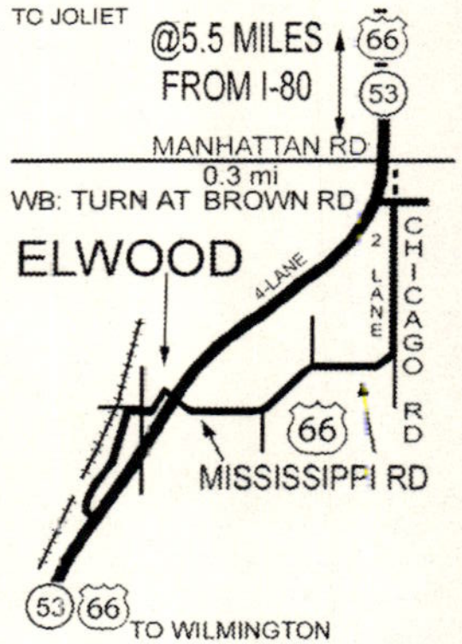

OPTION: Follow **Early 66** in **JOLIET**: **WB (**headed south**)**: INSTEAD of following Hwy 53 onto Ottawa, follow **Chicago St** straight south into downtown. This will take you past the majestic **Rialto Square Theatre** at 102 N Chicago, built in 1926 (same year that 66 was born!). An amazing architectural presence, inside and out. Leaving, **One-way** streets cause extra turns: At **Jefferson (**Lincoln Hwy**)** turn **LEFT**, then **LEFT** on **Scott**, **LEFT** on **Clinton**, and **LEFT** back on **Ottawa** to continue south. **EB** (headed north): just turn **LEFT** from **Scott** onto **Van Buren**, then **RIGHT** on **Chicago**, north to **Ruby**. **GIANT ALERT**! A cousin of the three famous "Illinois 66 Giants" stands proud just off the route. You can see the **Joliet Jackhammer's** mascot from Clinton, east of Scott, at Silver Cross Field ballpark. South of town, save the speed for **Route 66 Raceway** and enjoy the drive thru **ELWOOD** and the **Joliet Arsenal** region, with its conservation areas. **ELWOOD OPTION**: Follow the detail map to drive the old **2-lane 66** north of town.

EB: Follow **Hwy 53** north from **WILMINGTON** for 15.5 mi (passing **ELWOOD** en route) to cross under I-80 into **JOLIET**, entering on **MLK Blvd/HWY53**. Approaching downtown, turn **RIGHT** on **Washington**, then **LEFT** on **Scott** (one-way NB). Pass downtown, then follow **Hwy 53** as it turns **LEFT** on **Columbia** and joins **Ruby St** across the **Des Plains River** to the stoplight at **Broadway**.

(see MAP # 1 on IL page-2)

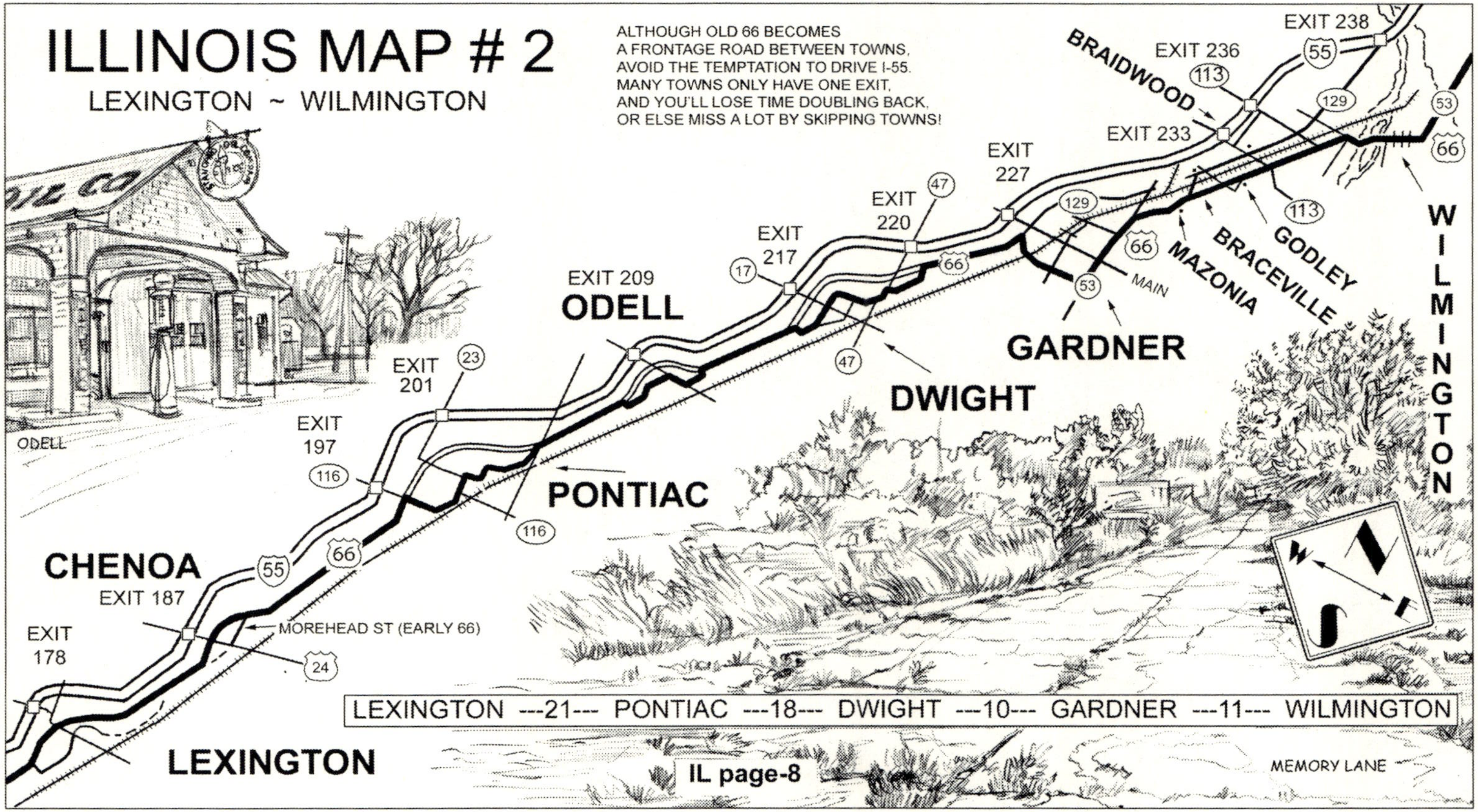
ILLINOIS MAP # 2
LEXINGTON ~ WILMINGTON
ALTHOUGH OLD 66 BECOMES
A FRONTAGE ROAD BETWEEN TOWNS,
AVOID THE TEMPTATION TO DRIVE I-55.
MANY TOWNS ONLY HAVE ONE EXIT,
AND YOU'LL LOSE TIME DOUBLING BACK,
OR ELSE MISS A LOT BY SKIPPING TOWNS!
ODELL
LEXINGTON
EXIT 178
CHENOA
EXIT 187
MOREHEAD ST (EARLY 66)
24
55
66
EXIT 197
116
EXIT 201
23
PONTIAC
116
EXIT 209
ODELL
EXIT 217
17
EXIT 220
47
47
DWIGHT
EXIT 227
129
66
53
MAIN
GARDNER
MAZONIA
BRACEVILLE
GODLEY
113
EXIT 233
BRAIDWOOD
EXIT 236
113
EXIT 238
55
129
53
66
WILMINGTON
LEXINGTON ---21--- PONTIAC ---18--- DWIGHT ---10--- GARDNER ---11--- WILMINGTON
MEMORY LANE

WB: Take **IL Hwy 53** thru **WILMINGTON**. Continue about 12 mi (thru **BRAIDWOOD**, **GODLEY** & **BRACEVILLE**) into **GARDNER**. Curve **RIGHT** with **Hwy 53**. Cross the RR tracks, then take the next **LEFT**. Follow the **Frontage Rd** southwest 6.5 mi to **Dwight Rd** (where the main road/Bypass 66 curves away), and turn **LEFT** to follow **Dwight Rd** into **DWIGHT**.

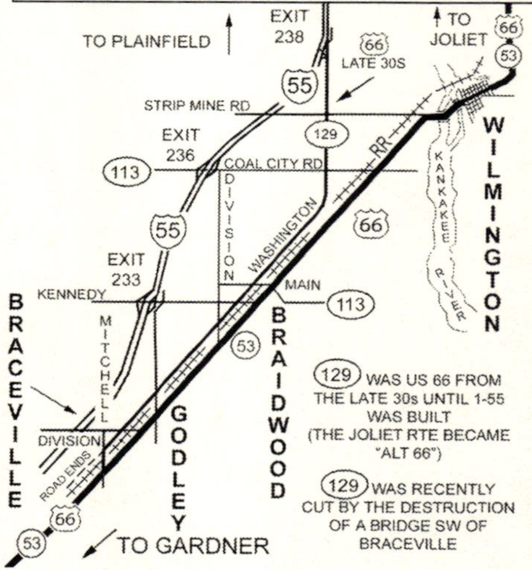

On **WILMINGTON**'s east side is a **GIANT ALERT**! One of three huge "brothers" on 66 in Illinois is the **GEMINI GIANT** at the **Launching Pad Drive In** (note: closed and for sale as of this writing…hope he doesn't fly). Look for the **Sinclair Dino** at G&D Tires, Main & Hwy 53.

SIDE TRIP: West of the **Kankakee River**, the later version of '66 comes in from I-55 (EXIT 238) as **Hwy 129**, to parallel **Hwy 53** (with the RR tracks in-between). Sadly, the removal of a classic bridge cut this latter-day routing beyond **BRACEVILLE**, where the lower end is reached via **Mitchell St**. Access the upper end of this section from **Hwy 53** via Strip Mine Rd.

Back on **HWY 53** in **BRAIDWOOD**, check out the **Polka Dot Drive In** with its '50s décor, then cross the tracks on **Hwy 113** to see the **1939 station** that houses **Lucenta Tire**. NOTE: the **Riviera,** a historic 1928 speakeasy, is gone.

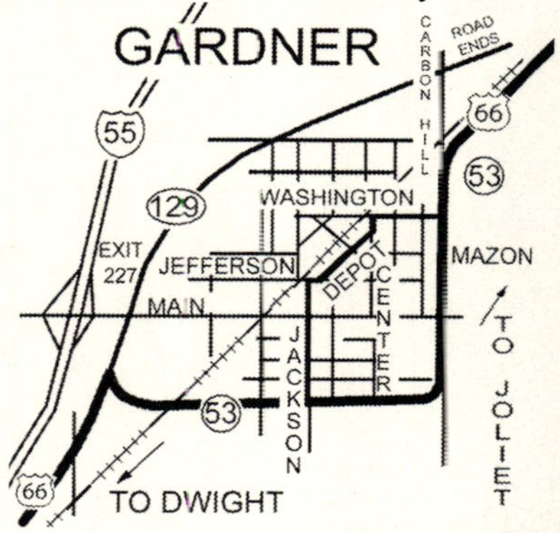

OPTION: See the map to follow the early route thru **GARDNER**, a rewarding drive that winds its way thru "downtown" via Washington, Center, Depot, Jefferson and Jackson streets. Near Mazon and Center are the 1906 **2-cell jail**, a **restored street car**, and a memorial to **Christian Christiansen**, who helped derail the Nazi's intended use of heavy water for their atomic bomb effort in WW2! Wow!

EB: From **Dwight Rd** follow the **Frontage Rd** northeast for 6.5 mi. At the **Hwy 53** JCT (near EXIT 227, **BEFORE** Main St) turn **RIGHT** and cross over the RR tracks into **GARDNER**. Follow **Hwy 53** as it curves **LEFT,** and continue from here about 12 mi (thru **BRACEVILLE**, **GODLEY**, & **BRAIDWOOD**) to continue thru **WILMINGTON**.

WB: Curve **RIGHT** to **Hwy 47**, then **LEFT**, along the RR on **Macnamara**. After Hwy 47 branches off (no turn), curve **RIGHT** onto **Waupansie**, then curve **LEFT**. At Hwy-17/Mazon Ave STOP, continue **AHEAD** on "**Old Route 66**" for 1 mi. Turn **LEFT**, back on main road (becomes **Frontage Rd**). Go **5.7 mi**, then **LEFT** on **Odell Rd** (becomes **West St**). Curve thru **ODELL**, leaving on **Odell Rd**. Turn **LEFT** on main road (Frontage Rd). Go 8.2 mi to **Pontiac Rd.** Turn **LEFT**, then curve **RIGHT** along the RR towards **PONTIAC.**

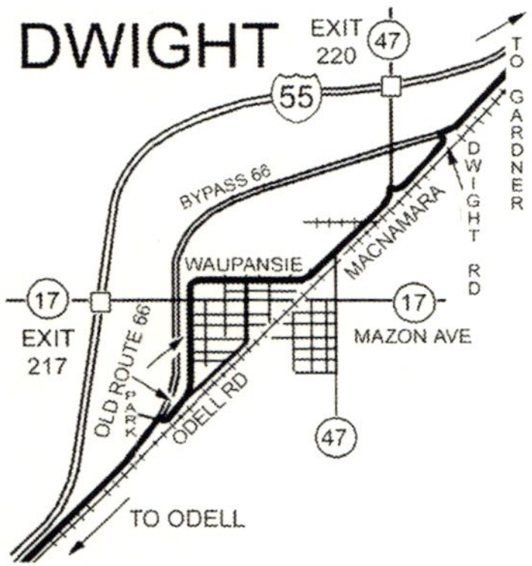

At the junction of Hwy 17 in **DWIGHT** is the old **Becker's Marathon Station** (1933). On the "National Register" as "**Ambler's Texaco,**" an earlier incarnation, it has been beautifully restored. **PHOTO OP**! At 105 S. Old 66 is Old Route 66 Family Restaurant. Next door to **Route 66 Tire & Auto** is a charming display of old gas pumps and signs. **SIDE TRIPS**: **Downtown** has a depot museum and other attractions. **Lions Lake Park**, on the south side, is a nice place to stop and rest, with bathrooms and a jogging track. Town INFO: **(815) 584-2091**

ODELL boasts a classic **1932 Standard Station** (also on the Register), restored due to heroic volunteer effort and donations, a great showpiece (815) 998-2133 or (815) 458-6616. **SIDE TRIP**: See the detail map for an older (pre-66) route thru "downtown." **SCAVENGER HUNT**: What **tire brand** is advertised on **Odell Station**? ______________

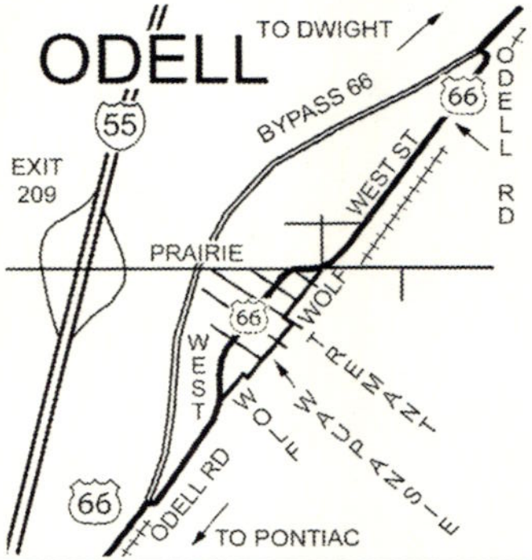

South of **ODELL**, watch for a pullout to view a rare, restored "**Meramec Caverns**" barn sign, and then note the rustic old grain elevator at "**Cayuga.**"

EB: Follow the **Frontage Rd** 8.2 mi, then **RIGHT** to curve onto **Odell Rd/Historic-66** into **ODELL**. Bear **LEFT** at Y on **West St**, and curve thru town, then along the RR (becomes **Odell Rd** again). Turn **RIGHT** on main road (becomes **Frontage Rd)**. Go 5.7 miles, then **RIGHT** onto "**Old Route 66"** in **DWIGHT.** At the "Y" with Odell Rd, bear **LEFT** with "**Old Route 66"** to the Hwy 17/Mazon Ave STOP. Cross onto on **Waupansie St**, which quickly curves **RIGHT**, then curve **LEFT** onto **Macnamara,** along the RR. Hwy 47 joins (no turn), follow as it curves **LEFT** towards I-55, but quickly turn **RIGHT** to join **Dwight Rd.** At the **Frontage Rd**, turn RIGHT.

WB: Take **Pontiac Rd** into **PONTIAC**. Follow the gradual curve **RIGHT,** then curve **LEFT** onto **Division St**. Cross North Creek, then curve **RIGHT** onto **Lincoln**, and **LEFT** onto **Ladd** St. Cross the JCT with Howard (**Hwy 116 east**). At **Reynolds**, turn **RIGHT**. Turn **LEFT** at stoplight onto **Bypass 66** and follow the **Frontage Rd** for about 25.7 mi, thru **CHENOA** and **LEXINGTON** to **TOWANDA**.

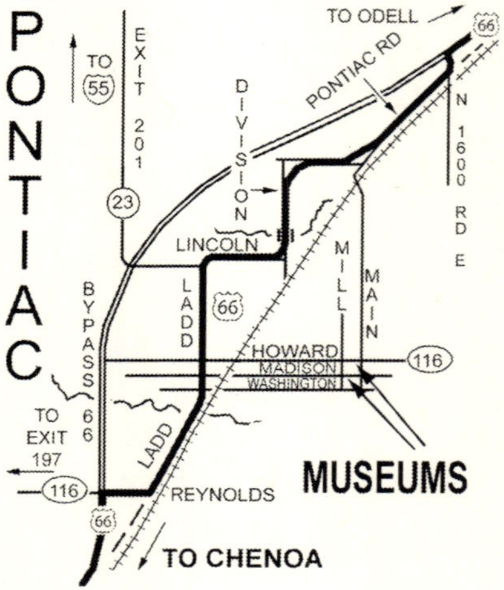

At the **Pontiac Rd** turnoff sits the **Old Log Cabin Restaurant**, dating back to 1926 and the birth of 66. Originally, it fronted the old pavement but spun around to face the 4-Lane 66 bypass.

MANDITORY SIDE TRIP: Be **SURE** to visit **PONTIAC**'s great **MUSEUMS**: **Route 66 Hall of Fame and Museum** downtown at **110 W Howard St** (memorabilia of **Hall of Fame** members, late artist **Bob Waldmire**'s van and bus and an upstairs photo exhibit) **(815) 844-IL66**. **Walldog Mural Museum** at 217 N Mill (815) 822 1848. The **Pontiac-Oakland Auto Museum** at 205 N Mill (815) 842 2345. Also the **War Museum** above **Old City Hall Shoppes** at 321 N Main. Plan on loitering in downtown a while! An "**early 66**" route posted to downtown **MIGHT** have been a detour while a bridge was being built in 1927. On the **tour route** (Division St), check out the recently rebuilt **North Creek Bridge**. The painted 1926 **Hwy 4 marker** (this became US 66) is preserved.

SIDE TRIP: Early 66 took **Morehead St** thru **CHENOA**; the southern extension is abandoned. US **24** will take you east to the town's historic, picturesque downtown area.

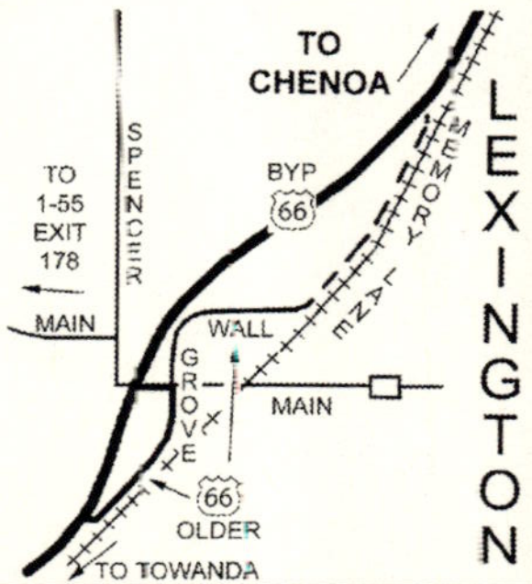

Just north of **LEXINGTON** is an old stretch called "**Memory Lane**" usually open for hiking, and sometimes to cars. A restored **neon arrow sign** at Main St points the way towards picturesque downtown.

EB: Continue 7.8 mi to **CHENOA** (at US 24-no turn). Continue 10.2 mi into **PONTIAC**. At **Reynolds St,** turn **RIGHT**, then **LEFT** on **Ladd St**. Stay **AHEAD** across Howard St (**Hwy 116 east**). Follow the curve **RIGHT** onto **Lincoln**, then **LEFT** onto **Division**. Take the next curve **RIGHT,** then a gradual curve **LEFT** onto **Pontiac Rd**, along the RR. Curve up to **BYP 66**, and turn **RIGHT** towards **ODELL**.

(see MAP # 2 on IL page-8)

ILLINOIS MAP # 3

SHERMAN ~ TOWANDA

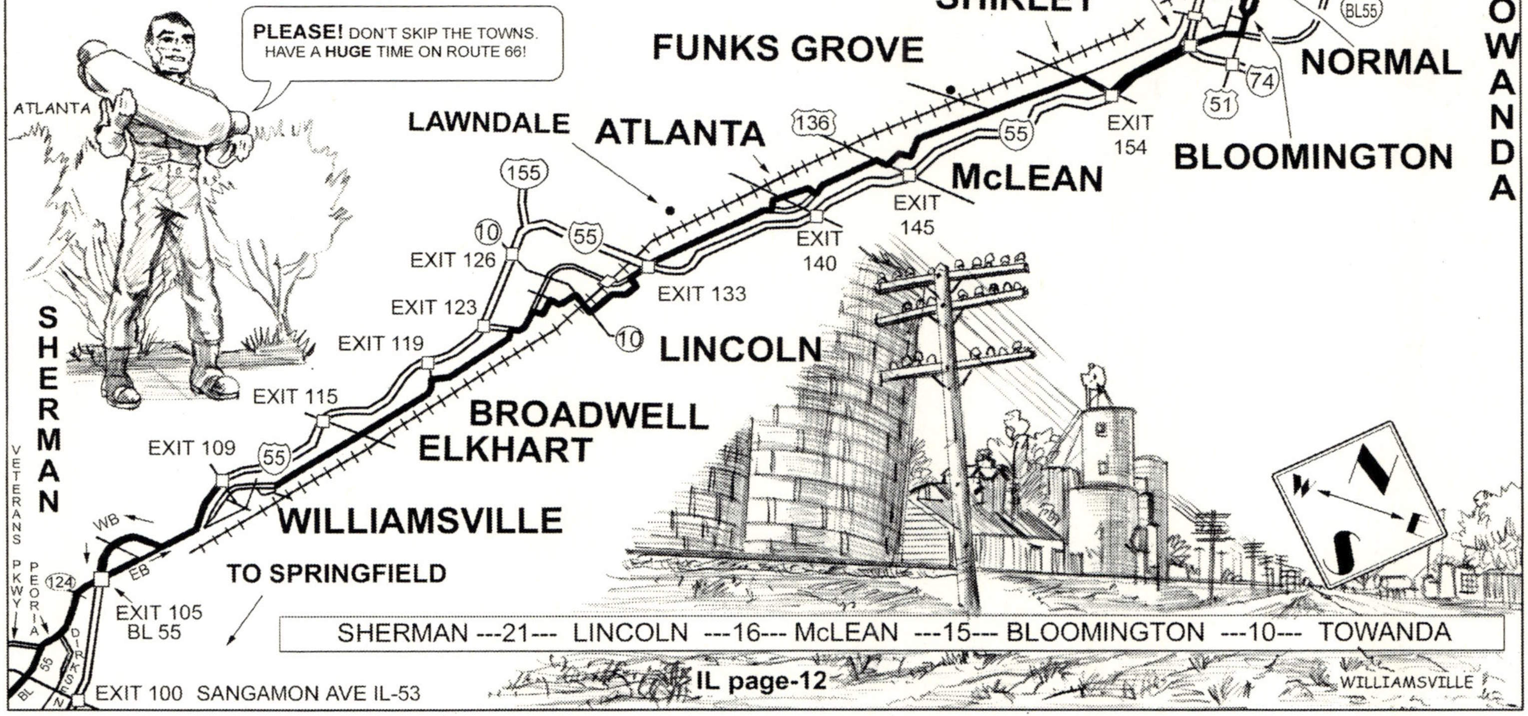

WB: Continue (no turn at STOP) from **TOWANDA**. Go 3.7 mi and pass under Veterans Pkwy. Old 66 is cut 0.5 mi ahead; curve onto **Shelbourne Dr**. Go 0.5 mi (continue across Towanda Dr), then turn **LEFT** on **Henry St**. Go 0.4 mi, then curve **RIGHT** onto **Pine St**. Go 0.8 mi, then **LEFT** on **Linden**. At the next light, turn **RIGHT** on **Willow**. Go 0.7 mi. **LEFT** on **Main St/US 51B** in **NORMAL**.

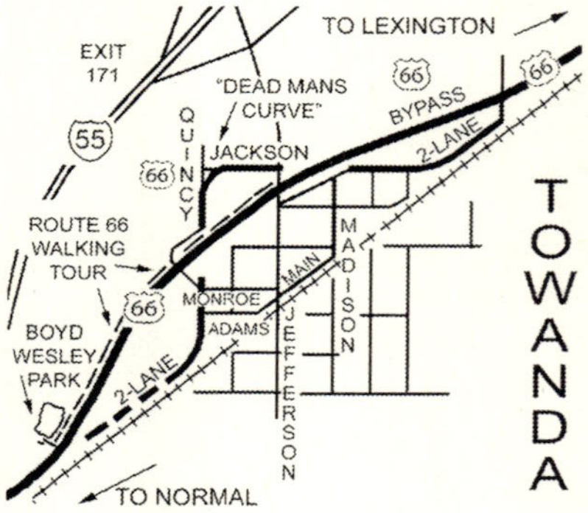

Tiny **TOWANDA** is rich in old 66 alignments, including infamous "**Dead Man's Curve**", where **Jackson St** bends sharply onto **Quincy** (see the **detail map** for this **SIDE TRIP** and two more old fragments). The town made good use out of the abandoned westbound lanes of former 4-Lane 66, by creating a 1.6 mi **Walking Tour** along the defunct roadway. Titled **Historic Rte 66 Illinois "A Geographic Journey**," the trail is complete with displays honoring all eight states and "Burma Shave" signs. They even had fliers printed in various languages. The tour begins at **Jefferson St** and ends at **Boyd Wesley Park**, which has toilets and a fishin' hole.

"**Veteran's Parkway**," the I-55 Business Loop that bypasses **NORMAL** and **BLOOMINGTON**, handled the main US 66 traffic since 1941, but more old-time flavor remains on the early route. The road seems to sneak into **NORMAL** by the back door, passing the attractive **1931 Sprague Super Service Station** and **Café** at Pine and N Walnut, now under restoration. The route slips by **Illinois State University** before turning south on **Main Street**, which it shares with its bigger neighbor to the south. At 1219 S Main and Virginia Ave is the site of the FIRST Steak 'n Shake, circa 1934 (now a pizza joint).

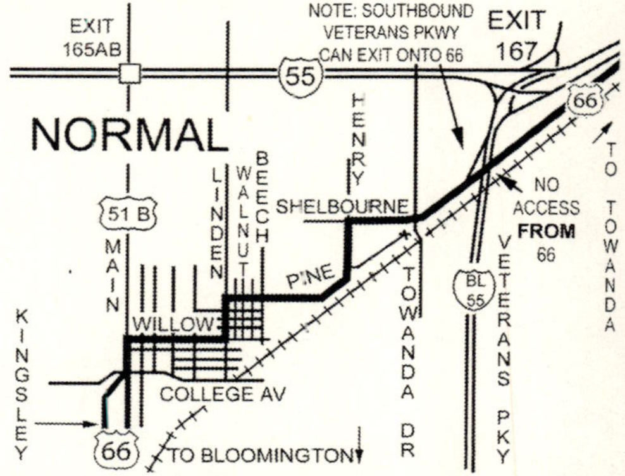

EB: Turn **RIGHT** on **Willow St**. Go 0.7 mi, turn **LEFT** at the **Linden St** stoplight. At next light, turn **RIGHT** on **Pine St**. Go about 0.5 mi (66 is cut ahead) then follow the curve **LEFT** onto **Henry St**. Go about 0.5 mi, then **RIGHT** on **Shelbourne Dr**. Go about 1 mi (curving back onto "**Old Route 66**" by the tracks) to pass under Veterans Pkwy (no access from 66), and continue for 3.7 mi to pass thru **TOWANDA**. Continue about 7.7 mi to pass thru **LEXINGTON**.

WB: Follow **Bus US 51** south (One-Way) from Willow St for 3.8 mi, past downtown **BLOOMINGTON**. Turn **RIGHT** with **Veterans Pkwy/BL- 55**. Go 2 mi. Join **SOUTH I-55** ("Springfield"). Take **EXIT 154**. From the offramp, turn **RIGHT**, then **LEFT** onto **Old Route 66/N Frontage Rd** near **SHIRLEY**. Take the **Frontage Rd** west along the railroad tracks about 4.2 mi, past **FUNKS GROVE**.

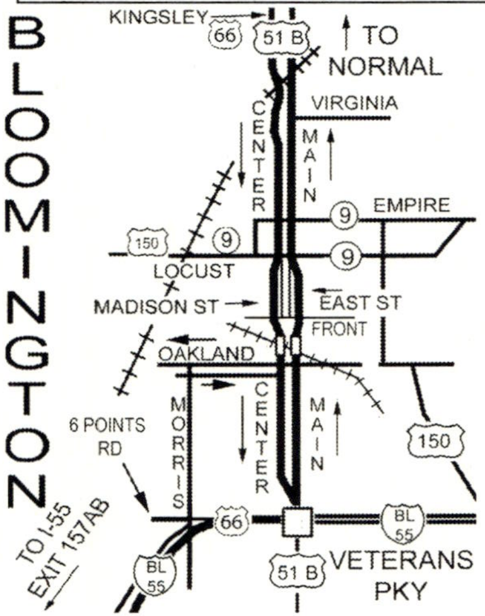

BLOOMINGTON has many claims to fame. It is the hometown of **M*A*S*H***s "Colonel Blake" (the actor, **McLean Stevenson**, grew up here, as did his kin, **Adlai** who is buried here). Here is also the world's sole source for "**Beer Nuts**." For those with a sweet tooth, there is the **Nestle** (formerly **Beich) Candy Factory**. Fill up on history at the **McLean Co Museum of History** (200 N Main) in the old 1903 courthouse downtown. Or, head to 1000 E Monroe St, for the "**David Davis Mansion State Historic Site**" where you can tour this 1872-era Victorian masterpiece. Visitor Info: (309)-665-0033.

OPTIONS: **Downtown** (**EB only**): From **US 51B**, pass Oakland, turn **LEFT** on **Front**, right on **Main**. Rejoin **US 51B**. **South of downtown (WB only):** Take **Oakland** (**One-Way WB**) and **Morris** streets (detail map). Near Wood and Morris is **Miller Park** (1887), home to a zoo, war memorials, an 18-acre lake and a restored dance pavilion. **West Side**: **Fox Creek Rd** (a substitute) runs from Veterans Pkwy (just east of EXIT 157), across I-55 to **Beich Rd** and along I-55('66 path joins) to **SHIRLEY**.

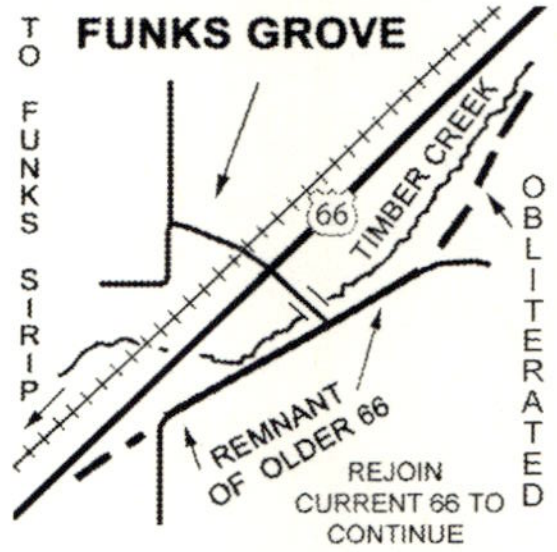

FUNKS GROVE SIDE TRIP: The village is across the tracks at the crossroads, but a turn east across **Timber Creek** leads quickly to a short, bypassed strip of older 66 in the woods. Look for signs on **current 66** for the home of **Funks Grove Maple "SIRUP"** (spelled thusly), sold since 1891 (March-August season). **GIFT SHOP ALERT** (309) 874-3360

EB: Join **NORTH I-55** at **EXIT 154** in **SHIRLEY**. At the **I-55 & I-70 JCT**, follow the signs at **EXIT 157B** to exit onto **Veterans Pkwy/BL-55** into **BLOOMINGTON**. Go 2 mi. **EXIT** at **Main St/Bus 51**. Turn **LEFT**. Follow **Main St/Bus 51** north (becomes One-Way) for 3.6 mi (past downtown) into **NORMAL**. Continue 0.2 mi past College Ave. (prepare for a **RIGHT** turn onto **Willow St**).

WB: Stay on **Frontage Rd** 4.2 mi to **McLEAN**. Curve away from the RR, then **RIGHT** on **Carlisle** St. Turn **LEFT** on **Main St**, then **RIGHT** on **US 136**. Turn **LEFT** just before the RR tracks and continue 4.1 mi to **ATLANTA**. Turn **RIGHT** with the "Atlanta" sign and curve **LEFT** to follow **Arch St** thru downtown. Cross the Hwy 25 JCT and continue on **SW Arch St** to the **Frontage Rd**: turn **RIGHT.**

The **Dixie Travel Plaza** in **McLEAN** began as the **Dixie Truckers Home** in 1928, and was the original host to the "Route 66 Hall of Fame." Model railroad fans should check out **McLean Depot Train Shop**, in the historic former depot across from the Dixie. mcleandepot.com (309) 244-5900

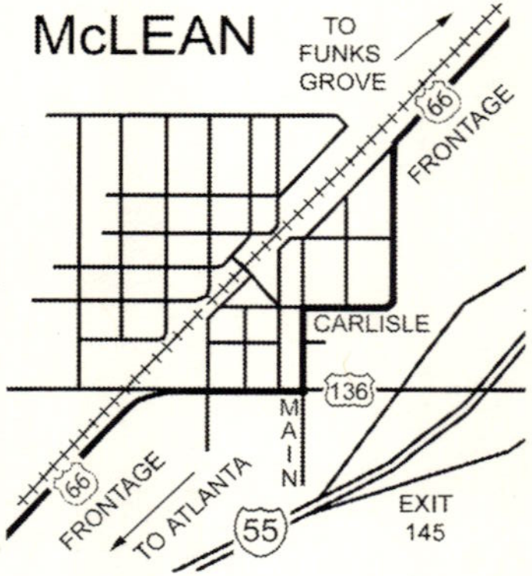

DO NOT skip downtown **ATLANTA**! There's much of interest in this friendly little town. **GIANT ALERT**: The **Bunyon Giant** (formerly of Cicero, IL and brother to the Gemini Giant) found a new home in town, along with a **Giant Hot Dog**. Across the street is **Memories**, Mike Evan's personal collection of Rte 66 era relics. Call (309) 275-1920. Near the **Atlanta Public Library** is the **J.H. Hawes Grain Elevator Museum** at Race and 2nd. How did a 1903 era grain elevator work? If you're lucky, you'll get to watch the fascinating workings from the inside. They are normally open on weekends, but do try calling (217) 648-2056 to arrange a tour.

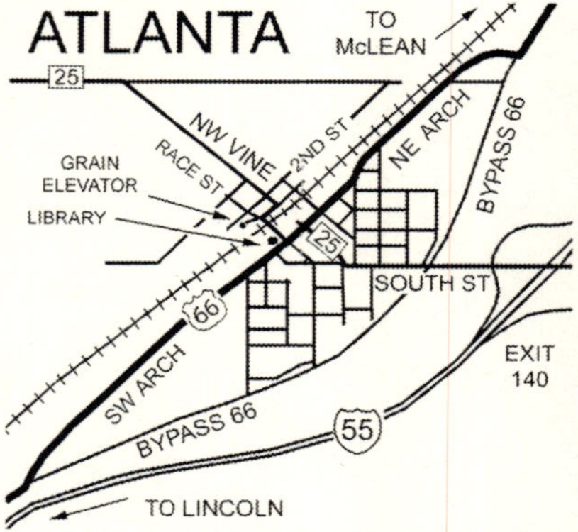

The town's **1908 Library** is **OCTAGONAL** in shape, and out front stands a **40-foot clock tower**, wound by **hand** every 8 days (you can see the "works" thru a window in the door). The town museum is downtown, near the great, recently restored **Palm Grill Café**. Don't miss the many downtown **murals**, or the yellow **water tower** with a **GIANT SMILEY FACE** atlantaillinois.org/rt66/tourist_rt66.html To the west, little **LAWNDALE** has an old grain elevator of its own across the tracks.

EB: Nearing **ATLANTA,** turn **LEFT** and follow **SW Arch St** into town. Cross the JCT of Hwy 25, and continue on **NE Arch St**. Curve back to the **Frontage Rd,** turn **LEFT**. Go 4.1 mi to **McLEAN**. Turn **RIGHT** on **US 136**. Cross East St, then turn **LEFT** on **Main St**. **RIGHT** on **Carlisle St**, then curve **LEFT**. Go 8.4 mi (passing **FUNKS GROVE**) to **SHIRLEY**, and turn **RIGHT on CO 34** to join I-55.

WB: Continue 6 mi. Pass under I-55 (EXIT 133) onto **BL 55/Lincoln Pkwy**. Go 1.4 mi into **LINCOLN**. Turn **LEFT** with the signs and curve with **BL 55** onto **Kickapoo St**. Turn **RIGHT** on **Keokuk**, cross the tracks, then **LEFT** on **Logan** (still **BL 55**). Cross Broadway, then curve **RIGHT** across Clinton onto **5th St**. Past Jefferson St, turn **LEFT** on **Washington**. Cross the tracks (now **Stringer St**). Go 0.3 mi, then **LEFT** to join **BL 55 (Lincoln Pkwy)**. Go 2 mi. Before reaching I-55, turn **LEFT** at "**Frontage Rd Entrance**." Go 3.5 mi. Curve to a **STOP** (near EXIT 119), then **LEFT** on the **Frontage Rd** for 9.7 mi (thru **BROADWELL** and **ELKHART**) to **WILLIAMSVILLE**.

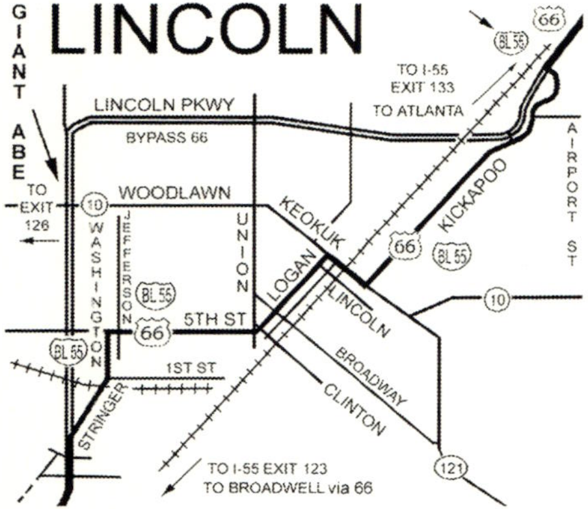

LINCOLN, named for Honest Abe, has plenty of historic sites, plus the **Lincoln College Museum** (300 Keokuk). A replica of the 1841 Postville Courthouse is sited on 5th St.

GIANT ALERT SIDE TRIP! The **GIANT Abe Lincoln** and wagon, formerly of Divernon, Illinois has once again moved, this time to the corner of Lincoln Pkwy (BYP 66) and County Rd (a few blocks south of Hwy 10). Hope he sits still a while. Another Lincoln site is the place where he christened the town with watermelon juice (from a cup!) in 1853 (Broadway and Chicago St). Lincoln INFO: www.lincolnillinois.com (217) 735-2385. **The MILL** at Stringer and First, a restaurant dating back to 1929 and sporting a replica windmill, is being restored.

Itty-bitty **BROADWELL** has lost the **Pig Hip Museum** to a fire. This was in the famed café dating back to 1937, home of the "Pig Hip Sandwich" and the late **Ernie Edwards** ("the Old Coot on Route 66"). Grain elevators still dominate the skyline of **ELKHART** (its charming downtown is across the tracks) and an old stretch of '66 concrete switches sides thru town.

EB: Take the **Frontage Rd** for 9.7 mi (thru **ELKHART** and **BROADWELL**). Nearing the EXIT 119 overpass, turn **RIGHT** at "**Frontage Rd Entrance**." Go 3.5 mi. Turn **RIGHT** (near EXIT 123) onto **BL 55/Lincoln Pkwy** into **LINCOLN**. Go 2 mi (cross Salt Creek) then **ANGLE RIGHT** onto **Stringer St**. Cross the tracks (now **Washington St**), go 0.3 mi then **RIGHT** on **5th St/BL 55**. Past Union, **ANGLE LEFT** onto **Logan**. Cross Lincoln Ave and turn **RIGHT** on **Keokuk**. Cross the tracks, then **LEFT** on **Kickapoo** (still **BL 55**) to **Lincoln Pkwy**: turn **RIGHT**. Pass under I-55 at EXIT 133, continue on the **frontage rd** for 6 mi to the turn for **ATLANTA**.

WB: Enter **WILLIAMSVILLE** on **Oak St (BYP 66)**. **LEFT** on **Elm**. Cross Main and curve along the tracks with **Spur 66**. At the end of Elm turn **RIGHT**, then **RIGHT** on Oak. At **Stuttle Rd**, turn **LEFT**. JOIN **WEST I-55**. Take **EXIT 105** and JOIN **BL 55/Sherman Blvd** thru **SHERMAN** (becomes Peoria Rd). Stay on **BL 55** for 4.6 mi (past Dirksen Pkwy). Be in the **LEFT LANE** under the RR tracks, and turn **LEFT** on **BL 55/Peoria Rd** from the Veteran's Pkwy stoplight. **AVOID** the H-66 sign/turn for Taintor Rd. Continue past Sangamon Ave and onto 9th St in **SPRINGFIELD**.

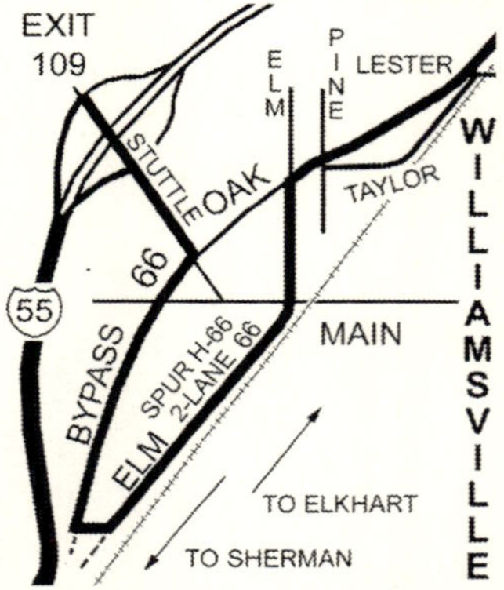

WILLIAMSVILLE is small enough that the guide takes you on a "loop" thru town, along two versions of '66. At 117 N Elm is a 1930's era gas station filled with toy cars and collectibles, plus old gas pumps and signs on view outside. **SCAVENGER HUNT!** What **name** is (hopefully) painted on the old **boxcar** that houses the **Williamsville Museum** near Elm and Main?

SIDE TRIP: The old route thru **SHERMAN** went west on **Hwy 124** (Andrew) and south on **Old Tipton School Rd** (see detail map).

NOTE: Dirksen Pkwy was a US 66 bypass around **SPRINGFIELD**. Some motel relics remain, but the road is **rough** in places. On the **tour route**, south of the **Illinois State Fairgrounds,** at 2075 Peoria Rd, is **Shea's Historic Route 66 Museum**. Contained in this former fuel-outlet is the long-time owner's extensive personal collection of photos and gas station goodies. An older station was relocated and restored. (217) 522-0475

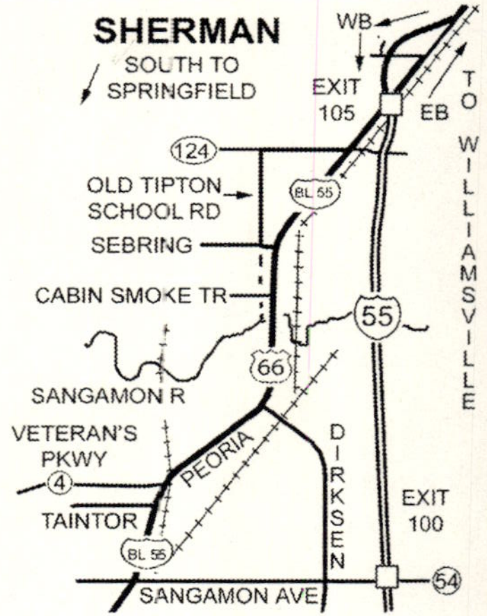

NOTE: Despite the signs, Taintor Rd was evidently **NOT** "1926-'30" US 66.

EB: Follow **BL 55/ Peoria Rd** past Sangamon Ave. Turn **RIGHT** with **BL 55** at **Veteran's Pkwy**, cross under the RR. Pass the JCT with Dirksen Pkwy. Across the Sangamon River, Peoria becomes **Sherman Blvd/BL 55** thru **SHERMAN**. At **EXIT 105**, cross under **I-55**, and stay **AHEAD** along the RR. **Merge onto EAST I-55**. Take **EXIT 109** at **WILLIAMSVILLE**, turn **RIGHT** on **Stuttle**, then **RIGHT** on **Oak** (BYP 66). At Oak's end, turn **LEFT**, then **LEFT** onto **ELM**. Curve up to cross Main. At **Oak**, turn **RIGHT** onto **Frontage Rd**.

(see MAP # 3 on IL page-12)

ILLINOIS MAP # 4

STAUNTON ~ SHERMAN

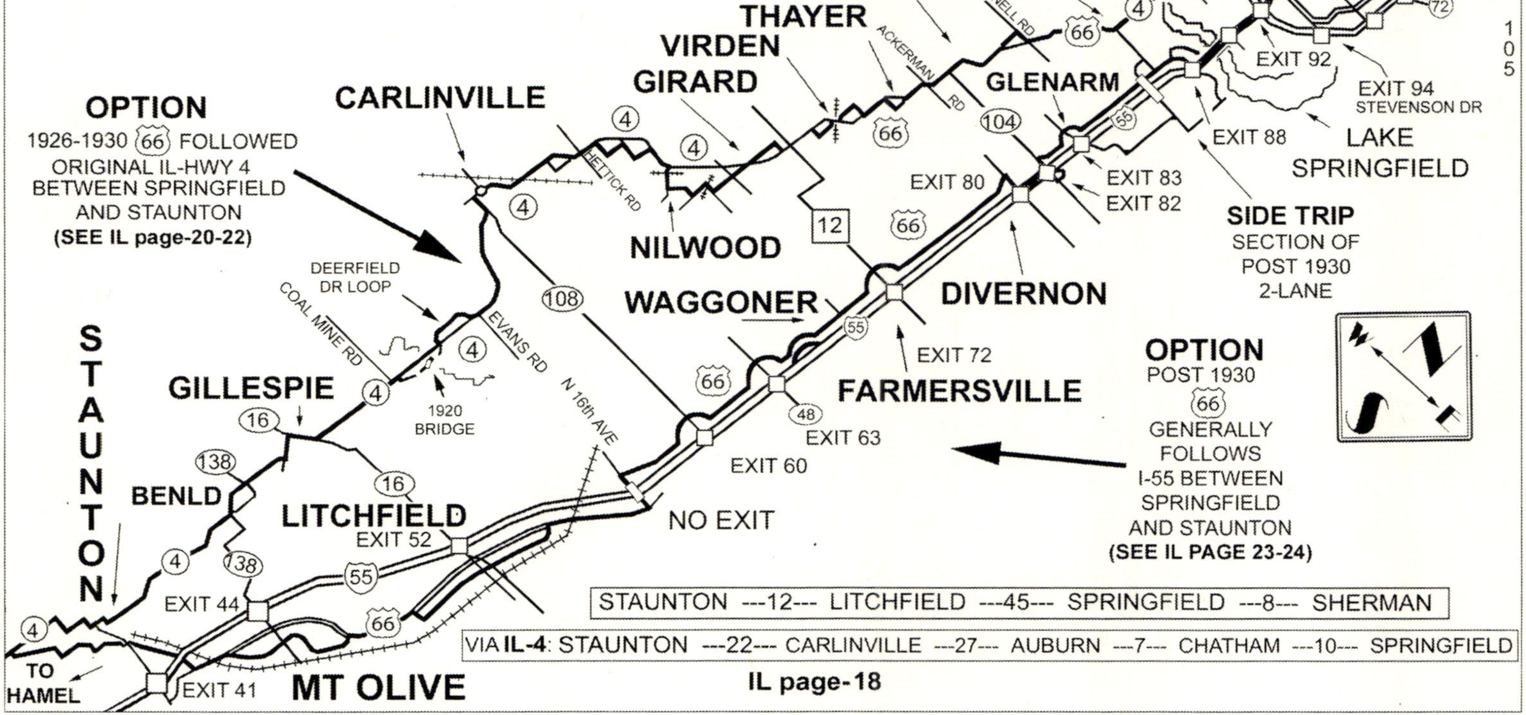

WB: Follow **9th St /BL 55** south past downtown **SPRINGFIELD**. (**NOTE**: see **IL page-20** for the **OPTIONAL 1926-1930 Route** that departs 9th St at Capitol Ave) Cross South Grand. Turn **RIGHT** on **Spruce** (One –Way), then **LEFT** on **5th St** (One-Way). Continue with **BL 55 south** past Stevenson Dr to **EXIT 92** and JOIN SOUTH **I-55**. Then go to **IL page-23** to continue via this **Post-1930 OPTION**.

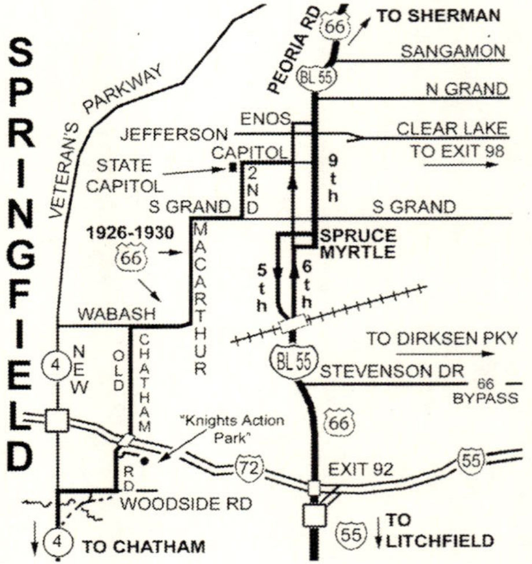

If you want Abe Lincoln sites, then **SPRINGFIELD** has 'em! The **Lincoln Home, Tomb** and **Presidential Library** for starters. Of course, there's a statue of Abe at the Capitol, but at only 10 and a half feet, it's not very exciting. **GIANT ALERT #1:** Thankfully, a **30-foot statue** of a young, skinny Lincoln stands near Gate #1 of the Fair Grounds. Very picturesque is the **OLD State Capitol** at Adams and 6th St, and there's plenty more. City INFO: (217) 525-1173.

OPTION: **EB** you can follow the **1930-era Route** along **6th St** (One-Way) north from Myrtle thru downtown. Then turn right on **Enos St** to rejoin **BL 55**.

Don't miss the famed **Cozy Dog Drive-In** (family of late Route 66 artist **Bob Waldmire**) on 6th /BL 55 north of Stevenson Dr, south side of town. **SIDE TRIPS**: West, off I-72, is the **"Route 66 Drive-In Theatre"** (not on 66 but close to Old Chatham Rd) at **Knights Action Park**. **GIANT ALERT #2** I never get "tired" of the **Lauterbach Giant** at Lauderbach's Tire and Auto Service on the north side of Wabash St (the 1926-'30 **OPTIONAL** route). He's one of the three giant "brothers' on '66 in Illinois.

WB OPTION: **Hwy 4** carried '66 from **1926 to 1930** (**IL page-20**). This route offers many zigzag turns on old concrete-slab roads (plus some **brick road**) thru charming towns. The **Post-'30** route, along I-55 thru **LITCHFIELD** and **MT OLIVE**, also has much to offer (**IL page-23**). If you decide on **Hwy 4**, try to cut over on **Hwy 16** to these two towns, at least.

EB: From I-55, take **EXIT 92** (LEFT EXIT) and follow **BL 55** north into **SPRINGFIELD**. Pass Stevenson Dr, then follow the split onto **6th St** north (One-Way). Turn **RIGHT** on **Myrtle** (One-Way) or **Laurel**, then **LEFT** on **9th St**. Follow **9th /BL 55** north, past downtown. (**OPTIONAL 1926-30 ROUTE** rejoins here)

<u>OPTIONAL 1926-'30 ROUTE WB:</u> In **<u>SPRINGFIELD</u>**, follow **Capitol Ave** west from **9th St**. (map **IL page-19**). Turn **LEFT** on **2nd** at the **Capitol**. Turn **RIGHT** on **S Grand**. Turn **LEFT** on **Macarthur**. Turn **RIGHT** on **Wabash**. Turn **LEFT** on **Old Chatham Rd**, go 3 mi (crossing I-72) to **Woodside Rd**: turn **RIGHT**. At **Hwy 4**, turn **LEFT**. Take **Hwy 4** for <u>7.6 mi</u> (passing **<u>CHATHAM</u>**). Turn **RIGHT** on **Snell Rd** (past **Ostermeier Rd)**. Curve left on **Curran Rd**. Rejoin **Hwy 4** south thru **<u>AUBURN</u>**, **<u>THAYER</u>** & **<u>VIRDEN</u>** to **<u>GIRARD</u>**.

NOTE: SEE the detail maps for **<u>OPTIONAL</u>** "dog-leg" sections of **Pre-'30 66**.

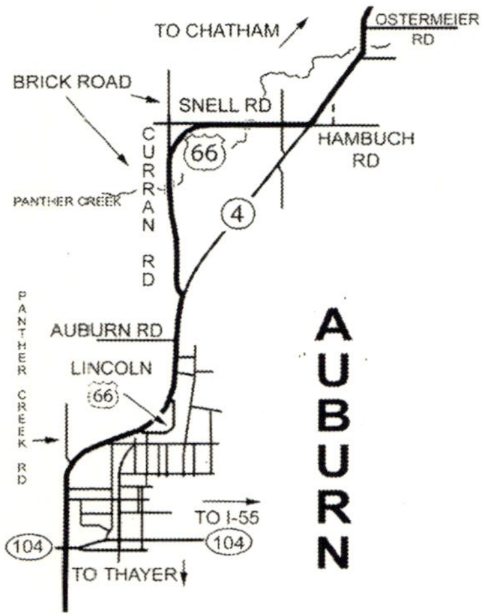

Leaving **<u>SPRINGFIELD</u>**, wave "Bye" to **Lauterbach Giant** on Wabash. **<u>SIDE TRIP</u>**: Off **Woodside Rd** (0.4 mi west from Chatham Rd) a dead end section of "**Old Chatham Rd**" runs for under a mile, ending at a swampy area and the closed "**Snake Bridge**" over Lick Creek.(map IL-page 19) **<u>CHATHAM</u>** has a marked dog-leg on Walnut and Church streets.

On **Snell** and **Curran Road,** between **<u>CHATHAM</u>** and **<u>AUBURN</u>,** is a rare 1.4-mile stretch of **BRICK** road. **Becky's Barn** (first right WB on Snell Rd (last left EB)to end of road) has really cool gifts and antiques. 10-5 Thurs-Sun. (217) 836 3043 for appointments other times. Look carefully for two short doglegs (**Planter** and **Tiller Roads**) at a curve centered on **Ackerman Rd** (2 mi south of Hwy 104). The map shows a dogleg in **<u>THAYER</u>. <u>VIRDEN's</u>** town square has the **Battle of Virden Monument**, memorializing a bloody struggle between coal miners and mine owners back in 1898. See the map for 2 sections of old road in **<u>VIRDEN</u>**.

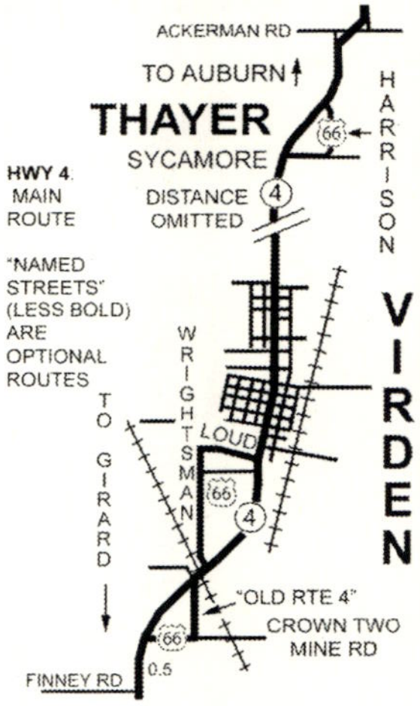

EB: Follow **Hwy 4** thru **<u>VIRDEN</u>** & **<u>THAYER</u>** to HWY 104 in **<u>AUBURN</u>**. Stay with **HWY 4** for <u>1.5 mi</u>, and turn **LEFT** onto **Curran Rd.** Curve **RIGHT** on **Snell Rd**. Rejoin **Hwy 4** north for 7.5 mi (thru **<u>CHATHAM</u>**). Turn **RIGHT** on **Woodside Dr**. Go 0.7 mi, then **LEFT** on **Chatham Rd**. Go 3 mi (crossing I-72) into **<u>SPRINGFIELD</u>** (see map on **IL Page-19**). Turn **RIGHT** on **Wabash**. Turn **LEFT** on **Macarthur**. Turn **RIGHT** on **South Grand**, then **LEFT** on **2nd**. At **Capitol Ave**, turn **RIGHT**. Turn **LEFT** on **9th St/BL-55**.

WB: In **GIRARD**, turn **RIGHT** on **Madison St**, and **LEFT** on **6th St**. Continue across Hwy 4 & RR on **Cambridge Rd.** Turn **RIGHT** on **Wylder**, then **LEFT**, past the RR underpass. Turn **RIGHT** on **Morean Rd**. Turn **LEFT** on **Pine** and **RIGHT** on **Morean St** in **NILWOOD**. At **Hwy 4** turn **LEFT**, go **1.8 miles**, then **LEFT** on **Donaldson Rd**. Follow the next corner **RIGHT**. Approaching Hwy 4, curve **LEFT** again with **Donaldson Rd (**see turkey tracks**)**. Turn **RIGHT** at **Allen Rd**, and **LEFT** on **Hwy 4** to **CARLINVILLE**.

CAUTION: The Allen Rd section is **ROUGH**. Go **SLOW**! Bike **ALERT**.

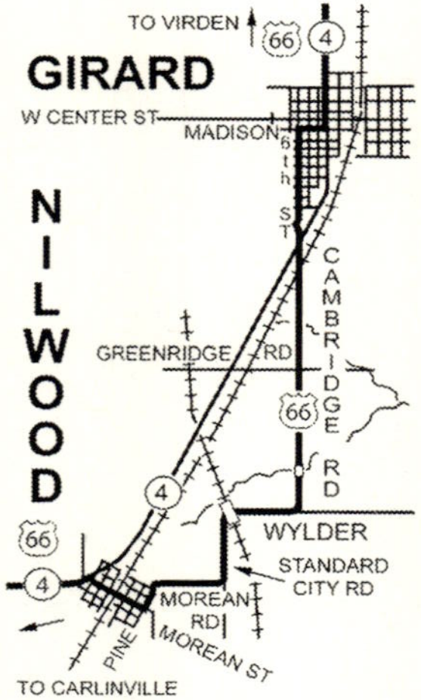

The section from **GIRARD** to **NILWOOD** is fantastic, a slice of the 1920s winding tipsy thru the farmland. Frequently a crack, like the snaking course of a river, meanders along the middle of this evocative concrete road.

West of **NILWOOD,** the **Donaldson Road** zigzags are a great **SLOW** drive. Look for the **TURKEY TRACKS**, highlighted in white, in the concrete on Donaldson Rd about 0.3 miles north of Allen Rd. Also look for dog (?) tracks to the south! Woof!

OPTION: About 0.8 of a mile south of Hettick Rd, **Harvest Rd** performs yet another quaint dogleg.

CARLINVILLE's brick-lined square defines picturesque, as does the impressive domed **courthouse** from 1870. **Cherry Tree Gifts** at 236 East Side Square has '66 items. The Standard Addition neighborhood has 152 "**Sears Houses**" in a 12 block area (ask).

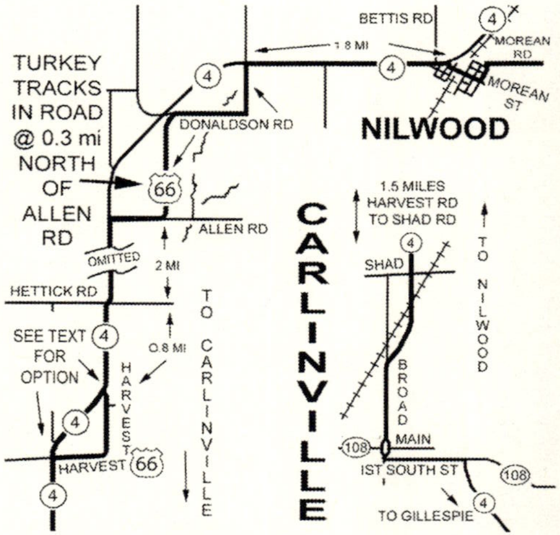

EB: Take **Hwy 4** from **CARLINVILLE**. Cross Hettick Rd. Go **2 miles**, turn **RIGHT** on **Allen Rd** (**SLOW**) then **LEFT** on **Donaldson Rd**. Nearing Hwy 4, curve **RIGHT** with **Donaldson Rd**, then curve **LEFT** up to **Hwy 4**: turn **RIGHT**. In **NILWOOD**, turn **RIGHT** on **Morean St**, then **LEFT** on Pine. Turn **RIGHT** on **Morean Rd**, then **LEFT** on **Standard City Rd**. Curve **RIGHT** on **Wylder**, under the RR, then **LEFT** on **Cambridge Rd**. Cross Hwy 4, stay **AHEAD** on **6th St** into **GIRARD**. **RIGHT** on **Madison**, then **LEFT** on **Hwy 4**.

WB: In **CARLINVILLE**, follow **Hwy 4** thru the square, then **LEFT** on **1st South St (Hwy 108)** for 0.5 mi. Turn **RIGHT** on **Hwy 4**, go 11 mi to **GILLESPIE**. Stay on **Hwy 4/H-66** as it turns thru town. Take **Hwy 4** south for 9 mi (thru **BENLD** & **SAWYERVILLE**) to **STAUNTON**. Turn with **HWY 4** thru town. Leave on **HWY 4** (**Post-1930 66** joins-see map below, and see **IL page-26** to continue)

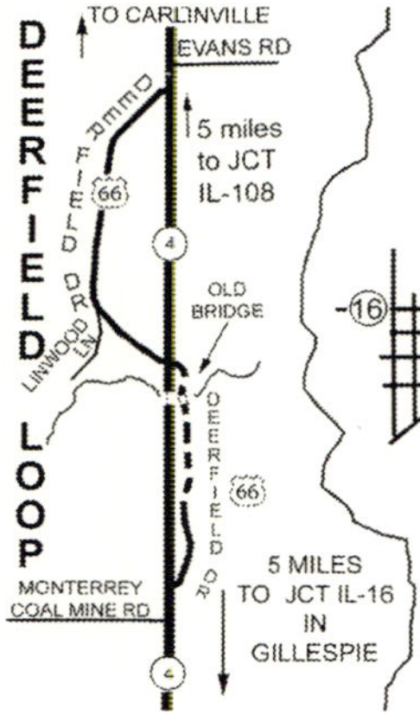

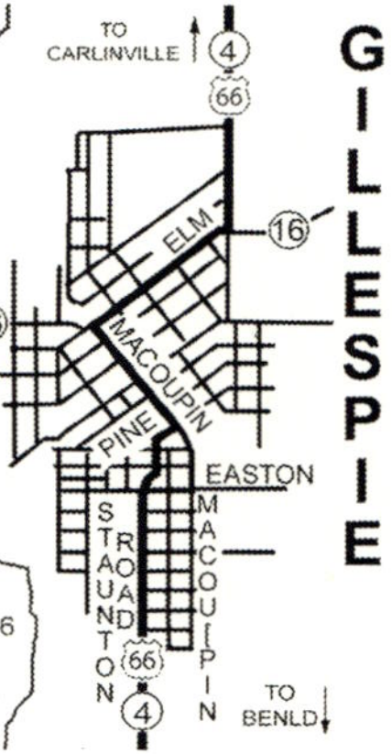

Carlinville's **Carlin-Villa Motel** (217 854-3201) on the south side (south of HWY 108) is a good choice. Watch for **abandoned sections** of road along this stretch.

OPTION: (a bit ROUGH) **WB**: 5 miles south of Hwy 108 (**CARLINVILE**) **EB**: 5.5 miles north of Hwy 16 (**GILLESPIE**) Follow **Deerfield Dr** as the road curves along a short scenic section thru forest and hills (SEE MAP). The currently-blocked southern loop crosses a stout (but endangered) little concrete bridge from 1920.

OPTIONS: MORE old dog-leg loops: **North Hardroad** in **BENLD**, and **Fritz Lane** in **SAWYERVILLE**. Look for the Historic 66 signs (both on east side of HWY 4).

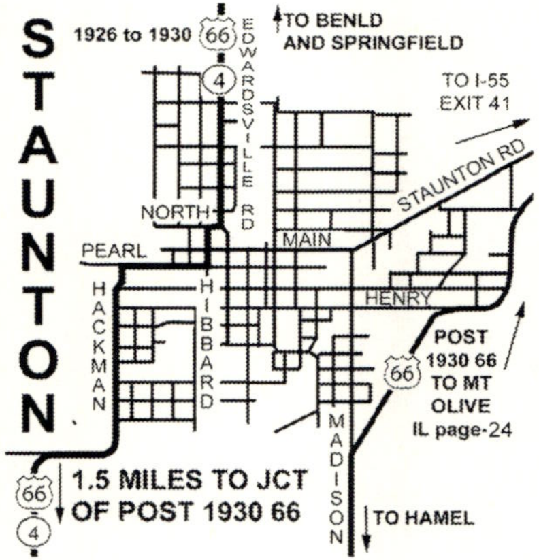

The former **Coliseum Ballroom,** south of **BENLD**, a historic structure dating to 1924, has burned down. The Pink Elephant and Giant Surfer are now on the 1950s route in **LIVINGSTON** (see IL page-26) **STAUNTON** has two glazed-brick former gas stations on Hwy 4, a great downtown, just off the route, plus a collection of rabbits and camels on the **POST-1930 ROUTE**! (be sure to see **IL page-24**)

EB: **1926-'30 OPTION** (see **IL page-24** for **Post-1930 OPTION**): Take **Hwy 4** north to **STAUNTON**. Turn with **Hwy 4** thru town, then follow it for 9 mi (thru **BENLD** & **SAWYERVILLE**) to **GILLESPIE**. Follow **HWY 4** as it turns thru town. Stay on **HWY 4** for about 11 mi. At **Hwy 108** (**1st South St**) turn **LEFT** into **CARLINVILLE**. Go 0.5 mi. Turn **RIGHT** on **Broad St/HWY 4**. Go thru the square.

WB: (POST 1930 OPTION) Take **I-55 Exit 88**, turn **RIGHT** and take the **Frontage Rd** for 7 mi (thru **GLENARM**). You must JOIN **SOUTH I-55** at **EXIT 82**. Take **EXIT 80** at **DIVERNON**. Turn **RIGHT**, then first **LEFT** to follow the **West Frontage Rd** for almost 21 mi (past **FARMERSVILLE** & **WAGGONER**) to cross HWY 108 (EXIT 60). Continue on the frontage rd for 3.2 mi, then cross over I-55 at **N 16th Ave** (no exit). Turn **RIGHT** on "**Old Route 66**." Go 3.3 mi, across the RR overpass, then quick-**LEFT** on "**1930-40 66**" into **LITCHFIELD**. Cross Hwy 16, continue on "**1930-40 66**" for 2 mi. At **N 10th Ave**, turn **RIGHT**, then **LEFT** on **"Route 66."**

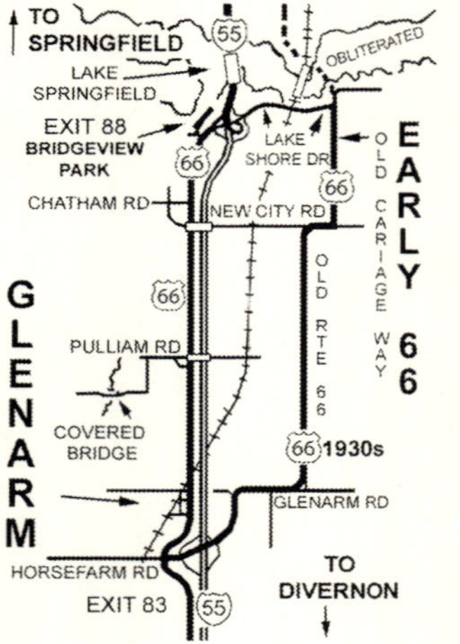

ADVISORY: Parts of the **Frontage Rd** south of **EXIT 80** can be quite **bumpy**.

SIDE TRIP #1: East of I-55 between **EXIT 88** and **83,** you can drive old **2-Lane 66** (circa 1930) by following the detail map. Or, in **Bridgeview Park** off **EXIT 88** is a dead-end section of **4-Lane 66**, just south of **Lake Springfield** (which cut the route).

SIDE TRIP #2: Follow the signs on **Ponyshoe Lane** and **Pulliam Rd** to **Sugar Creek Covered Bridge**, just over a mile west, to walk this **1880** span.

In **FARMERSVILLE** is the oft-photographed sign of the newly remodeled **Art's Motel**. South from **WAGGONER** is **"Our Lady of the Highways"** shrine, blessing the road since 1959. A series of signs along a nearby fence recite the "**Hail Mary**."

Linger in **LITCHFIELD** for the classic **SkyView Drive-in Theatre** (one of few left on 66) and well-preserved and recommended **Ariston Café** from 1931. A new **Litchfield Museum** and **Rte 66 Welcome Center** is being built. www.litchfieldmuseum.org

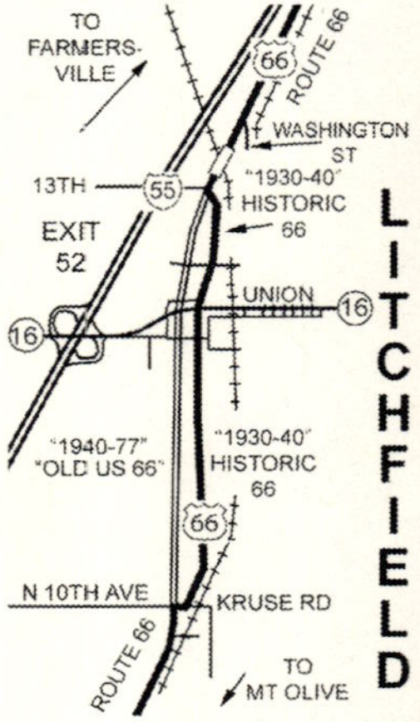

EB: Turn **RIGHT** at **N 10th Ave**, quick curve **LEFT** onto "**1930-40 66**" into **LITCHFIELD**. Continue past Hwy 16 for 0.8 mi. Curve **LEFT** then **RIGHT** on **Route 66/ Frontage Rd.** Go 3.3 mi, then **LEFT** on **N 16th Ave**, across **I-55** and **RIGHT** on "**Old Rte 66**" (**West Frontage Rd**). Go 24 mi (past **WAGGONER** & **FARMERSVILLE**). At **DIVERNON,** cross and JOIN **NORTH I-55 (EXIT 80)**. Take **EXIT 82**, turn **RIGHT** on **Hwy 104**, and cross under I-55. Turn **RIGHT** to rejoin the **W Frontage Rd** thru **GLENARM** for 7.5 mi. At **EXIT 88**, join **I-55 north** to **EXIT 92**.

(See IL page-19 to continue to SPRINGFIELD)

WB: Go 4.4 mi, then turn **LEFT** on "**Old Rte 66 St**" into **MT OLIVE**. Follow "**Old Rte 66 St**" across the JCT of Hwy 138 and on out of town. At "**US Hwy 66 St**" (BYP 66) turn **LEFT**. Cross under the RR overpass, then turn **RIGHT** on "**Old Rte 66.**" Cross I-55 (no exit). At the JCT of Staunton Rd, cross over onto "**Historic Old Rte 66 St,**" which curves along the edge of **STAUNTON**. Leave on **Madison St** (becomes **Sievers Rd**), and follow the curve **RIGHT** onto **Williamson Rd**. At **Hwy 4**, turn **LEFT** towards **HAMEL**.

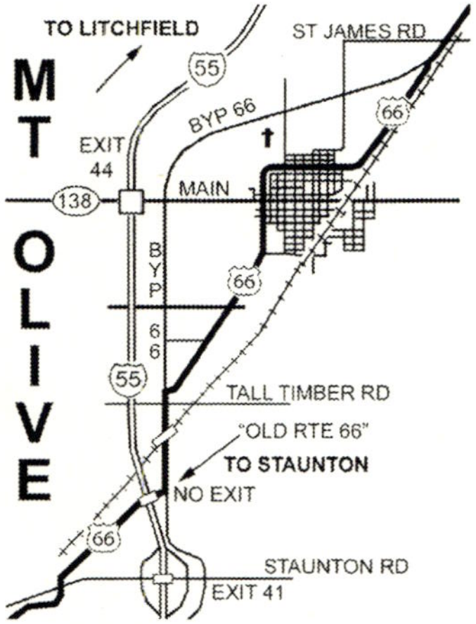

PHOTO OP! The gem of **MT OLIVE** is the restored **Soulsby Station**. Resplendent with its antique red and yellow Shell gas pumps, the station, dating from 1926, sold gas along the road for 65 years. Also, you might visit the **Mother Jones Monument** in the Union Miner's Cemetery on the north side of town.

STAUNTON is where the **PRE and POST-1930** routes of US 66 meet/diverge. (**EB**: see **IL page-22** for the **1926-'30 Route**). The **POST-1930** road, which staggers along the edge of town, was in turn bypassed in **1940** by a route thru **LIVINGSTON** along I-55. But Old 66 is really hopping in **STAUNTON**, at **Henry's Rabbit Ranch & Route 66 Emporium**, near Madison St on **POST-'30 66**. Check out the cute critters, and admire the truck and trailers bearing the likeness of "**Snortin' Norton,**" beloved mascot of the defunct **Campbell 66 Express** truck line. **GIFT SHOP ALERT!**

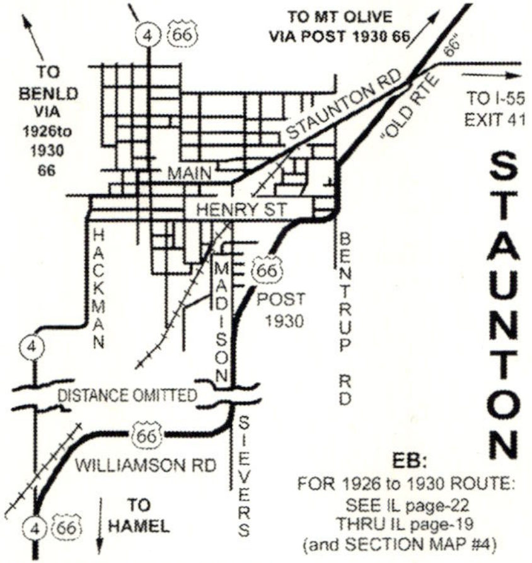

EB: (See **IL page-22** for **1926-'30 OPTION**). Take **Hwy 4** north **3 miles**, then turn **RIGHT** onto **Williamson Rd**. At **Sievers Rd**, curve **LEFT** (becomes **Madison**) into **STAUNTON**. At the "**Y**," follow "**Historic Old Rte 66 St**" as it angles **RIGHT**, to curve along the edge of town. Angle to the JCT with Staunton Rd. Cross onto "**Old Rte 66"** and then cross I-55. Turn **LEFT** on **East Frontage Rd**, and pass under the RR overpass. Prepare for a quick **RIGHT** turn onto **Mt Olive Rd/Old Rte 66**. Enter **MT OLIVE**, cross the JCT with Hwy 138, and curve thru town to the JCT with "**US Hwy 66 St**" (Bypass 66): turn **RIGHT for** 4.4 mi to the turn into **LITCHFIELD**.

(see MAP # 4 on IL page-18)

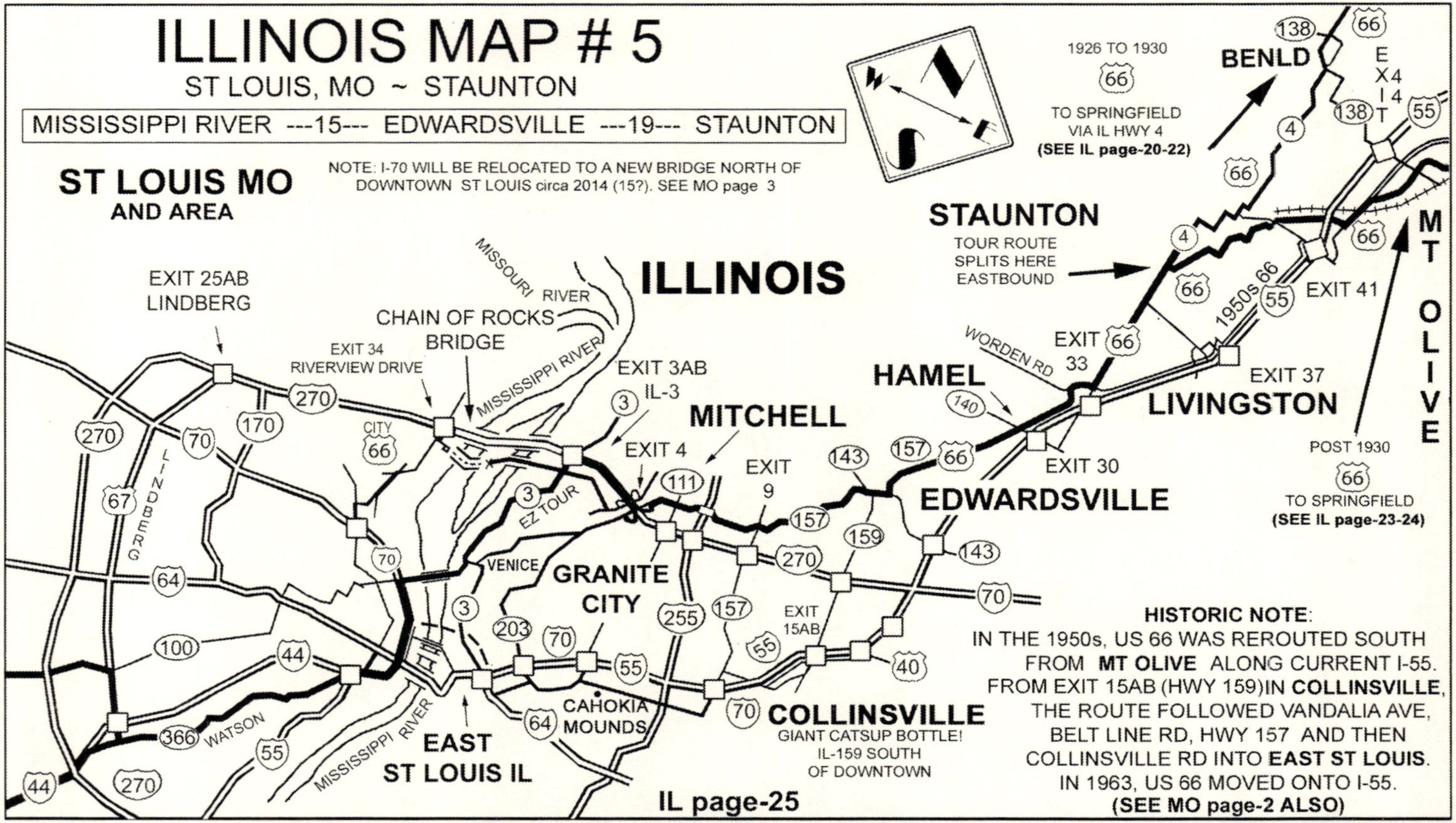
ILLINOIS MAP # 5
ST LOUIS, MO ~ STAUNTON
MISSISSIPPI RIVER ---15--- EDWARDSVILLE ---19--- STAUNTON
ST LOUIS MO
AND AREA
NOTE: I-70 WILL BE RELOCATED TO A NEW BRIDGE NORTH OF DOWNTOWN ST LOUIS circa 2014 (15?). SEE MO page 3
1926 TO 1930
66
TO SPRINGFIELD
VIA IL HWY 4
(SEE IL page-20-22)
BENLD
STAUNTON
TOUR ROUTE
SPLITS HERE
EASTBOUND
ILLINOIS
EXIT 25AB
LINDBERG
CHAIN OF ROCKS
BRIDGE
MISSOURI RIVER
MISSISSIPPI RIVER
EXIT 34
RIVERVIEW DRIVE
CITY 66
EXIT 3AB
IL-3
EXIT 4
MITCHELL
EXIT 9
HAMEL
WORDEN RD
EXIT 33
EXIT 30
1950s 66
EXIT 41
EXIT 37
LIVINGSTON
EXIT 44
MT OLIVE
POST 1930
66
TO SPRINGFIELD
(SEE IL page-23-24)
EDWARDSVILLE
LINDBERG
EZ TOUR
VENICE
GRANITE CITY
EXIT 15AB
CAHOKIA MOUNDS
WATSON
EAST
ST LOUIS IL
COLLINSVILLE
GIANT CATSUP BOTTLE!
IL-159 SOUTH
OF DOWNTOWN
HISTORIC NOTE:
IN THE 1950s, US 66 WAS REROUTED SOUTH FROM MT OLIVE ALONG CURRENT I-55. FROM EXIT 15AB (HWY 159)IN COLLINSVILLE, THE ROUTE FOLLOWED VANDALIA AVE, BELT LINE RD, HWY 157 AND THEN COLLINSVILLE RD INTO EAST ST LOUIS. IN 1963, US 66 MOVED ONTO I-55.
(SEE MO page-2 ALSO)
IL page-25

WB: (PRE-1930 OPTION joins) Go 3 mi on **Hwy 4**. Nearing EXIT 33, turn **RIGHT (Worden Rd**-see map**)**, then quick **LEFT** onto the **Frontage Rd** for 4 mi to **HAMEL**. Cross Hwy 140 and join **Hwy 157** AHEAD for 8 mi to **EDWARDSVILLE**. In town, turn **RIGHT** with **Hwy 157**, go 0.9 mi, past downtown, then turn LEFT with **Hwy 157** at **West St**. After 4.6 mi, continue thru the stoplight at S University Dr (no turn) and curve onto **Chain of Rocks Rd**. Go 4 mi, passing I-255 (no exit) and the Hwy 111 JCT, into **MITCHELL**.

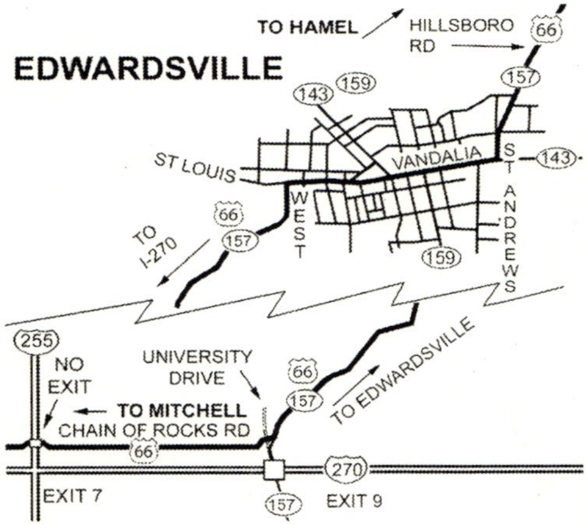

South of **STAUNTON** is **Decamp Junction**, a classic roadhouse from way back. A "roadhouse" of worship is the **St. Paul Lutheran Church** with the **Neon Cross of Route 66**.

GIANT ALERT SIDE TRIP: Use **Livingston Dr** (between **STAUNTON** and **EXIT 33**) to visit **Pink Elephant Antiques** in **Livingston** (on "1950s 66" near I-55 EXIT 37) The **Giant Surfer** and **Pink Elephant** of the former Coliseum (near Benld) live here now with other cool stuff. Or head back up the Frontage Rd from EXIT 33. Then either follow the Frontage Rd down to EXIT 33, or go back on Livingston Dr to IL 4.

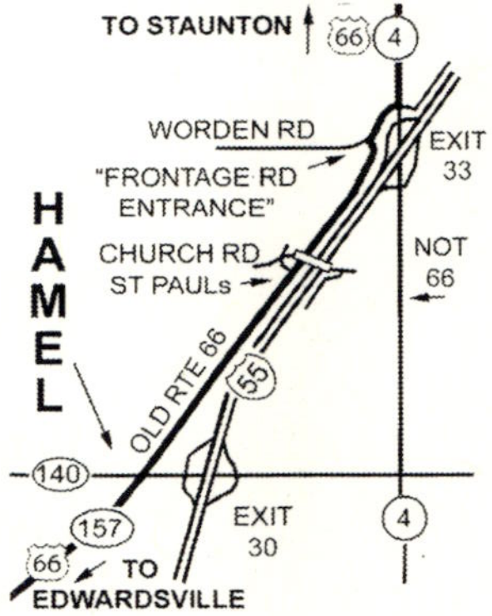

A driver-fuel stop is **Weezy's Route 66 Grille** in **HAMEL**. Look for the old **interurban right-of-way** (culverts and such) along 157 to **EDWARDSVILLE**. The **Stagger Inn** on Vandalia offers live music for a diverse crowd.

EB: From **MITCHELL** take **Chain of Rocks Rd** for 4.4 mi, past the Hwy 111 JCT and I-255(no exit). At the **Hwy 157**/S University light, follow **Hwy 157** uphill (no turn) 4.6 mi into **EDWARDSVILLE**. Turn **RIGHT** with **Hwy 157** onto **St Louis St**, then bear **RIGHT** at the "**Y**". Stay on **Hwy 157(Vandalia St)** for 0.6 mi, thru downtown. Turn **LEFT** with **Hwy 157**. Go 8 mi to Hwy 140 in **HAMEL**. Continue **AHEAD** with "**Old Rte 66**" (Frontage Rd) for 4 mi. Nearing EXIT 33, turn **RIGHT (Worden Rd)**, then **LEFT** on **Hwy 4**.

WB: From **<u>MITCHELL</u>**, turn **LEFT** (just before reaching the overpass) onto the ONRAMP and follow the signs to join **WEST I-270** ("Kansas City"). **AVOID** Old Alton Rd (and the Historic-66 sign here). Go 1.5 mi, then take **EXIT 3A (AVOID** 3B), and join **Hwy-3 SOUTH** (this is a substitute-not 66) past Chain of Rocks Rd (SEE **SIDE TRIPS)**. Take **HWY 3** for 7.3 mi, then continue **AHEAD** (**AVOID** the Hwy 3 turn at the Broadway light) to follow the divided 4 lane as it curves up to enter **<u>MISSOURI</u>** via **McKinley Bridge** (a stoplight past this 2 lane bridge may cause back-up at rush hour: see **NOTE** below for ALTERNATE routes- also see map **MO page-2)**

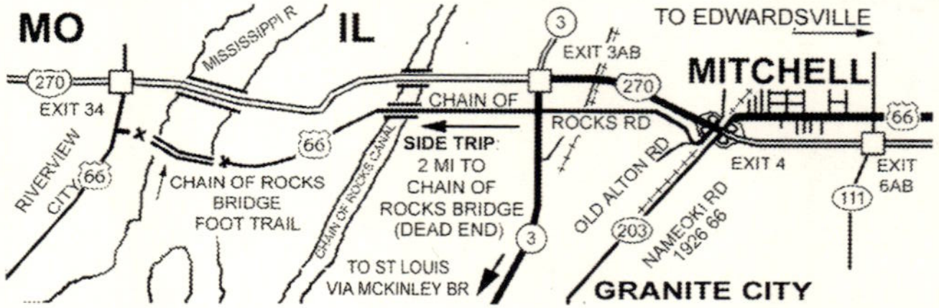

Some Rte 66 atmosphere remains on **Chain of Rocks Rd**, with old motels and signs along the way. **<u>MITCHELL</u>**'s **Luna Café** (1924) has a great restored neon sign and quite a history, involving gangsters (Al Capone drove 66!) gambling and "ladies of the night," whose presence was suppposedly announced by lighting the "cherry" on the neon sign. Its much tamer, now.

<u>Chain of Rocks SIDE TRIP #1</u>: Head west on **SPUR 66/Chain of Rocks Rd** from HWY 3 (just south of EXIT 3A) to the **ILLINOIS** end of **Chain of Rocks Bridge** (a 4-mile round trip). A one-lane bridge en route requires a delay at a traffic light. HIKE across the famous "bent" bridge from the parking lot. As always, safeguard your stuff.
<u>SIDE TRIP #2</u>: **Route 66/Chain of Rocks Rd** runs for 1.5 mi east from HWY 3. Double back (carefully) at Old Alton Rd.

<u>NOTE</u>: **Route 66** evolved a bewildering tangle of "main" and "city" routes to cross into **MISSOURI**, many of which are difficult or not "tourist friendly" (too complicated, rough, etc). The **1926** route took HWY 203/Nameoki Rd thru **<u>GRANITE CITY</u>**, and passed thru **<u>MADISON</u>** to cross the **Mickinley Bridge** in **<u>VENICE</u>** (see **MO map** #1) In **1929**, US 66 used **Hwy 3** (and also **Hwy 203**) south from **<u>VENICE</u>** to **<u>EAST ST LOUIS</u>**. Matters are just as complex on the other side of the river, so stick to the **EZ tour** via **IL 3** and **I-70** (modern substitutes), or, as an **ALTERNATE**, double back on I-270 to use **I-255** and **I-55** to cross the Mississippi. Or use **I-270** (path of **POST-1936 US 66**) or **I-255 / I-270** to circle past the river area, if **time** or **traffic** require (expect traffic!). Be sure to double back into **<u>ST LOUIS</u>**.

EB: At the Broadway light, continue **AHEAD** onto **Hwy 3** (NO turn). Go 7.3 mi, cross Chain of Rocks Rd (SEE **SIDE TRIPS**) then quickly **JOIN EAST I-270** at **EXIT 3**. Take **EXIT 4 (AVOID** Old Alton Rd**)** to **Hwy 203** ("Granite City"). Curve down, then turn **RIGHT** on HWY 203, cross under I-270, and curve onto **Chain of Rocks Rd** in **<u>MITCHELL</u>** (note Luna Café for next mileage reading).
(see **Illinois INTRO on IL page-1)**

(see MAP # 5 on IL page-25)

SHOW ME MISSOURI!

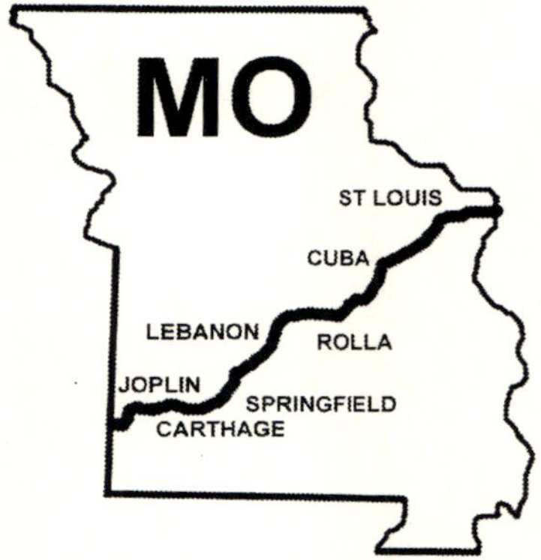

MISSOURI sure has plenty to show the Route 66 road warrior. From the sprawling city and suburbs of **ST LOUIS**, to the former mining region of **JOPLIN**, with the forested limestone hills of the **Ozarks** in between, **MISSOURI** loves company.

US 66 inherited the path of **State HWY 14**, then was upgraded and finally 4-laned for much of the over 300-mile length in the 1950s. Some of this **4-Lane 66** was later rebuilt to I-44 standards, while other sections, such as near **DEVILS ELBOW**, survive, as do many miles of multi-generation **2-lane road**.

ST LOUIS, gateway to the west, nests in a tangled web of roads and freeways. Over the decades, **US 66** used a bewildering variety of streets thru the region: main, city, truck, bypass and optional routes made worse by later road building and One-Way streets. The maps that follow this urban area show **SOME** of those bygone alignments, but **NOT** all the myriad routes. To make it a bit **EZ**-er, the official tour uses a substitute combo of **IL HWY 3** and **I-70** (across Mckinley Bridge, the 1926 crossing) to connect **Chain of Rocks Bridge** to downtown. If time or traffic conditions require you to cross the area quickly, use I-270 around the north (the path of **Post 1936 Route 66)**, then follow US 67 south from Exit 25AB to Watson Rd, and double back as needed. Optionally, I-255 heads south to connect with I-270, then joins I-44. To the west, see **MO page- 8** for the **PRE-1932 OPTION** along **MO HWY 100**.

Most of **Route 66** thru the state is more serene, including many scenic wooded drives thru hills and valleys out of sight of the superslab. The people are friendly and history abounds, as do relics of the roadside past. Enjoy what **MISSOURI** has to show. **CAR GAME**: "**Historic Byway**." Look for blue and white "**Historic 66 Byway**" signs. **FIRST** to spot one gets a letter. Spell "**HISTORIC**" to win!

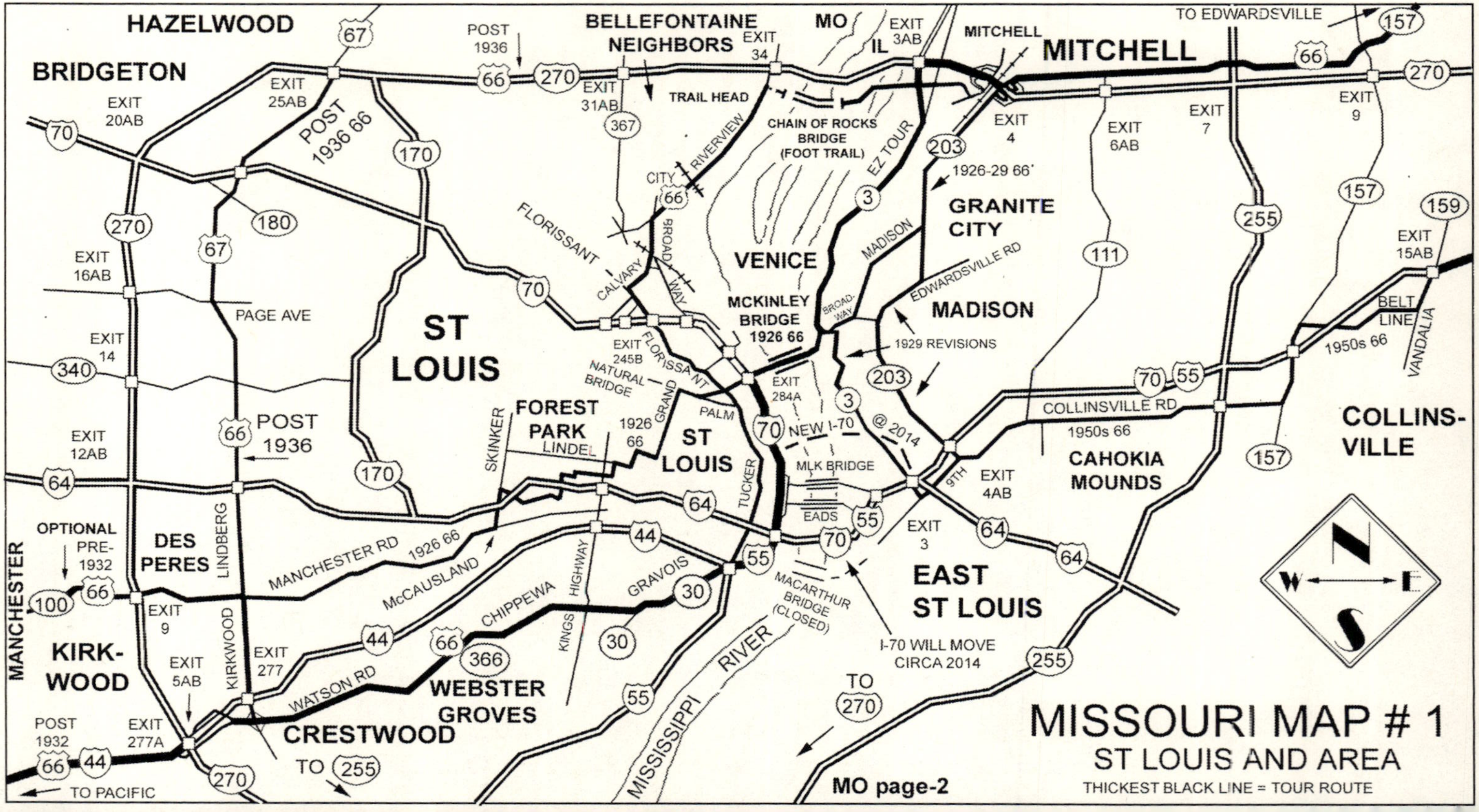
MISSOURI MAP # 1
ST LOUIS AND AREA
THICKEST BLACK LINE = TOUR ROUTE
MO page-2
HAZELWOOD
BRIDGETON
BELLEFONTAINE NEIGHBORS
MO
IL
MITCHELL
GRANITE CITY
VENICE
MADISON
ST LOUIS
FOREST PARK
EAST ST LOUIS
CAHOKIA MOUNDS
COLLINS-VILLE
DES PERES
KIRK-WOOD
WEBSTER GROVES
CRESTWOOD
MANCHESTER
TO EDWARDSVILLE
TO PACIFIC
TO 255
TO 270
POST 1936
POST 1936 66
POST 1932
OPTIONAL PRE-1932
1926-29 66
1929 REVISIONS
1926 66
1950s 66
TRAIL HEAD
CHAIN OF ROCKS BRIDGE (FOOT TRAIL)
EZ TOUR
MCKINLEY BRIDGE 1926 66
NEW I-70
@ 2014
MLK BRIDGE
EADS
MACARTHUR BRIDGE (CLOSED)
I-70 WILL MOVE CIRCA 2014
MISSISSIPPI RIVER
RIVERVIEW
CITY
BROADWAY
FLORISSANT
CALVARY
NATURAL BRIDGE
GRAND
PALM
TUCKER
SKINKER
LINDEL
MANCHESTER RD
McCAUSLAND
CHIPPEWA
GRAVOIS
KINGS HIGHWAY
WATSON RD
LINDBERG
KIRKWOOD
PAGE AVE
EDWARDSVILLE RD
COLLINSVILLE RD
9TH
BELT LINE
VANDALIA
EXIT 20AB
EXIT 25AB
EXIT 31AB
EXIT 34
EXIT 3AB
EXIT 4
EXIT 6AB
EXIT 7
EXIT 9
EXIT 15AB
EXIT 16AB
EXIT 14
EXIT 12AB
EXIT 245B
EXIT 284A
EXIT 3
EXIT 4AB
EXIT 9
EXIT 5AB
EXIT 277
EXIT 277A
N
S
E
W

WB: Cross **McKinley Bridge** into **<u>MISSOURI</u>**. (2-lane bridge-traffic ALERT) Follow the signs "**To East I-70**," cross I-70, then **quick LEFT** onto **11th** to join **EAST I-70** south towards downtown **<u>ST LOUIS</u>**. (see **MO page-4** for directions to the arch and downtown).

<u>**ADVISORY**: I-70 will be rerouted across the river north of downtown circa 2014-15. I-44 will connect directly thru downtown.</u>

Like all big cities, **ST LOUIS** can dish out the traffic jams, so plan your trip accordingly (and be very careful in unfamiliar urban areas). The two-lane **McKinley Bridge** (1926 '66) can slow due to stoplights. **<u>SIDE TRIP</u>**: The **Chain of Rocks Bridge** (with the 22-degree turn in the middle) was built in 1929 and became part of US 66 in 1936, but was abandoned in 1968. **Trailnet Inc** began refurbishing the bridge in 1997, now open only to hikers and bikers. www.trailnet.org Until <u>safety issues</u> are solved at the Missouri end, park on the Illinois side (SEE **IL page-27**).

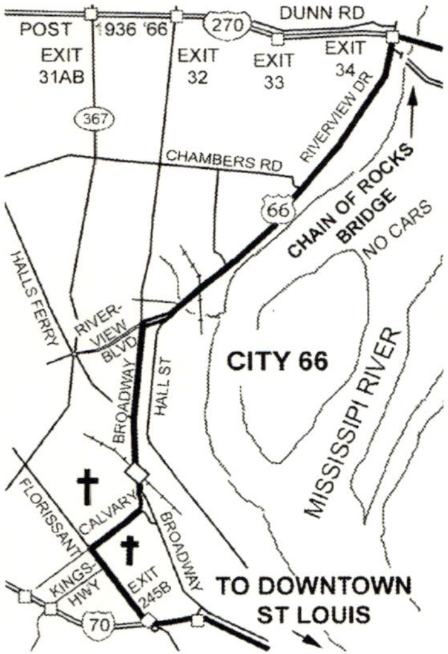

<u>HISTORIC NOTE</u>: "**City 66**" ran from Chain of Rocks to downtown (see map at left). South past **I-70 EXIT 245B**, the route narrows as it winds thru a decayed region of empty lots and boarded-up row houses, churches and stores, the ghosts of once lively neighborhoods. The <u>many</u> **STOP** signs are annoying, and it is easy to turn wrong (I have). Chance this stretch if you wish, but the "**Official**" **EZ Tour Route** makes it "EZ" for you to skip ahead to downtown and the Arch (**MO page-4**) by substituting **IL HWY 3** and **I-70**. It's OK, just this once.

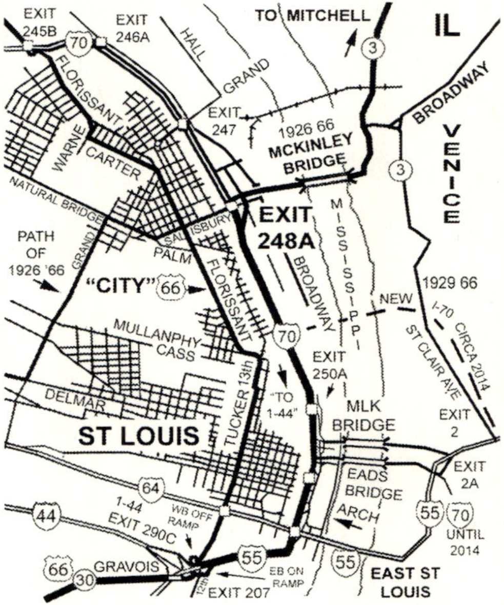

EB: Take **WEST I-70** north from downtown **<u>ST LOUIS</u>**. Take **EXIT 248A**, cross Salisbury, then **quick RIGHT** on **McKinley Bridge**, across the river into **<u>ILLINOIS</u>** (2-lane bridge traffic ALERT). Curve down onto **Cedar St** and past the Broadway light (**NO** turns).

WB: (SEE ARCH SIDE TRIP) From **EAST I-70** near downtown **ST LOUIS**, follow the "**To I-44**" signs towards **SOUTH I-55**. Pass **EXIT 208**, then **KEEP RIGHT** on **WEST I-44** ("TULSA") at **EXIT 207**. Stay in the **RIGHT** lane, and **QUICKLY** take **I-44 EXIT 290C** (12th St/Gravois). Curve around onto **Tucker St**, cross the freeways, and bear **RIGHT** at the 12th ST stoplight onto **Gravois/HWY 30**. Go 3 mi (across Grand Blvd), then, at the **Chippewa St** stoplight, turn **RIGHT** with **Chippewa/HWY 366**.

ADVISORY: I-70 will be routed across a new bridge from E St Louis to north of downtown by 2014-15.

Curving skyward between the muddy **Mississippi River** and downtown **ST LOUIS** is the shining **Gateway Arch**, built on the riverfront in **Jefferson National Expansion Memorial** to commemorate the western growth of the US. You can ride an internal tramcar to the tip-top of the 630-foot monument, completed in 1965, for a dizzy panoramic view of the area. Under the arch lies the **Museum of Westward Expansion**. **GIFT SHOP ALERT**! Two blocks west, the **Old Courthouse** dates to 1839. www.gatewayarch.com www.nps.gov/jeff/mus-tour.htm As usual, safeguard your stuff when parked.

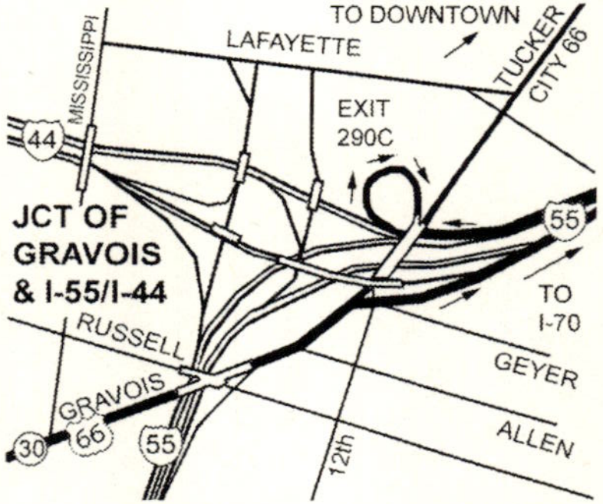

ARCH SIDE TRIP: From the **NORTH**, take I-70 **EXIT 250A** (exit # may change) "MLK Bridge /ARCH." Follow the ARCH signs, curve under I-70, bear **RIGHT** at the light onto **Laclede's Landing Blvd (AVOID the MLK Bridge)**. **RIGHT** on **N Leanor K Sullivan Blvd**. Park in the garage on Washington, or try the riverfront parking.

From the **SOUTH**: From I-55, use **EXIT 209A** ("Downtown") or I-70 **EXIT 251C** and join **Memorial Drive** (follow "ARCH" signs) to **Washington**. **RIGHT** to the riverfront. **BOTH WAYS**: After, take **Poplar** back to **Memorial Dr** and follow signs to **JOIN I-70 N or S**.

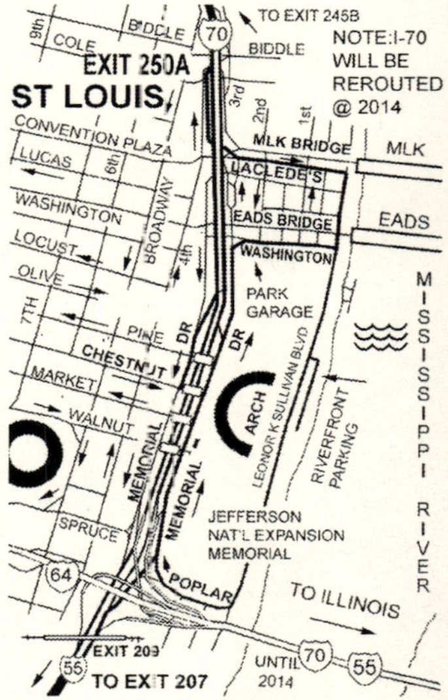

EB: **LEFT** on **Gravois/HWY 30**. Go almost 3 mi. Past the light at Russell Blvd, get in the right lane and follow signs "**TO I-55 North**." **JOIN NORTH I-55** (SEE **ARCH SIDE TRIP**). Stay in the **LEFT** lanes and **JOIN WEST I-70** (going north) at **EXIT 209B** (this I-70 section will be signed "I-44" & "To I-70" after the relocation circa 2014). Go past downtown **ST LOUIS** about 3 mi to take **EXIT 248A**.

WB: Follow **Chippewa/HWY 366** for 9 mi (Chippewa becomes **Watson Rd** en route) thru **SHREWSBURY**, **MARLBOROUGH**, **WEBSTER GROVES** and **CRESTWOOD** to cross **Kirkwood Rd/US 67** (NOTE: south of I-40 EXIT 277). See **OPTION** MO page-8

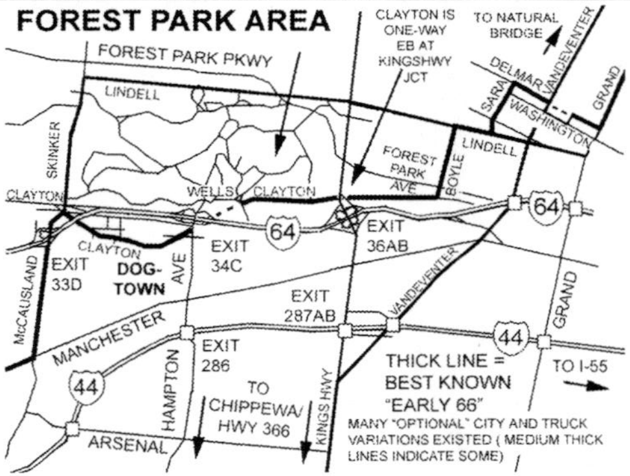

The route along **Gravois** and **Chippewa** runs thru interesting neighborhoods lined with old businesses and charming houses, with variations of cottage styles, differing in the details. **Ted Drewes Frozen Custard** at 6726 **Chippewa** (between Lansdowne & Jamieson) is the major tourist attraction, selling their thick "concretes" since about 1941. http://www.teddrewes.com/

SIDE TRIP: **Forest Park** is a historic area that early 66 ran thru. Its many attractions include the **Missouri History Museum**. A profusion of short lived "optional," "city," and "truck" routes add to the confusion created by cut streets and a One-Way section as older 66 zigs up to McKinley Bridge (**NOT** part of TOUR: shown for historic purposes). **DOGTOWN**, on Clayton, is a lively neighborhood of old buildings. **GIANT ALERT**! Watch for the **GIANT AMOCO SIGN** at Clayton and McCausland. Its ancestor dated back to old 66!

GIANT ALERT! **Giant Farmer and Son** at Sappington Farmers Market in General Grant Center, 8400 Watson Rd. The **Crestwood Bowl** sign (9822 Watson) is being restored. In **MARLBOROUGH** was the site of the now-demolished **Coral Court Motel**. Shame they destroyed this "Streamline Moderne" masterpiece. See a preserved example of one of the 1941 bungalows at the **Museum of Transportation**, where the rebuilt unit is on "semi-permanent" display, along with many old trains and other transport relics. **Directions**: From I-270 EXIT 8 at Dougherty Ferry Road, head west for a mile to Barrett Station Road, then turn left for one-half mile (see map on MO page-8). **INFO:** http://www.museumoftransport.org/welcome.htm or (314) -965-7998.

EB: (**PRE-32 OPTION** from MO page-8 **REJOINS** here) From the JCT with **Kirkwood Rd/US 67** (NOTE: south of I-44 EXIT 277) follow **Watson Rd/HWY 366** for 9 mi, thru **CRESTWOOD**, **WEBSTER GROVES**, **MARLBOROUGH** and **SHREWSBURY** into **ST LOUIS** (en route, Watson Rd becomes **Chippewa St**) to the JCT with **HWY 30/Gravois St** (prepare for left turn).

(see MO MAP # 1 on Mo page-2)

MISSOURI MAP # 2

BOURBON ~ I-270

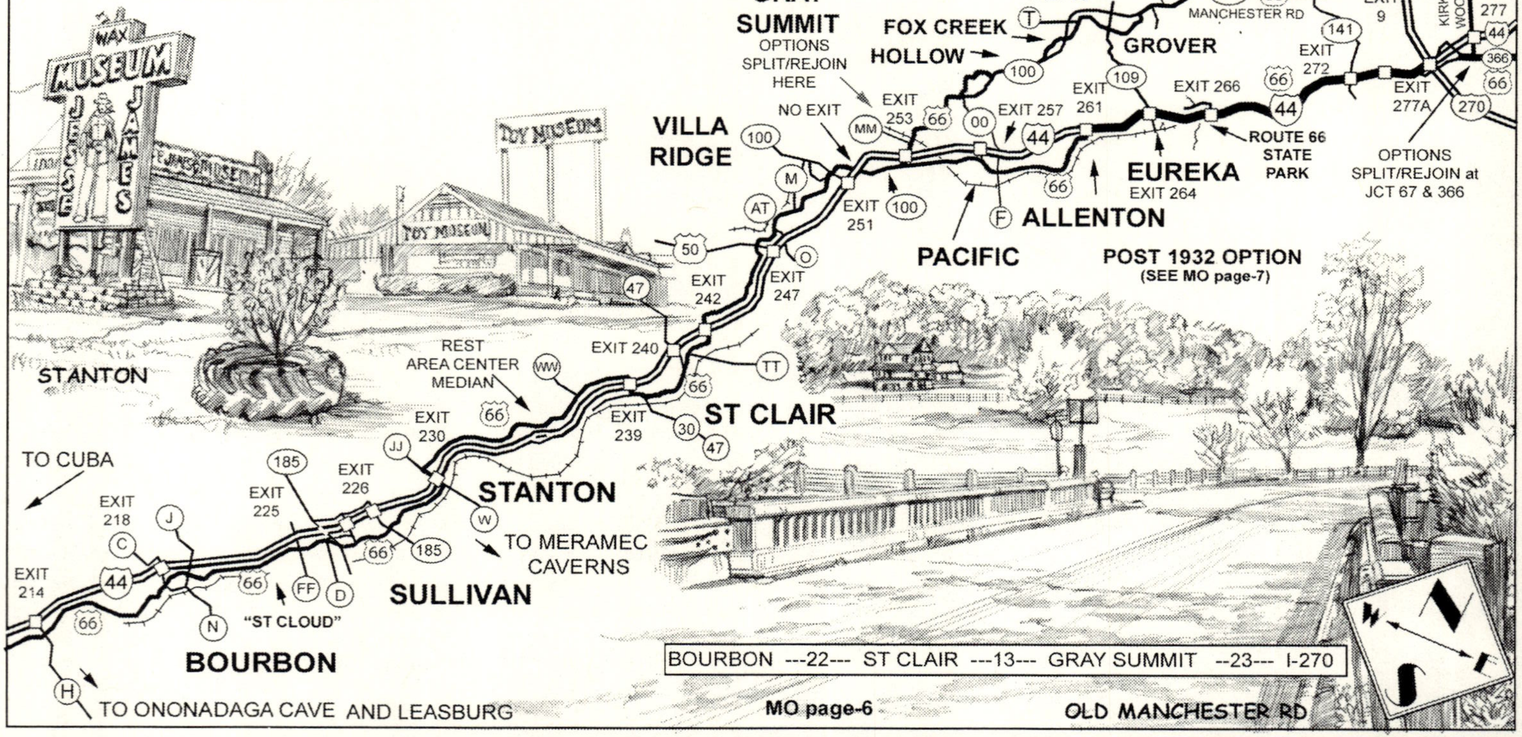

BOURBON ---22--- ST CLAIR ---13--- GRAY SUMMIT --23--- I-270

WB: Continue on **Watson** past Kirkwood (US 67) to join **I-44 WEST ("Tulsa")**. Take **I-44** past the I-270 JCT, EXIT 266 (**Route 66 State Park**) and EXIT 264 (**EUREKA**) to take **EXIT 261** (**ALLENTON**). Cross under I-44 and follow **BL 44/Osage St** about 9 mi thru **PACIFIC** (no turns). Continue **AHEAD** when **HWY 100** joins at EXIT 253/**GRAY SUMMIT** (go to **MO page-9** to continue.)

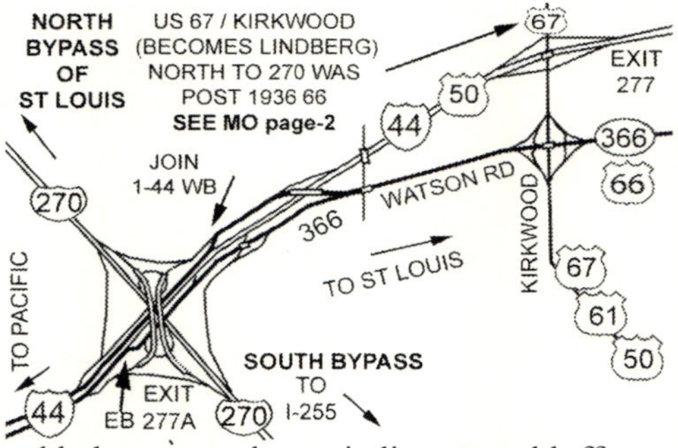

WB NOTE: **THIS** page covers the **POST 1932 ROUTE** along **I-44** west thru **PACIFIC** to **GRAY SUMMIT** (the **PRE-1932 OPTION via HWY 100** diverges at **Kirkwood Rd** and **Watson**…see **MO page-8** and choose your route). Some I-44 driving is required this page. West of **ST LOUIS**, the route slips thru a region of forested hills, with big cuts and steep grades. **Route 66 State Park**, east of **EUREKA** at Exit 266 is the site of former **Times Beach,** long abandoned and demolished due to dioxin contamination (quite safe now). A nifty **Route 66 Exhibit** is located there in the **Bridgehead Inn**, a former 1935 roadhouse east of the currently closed and partly demolished **Meramec River Bridge** (636) 938-7198. **ALLENTON** is home to Six Flags theme park, and is the eastern end of a section of **POST-'32 US 66** that winds with the railroad below rugged, scenic limestone bluffs thru **PACIFIC**. NOTE: The former Red Cedar Inn on the east side of town is now a business center.

EB NOTE: If time or traffic require you to get around to the other side of **ST LOUIS** quickly, try I-270 around the north of the city, or I-270 south to connect with I-255 (see **MO page-2**)

EB: if reading ahead, see **MO page-8** to compare **PRE-32 OPTION** from EXIT 253.

EB: (**Post-1932 OPTION**) From **EXIT 253** (JCT HWY 100) take the **S Outer Rd/BL 44/Osage St** about 9 mi (no turns) thru **PACIFIC**. Join **I-44 EAST** at **ALLENTON** EXIT 261. Go about 14 mi. At the I-270 interchange, take **EXIT 277A** (**366 East/Watson Rd**). Follow the signs for **366 East/Watson Rd** past Kirkwood Rd and continue with **Watson/Hwy 366** towards **ST LOUIS**.

WB: PRE-1932 OPTION: from Watson Rd, follow **Kirkwood/US 67** north for 3 mi to **HWY 100** in **DES PERES**. Turn **LEFT**, follow **HWY 100/Manchester Rd** across I-270, then go 7.5 mi (thru **MANCHESTER** & **BALLWIN**) to cross Hwy 340 in **ELLISVILLE**. Continue 2 mi, then **LEFT** with **Manchester Rd**. Go 4.6 mi (thru **GROVER**, across HWY 109, thru **POND** to **FOX CREEK**). Cross HWY 100, then **QUICK LEFT** onto **Old Manchester Rd**. Go less than 1 mi. At Melrose Rd, turn **LEFT**, then **RIGHT** on **HWY 100**. Go 2.4 mi (thru **HOLLOW**). Turn **RIGHT** on **Old Manchester Rd**, then 2 mi further, turn **RIGHT** on **HWY 100** (at the HWY "OO" JCT). Stay on **HWY 100** for 6 mi to **GRAY SUMMIT** (EXIT 253), **CROSS** I-44, turn **RIGHT** with HWY 100 (rejoin main tour).

The **PRE-1932 OPTION** on **THIS PAGE** is a mix of urbanized multi-lane strip thru **MANCHESTER**, and scenic two-lane stretches thru the hills of the Rockwoods Range west of **ELLISVILLE**.

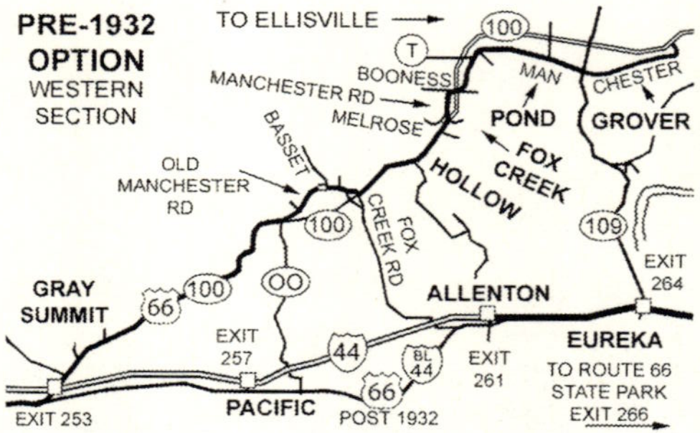

OPTIONAL SUGGESTION: Use **HWY 109** between Manchester Rd at **GROVER** and I-44 EXIT 264 at **EUREKA** as a connector to combine the scenic western portion of the **Pre-'32 Route** with the **Post-'32** section (and **Route 66 State Park** at EXIT 266) in one trip (you can double back to **MANCHESTER** or **PACIFIC** as desired). **NOTE**: Hwy 109 is **STEEP** north of **EUREKA**.

West of **POND** is **Big Chief Roadhouse**, in the former 1929 Big Chief Cabin Hotel.

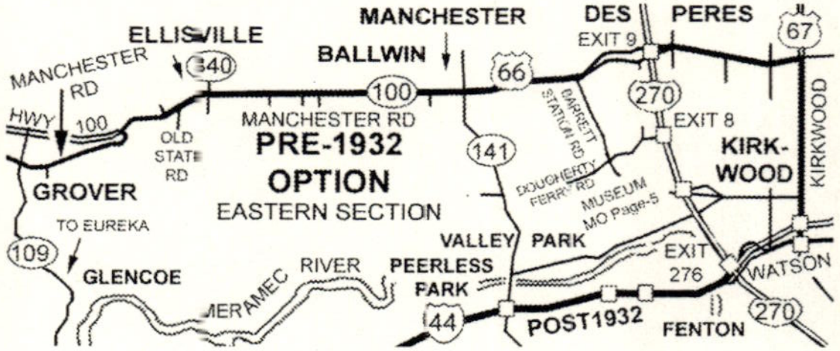

EB: PRE-1932 OPTION: Turn **LEFT** and follow **HWY 100** across I-44 at **EXIT 253** in **GRAY SUMMIT**. Continue almost 6 mi, and turn **LEFT** onto **Old Manchester Rd** (at the HWY "OO" JCT). Go 2 mi, turn **LEFT** onto **HWY 100**. Go 2.4 mi (thru **HOLLOW**) then turn **LEFT** and **QUICK RIGHT** onto **Manchester Rd**. Go 0.8 mi. **Cross** HWY 100 at **Booness Rd**, curve **LEFT** with **Old Manchester Rd** for 2.8 mi (thru **FOX CREEK** and **POND**) to HWY 109. Cross, then go 1.8 mi, turn **RIGHT** on **HWY 100 (Manchester Rd)**. Go 9 mi (thru **ELLISVILLE**, **BALLWIN** and **MANCHESTER**) to cross I-270. Continue 2.5 mi thru **DES PERES** to **Kirkwood Rd/US 67**: turn **RIGHT**. Go 3 mi (crossing I-44). At the HWY 366 JCT, take the off ramp, then turn **LEFT** onto **Watson Rd/Hwy 366**.

(**REJOIN** MAIN EB TOUR on **MO page-5**)

WB: Take **HWY 100** west from **<u>GRAY SUMMIT</u>**. **CROSS** I-44 (no exit) to the stoplight near EXIT 251 (HWY 100 turns). Continue **AHEAD** to JOIN **HWY AT** for 4.8 mi. **CROSS** US 50 to join the **North Outer Road** for 5 mi to **EXIT 242**. **CROSS** I-44, and turn **RIGHT** on the **South Outer Rd** to **<u>ST CLAIR</u>**. Continue with **Commercial Ave** at the **HWY 47** light. At the next light (1 mi), turn **RIGHT** with **N HWY 30**, then go 0.2 mi and turn **RIGHT**. **CROSS** I-44 @ **EXIT 239**, then **LEFT** with **HWY WW/N Outer Rd**. Stay with the **North Outer Rd** past the HWY WW turnoff, then **CROSS** I-44 at **EXIT 230** (HWY W) into **<u>STANTON</u>**.

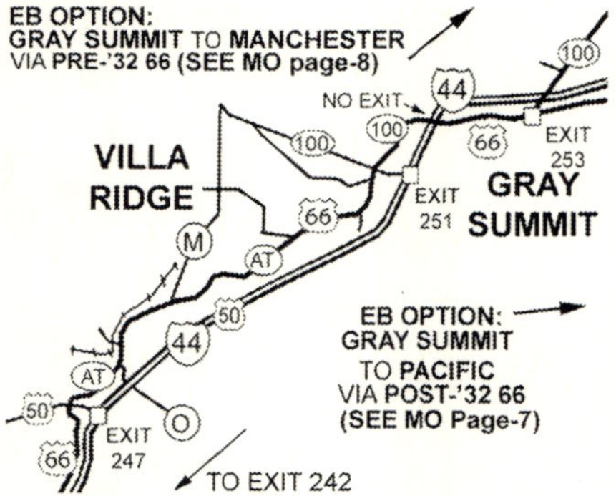

Since 1925, **<u>GRAY SUMMIT</u>** has been home to **Shaw Nature Reserve** (formerly the Shaw Arboretum), with 2,500 acres of natural Ozark landscape and plant collections. The many natural and landscaped settings, including 13 miles of trails, are open year round, 7 am to sunset (the visitor center has its own hours). Their 1879 **Joseph H. Bascom Manor House** contains exhibits titled "People on the Land" covering conservation issues (636) 451-3512.

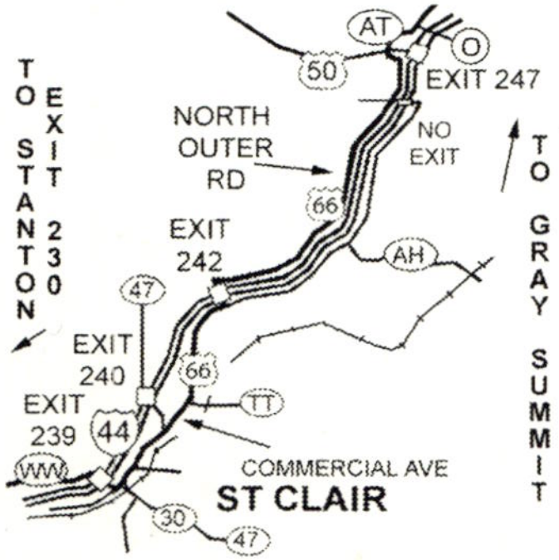

On Hwy 100 south of I-44, watch for the **Gardenway Motel's** classic neon sign as you drive past. On HWY AT (at the Y with old Hwy 100), the big bldg with rounded corners was home to the old **Diamonds Restaurant**. On the North Outer Rd just east of **EXIT 242**, view the "Indian" stuff from your car as you drive past. **<u>ST CLAIR</u>** has the **Lewis Café** on 145 S Main, and a **Museum** at 280 Hibbard St. West of town, 66 briefly continues along the tracks before ending. A few former motels still repose east of **<u>STANTON</u>**.

EB: Choose which **OPTION** to take at **<u>GRAY SUMMIT</u>**.

EB: In **<u>STANTON</u>**, **CROSS** I-44 at **EXIT 230**, then **RIGHT** on the **North Outer Rd** (becomes **HWY WW**). Go 8.8 mi. At **EXIT 239**, **CROSS** I-44 on **HWY 30**, then **LEFT** with **HWY 30** into **<u>ST CLAIR</u>**. Turn **LEFT** with **Commercial Ave/HWY 47** at the light. Go 1 mi, and continue past N Main (HWY 47 turns here to EXIT 240). Follow the **South Outer Rd** for 2.3 mi to **EXIT 242**. **CROSS** I-44, and take the **North Outer Rd RIGHT** for 5 mi. **CROSS** US 50 to join **HWY AT** for 4.8 mi. At the **HWY 100** stoplight (near EXIT 251) continue **AHEAD** (not turn) onto **EAST HWY 100**. **CROSS** I-44 (no exit) then continue 1.3 mi to EXIT 253 in **<u>GRAY SUMMIT</u>**.

(see **MO page-7** to stay on **POST-1932 '66**)

(see **MO page-8** to follow **PRE-1932 '66**)

WB: In **STANTON**, CROSS **I-44** at **EXIT 230**, then turn **RIGHT** on the **South Outer Rd**. Go 5.7 mi (becomes **Springfield Rd**) into **SULLIVAN**. Turn **LEFT** at the **3-Way Stop** on **N HWY 185**, then continue **AHEAD** with **Springfield Rd** (no turns) to join the **South Outer Rd.** Continue past S HWY D and past HWY FF, then thru **ST CLOUD**. Continue **AHEAD** at the HWY J JCT, to curve thru **BOURBON** on **"Old Hwy 66."** At W Pine St (HWY C to EXIT 218), continue **AHEAD** on **"Old HWY 66"** towards **CUBA**.

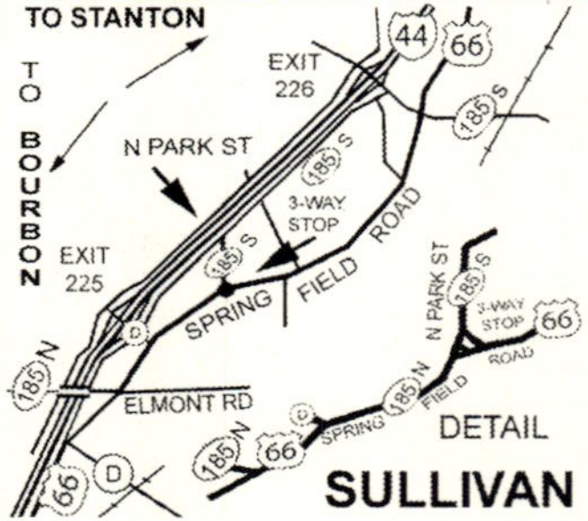

STANTON's proximity to **Meramec Caverns** brought in other tourist attractions. Near EXIT 230 is **Jesse James Wax Museum**, which claims the bandit died in 1952 under the name J. Frank Dalton (instead of being shot to death in 1881). Open everyday June-August (weekends otherwise) (573) 927-5233. En route to the cave (3 miles south on HWY W) is **Riverside Reptile Ranch**, an old-fashioned snake and gator roadside exhibit. **Meramec Caverns** itself is responsible for all those barn-side billboards along Route 66 (a restored example is in Illinois). The extensive caverns, along the banks of the Meramec River, are claimed to be a Jesse James hideout (573) 468-3166. **GIFT SHOP ALERTS**! (all of the above)

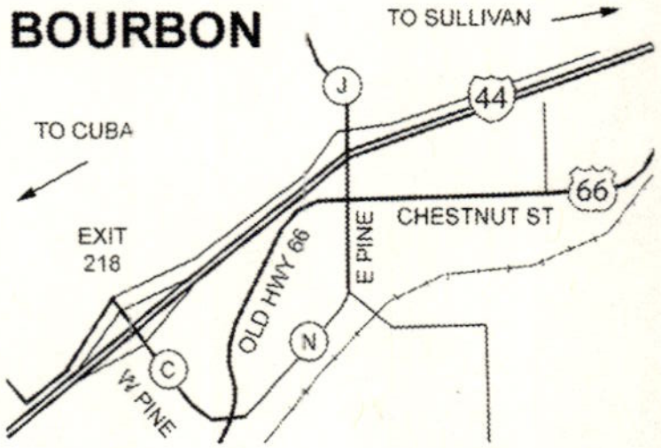

When US 66 was 4-laned in the '50s, the new WB lanes ran along what is now I-44 N Outer Rd thru **SULLIVAN**, right by Snell's Café (slogan: "Awful Good Food"). Snell's is long-gone, and the building (which began as an Alamo-style motel) is currently empty. Riverside camping and floating are available in the area. **BOURBON** is infamous for its water tower labeled "Bourbon" (to the delight of countless tourists). The **Circle Inn Malt Shop** on the west side has good roadfood.

NOTE: The intersections of **N & S Hwy 185** (and **HWY D**) in **SULLIVAN** can **confuse. NO TURNS** except at the **3-WAY STOP**.

EB: Follow **"Old HWY 66"** into **BOURBON**. At W Pine St (HWY C from EXIT 218), continue **AHEAD** on **"Old Hwy 66"**. At HWY J (E Pine St), continue **AHEAD** on '66, thru **ST CLOUD**. Cross the HWY FF JCT. Past the HWY D JCT (2 mi from FF), continue **AHEAD** with **Springfield Rd** (no turns) thru **SULLIVAN**. Turn **RIGHT** at the **3-Way STOP** (**AVOID** the left onto SOUTH 185) and then continue **AHEAD** with **Springfield Rd** (becomes the **South Outer Rd**) for 5.7 mi to **STANTON**.

(see **MAP # 2** on **MO page-6**)

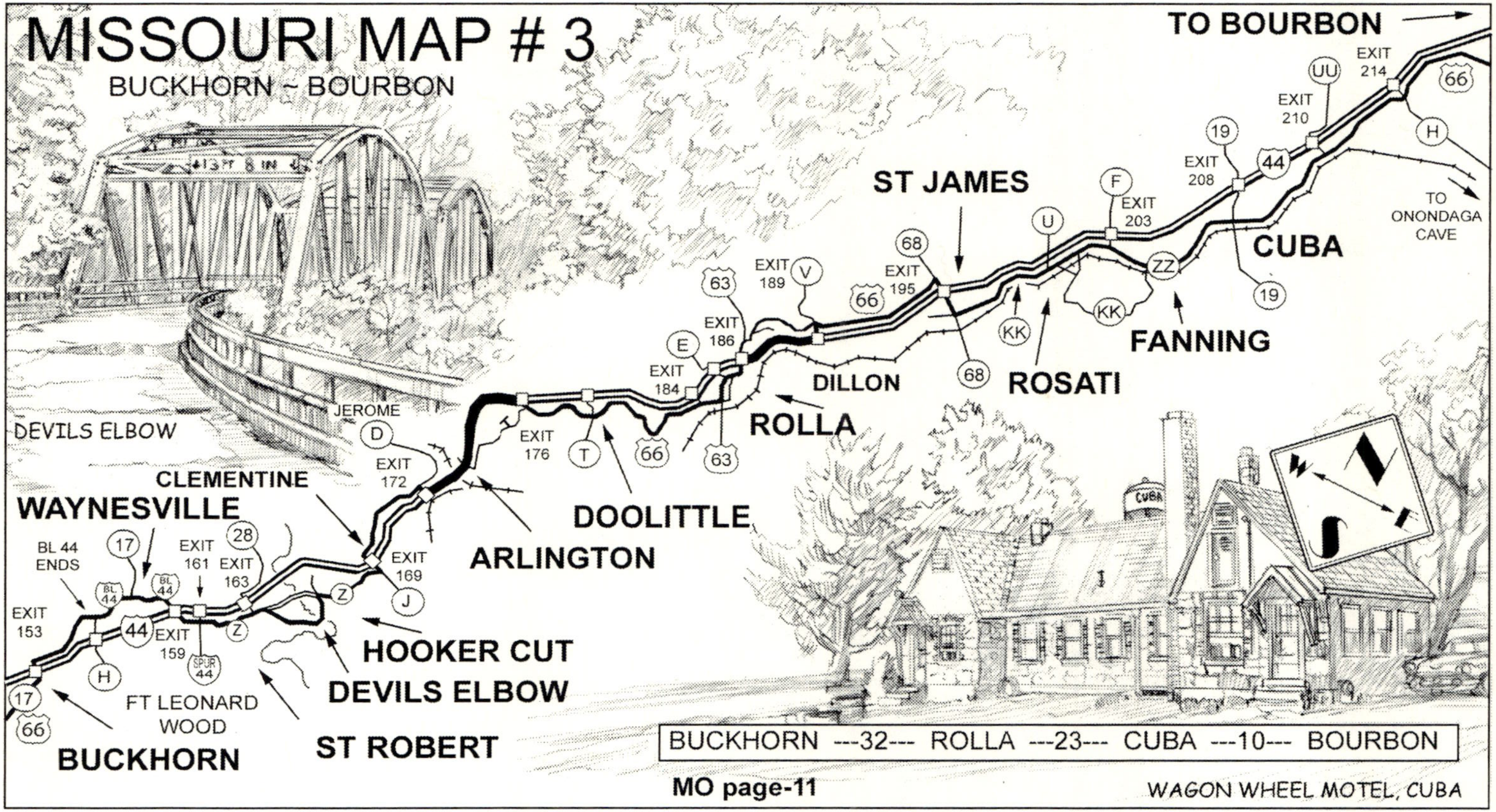
MISSOURI MAP # 3
BUCKHORN ~ BOURBON
TO BOURBON
DEVILS ELBOW
JEROME
CLEMENTINE
WAYNESVILLE
BL 44 ENDS
EXIT 153
EXIT 159
EXIT 161
EXIT 163
EXIT 169
EXIT 172
EXIT 176
EXIT 184
EXIT 186
EXIT 189
EXIT 195
EXIT 203
EXIT 208
EXIT 210
EXIT 214
ARLINGTON
DOOLITTLE
ROLLA
DILLON
ST JAMES
ROSATI
FANNING
CUBA
TO ONONDAGA CAVE
HOOKER CUT
DEVILS ELBOW
ST ROBERT
FT LEONARD WOOD
BUCKHORN
BUCKHORN ---32--- ROLLA ---23--- CUBA ---10--- BOURBON
WAGON WHEEL MOTEL, CUBA

WB: Take "**Old Hwy 66**" (becomes the S Outer Rd) from **BOURBON** for 11 mi into **CUBA** (becomes **Washington St**). Continue **AHEAD** at the JCT of Franklin St (HWY 19) and follow **Washington St** (becomes **HWY ZZ**) for 7.5 mi (past **FANNING**). Becomes **HWY KK** at **ROSATI**. Continue **AHEAD** (no turns) on **HWY KK** alongside I-44 for 5.6 mi into **ST JAMES** (becomes **James Blvd**). Turn **RIGHT** at **Jefferson St** (HWY 68) to cross I-44 at **EXIT 195.**

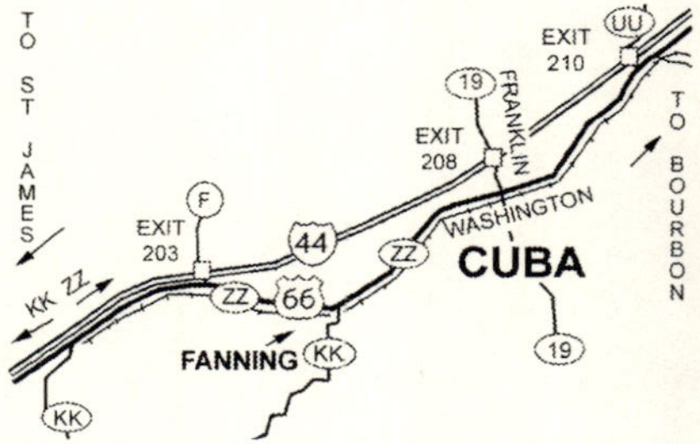

West of **BOURBON** is a nice little drive along the RR thru a green farm scene. HWY H leads to **Onondaga Cave State Park**, which also had some painted barn signs along '66 (not as many as Meramec Caverns). On the eastern outskirts of **CUBA**, **Missouri Hickory Bar B Q** greets you with their stereotypical sign of a coverall-clad Hillbilly, holding his favorite hog.

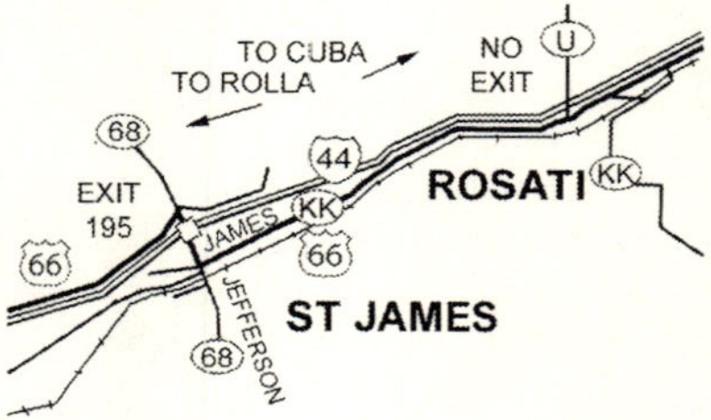

CUBA's recently and wonderfully restored **Wagon Wheel Motel** has a great neon sign and lots of atmosphere. Also in connection is **Connie's Shoppe** for gifts. (573) 885-3411 www.wagonwheel66cuba.com Proclaimed the "**Route 66 Mural City,**" **CUBA**'s MANY murals include a depiction of bygone "Al West Motor/Tractor Sales," and another of soldiers going off to war on the "FRISCO." **CUBA** still has a Drive-In Theatre, north on HWY 19. Downtown at HWY 19 and 66 is a beautifully restored and muraled **1932 Phillips 66**. **GIANT ALERT**! Giant **ROCKING CHAIR** at **US 66 Outpost** in **FANNING**. It's a nice drive betwixt **CUBA** and **ROSATI**, home to **Rosati** and **St James Wineries**. Many grape stands are open in season ("Grapes by Bushel, box or pound"). **ST JAMES** has an interesting downtown just off the route. **NOTE:** The divided, tree-lined alignment of 66 that continues to the west of Jefferson St is soon interrupted by I-44, requiring a jump up at EXIT 195 onto the N Outer Rd on the way to **ROLLA**.

EB: Take **Jefferson St** (HWY 68) south about 0.4 mi from **EXIT 195** into **ST JAMES**. Turn **LEFT** on **James Blvd/HWY KK** and continue for 5.6 mi to **ROSATI**. Here HWY KK turns south, continue **AHEAD**, joining **HWY ZZ** for 7.5 mi (past **FANNING**) into **CUBA** (becomes **Washington St**.) Continue **AHEAD** at the JCT of Franklin St (HWY 19) to follow **Washington St** (becomes **S Outer Rd**) for 11 mi, to **BOURBON**.

WB: CROSS I-44 at **EXIT 195**, then **LEFT** on **N Outer Rd** (first light). Go 6 mi to HWY V (EXIT 189). Turn **LEFT** then **RIGHT** on the onramp to join **WEST** I-44 to **ROLLA** (visit the MULE first!). Take **EXIT 186**. **LEFT** on **BL 44/Bishop Ave/ US 63**. Go 1.4 mi.

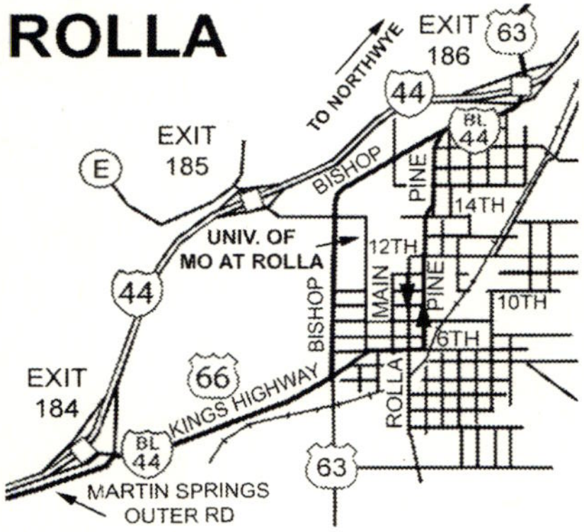

GIANT ALERT #1! On the **North Outer RD** west of **ST JAMES** is the **GIANT DRIPPING NEON FAUCET**. Also West on the **N Outer Rd** is **Route 66 Motors and Gift Shop**, brim full of old cars, signs, and antiques for sale.

Across I-44 at **EXIT 189** (HWY V) is the venerable **Mule Trading Post**, purveyor of Ozark souvenirs for many a year. **GIANT ALERT #2**: A **BIG HILLBILLY** at the **Mule** (all these giants…must be something in the water…see below).

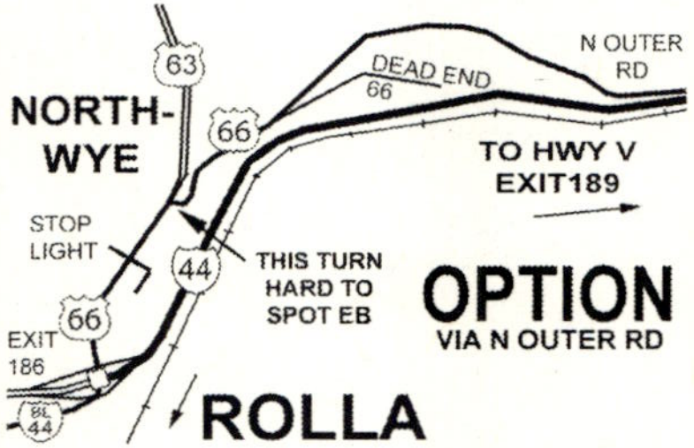

OPTION: **WB**: Continue to follow the **North Outer Rd** from the HWY V JCT to **US 63** (north of EXIT 186).Turn **LEFT** on **US 63** to rejoin the tour into **ROLLA**. **EB: From ROLLA, CROSS** I-44 on **US 63**. Go thru the next stoplight (store entrance). Past the "**NORTHWYE**" sign, turn **RIGHT (hard to spot)**. Curve with the main road (**BEAR LEFT** at the "**Y**.") Follow the **North Outer Rd** past HWY V to rejoin the tour.

Odd College Stuff! At 14th St and Bishop Ave in **ROLLA** is a half-scale replica of **Stonehenge**, carved with high-speed water jets. The **University** of **Missouri At Rolla** is also home to the FIRST **Nuclear Reactor** in Missouri, a "swimming pool" model located under water. NO SWIMMING. **OPTIONAL CITY ROUTE**: Best done **EASTBOUND** (due to a One-Way street). Continue on **Kings Highway** east across US 63/Bishop Ave. The road narrows, and then angles onto **6th St**. Pass Main and Rolla Streets, turn **LEFT** on **Pine (One-Way North below 12th St)** thru downtown. At the end of Pine, join **BL 44/ US 63**. Area INFO: (573) 364-3577. More **ROLLA** on **MO page-14**.

EB: Take **US 63 (Bishop Ave)** for 1.3 mi to **EXIT 186** (BL 44 ends). JOIN **EAST I-44**, then take **EXIT 189/HWY V**. **CROSS** I-44, and turn **RIGHT** on the **North Outer Rd**. Go 6 mi, to **EXIT 195** in **ST JAMES**. Turn **RIGHT** to **CROSS** I-44 on **Jefferson St** (HWY 68).

WB: From US 63 in **ROLLA**, turn **RIGHT** with **BL 44 / Kings Highway**. Go 0.7 mi, and curve thru the **roundabout** onto **Martin Springs Drive/Outer Rd.** After 5.5 mi, continue across the HWY T JCT at **DOOLITTLE** (becomes **Eisenhower St**). Continue 3.4 mi to JOIN **WEST I-44** at **EXIT 176**. Take **EXIT 172**, and turn **LEFT** on **Outer Rd West/ Powellville Outer Rd** (**ALERT**-choppy pavement). Go 3.6 mi, then, at HWY J/**EXIT 169 go ACROSS I-44** and (past the off ramp) turn **RIGHT** with **HWY Z**.

ADVISORY: A **drug sting** has at times operated at **EXIT 176 (EB)** to catch alleged culprits that exit here after a sign warns of an upcoming "checkpoint" on I-44. Route 66 tourists shouldn't worry (just don't carry illegal drugs!).

BIKE ALERT: Powellville Outer Rd is currently choppy with big sudden bumps.

EB: For **ROLLA** map and info see **MO page-13**. For food, try **Maid Rite** on **Kings Highway**. The long-lived **Totem Pole Trading Post** on Martin Springs Dr offers antiques and curios.

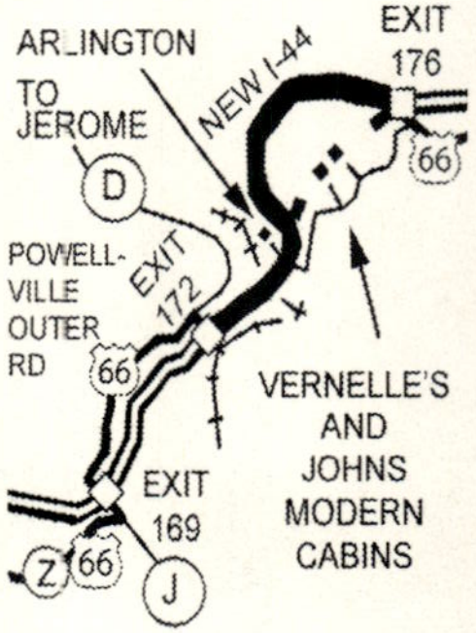

SIDE TRIP 1: Stranded on dead end **Arlington Rd** west of **EXIT 176** are the abandoned log ruins of **Johns Modern Cabins** and lonely **Vernelle's Motel**. The recent realignment of I-44 isolated them further. Cut off by earlier relocations of US 66 and I-44 is **ARLINGTON**, on the banks of the **Little Piney River** at the end of the access road. **SIDE TRIP 2**: West of the river, old 66 once followed **HWY D** a short way east from **EXIT 172**, the long-gone pathway now lost where the current road curves north to **JEROME**. **FOLK ART ALERT**! 0.3 mi east of the exit (private residence), an ornate rock arch gateway honors the "**Trail of Tears**" (the forced migration of the Cherokees). Nearby, a few old cabins and an old store are all that remain of the **Stony Dell** resort.

Back on the **TOUR ROUTE**: On **Powellville Outer Rd** (named for an old business) is the turnoff to **Onyx Mountain Caverns** (1 mi) for you cave buffs (573) 762-3341. **CLEMENTINE**, just east of **EXIT 169**, was a community famous for homemade baskets once sold on 66.

EB: **CROSS I-44** at **EXIT 169**, then **RIGHT** on **Powellville Outer Rd** (**ALERT**-choppy pavement). Go 3.6 mi to the HWY D JCT (EXIT 172), cross and JOIN **EAST I-44**. Take **EXIT 176** and JOIN **Historic 66**. After 3.4 mi, continue **AHEAD** with **Eisenhower St** at HWY T in **DOOLITTLE**. Go 5.5 mi (becomes **Martin Springs Outer Rd** and then **Martin Springs Dr)** towards **ROLLA**. At the **roundabout** (near EXIT 184), curve onto **Kings Highway/BL-44**. Go 0.7 mi and turn **LEFT** with **BL-44** onto **US 63 (Bishop Ave)**.

WB: Take **HWY Z** (becomes **4-Lane 66**) for 3 mi (thru **HOOKER CUT**). Turn **LEFT** onto **Teardrop Rd**. Cross the bridge into **DEVILS ELBOW**. Curve uphill, then turn **LEFT** onto **HWY Z** (becomes 2-lane). At HWY 28 (EXIT 163), continue 2.8 mi on **HWY Z** to **ST ROBERT**. At the "SPUR I-44" JCT, stay **AHEAD** onto **BL 44**. **CROSS I-44** at EXIT 159, then stay with **BL 44** for 2 mi into **WAYNESVILLE** (**HWY 17 joins-stay with BL 44**). When BL 44 turns, **stay AHEAD** on **HWY 17** ("**Historic 66 West**") to **EXIT 153.**

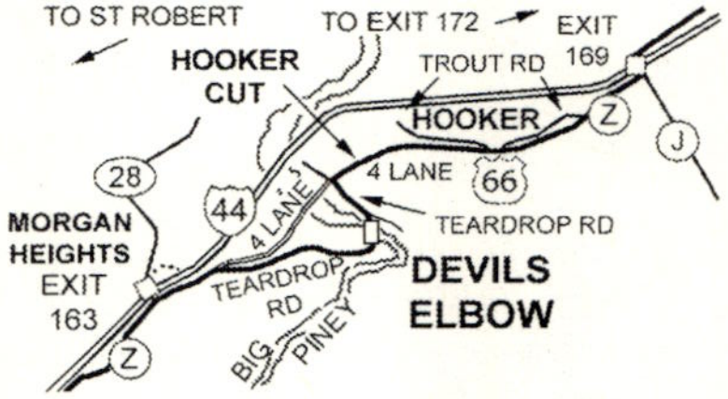

The stretch of **4-Lane 66** thru **HOOKER** was the FIRST on '66 in Missouri, built in 1941-45 for wartime traffic to **Ft Leonard Wood**. At 90 feet, kudzu-covered **HOOKER CUT** was once the deepest road cut in Missouri. Early 2-Lane 66 went around north of the ridge thru **HOOKER** (Trout Rd, north of HWY Z, is a remainder). The 4-Lane bypassed the **1923 Bridge** over the **Big Piney River** that leads to **DEVILS ELBOW**, and the steep slope to the west. **SIDE TRIP**: Double back to drive 4-lane 66 west of Hooker Cut. This relic of 4-lane 66 served until the early '80s.

NOTE: Repairs are planned for the **Devil's Elbow Bridge**. See **www.mcjerry66.com** for updates.

DEVILS ELBOW, named for a bend in the river that caused logjams, sits below 200-foot tall tree-lined bluffs. The **Elbow Inn Bar & BBQ** operates from the 1929 Munger Moss Sandwich Shop building. East of the river is the old **Allman's** (now Sheldon's) **Market** and P.O. A rock-walled pullout on old 66 up the hill provides a scenic view of the valley.

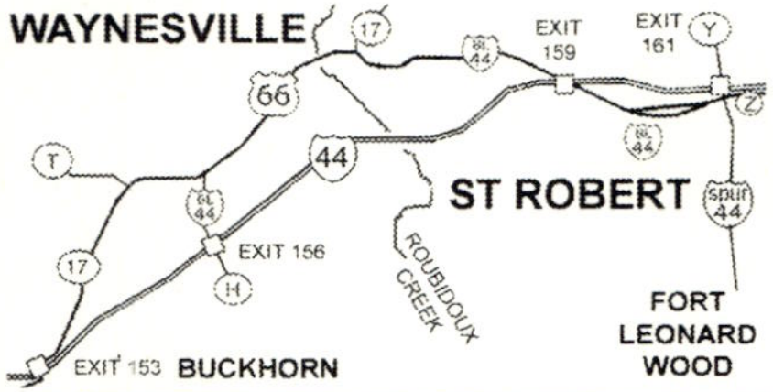

SCAVENGER HUNT! What military "vehicle" honors **Ft Leonard Wood** at **George M Reed Roadside Park** (w of Spur 44 in **ST ROBERT**)?__________ **GIANT ALERT**! Just east of **WAYNESVILLE**, a big boulder sticking out of the hill cut is painted like a **GIANT FROG**. Downtown has some neat buildings. **Go** to **oldstagecoachstop.org/** for info on this historic restored building. The classic concrete **1923 Rubidoux Creek Bridge** was recently restored.

EB: Take **HWY 17** for 3.5 mi into **WAYNESVILLE**. Join **BL 44 ahead** (at the Ichord Ave light-no turn). When HWY 17 turns, continue with **BL 44** thru **ST ROBERT** and **CROSS I-44** at **EXIT 159**. Continue from here on **BL 44** for 1.2 mi. At SPUR 44 JCT, stay **AHEAD** onto **HWY Z**. About a mile east of EXIT 163 (HWY 28) **ANGLE RIGHT** onto **Teardrop Rd**. Descend to **DEVILS ELBOW**, and cross the bridge. Turn **RIGHT** on **HWY Z (4-Lane 66**). Pass thru **HOOKER CUT**, and follow **HWY Z** for 3 mi to **EXIT 169.**

(see **MAP #3, MO page-11)**

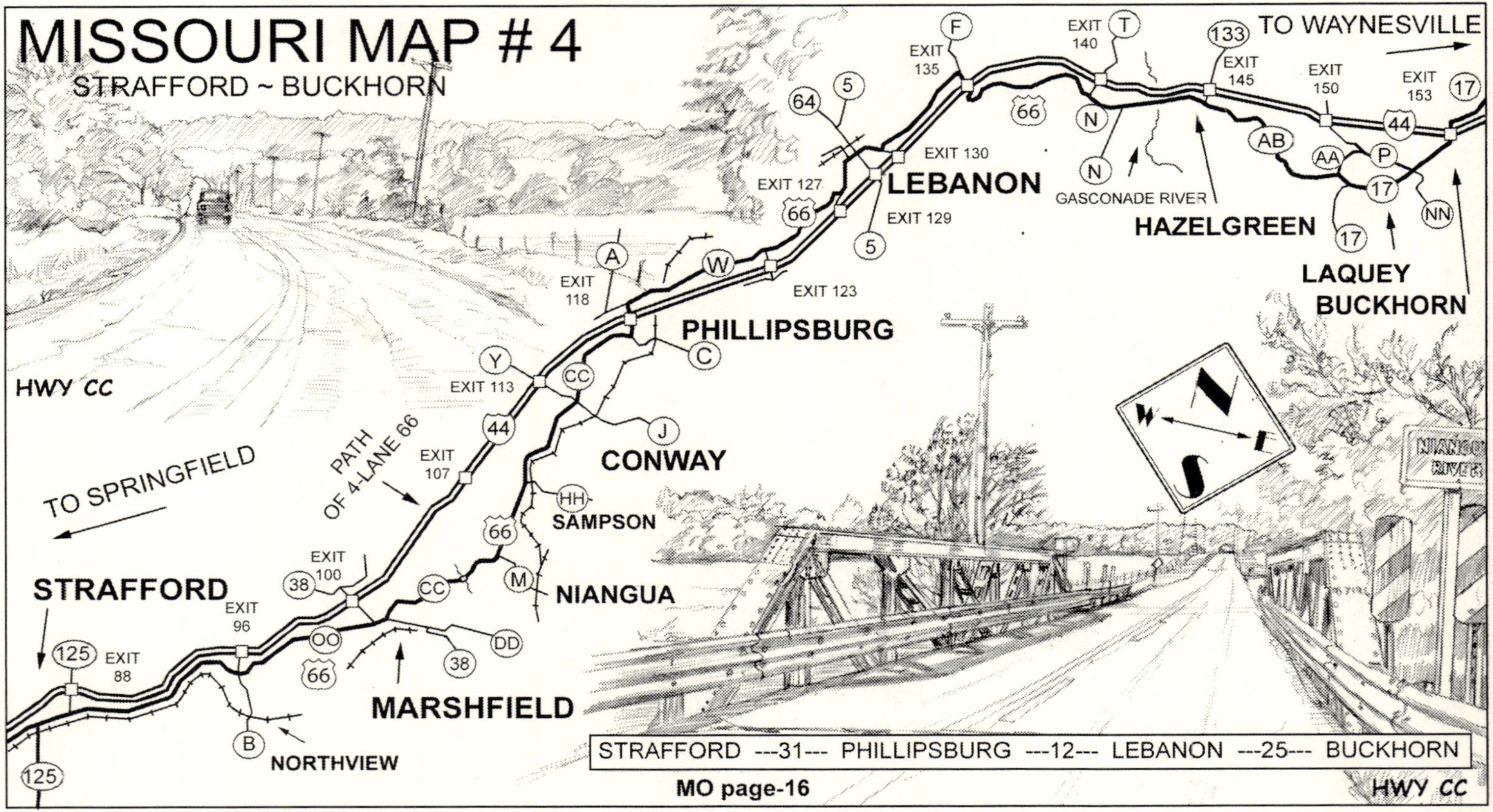
MISSOURI MAP # 4
STRAFFORD ~ BUCKHORN
TO WAYNESVILLE
TO SPRINGFIELD
PATH OF 4-LANE 66
STRAFFORD
MARSHFIELD
NORTHVIEW
NIANGUA
SAMPSON
CONWAY
PHILLIPSBURG
LEBANON
GASCONADE RIVER
HAZELGREEN
LAQUEY
BUCKHORN
HWY CC
HWY CC
EXIT 88
EXIT 96
EXIT 100
EXIT 107
EXIT 113
EXIT 118
EXIT 123
EXIT 127
EXIT 129
EXIT 130
EXIT 135
EXIT 140
EXIT 145
EXIT 150
EXIT 153
125
125
38
38
OO
66
B
DD
CC
M
HH
66
44
Y
CC
J
C
A
W
66
64
5
5
F
66
N
N
T
133
AB
44
AA
P
17
17
NN
17
STRAFFORD ---31--- PHILLIPSBURG ---12--- LEBANON ---25--- BUCKHORN

WB: CROSS I-44 at **EXIT 153** and continue with **HWY 17** for 1.3 mi (thru **BUCKHORN**). Turn **RIGHT** on **HWY P**. Go 1 mi, then **LEFT** on **HWY AA** in **LAQUEY**. Continue 1.6 mi to **HWY AB**, turn **RIGHT**. Go 6 mi to the HWY 133 JCT (near EXIT 145): continue **AHEAD** on the **S Outer Rd** for 10.7 mi (thru **HAZELGREEN**) crossing the **Gasconade River Bridge** enroute. At the **HWY F JCT**, go **ACROSS I-44**, then turn **LEFT** onto the **N Outer Rd West** ("Route 66").

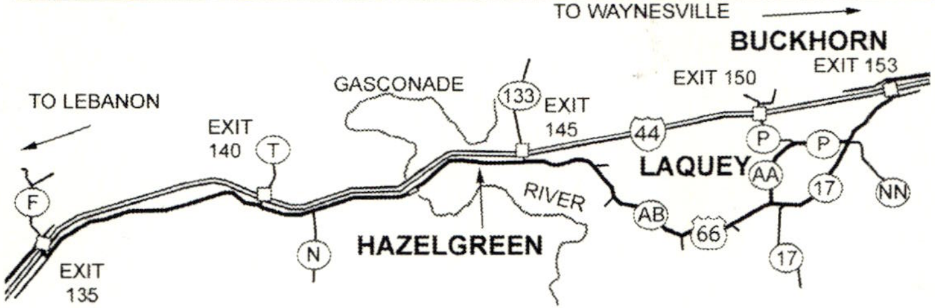

Just east of **EXIT 153** is a **GIANT ALERT**! See the **GIANT BOWLING PIN** (right beside the sign "Adult SUPER Store" for an interesting juxtaposition).

Across I-44, about the only thing named for little **BUCKHORN** is the Baptist Church. This is a nice drive, away from I- 44 for a bit, so savor it.

OPTION: Later US 66 looped south of **LAQUEY** via **Highway 17** between **HWY P** and **HWY AB** (see map) This is also a scenic drive, so I suggest looping back to drive it if you've time to do both.

East of the HWY 133 JCT (near EXIT 145) on HWY AB, you pass the former **Gascozark Trading Post**. At **HAZELGREEN**, several houses (some on stilts) and a charming Methodist Church perch on the edge of a steep drop. West of EXIT 145, a defunct Phillips 66 station serves as a trellis for a clinging kudzu coat. Three thru-truss spans (plus a small "pony" truss) of a magnificent **1923 bridge** carries Route 66 over the **Gasconade River.** **SCAVENGER HUNT!** What is the **NAME** of the **"Conservation Area"** just east of EXIT 135/HWY F?

EB: From **EXIT 135** (HWY F) curve down and turn **LEFT** on the **South Outer Rd**. Go 10.7 mi (crossing the **Gasconade River Bridge** enroute and thru **HAZELGREEN**). At the HWY 133 JCT (near EXIT 145) follow **HWY AB** away from I-44. Go 6 mi, then **LEFT** on **HWY AA**. Go 1.6 mi, then **RIGHT** on **HWY P** in **LAQUEY** for 1 mi. Turn **LEFT** on **HWY 17** for 1.3 mi to **EXIT 153** in **BUCKHORN**. Cross I-44, then continue **RIGHT** with **HWY 17** into **WAYNSEVILLE**.

WB: Follow the **N Outer Rd** ("Route 66") for 5 mi west from EXIT 135 to **LEBANON**. At the JCT of **BL 44**, (near EXIT 130) turn **RIGHT**. Follow **BL 44** as it curves for 3 mi thru town (crossing HWY 5-no turns) towards EXIT 127. Turn **RIGHT** at the light onto **HWY W** (opposite the exit ramps). Stay with **HWY W** for 9.5 mi (passing EXIT 123) to **EXIT 118**. **CROSS I-44** on **HWY C**.

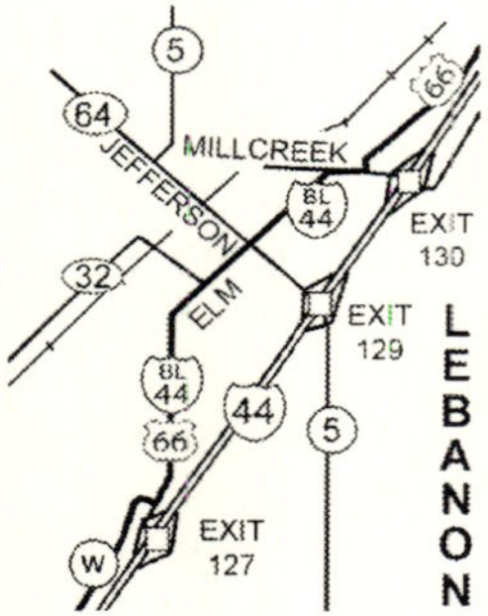

Near EXIT 135 is **I-44 Speedway**, a 3/8 mile "high bank clay oval" (shoulda' named it for Route 66!). Nearby is **Mr. C's RoutePost**, with unique gifts and collectibles, including a large variety of 66 stuff. Home of Route 66 Root Beer!

LEBANON is home to one of my "homes away from home," the famous **Munger Moss Motel** from 1946. Bob and Ramona (great supporters of '66) started there in 1971, renovating the units and maintaining the outstanding neon sign (if you can't stay, try the **GIFT SHOP**). They decorated many rooms in **Route 66 themes,** including the "pretty in pink" tribute to the bygone **Coral Court Motel**, with photos by famed Route 66 photographer Shellee Graham. In the TEXAS room, they hung prints of some of my artwork. Ramona and Bob deserve a rest, and the motel is up for sale. Hopefully their tradition will continue in the future with new owners. (417) 532-3111. www.mungermoss.com. The 'Moss sits on a great Route 66 street, with the **Starlite Lanes** across the road, plus another vintage motel. **Wrink's Market**, a small brick store of long-standing, has had many guises after the passing of Mr. Wrinkle.

SIDE TRIP: **LEBANON** is justly proud of their **Route 66 Museum** in the **Laclede County Library**. Inside are memorabilia and recreations of the'66 era, such as an old motel room, 50's diner and soda fountain. Go south from BL 44 on **HWY 5** to 915 S Jefferson (north of I-44) (417) 532-2148. There are loads of "**factory outlet**" and antique stores in town.

West of **LEBANON** at EXIT 123, a short bit of old 66 is cut off on the south of I-44, in front of nifty **Route 66 Antiques** and the **Caffeyville Country Store.** Between this exit and a **1926 RR overpass** to the west, is a pair of photogenic **Meramec Caverns Barns**.

EB: From **EXIT 118**, follow **HWY W** (**N Outer Rd**) 9.5 mi east to **LEBANON** EXIT 127. Curve to the **STOPlight**, then turn **LEFT** onto **BL 44 (Elm St)**. Follow **BL 44** for 3 mi (crossing Hwy 5-no turns) as it curves thru town towards EXIT 130. **BEFORE** reaching the ramps, turn **LEFT** onto "**Historic Route 66**" (becomes N Outer Rd), and continue 5 miles to **EXIT 135 (Hwy F)**. **CROSS I-44.**

WB: Take **HWY C** south from **EXIT 118** in **PHILLIPSBURG**. Quickly turn **RIGHT** on **HWY CC**. Go for 4.5 mi to **CONWAY**. Continue **AHEAD** at HWY J, and follow **HWY CC** for 14 mi into **MARSHFIELD**. At the light, stay right, and merge **RIGHT** onto **HWY 38**. Turn **LEFT** at the next light onto **HWY OO**. Go 12.3 mi to the HWY 125 JCT in **STRAFFORD**. Continue **AHEAD**.

Please note that old 66 on the north side of EXIT 118 goes to the WEST for a short bit. **HWY CC** connects to the continuation of 66 on the south, and offers an **excellent drive** over hills and thru woods and meadows. We can be grateful that **4-lane 66** (and later I-44) ran further west; leaving this section almost untouched (just a light coat of asphalt hides the original curbed concrete). **SCAVENGER HUNT**! Almost a mile west of the HWY CC JCT at **PHILLIPSBURG** is the location of a former roadside park (note the line of big trees and the old culvert on the south side). Whose **NAME** is listed on the small concrete marker as having donated the land for the defunct park? ______________

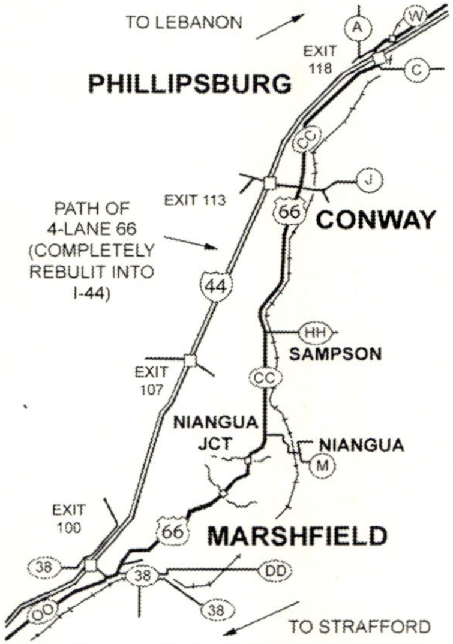

The **Niangua Junction Store** has guarded the JCT with HWY M since 1935. Further west, HWY CC crosses a small, picturesque green painted-girder bridge over the **Niangua River**. A former cottage-style gas station from 1925 sits just east.

MARSHFIELD's claim to fame is hometown boy **Dr Edwin Hubble**, the noted astronomer and namesake of the **Hubble Space Telescope**, a quarter-scale (1,200 lb) model of which is on display in the town square (east off MO 38). The town also has some bed and breakfasts, including **The Dickey House** in a 1913 mansion. (417) 468-3000. CITY INFO: 417-468-3943. Along the side of '66 between Marshfield and **STRAFFORD** is **Wild Animal Safari**, a large drive-thru wildlife park. (417) 859-5300.

EB: Stay on **HWY OO** east from the N HWY 125 JCT in **STRAFFORD**. Go 12.3 mi to **MARSHFIELD**. At the light, turn **RIGHT** onto **HWY 38**. At the next light, be in the left lane and turn **LEFT** onto **HWY CC**. Bear **LEFT** with **'CC** at the next "Y." Stay with **HWY CC** for 13.8 mi to **CONWAY**. Continue **AHEAD** at HWY J, and follow **HWY CC** for 4.5 mi to the JCT of **HWY C** in **PHILLIPSBURG**: turn **LEFT** and **CROSS I-44** at **EXIT 118**, then turn **RIGHT** on **HWY W** (N Outer Rd).

(see **MAP # 4**, **MO page-16**)

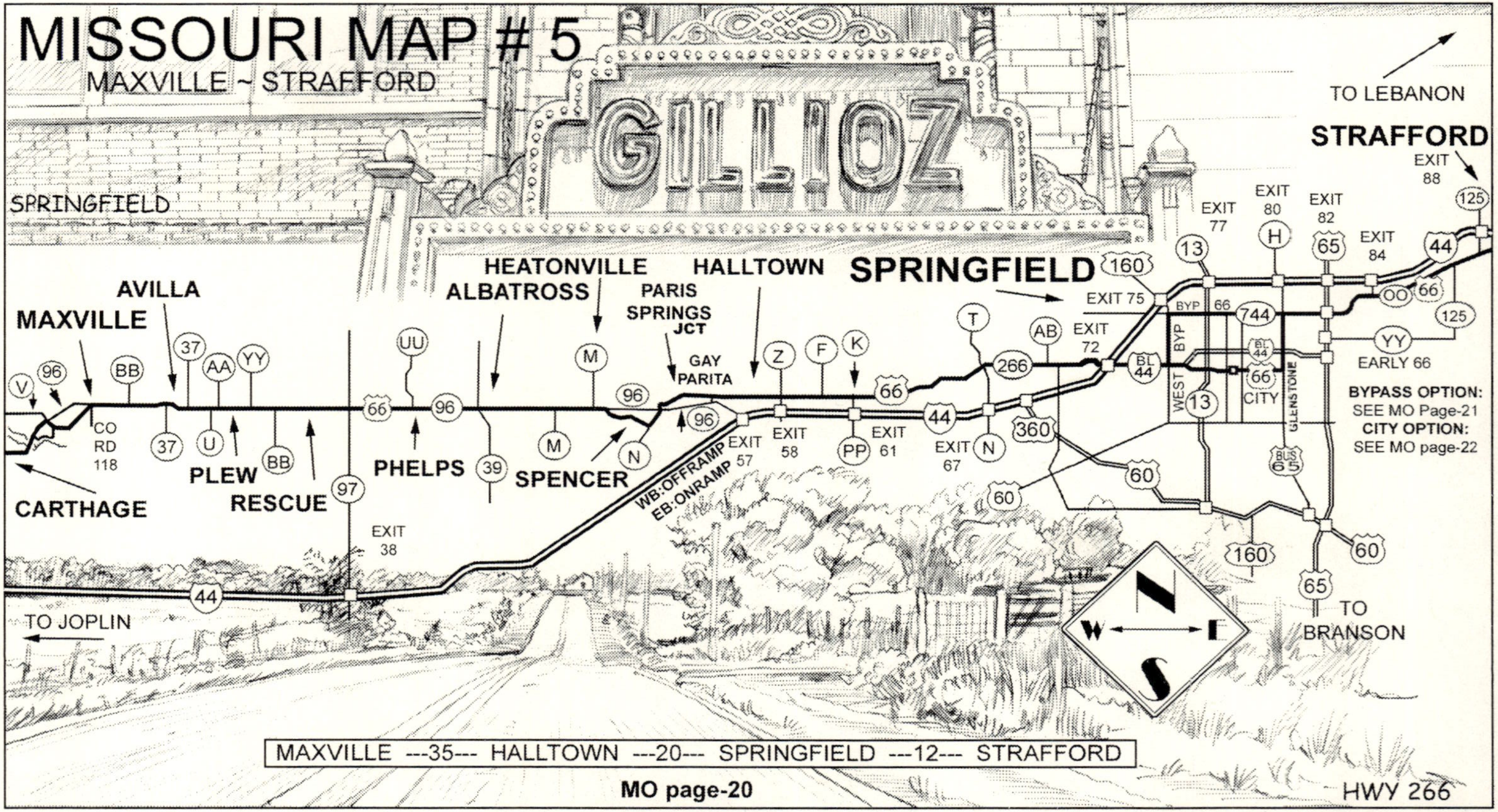
MISSOURI MAP # 5
MAXVILLE ~ STRAFFORD
SPRINGFIELD
GILLIOZ
TO LEBANON
STRAFFORD
EXIT 88
EXIT 77
EXIT 80
EXIT 82
EXIT 84
SPRINGFIELD
EXIT 75
EXIT 72
BYP 66
WEST BYP
CITY
GLENSTONE
EARLY 66
BYPASS OPTION:
SEE MO Page-21
CITY OPTION:
SEE MO page-22
HEATONVILLE
ALBATROSS
HALLTOWN
AVILLA
MAXVILLE
PARIS SPRINGS JCT
GAY PARITA
CO RD 118
PLEW
RESCUE
PHELPS
SPENCER
CARTHAGE
WB:OFFRAMP
EB:ONRAMP
EXIT 57
EXIT 58
EXIT 61
EXIT 67
EXIT 38
TO JOPLIN
TO BRANSON
W E N S
MAXVILLE ---35--- HALLTOWN ---20--- SPRINGFIELD ---12--- STRAFFORD
HWY 266

WB: From **STRAFFORD**, continue **AHEAD** with **HWY OO** and **HWY 125**. HWY 125 soon turns south, continue with **HWY OO**. Continue when **HWY 744** joins near EXIT 84 (becomes **Kearney St**) and **CROSS** US 65 into **SPRINGFIELD**. (See **CITY OPTION**, **MO page-22**). Stay **AHEAD** with Kearney at the **Glenstone** (BL 44) JCT. Go 4.8 mi. Turn **LEFT** on **West Bypass** (US 160). Go 2 mi. At the **Chestnut Expwy** (BL 44) JCT, turn **RIGHT**. Cross I-44 at EXIT 72. Continue on **MO HWY 266**. (go to **MO page-23**)

NOTE: THIS page covers the **MAIN 1936 BYPASS ROUTE** (west from the JCT of Glenstone and Kearney). See **MO page-22** for the earlier **CITY OPTION** thru downtown. Serving as the main route since **1936**, the **BYPASS** has many remaining vestiges of old 66 to spot, like the majestic neon sign at the **Rest Haven Court** (2000 E Kearney). Its OK, but you might check the room first if picky (417) 869-9114.

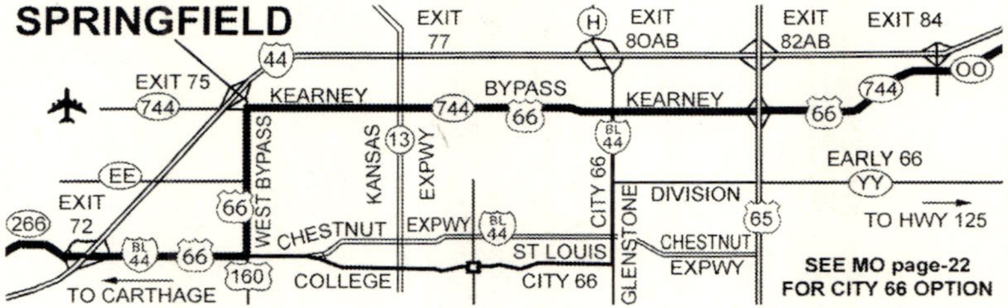

OPTION: Early 66 went down **HWY 125** From **STRAFFORD**, then west to Glenstone via **HWY YY** (Division St). On Division was headquarters of the late **Campbell 66 Express**, whose camel mascot, **"Snortin Norton,"** humped along '66 for years.

If you're wondering about that **"Branson"** place on all the billboards, why, it's the Musical Mecca of Country Music, about 35 mi south on US 65. INFO: (800) 961-1221. **SPRINGFIELD** is chock-full of area attractions, including **Fantastic Caverns** (why walk thru a cave, when you can ride?) and **Bass Pro Shops Outdoor World**. www.springfieldmo.org or (800) 678-8767.

GIANT ALERT! Beware of the **GIANT PISTOL** at 810 Kearney. Just south on **West Bypass**, a classic 1932-era "cottage" houses **Rex Smith Oil Co**. West out of town on **Chestnut Expwy** are more old motels and a few neon signs. Too bad that **Red's**, the famed burger joint with the "Giant Hamburg" sign and '55 Buick adorned with whirling tinfoil-balls, is long gone.

EB: Take **BL 44/Chestnut Expwy** for 2 mi past I-44. At **West Bypass/US 160**, turn **LEFT**. Go 2 mi, then **RIGHT** on **HWY 744 (Kearney St)** for 4.8 mi. Continue **AHEAD** at BL 44/Glenstone (**City OPTION** joins). Follow **HWY 744 (Kearney)** across US 65. Join **HWY OO AHEAD** when HWY 744 turns (EXIT 84). Follow **HWY OO** past S HWY 125 and then past N HWY 125 in **STRAFFORD**.

WB: <u>CITY OPTION</u>: From **Kearney**/HWY 744, turn **LEFT** on **Glenstone**/BL 44. Go 2 mi (past Chestnut Expy-BL 44 turns). Cross the RR, then prepare to turn **RIGHT** on **St Louis St**. Go 1.5 mi. Continue past Jefferson and enter the square on Park **Central East**. Turn **RIGHT** on **Park**, then **LEFT** along the north side of the square, then **LEFT** again and **RIGHT** on **Park Central West**. Continue onto **College St**. Go 2.2 mi to next turn. Cross West St, then curve up to the JCT of **Chestnut Expwy (BL 44)**: turn **LEFT**. Continue past the West Bypass stoplight (**Main Bypass Route** joins here), and cross under I-44 at EXIT 72. Stay **AHEAD** with **MO HWY 266.**

RV ALERT! The downtown **Park Central Square** has tight turns: take the **BYPASS (MO Page-21).**

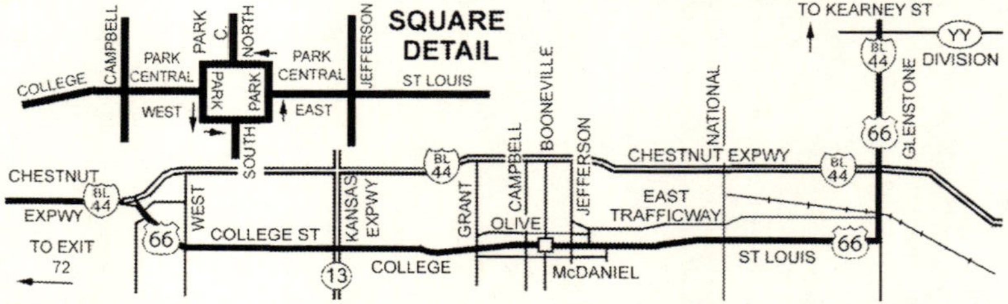

Glenstone Ave still has some 66-era motels. The **Best Western Route 66 Rail Haven** at Glenstone and St Louis is great, with plenty of history, having opened in 1938. A split rail fence bordered the original cottages, hence the name (417) 866-1963. On St Louis at National is a classic **Steak & Shake**, with its slogan-covered exterior ("TAKHOMASAK").

Streets enter Downtown's **Park Central Square** in the middle, requiring some tight turns to continue. **Park Central East** and **West** are now "winding" mall-like streets. **<u>SCAVENGER HUNT</u>**! Who did **"Wild Bill" Hickok** shoot here in the 1860s?______? Park and look for the marker on the south side of the square. On the east side is the **1926 Gilloz Theatre**. West on **College St** a series of tile mosaics enlivens a retaining wall on the south. Many roadside remnants of former stations and motels await the discerning eye. East of Kansas Expwy the **College St Café** welcomes smokers, while **College St Body Shop** has a big car-shaped sign. The well-kept half-circle of cabins near West St (now apartments) were the **Rock Fountain Court**. **NOTE**: MO 266 was rebuilt at I-44, cutting off a bit of 66. Directions are the same.

EB: CITY OPTION: (OR see **Main Bypass Route**: **MO page-21**) **RV ALERT**! Take **BL 44/Chestnut Expwy** into **<u>SPRINGFIELD</u>**. Cross West Bypass/US 160. Go 0.9 mi. Veer **RIGHT** onto **College St** (before the stoplight). Continue on **College St** at Kansas Expwy (avoid turn lane). Cross Campbell St and continue onto **Park Central West**. Turn **RIGHT** (One-Way) at the Square, then quick **LEFT** along the south side and **LEFT AGAIN**. Next **RIGHT** on **Park Central East**. Continue across **Jefferson** (careful) onto **St Louis St**. Go 1.5 mi, then **LEFT** at **Glenstone Ave** (becomes **BL 44)**: Continue 2.1 mi to **Kearney St (HWY 744):** turn **RIGHT** (join **Bypass Route**).

WB: Take **MO 266** for 14 mi to **HALLTOWN**. Continue 2.5 mi, then **AVOID** the left "TO HWY 96." Continue **AHEAD** thru **PARIS SPRINGS**. **CROSS** HWY 96, and briefly join **HWY N**. Turn **RIGHT** at first chance onto **Farm Rd 2062**: cross the bridge and pass **SPENCER**. Turn **LEFT** on **HWY 96**. It is 30.1 mi to the **next** turn (past **HEATONVILLE**, **ALBATROSS**, **PHELPS**, **RESCUE**, **PLEW**, **AVILLA** & **MAXVILLE**). Turn **LEFT** on **CO RD 118**, then **QUICK RIGHT** onto "**Old 66 Blvd**."

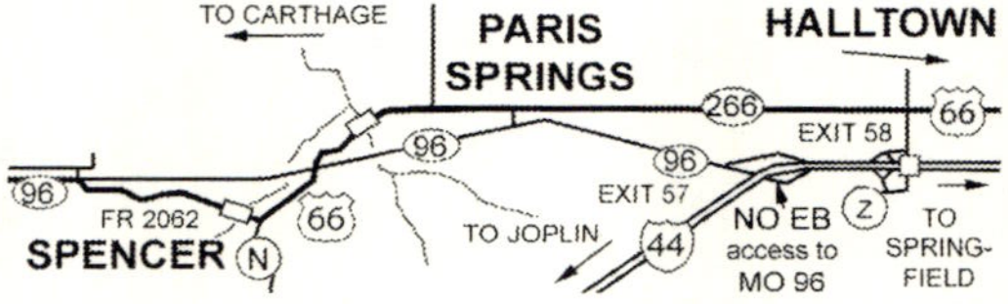

Route 66 from **SPRINGFIELD** to **CARTHAGE** is a special, I-44-free drive. Reminders of old roadside culture are frequent. The directions are **EZ** so get your head out of the guide and enjoy. **HWY 266** winds thru pastoral settings of rolling wooded hills and green fields, peppered with churches, barns, and roadside remnants. Look for a hillside tableau of an old **Texaco sign** and **pumps** just east of HWY T. In **HALLTOWN**, **Whitehall Mercantile** has long been a great spot to find antiques.

A newer icon with old-time feel is the **Gay Parita Sinclair Station** at **PARIS SPRINGS**. Friendly **Gary Turner** built this beautiful gas station replica complete with vintage trucks on the site of a long-gone station, named for the early owner's wife. He welcomes visitors, so do stop by for a nice long friendly chat and **PHOTO OP**. The winding road west crosses a **1923 "pony" bridge** over Turnback Creek, and a picturesque **1926 thru-truss** bridge over Johnson Creek on the way to the recently restored, photogenic remains of little **SPENCER**.

OPTION: The 2-mile frontage road (**CO RD 2059**) between South HWY M and the **SPENCER** turnoff (east of N HWY M) was old 66. **HWY 96** traffic can be fast and furious, (and farm vehicles go 35 in a 65 mph zone!) so be alert. All the tiny towns strung along '66 have remains of old businesses. Many had been "rocked", like the old garage in **HEATONVILLE**. Either side of **PLEW**, one runs a gauntlet of religious Burma Shave-style signs and billboards. **AVILLA** has a row of rustic old structures, including the **Route 66 Bar**.

EB: Take **HWY 96** for almost 30 mi (thru **AVILLA**, **PLEW**, **RESCUE**, **PHELPS**, **ALBATROSS** & **HEATONVILLE**). Half a mile east of HWY M North, turn **RIGHT** downhill **(**across from **FR 2059)** on **Farm Rd 2062**, and pass by **SPENCER**. Cross the bridge, then turn **LEFT** on **HWY N**. Go across HWY 96 and follow "**Old 66**" thru **PARIS SPRINGS**. At the **STOP**, merge **AHEAD** onto **HWY 266** for 14 mi (thru **HALLTOWN**) to cross under I-44 at EXIT 72. Continue on **BL 44/Chestnut Expwy** into **SPRINGFIELD**.

(see **MAP # 5 MO page-20**)

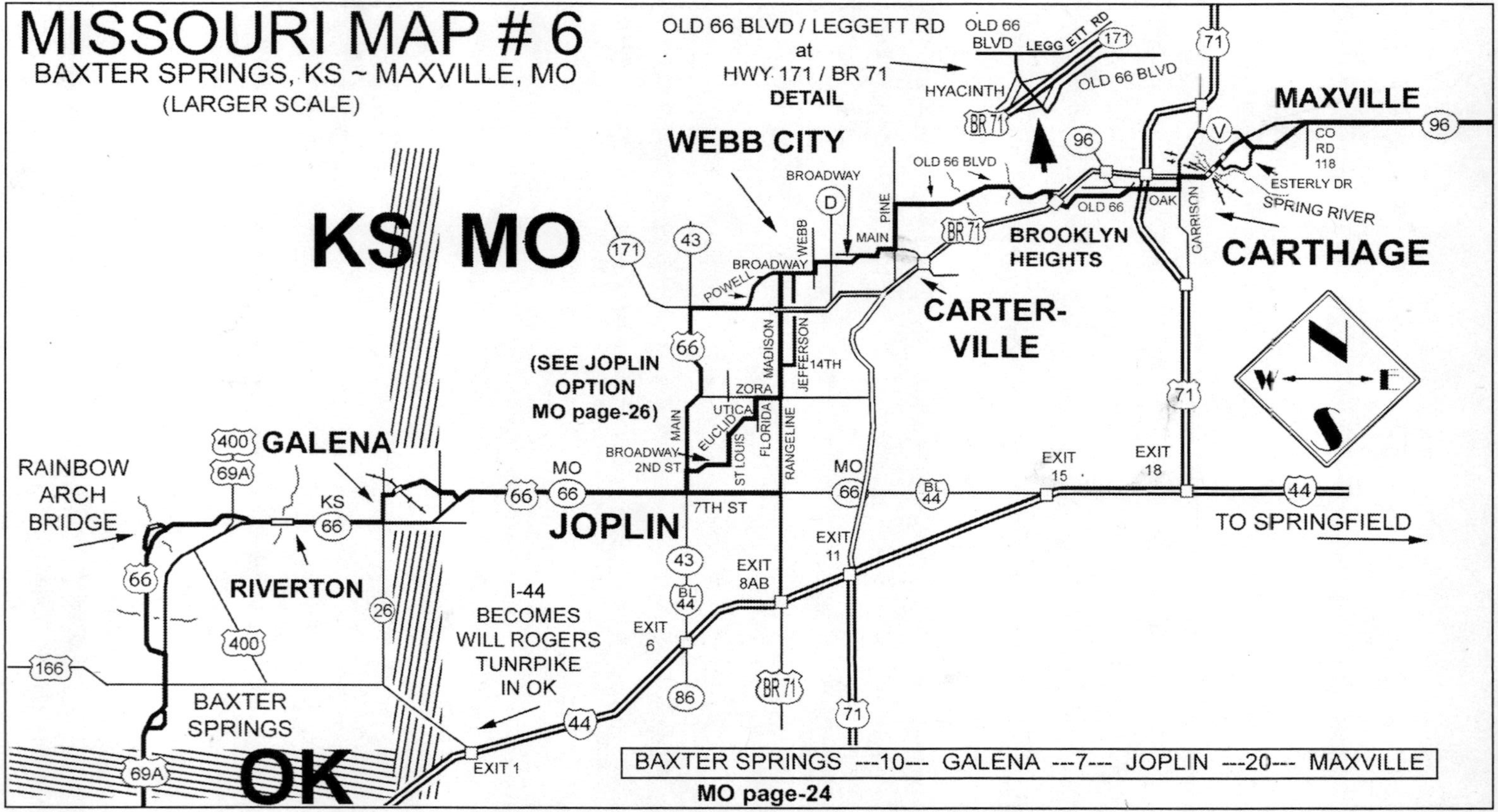
MISSOURI MAP # 6
BAXTER SPRINGS, KS ~ MAXVILLE, MO
(LARGER SCALE)
OLD 66 BLVD / LEGGETT RD
at
HWY 171 / BR 71
DETAIL
OLD 66 BLVD
LEGGETT RD
171
OLD 66 BLVD
HYACINTH
BR 71
71
MAXVILLE
96
CO RD 118
V
ESTERLY DR
SPRING RIVER
CARTHAGE
96
OLD 66 BLVD
OAK
OLD 66
CARRISON
WEBB CITY
BROADWAY
D
PINE
MAIN
WEBB
BROADWAY
BR 71
BROOKLYN HEIGHTS
KS
MO
171
43
POWELL
CARTER-
VILLE
66
MADISON
JEFFERSON
14TH
(SEE JOPLIN
OPTION
MO page-26)
ZORA
UTICA
EUCLID
FLORIDA
MAIN
ST LOUIS
RANGELINE
BROADWAY
2ND ST
71
W
E
N
S
400
GALENA
69A
RAINBOW
ARCH
BRIDGE
KS
66
MO
66
66
7TH ST
JOPLIN
MO
66
BL 44
EXIT 15
EXIT 18
44
TO SPRINGFIELD
66
RIVERTON
26
43
BL 44
EXIT 8AB
EXIT 11
I-44
BECOMES
WILL ROGERS
TUNRPIKE
IN OK
EXIT 6
400
166
BAXTER
SPRINGS
86
BR 71
71
44
69A
OK
EXIT 1
BAXTER SPRINGS ---10--- GALENA ---7--- JOPLIN ---20--- MAXVILLE
MO page-24

WB: From **MAXVILLE**, follow "**Old 66 Blvd**" 1.5 mi to the JCT with **HWY 96** (at HWY V) (see **OPTION**). Turn **LEFT** on **HWY 96** for 1.6 mi to **CARTHAGE** (joins **Central Ave**). At **Garrison**, turn **LEFT** for two blocks, then **RIGHT** on **OAK St**. Cross under US 71, then **BEAR LEFT** at the "**Y**" and stay with "**Old 66 Blvd**" for 2.8 mi to the JCT with Bus 71 (HWY 171) in **BROOKLYN HEIGHTS**.

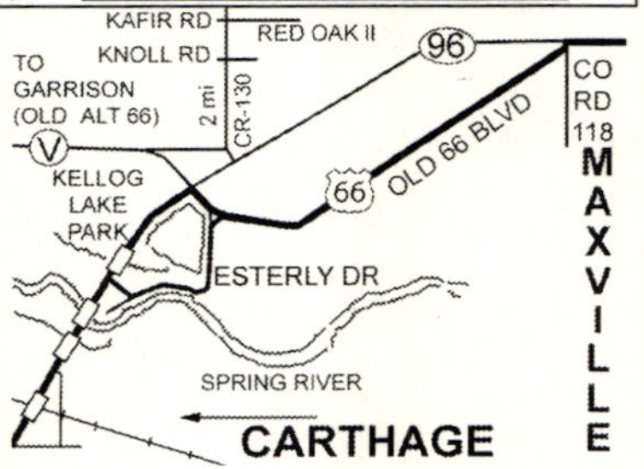

FOLK ART ALERT/SIDE TRIP: At HWY V and HWY 96, the **Flying W Store** has a "flying manure spreader" sculpture by artist Lowell Davis named the "**Crap Duster**. Mr. Davis created nearby **Red Oak II**, a fantastic site full of relocated and restored old buildings and private residences (including 2 gas stations originally from '66) About ¾ mi east of CR-130 on Kafir Rd (See map). http://redoakii.com

OPTION: **OLD 66 thru KELLOGG LAKE PARK**. Follow **Esterly Drive** from **HWY 96** on the west side, and "**Old 66 Blvd**" on the east, for a scenic, peaceful drive along the **Spring River** (which runs barely below the south shoulder at times!). Old 66 dead ends at the west end of the park past Esterly Dr.

CARTHAGE's classic **Boots Motel**, world famous for its architecture, neon and history is now being restored to its Route 66 glory. Five rooms are open as of this writing. Contact bootsmotel@hotmail.com or call (417) 310-2989. Down Garrison, the **Pancake Hut** has a mechanical "**Chicago Band Box**" that they'll play for you (good food too). The **Civil War Museum** (205 Grant St) has dramatic murals of "**The Battle of Carthage**" and more, near the **Historic Square**. City INFO: (417) 358-2373.

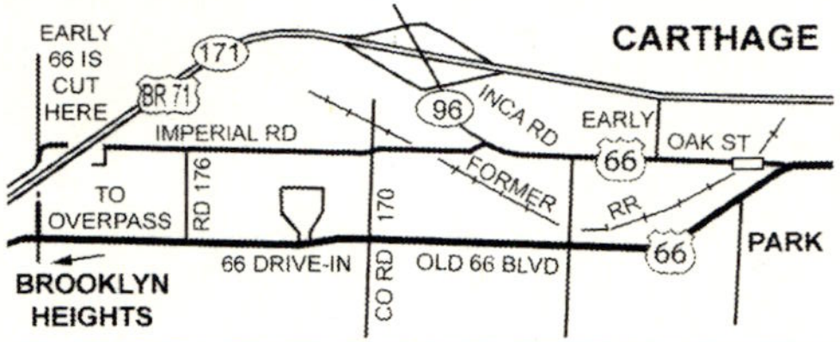

SIDE TRIP: Old 66 continued west on Oak, (across a 1936 RR viaduct) behind the **66 Drive In**, but it dead-ends now. Speaking of the **66 Drive-In**, this roadside theatre, restored after years of being a junkyard, is a **MUST** if you're overnighting in the area. Too precious is **Precious Moments Park**, south of town off US 71, with tours, shopping and **The Chapel**.

EB: Take "**Old 66 Blvd**" for 2.8 mi, then curve onto **Oak St** in **CARTHAGE**. After 0.5 mi, cross under US 71. Go 1 mi, turn **LEFT** on **Garrison Ave**, then 2 blocks and **RIGHT** on **HWY 96** (Central Ave). Take **HWY 96** for 1.6 mi to the JCT of HWY V, but turn **RIGHT** and join "**Old 66 Blvd**" for 1.5 mi to **CO RD 118** (see **OPTION**). Turn **LEFT**, then quick **RIGHT** on **HWY 96** in **MAXVILLE**.

WB: CROSS Bus 71/HWY 171 and stay **AHEAD** (NO turns) to the "T" JCT with "**Old 66 Blvd**," turn **LEFT**. Go 2.6 mi to **Pine St**, turn **LEFT**. Cross the RR into **CARTERVILLE**. At **Main St** turn **RIGHT** thru downtown, then curve **LEFT** on **Carter**, and **RIGHT** at **Lewis**. Cross the RR, then **bear LEFT** at the "**Y**" onto **Broadway** in **WEBB CITY**. Stay **AHEAD** on **Broadway** at Main, then **LEFT** on **Webb St**, and quick **RIGHT** back on **Broadway**. After 8 blocks, continue **AHEAD** past Madison St or see **JOPLIN OPTION**

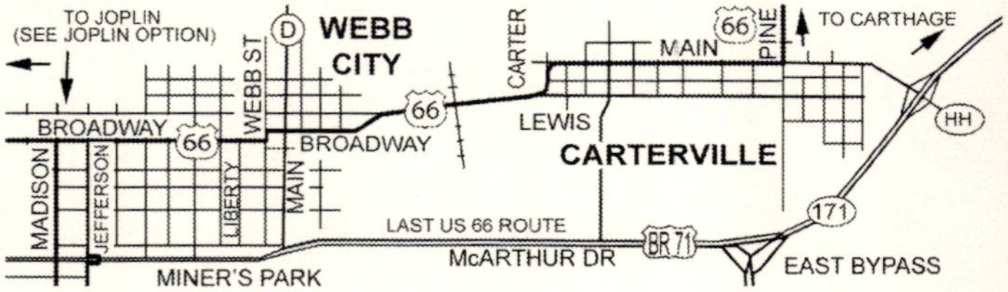

"**Old 66 Blvd**" is a pleasant drive on curvy, narrow pavement, across a **1922 bridge**. **CARTERVILLE**'s "**SuperTAM on 66" Ice Cream Parlor** has a 30-year collection of Superman ™ memorabilia. Call ahead for evening hours: (417) 392-7405. Look for the **bear statue** at **Stewarts Café** (Pine and Main).

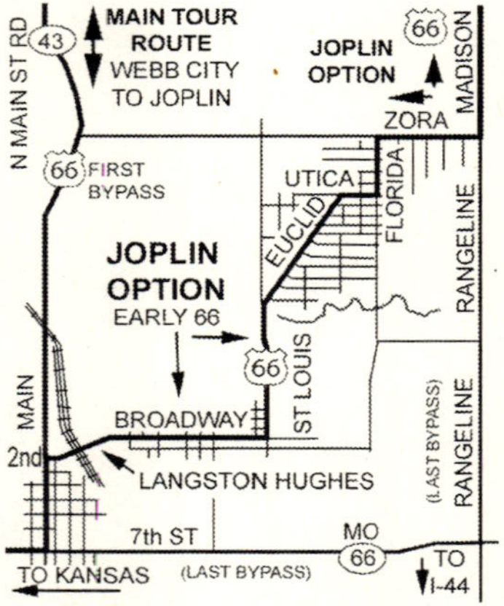

Once a busy mining area, old mining scars mark the way into **WEBB CITY**, where the **Bradbury Bishop Deli** at 201 N Main is currently closed/for sale. An old gas station at Webb and Broadway houses "**Route 66 Center**." **GIANT ALERT SIDE TRIP**! **PRAYING HANDS** on **Macarthur Dr** (final US 66 between Carthage and Joplin) near S Main St in **Miner's Park**.

JOPLIN OPTION: (many turns, but very **Recommended**) South from Broadway in Webb City, Early 66 took **Jefferson** to **14th** to **Madison**. Since **Macarthur** now blocks **Jefferson**, take **Madison** south instead. Follow the detail map along **Zora**, **Florida**, **Utica**, **Euclid**, **St Louis** and **Broadway**, then veer onto **2nd** to join **Main St** in downtown **JOPLIN**. (EB reverse) This is a surprisingly nice drive thru residential areas, with many reminders of old 66. Watch for a former gas station on Broadway and one on Utica.

EB: Take **Broadway** past Liberty St, then turn **LEFT** on **Webb St**. **QUICK RIGHT** back on **Broadway**. Cross Main and stay with **Broadway** as it curves towards **CARTERVILLE** (becomes **Lewis St**). Curve **LEFT** on **Carter** and **RIGHT** on **Main**. Thru downtown, turn **LEFT** on **Pine St**. Cross the RR, and take the first **RIGHT** on "**Old 66 Blvd**" (See detail map: **MO page-24)**. Go **2.6 mi**, then turn **RIGHT**, cross **OVER** Bus 71 (HWY 171), and follow the frontage road curve onto "**Old 66 Blvd**" in **BROOKLYN HEIGHTS**.

WB: After 4 blocks, **Bear LEFT** with **Broadway** across College Ave, then quickly **Bear LEFT** at the next "Y" onto **Powell St**. Go 0.4 mi, then turn **RIGHT** on **Macarthur Blvd** (**HWY 171**) for 1.3 mi. At the **HWY 43 (N Main St Rd**) JCT, turn **LEFT**. Follow **HWY 43/Main** south for 4 mi to and thru downtown **JOPLIN**. Turn **RIGHT** on **7th St/MO HWY 66** for 5 mi, and cross Malang Rd (prepare for right turn). After the sign "**Old 66 Next Right**", turn **RIGHT** and join "**Old 66 Blvd**" to **KANSAS**.

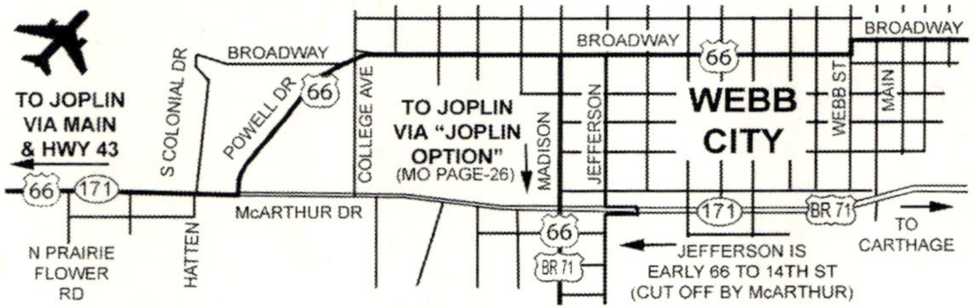

Relics of former motel units and gas stations crop up among homes along **Broadway** west from Webb City.

HWY 171 west of **WEBB CITY**, and Main St (HWY 43 S), bypassed the original "**City" 66** thru **JOPLIN** in the 1930s. Former gas stations and an **ARMY TANK** (this at Veteran's Way) decorate the route, a more peaceful drive than the **FINAL** route of US 66 along urbanized **Madison / Rangeline** south to **7th Ave**. The devastating 2011 tornado ran south of 7th Ave.

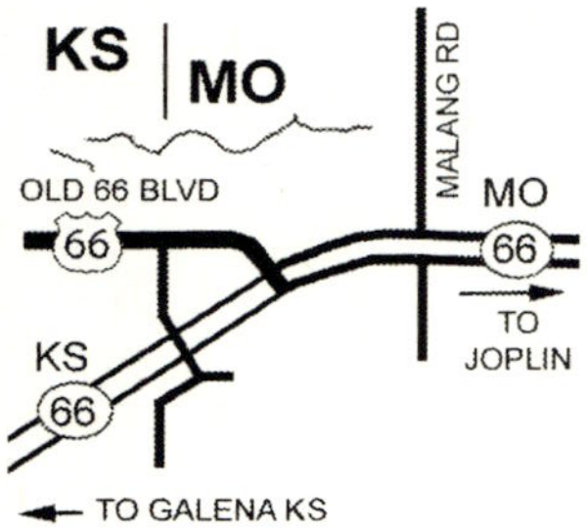

GIANT ALERTS! Giant Coke Bottle (at Woody's) and **Giant Crayon** on **West 7th**. The **Joplin Museum Complex**, off 7th in **Shifferdecker Park**, has a cool lil' museum dedicated to **Cookie Cutters** plus the **Tri State Mineral Museum**, **Hoover Historical Museum**, **Empire District Electric Company Museum** and the **Joplin Sports Authority Hall of Fame** (whew!) www.joplinmuseum.org/about.html. City INFO: (800) 657-2534. West on **MO HWY 66** is **66 Carousel Park**, a local amusement park, on the left. **WB**, don't miss the turn for Old 66 into **KANSAS**, then pass **Paddock Liquors** (2 "visible" gas pumps in front) to the State Line.

EB: Curve to the JCT of **MO HWY 66** and turn **LEFT** (becomes **7th St**). Go 5 mi into **JOPLIN**. Turn **LEFT** on **Main St** (**HWY 43**) in downtown. (**SEE JOPLIN OPTION** on **MO page-26**, or stay **AHEAD** on **Main St.)** 4 mi later, turn **RIGHT** at the **HWY 171 JCT**, (becomes **McArthur**) and continue for 1.3 mi, then turn **LEFT** on **Powell Drive**. Follow the curve onto **Broadway** (past College St). Continue for about 11 blocks into **WEBB CITY** (**JOPLIN OPTION** rejoins at Madison St) and prepare for a left turn after Liberty St.

WB: Continue **AHEAD** past State Line Rd into **KANSAS**. Cross the RR viaduct, then turn **LEFT** on **Main St**, and pass thru downtown **GALENA**. Turn **RIGHT** on **7th St/KS HWY 66**. Continue for 4.2 mi, thru **RIVERTON** to the JCT with US 400 / 69A.

CUT the CORNER of KANSAS on ROUTE 66

The **Mother Road** only traverses about 13 miles of the **Sunflower State**, the **ONLY** Route 66 state entirely bypassed by an interstate highway. This makes **KANSAS** the sole '66 state thru which it is possible to drive **without** encountering any sign of the superslab. Although short on miles, Route 66 thru **KANSAS** is long on charm and history, so plan to linger and enjoy this small corner of Old 66 (turn to **OK page-3** for info on the **Tri-State Spooklight**, which is in the corner of **KS**, **MO** and **OK** about 10 miles south of **GALENA**).

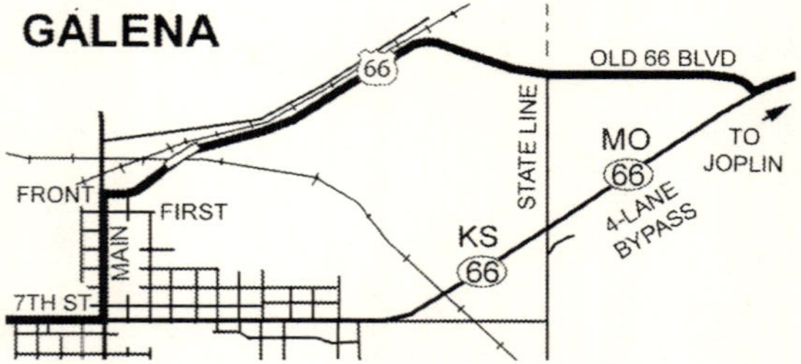

Westbound, your first taste of **KANSAS** is the **State Line Bar**, past which old 66 curves along with the railroad thru a desolate former mining area (where an old train and caboose are on display). West of a vintage concrete-post viaduct above the tracks, a quaint 90-degree turn takes old 66 into downtown **GALENA**. On this corner (119 North Main) is "**4 Women on The Route**" in a beautifully restored Kan-O-Tex gas station, featuring "Tow Tater," the inspiration for 'Mater from the movie *CARS*. **GIFT SHOP ALERT**! Friendly folks, and a must stop! (620) 783-1366. A Victorian house nearby may become a B&B and tearoom. **Howard Litch Park**, downtown, has a **Will Rogers Hwy** marker. The town gem is the **Galena Museum** at 319 W 7th St, in the old KATY (M.K.T. RR) depot, housing a fascinating collection of area history. Outside are a restored **ARMY TANK**, switch engine and caboose. Inside are exhibits honoring the history of this mining region, including a room full of ore samples. Admire the ancient horse-drawn hearse, and let the kids try to figger out what all those old contraptions did. Summer hours: Mon-Sat 9-3:30 (closed for lunch). Call (620) 783-2192 off-season.

EB: Continue with **KS HWY 66** (7th St) to **GALENA**. Turn **LEFT** on **Main St** thru downtown. Cross First St, then turn **RIGHT** on **Front St**. Cross the RR viaduct, then continue past State Line Rd with **Old 66 Blvd** into **MISSOURI** to join **MO 66** toward **JOPLIN**.
(see Missouri INTRO on MO page-1)

(see MO MAP # 6, MO page-24)

WB: West of **RIVERTON**, curve to the US 400 / 69A JCT (KS HWY 66 ENDS): curve thru the **circle** onto **Beasley Rd** / Historic-66. Continue 1.4 mi (pass the **STOP** at 60th) and cross Brush Creek (see **BRIDGE DETOUR**). Follow the curve south onto **50th St**, continue for 2.7 mi (becomes **Willow St**). Curve **LEFT** to join **3rd St**, then turn **RIGHT** onto **US 69A** (**Military Ave**) thru **BAXTER SPRINGS**. (SEE **OLD 66 OPTION**) Continue south past the US 166 JCT for 2.5 mi to **OKLAHOMA**.

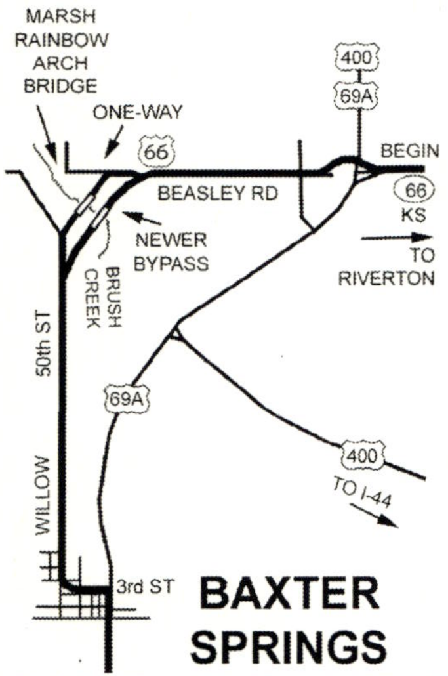

Check out the famous **Eisler Bros** (now **Neilson's**) **Grocery and Deli** in **RIVERTON**. **GIFT SHOP ALERT!** Scope out the original embossed tin ceiling of the 1925 store and an old outhouse in back.

RAINBOW BRIDGE DETOUR: You **MUST** take the short loop across this historic unique bridge, in a lush setting at Brush Creek. This is the **LAST** of three "Marsh Arch" bridges (named for their designer) that once graced US 66 in **KANSAS**. "Progress" claimed the others; preservation saved this one. Look for the "**Field of Dreams**" baseball field on 50th St south from the bridge.

In historic **BAXTER SPRINGS,** a restored 1930s-era **Phillips 66 Station** at 940 Military (on the National Historic Register) houses a great **Route 66 Visitor Center**. Downtown, check out the **Little Brick Inn** which occupies a former bank (robbed by Jesse James in 1876). The **Baxter Springs Museum** at 740 East Ave is great. baxterspringsmuseum.org/ (620) 856-2385.

OLD 66 OPTION: Since **KANSAS** has so few Route 66 miles, be sure to follow the map to drive this short stretch on the south side of **BAXTER SPRINGS**, along Roberts Rd and 30th St, behind the Wal Mart and McDonalds.

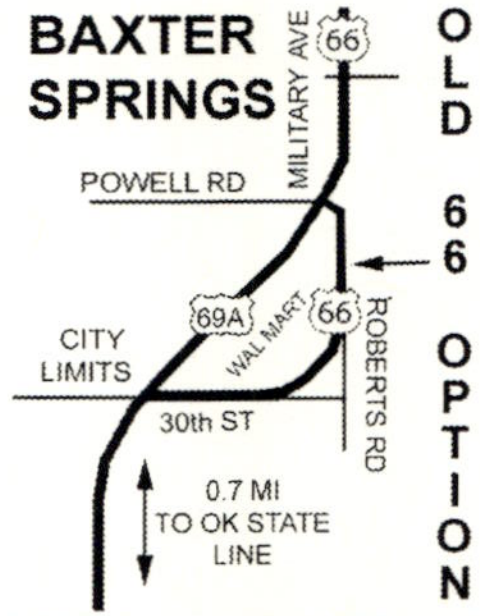

EB: Follow **US 69 ALT** into **KANSAS**. Becomes **Military Ave** in **BAXTER SPRINGS** (SEE **OLD 66 OPTION**). Stay **AHEAD** thru downtown, past the US 166 JCT. Go 0.7 mi, and turn **LEFT** on **Third St**. Follow the curve **RIGHT** onto **Willow Ave** (becomes **50th St**). Go 2.7 mi, curve across Brush Creek (see **BRIDGE DETOUR**) then continue for 1.4 mi on **Beasley Rd** (pass the **STOP** at 60th St). Curve to the **circle** at US 400 / 69A, then curve with Historic-66 onto **KS HWY 66**. Continue 4.2 mi, thru **RIVERTON**, to **GALENA**.

(see **MO MAP # 6, MO page-24**)

ON the ROAD thru OKLAHOMA

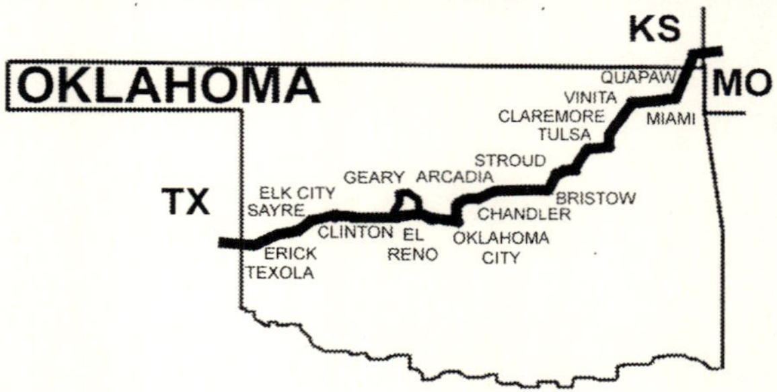

Route 66 traces a long jagged path across **The Sooner State**, entering at the very NE corner, and zigzagging its way down to the middle before taking off for **TEXAS**. In **1926,** US 66 was plotted for about 415 miles across **OK**. By 1937 this had been reduced to about 383 miles of first generation paving (including the 9-foot wide "Sidewalk Highway" between **AFTON** and **MIAMI**).

There are still **PLENTY** of places to see and visit along OK 66. You can just about go across the whole state without hitting an interstate but you do drive on some upgraded 4-lane sections, especially in the east, where the "free road," bypassed by the turnpikes, still gets plenty of use. Be sure to visit **EZ 66 author** and Route 66 artist **Jerry McClanahan** (me!) in **CHANDLER** (see OK page 16 if you want to call ahead). Across the **Western** half of the state are extensive sections of pristine, original **Portland concrete**, complete with curbs. You must hop back and forth across I-40 to follow the old pavement, but the "kathumpety-thump" as you roll over the concrete joints is worth the trouble. Western OK is fortunate to have two excellent Route 66 museums, The **OK Route 66 Museum** at **CLINTON**, and the **National Route 66 Museum** in **ELK CITY**. Very well done and friendly: see both!

As you motor among red hills, plains, grasslands, woods and rivers keep your eye out for the splendid history of OK, thru small towns connected to the world by a thin ribbon of concrete. **CAR GAME: CREEK CRITTERS: OK HWY 66** crosses many creeks in between **MIAMI** and **LUTHER**, some named after animals. See who is the **FIRST** to spot the following creeks: (WB order) Horse, Bird, Polecat (little and big) Catfish, and Wildhorse Creeks. The one who spots the most on the list wins! (hope the SIGNS are still visible!)

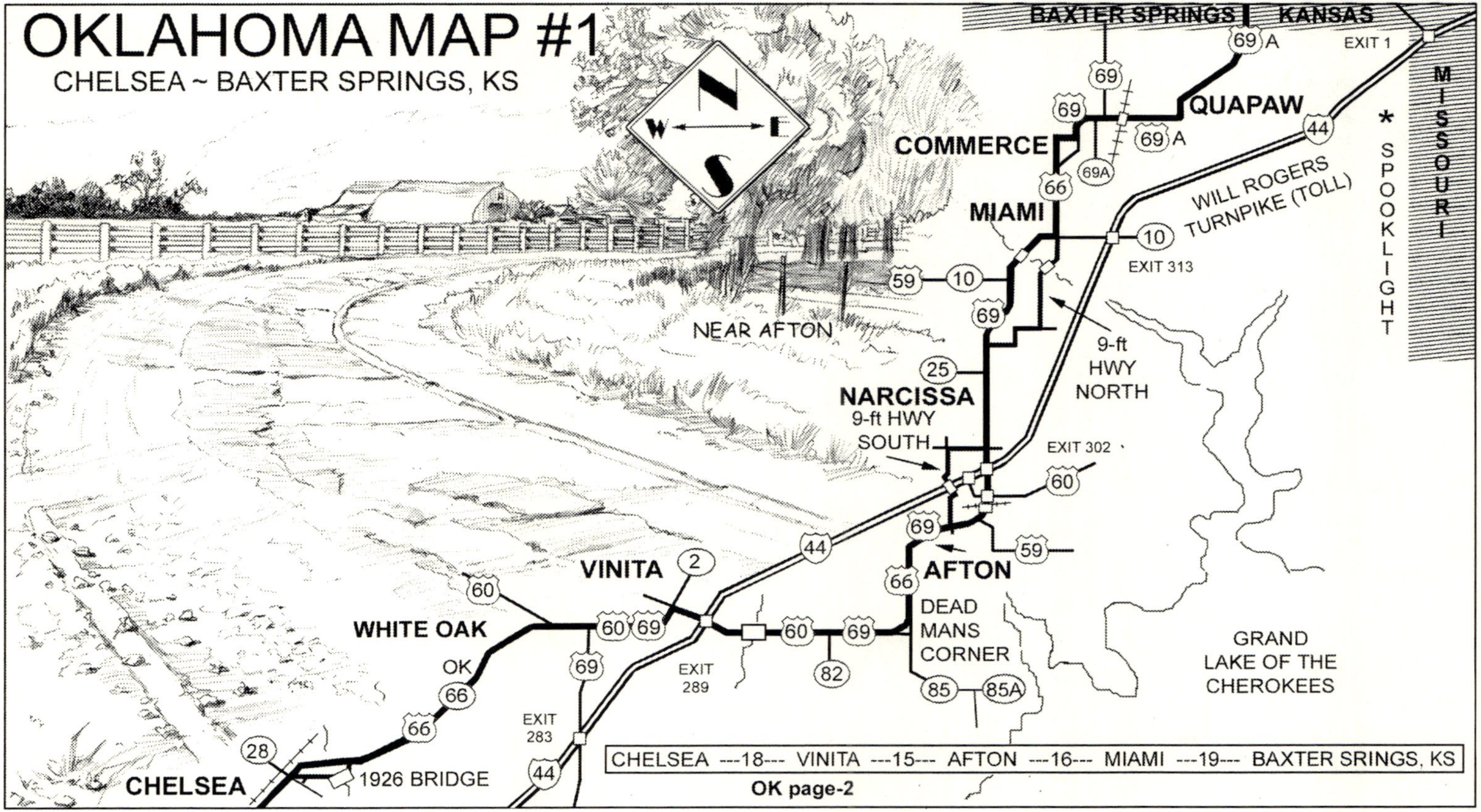
OKLAHOMA MAP #1
CHELSEA ~ BAXTER SPRINGS, KS
N
W
E
S
BAXTER SPRINGS
KANSAS
MISSOURI
EXIT 1
69 A
69
QUAPAW
69 A
69A
COMMERCE
66
MIAMI
44
WILL ROGERS TURNPIKE (TOLL)
10
EXIT 313
* SPOOKLIGHT
59
NEAR AFTON
25
NARCISSA
9-ft HWY SOUTH
9-ft HWY NORTH
EXIT 302
60
AFTON
DEAD MANS CORNER
GRAND LAKE OF THE CHEROKEES
VINITA
2
WHITE OAK
82
85
85A
EXIT 289
EXIT 283
OK
1926 BRIDGE
28
CHELSEA
CHELSEA ---18--- VINITA ---15--- AFTON ---16--- MIAMI ---19--- BAXTER SRINGS, KS
OK page-2

WB: Take **US 69A** into **OKLAHOMA** for about 10 mi, curving thru **QUAPAW** (west of town the route becomes **SOUTH US 69-** continue ahead…no turns) to enter **COMMERCE** on **Mickey Mantle Blvd**. Turn **RIGHT** on **Commerce St**, thru downtown for 0.6 mi, then **LEFT** at the "T" on **Main St**. After 0.8 mi, continue **AHEAD** from the **STOP** back onto **South US 69** in **NORTH MIAMI**.

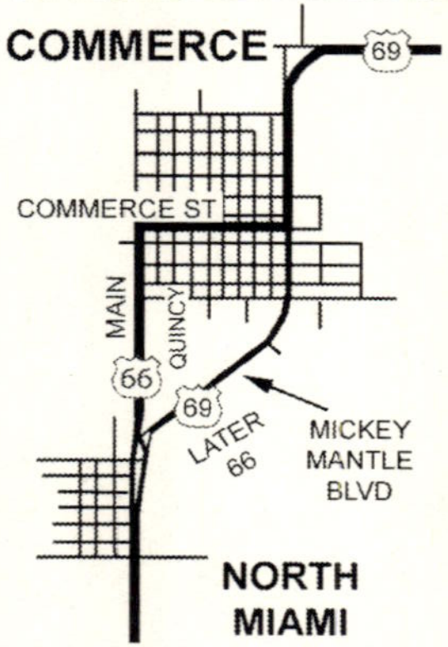

Over the line, more "chat piles" (old mining tailings) greet you in **OKLAHOMA**. Several (deteriorating) murals decorate quaint **QUAPAW**. One honors the coal mining days with a scene of miners and mine works, while others show scenes of a steam engine at the train depot and an old gas station. The **Dallas Dairyette** offers small-town eats.

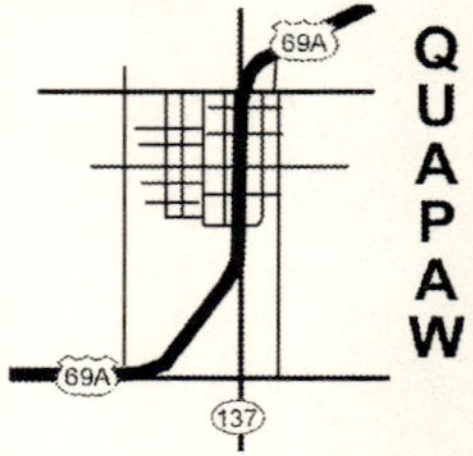

SIDE TRIP: About 11 miles east of **QUAPAW** is the infamous **SPOOKLIGHT**. Folks have seen "ghostly" lights here since Indian days, but modern sightings are likely to be the lights of cars on Old 66. Paranormal, or "para-headlights," you decide. The site is located just inside **OK** on **CO RD E50**. You'll need local directions (or "google" it) to find the spot. Try **Neilson's** (old Eisler Bros) in **RIVERTON**, **KS** or **Waylan's Ku-Ku Burger** in **MIAMI** for maps. **NOTE**: The **Oklahoma Route 66 Association Guide** says: "…local police discourage people from going." So spot the spooks at your own risk!

COMMERCE was **Mickey Mantle's** hometown. His **childhood home** (no exhibits) is at 319 S Quincy (3 blocks south of Commerce St on Main, then 2 blocks east on C St, on the corner of C St and Quincy). North on Main St (from Commerce St) is **Mutt Mantle Field**, named for his dad. A **statue** of Mantle is at **Mickey Mantle Field** at Commerce High School. At Commerce and Main, in a 1925-era Marathon station, is the **Dairy King**, a great little small town burger joint. Across the street a picturesque former cottage-style gas station that appears to be "sunken" halfway into a brick wall, houses **Allen's Fillin' Station**, a worthy photo stop even if you don't catch them open. Call (918) 533-2079 for an appt.

EB: Continue on **US 69 (Main St)** for 3.4 mi (thru **NORTH MIAMI**). As US 69 begins to curve right, be in the **LEFT TURN** lane. **AVOID** the first chance to turn, then **CURVE LEFT** at the **"Y"** and **STOP** in the center median. Cross the WB lanes, then continue 0.8 mi on **Main St** into **COMMERCE**. Turn **RIGHT** on **Commerce St** thru downtown for 0.6 mi, then **LEFT** on **US 69 / Mickey Mantle Blvd**. At the NORTH US 69 JCT, continue **AHEAD** (no turn) onto **US 69A**. Curve thru **QUAPAW**, then go about 4.3 mi to **KANSAS**.

WB: Take **US 69 South** for 3.3 mi thru downtown **MIAMI**. At **Steve Owens Blvd** (HWY 10), turn **RIGHT** and follow **US 69 South** from town for 11.4 mi (thru **NARCISSA**). Pass under I-44, and under the overpass at the US 60/I-44 JCT. Continue with **US 69** across the RR overpass, and bear **RIGHT** at the US 59 JCT. Continue on **US 69** for 2 mi, into **AFTON**.

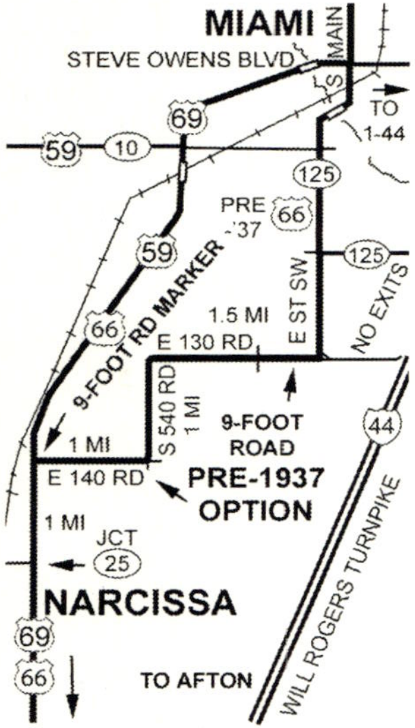

On **MIAMI's** (say My-am-uh") north side is **Waylan's Ku Ku Burger**, and their great neon sign. **GIANT ALERT**! A **GIANT Ku Ku** is posed as if it just popped out of the building (think coo-coo clock). Downtown at 103 N Main sits the proud **Coleman Theatre Beautiful**, a restored 1929 Spanish mission-styled showpiece, with tours (918) 540 2425. At 128 S Main is the cool **Route 66 Vintage Iron Motorcycle Museum** (918) 542 6170 **MIAMI** INFO: (918) 542-4435.

PRE-1937 OPTION (follow the maps): South from **MIAMI**, remnants of the famous **9-foot Hwy** (**AKA**: Sidewalk Hwy) zigzag towards **AFTON**. This narrow strip, with concrete base and curbs and an asphalt road surface paved in 1922, served until 1937. **NOTE: VERY ROUGH GRAVEL** covers some sections so go **SLOW**. The road is fragile, so no heavy rigs. The **NORTH** section begins as blacktop (past an old "Colonial" style gas station on S Main), then reverts to one-lane road past HWY 125. **NARCISSA** sits on US 69 between the surviving segments. The **SOUTHERN** section starts at the NE Technology Center turnoff, and curves south, across I-44 and the RR, ending back at US 69 east of **AFTON**.

CURRENT ROUTE: If you can't drive either stretch, see the **marker** at the JCT of E 140 RD and US 69 near **NARCISSA**, or the **Will Rogers Hwy Marker** on the south side of 66 about a half mile east of **AFTON** where the southern section ends (see map). Between the US 60 overpass and US 59 is **Buffalo Ranch**. A new multi-purpose facility has replaced the original complex, but they DO keep some **LIVE BUFFALO** on hand for modern tourists.

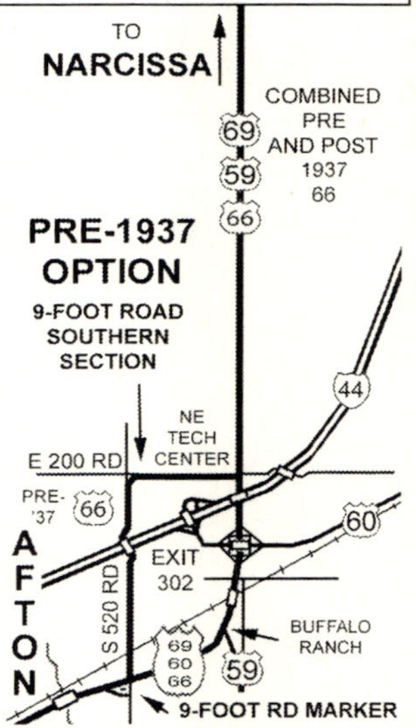

EB: Follow **US 69** north from **AFTON** for 15 mi (over the RR overpass and under the US 60/I-44 overpasses, and thru **NARCISSA**) into **MIAMI** (becomes Steve Owen Blvd). Turn **LEFT** on **Main St**. Follow **US 69** for 3.4 mi north (thru downtown) from this turn.

WB: Follow **US 69 & 60** for 14 mi from **AFTON**. Cross under I-44 and go 1.3 mi, entering **VINITA** on **Illinois St** (**US 69 & 60**). Turn **LEFT** on **Wilson** with **69/60**, then curve out of town. Stay **AHEAD** past the SOUTH US 69 JCT. About a mile further, at the WEST US 60 JCT, continue **AHEAD** (no turns) with **OK HWY 66**, and continue 1.6 mi, passing thru **WHITE OAK**.

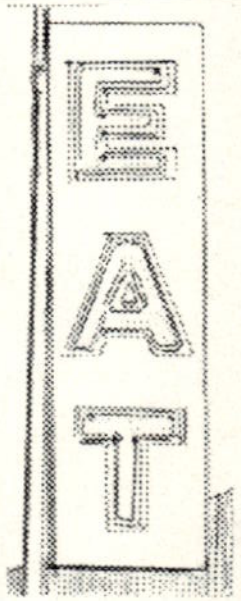

Near **Buffalo Ranch** (JCT US 59) is the charming **Route 66 Motel**, with theme rooms (918) 257 8313. Just east of **AFTON** you'll cross the **Horse Creek Bridge**, with its built-in sidewalks. The **PACKARD** sign downtown marks **Afton Station/Route 66 Packards**, the former **DX gas station** rehabilitated to house Laurel Kane's collection of Route 66 postcards and Buffalo Ranch memorabilia, plus David Kane's antique **Packards**. Do **call ahead** to (918)-382-9465 or (918) 787-8903 for info on hours and open days. Sometimes Ron Jones, "Tattoo Man" is there! **GIANT ALERT**! **GIANT PENGUIN statue** decorated with names of all the Oklahoma Route 66 towns. **SIDE TRIP**: South of **AFTON** is **Grand Lake O' the Cherokees**, 1,300 miles of shoreline among the foothills of the Ozarks.: At "Monkey Island" near Bernice, **Darryl Starbird's Custom Car Museum** (Hwy 85A) features 40 exotic vehicles, including "bubble-top" customs (918) 257-4234.

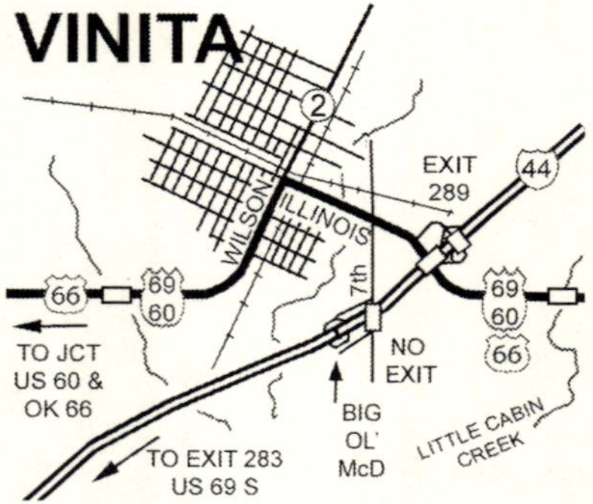

Between **Dead Man's Corner** (self-explanatory) and I-44 are the pecan groves of **Little Cabin Pecan Co**, with pecans and pottery. (918) 256-2218 **GIFT SHOP ALERT**! Look for the bypassed truss bridge over Little Cabin Creek east of **VINITA**. In town is the classic neon **EAT** sign at **Clantons Café** (owned by the same family since 1927). Downtown offers antiques and old gas station relics. Some Mom and Pop motels are listed in the Federation guide.

GIANT ALERT! The **World's LARGEST McDonalds** (formerly the Glass House) straddles I-44 between Exits 289 and 283. If you want to stand in the middle and watch all the traffic zoom by underneath, sneak south from Illinois St on 7th St (just west of EXIT 289). Mid-September brings the **Worlds LARGEST Calf-Fry Festival** to town (you know what a "calf-fry" is, right?) City INFO: www.vinita.com

EB: Follow **OK 66** 1.6 mi from **WHITE OAK**. Continue, as both **US 60 & US 69** join, for 4 mi into **VINITA**. Curve with **60/69** onto **Wilson St**, thru downtown, then turn **RIGHT** with **60/69** onto **Illinois St**. Cross under I-44, follow **US 69 & 60** for 14 mi into **AFTON**.

(see **MAP #1 OK page-2**)

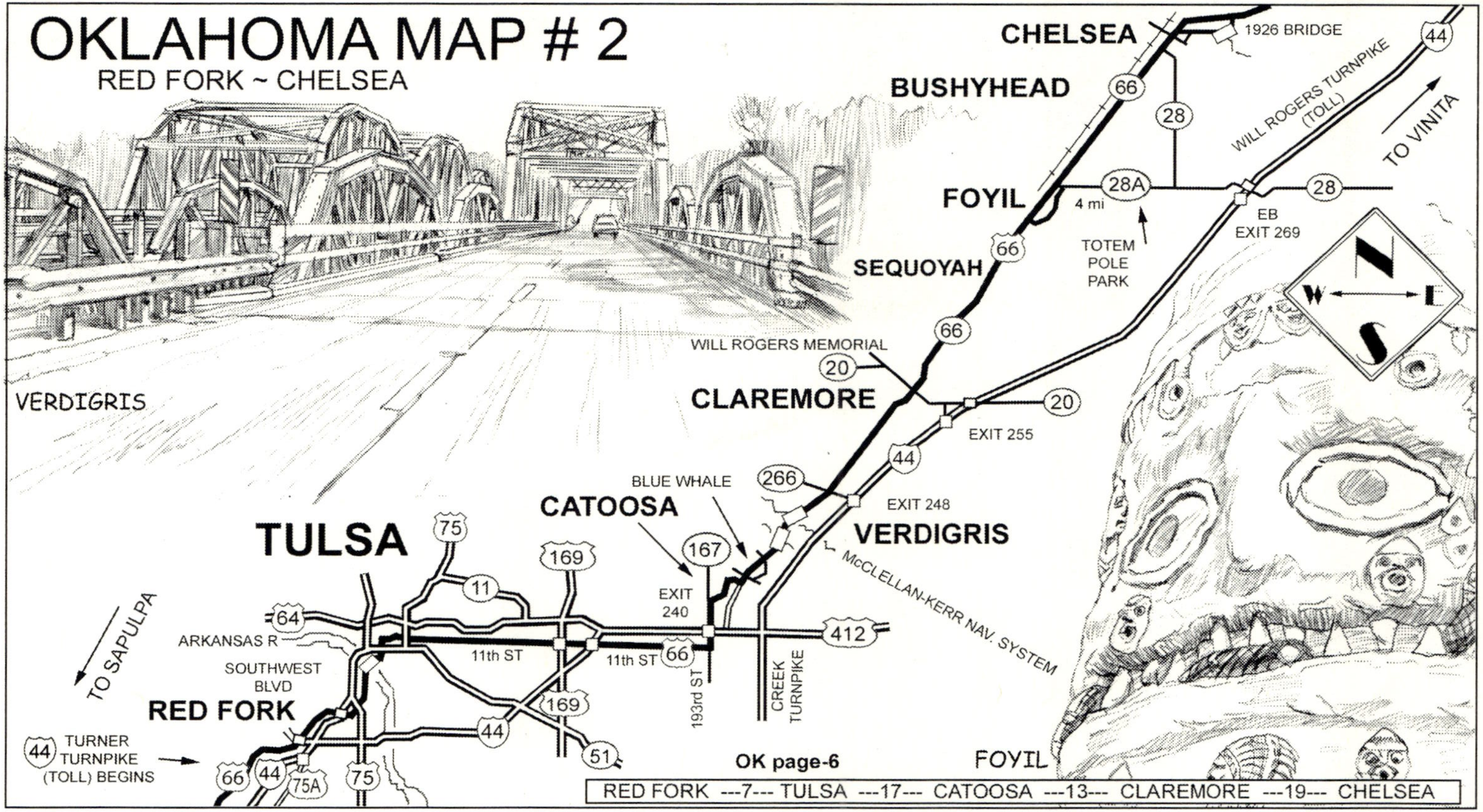
OKLAHOMA MAP # 2
RED FORK ~ CHELSEA
CHELSEA
1926 BRIDGE
BUSHYHEAD
WILL ROGERS TURNPIKE (TOLL)
TO VINITA
FOYIL
4 mi
28A
TOTEM POLE PARK
EB EXIT 269
SEQUOYAH
WILL ROGERS MEMORIAL
CLAREMORE
EXIT 255
VERDIGRIS
BLUE WHALE
CATOOSA
EXIT 248
VERDIGRIS
McCLELLAN-KERR NAV. SYSTEM
TULSA
EXIT 240
ARKANSAS R
SOUTHWEST BLVD
11th ST
11th ST
193rd ST
CREEK TURNPIKE
TO SAPULPA
RED FORK
TURNER TURNPIKE (TOLL) BEGINS
OK page-6
FOYIL
RED FORK ---7--- TULSA ---17--- CATOOSA ---13--- CLAREMORE ---19--- CHELSEA

WB: From **WHITE OAK**, take **OK HWY 66** for 30 mi thru **CHELSEA**, **BUSHYHEAD**, **FOYIL** & **SEQUOYAH** to **CLAREMORE**.

WHITE OAK has an old mill across the tracks. In **CHELSEA** at 10th and Olive is a vintage house mail-ordered from the Sears Catalog in 1913 (tours by appointment only). The former Chelsea Motel still has a picturesque old sign, but the **Chelsea Motor Inn** is a nice place to stay (918) 789-3437. A mural of OK's **oldest oil well** is across the tracks downtown. The 1932 pony bridge (see map at right) is doomed. **OPTION**: Use the detail map to drive across a **1926 iron bridge** over **Pryor Creek** (partly gravel road).

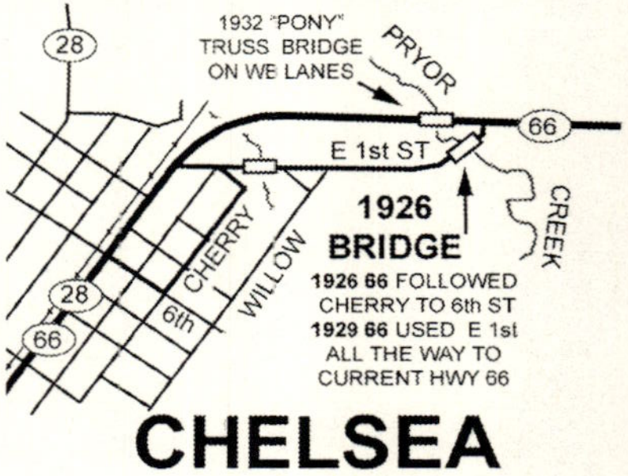

GIANT ALERT SIDE TRIP! Just 4 miles east of HWY 66 on **HWY 28A**, (northeast of **FOYIL**) is **Totem Pole Park**, site of the **World's LARGEST Totem Pole** (90 feet), created over 11 years by the late Ed Galloway and recently restored. **FOLK ART ALERT**! The property contains a colorful collection of smaller concrete totems, covered in countless critters, plus the 11-sided "Fiddle House" (once housed almost 400 hand-carved violins). Truly a worthy **PHOTO OP**! INFO: (918) 342-9149

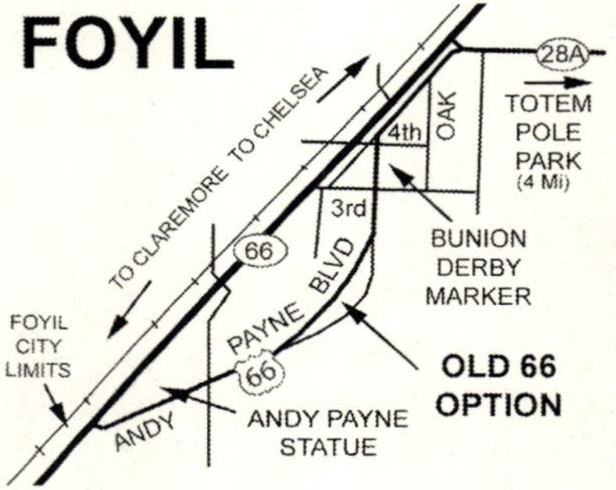

FOYIL was home to **Andy Payne**, winner of the 1928 "**Bunion Derby**," the Transcontinental Foot Race from LA to New York City that followed US 66.

OPTION (recommended): Drive **Old 66** thru **FOYIL** along **Andy Payne Blvd**, past the **Bunion Derby Historic Marker**, and the **Andy Payne Statue**. **WB**: The north end of this loop is at 4th St, about 0.2 mi past HWY 28A (see map). **EB**: if you miss the first access, double back from 4th St (it's a short loop).

SCAVENGER HUNT! Between **FOYIL** and **SEQUOYAH** is a store called **Kong's Kafe**. What does the "statue" out front depict? ______________

EB: From **CLAREMORE**, take **OK HWY 66** 30 mi, thru **SEQUOYAH**, **FOYIL**, **BUSHYHEAD** and **CHELSEA** to **WHITE OAK**.

WB: Follow **OK HWY 66** (becomes **Lynn Riggs Blvd**) thru **CLAREMORE** (see **PRE-1958 OPTION**). Continue on OK 66 for about 5 mi, crossing the Hwy 266 JCT. (next turn is about 5.7 mi ahead from JCT).

CLAREMORE once was famous for "radium" baths, piped in mineral water discovered in 1903. One dispenser of this "miracle water" was the grand **Will Rogers Hotel**, 6 stories and 78 rooms of opulent Spanish decor (now restored as senior living). **SCAVENGER HUNT**! What **SIGN** is painted at the top of the backside of the former hotel (now the **Will Rogers Center and Apartments)**? ________________

OPTION: PRE-1958 66 followed **J. M. Davis Blvd**, one block west and parallel to current HWY 66. This connects to Lynn Riggs on the north side at the Stuart Roosa stoplight, and on the south, below Claremore St. **PRE-'58 66** features several old road relics, including the **Adobe Village Apts**, which once were the El Sueno Courts, a former Alamo-style motel. Try to loop on both routes.

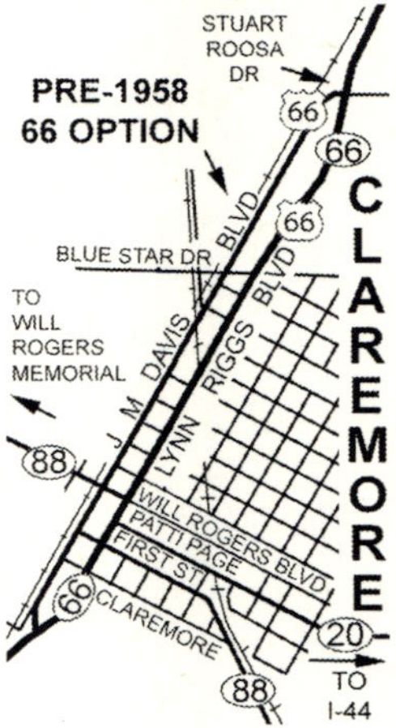

This town is loaded with memorials (even the street names). The **Will Rogers Memorial and Museum** at 1720 W **Will Rogers Blvd** honors the celebrated movie and stage star and author, who never met a man he didn't like. (800) 324-9455. Another name promoted for Route 66 is "**Will Rogers Hwy,**" as evidenced by many markers, old and new, along the route to California. Also on **Will Rogers Blvd** is a statue of Will sitting on a park bench.

20,000 guns (and other artifacts) wait at the **J M Davis Arms and Historical Museum**, the **Worlds LARGEST Private Firearm Collection (**plus an **ARMY TANK**) at 333 N Lynn Riggs. Beware those guns that were formerly owned by outlaws and bandits! (918) 341-5707. Less military is the **Lynn Riggs Memorial**, at 121 N Weenonah, honoring the author who inspired the musical ***Oklahoma*** (the original "Surrey with the fringe on top" from the movie is here) (918) 627-2716. **CLEVER NAME**! "Spirits of 66" liquor store. For eats try **Ron's Hamburgers and Chili**. To rest up and dream about Will, try the **Best Western Will Rogers Inn** (918) 341-4410 or the **Claremore Motor Inn** (800) 828-4540 (both are in the Federation Guide). City INFO: (918) 341-2818 or www.claremore.org

EB: Follow **OK HWY 66** (becomes **Lynn Riggs Blvd**) thru **CLAREMORE** (see **PRE-1958 OPTION**).

WB: From the HWY 266 JCT, continue on OK 66 for 5.7 mi (the Blue Whale is 5 mi on the right), then curve **RIGHT** on **Ford St** into **CATOOSA**. Turn **LEFT** on **Cherokee**, and continue 1.6 mi to the HWY 167 (193rd St) JCT.

Near **VERDIGRIS**, **The Nut House** ("Pecans and other nuts") is decorated inside and out with antiques. (918) 266-1604. Since the late '60s, **HWY 66** has crossed over the **McClellan-Kerr Navigation System**, a 445-mile waterway that links Tulsa to the Gulf. The formerly photogenic pair of "almost" Twin Bridges across Bird Creek were ruined with the removal of the 1936 WB span, leaving behind its lonely 1957 sibling (added for 4-lane 66). Sections are preserved in a park on the east side of the creek, plus as the entrance to **Molly's Landing Restaurant** on the west side.

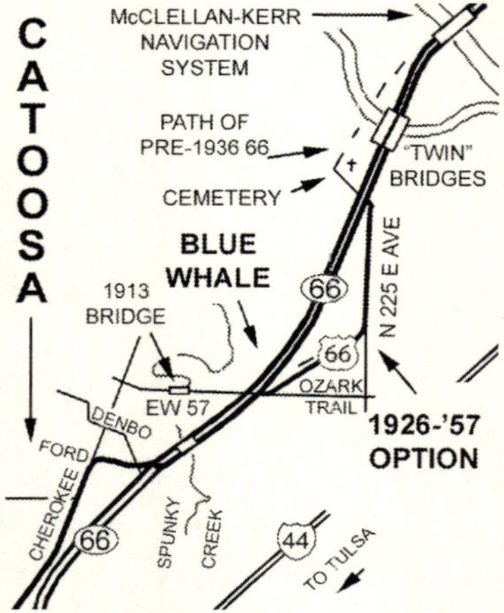

1926-1957 OPTION: Just west of the former Twin Bridges, an older loop of 66 turns off to the south. Its pavement follows **N 225 E Ave** (**WB**: access from next x-over), cuts the corner of the older Ozark Trail to hit **EW 57**, then rejoins **OK HWY 66**. Along the way, the route passes the front of the former **Arrowood Trading Post** (now a garage). The **Ozark Trail** (Pre-US 66) continued across the 4-Lane on EW 57 (Rice St), but the **1913 one-lane "beadstead" bridge** is now closed.

If you drive the **OPTION**, be sure to double back on **4-lane 66**, to visit the **BLUE WHALE**, the grinning star of a former swimming hole, now renovated as a small park (no swimming!). **PHOTO OP**! On the other side of 4-lane 66 is the picturesque "back" facade of **Arrowood**, with paintings of Indian dancers and its name in huge letters. **CATOOSA** itself has a **Historical Museum** in an old RR depot, with a "Ship it on the Frisco" caboose, on Cherokee. **SCAVENGER HUNT**! What is the caboose's 4-digit number? (may have been painted over). In town on Pine St, just west off 66, is the **DW Correll Museum**, full of old cars, toys, bottles 'n rocks (and a nifty **mural** facing 66). (918) 266-3612 The nearby **Port of Catoosa** is billed as the **furthest inland seaport** in the US!

EB: Continue thru **CATOOSA**, then curve **RIGHT** on **Ford St**. At **OK HWY 66**, carefully cross and turn **LEFT** onto the EB lanes, and continue 11.4 mi (the **Blue Whale** is 0.7 mi from this turn on the left) into **CLAREMORE** (becomes **Lynn Riggs Blvd**).

WB: Turn **LEFT** on **HWY 167 (193rd E Ave)**. Continue under I-44 with **193rd E Ave**. Go 1 mi (passing Admiral Place), then **RIGHT** on **11th St**. Go 4.8 mi and continue with 11th under I-44 (**IGNORE** the "OK Hwy 66" sign). After 0.7 mi, cross under US 169/Mingo Expwy. Continue on **11th St** for 6.6 mi, then cross under US 75 and continue on 11th into **TULSA.**

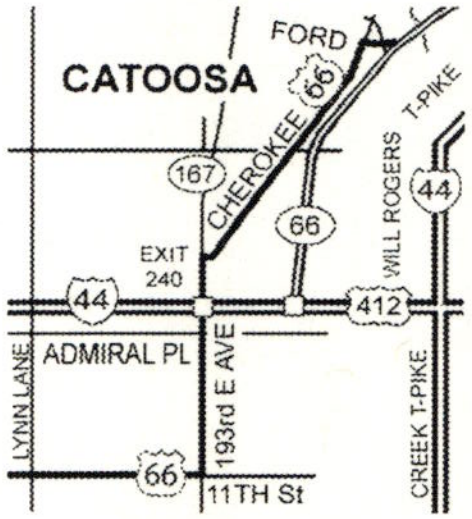

66 runs straight on **11th St** to downtown **TULSA**. The east part is 2-lane country road, but grows into a busy artery. **SIDE TRIP**: **PRE-32 '66** turns up **Mingo Rd** to **Admiral Place**, where it spins "roundabout" a traffic circle. **Cyrus Avery**, "The Father of 66" arranged for '66 to pass by his (gone) business, the Old English Inn, at this point! This route followed **Admiral Place** west to **Lewis**, then south to **2nd**, but a detour off 2nd and one-way streets now hamper this way into downtown. At 7355 E Easton St (north of I-244) is the reborn **Admiral Place Drive-In Theatre**.

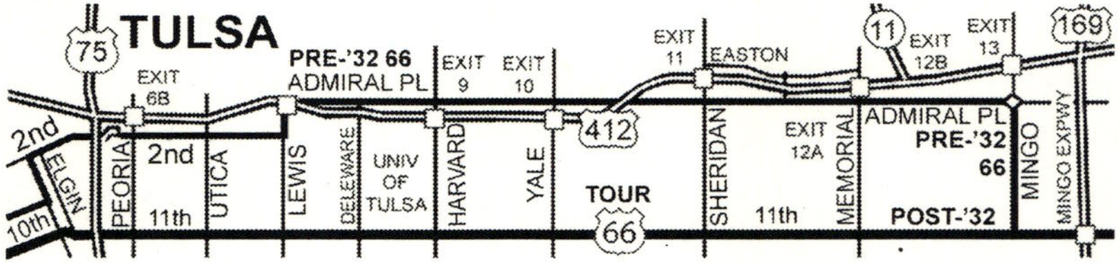

Several old motels still exist on 11th, some with classic signs but untapped potential. The **Desert Hills**, east of Yale, has a great neon sign, but reviews differ widely on this place. You might ask to see a room near the office. A restored 1927 bldg at 2636 11th houses the well-reviewed **Campbell Hotel**. www.thecampbellhotel.com. Good eateries include **Talley's Café** at Yale, the **Corner Café** at Peoria, and the **Rancho Grande**, with its vintage neon sign of a lasso-twirling vaquero, west of Utica St. From Yale to Peoria St, the sidewalks are lined with paving blocks bearing the US 66 shield. **GIANT ALERT SIDE TRIP**! Well south of 66, but worth a detour for giant fans, is **The Golden Driller**, a 76-foot tribute to **TULSA**'s oil heritage (the former "Oil Capitol of the World"), at 21st St west of Yale. Also well south of 11th is **Route 66 Harley-Davidson Dealership** at the JCT of Broken Arrow Expressway and Memorial Dr. They have a Route 66 exhibit. 918 622 1340. The historic and spectacular Meadow Gold Neon Sign is in its new '66 home at 11th and Quaker, between Utica and Peoria east of downtown.

EB: Follow **11th St** for 6.6 mi, crossing under US 169/Mingo Expy. Continue 0.7 mi and cross under I-44 (**IGNORE** "OK HWY 66" sign). Continue on **11th St** for 4.8 mi, then turn **LEFT** on **193rd E Ave**. **AVOID** the "turn lanes" at the I-44 JCT: continue with **HWY 167** (**IGNORE** the "OK HWY 66" sign at the onramp) for 0.3 mi, then **RIGHT** at the light onto **Cherokee St**, into **CATOOSA**. Go 1.6 mi.

WB: Briefly stay with **11th St**. Curve thru the roundabout (past Elgin Ave) onto **10th St**. West of Boulder Ave the route curves back onto **11th St**. Past Denver Ave, curve to the **LEFT** and cross US 75/64, then follow the curve onto **12th St**. Turn **LEFT** at the "T" onto **Southwest Blvd**. Go about 2.5 mi, then follow **Southwest Blvd** under US 75, and continue across I-244 in **RED FORK**.

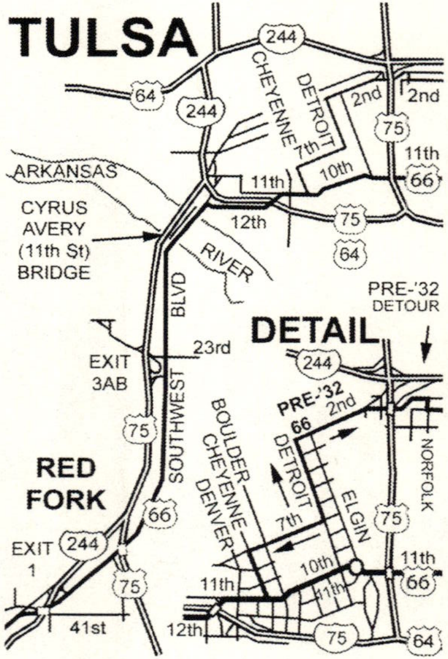

TULSA is famous for abundant Art Deco architecture. **11th St** has many examples, including the "Streamline" styled **Tulsa Monument Building**, east of Utica. The "ZigZag" tower and terra-cotta details of the preserved 1929 **Warehouse Market Building** at the Elgin Street intersection bear close examination. Former tenants **Tulsa Treasures** (gifts and collectibles) and **Lyons Indian Store**, which boasts a selection of Indian goods, have moved to 111 S Detroit, in the **Blue Dome District**. More "Zigzag" style and colorful terra-cotta tiles abound in downtown, including the **Boston Ave Church**. For info check www.tulsaarchitecture.com or call for info on a walking tour: (800) 558-3311.

SIDE TRIP: detour up to **PRE-'32 66** to ogle the 1925 **Blue Dome gas station** (topped by a blue dome, of course) at **2nd** and **Elgin**. One-way streets (and a detour of 2nd St at US 75, via 1st and Norfolk) make the **PRE-32** route via **Admiral Place** harder to follow. Among area attractions are the **Gilcrease Museum** of western art/artifacts and the **Philbrook Museum of Art**. INFO: www.visittulsa.com.

The long-closed **Cyrus Avery (11th St) Bridge,** a 1916 Art Deco concrete masterpiece, still spans the **Arkansas River**. At its east end, **Cyrus Avery Centennial Plaza** features a huge bronze statue "**East meets West**" featuring "The Father of 66," plus a "66 Arch" over the road. Across the river, stop at **Route 66 Village** at 3770 **Southwest Blvd** for the restored **Frisco 4500 steam engine** and train cars, plus a 194 foot tall **oil derrick**, honoring the transportation and oil industry heritage of the corridor.

EB: Cross under US 75 and continue on **Southwest Blvd** for 2.5 mi to cross the river into **TULSA**. Turn **RIGHT** on **12th St**. Angle across US 75/64 (no choice) then curve right onto **11th St**. Past Cheyenne St, follow the main street as it bears **LEFT** onto **10th** (thru Boulder). Past Detroit Ave, curve partway around the roundabout onto **11th St**. Follow **11th St** under US 75.

(see **MAP # 2 OK page-6**)

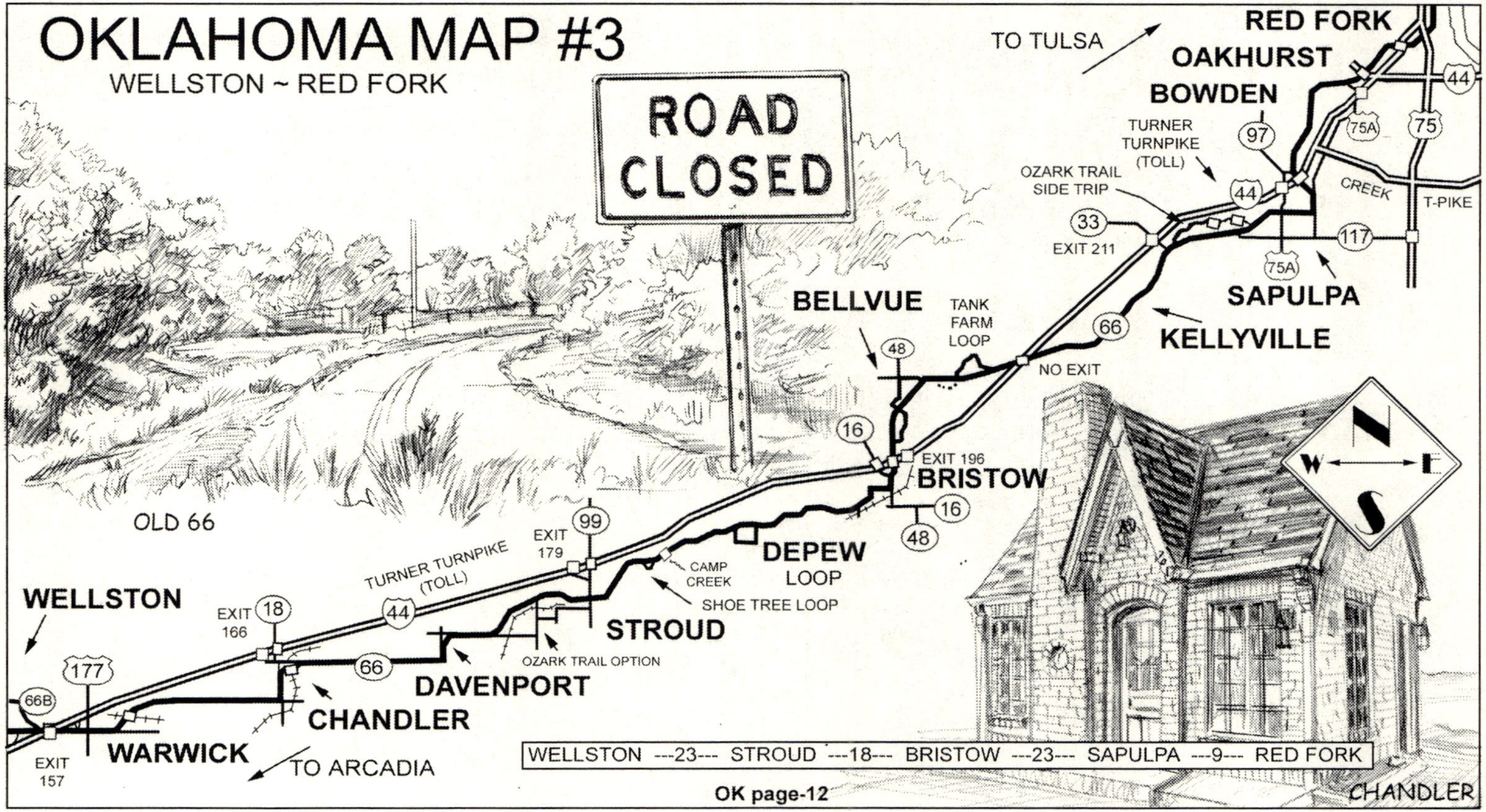
OKLAHOMA MAP #3
WELLSTON ~ RED FORK
ROAD CLOSED
OLD 66
TO TULSA
RED FORK
OAKHURST
BOWDEN
TURNER TURNPIKE (TOLL)
OZARK TRAIL SIDE TRIP
33
EXIT 211
97
44
75A
75
CREEK
T-PIKE
117
SAPULPA
KELLYVILLE
66
NO EXIT
TANK FARM LOOP
BELLVUE
48
16
EXIT 196
BRISTOW
16
48
DEPEW
LOOP
CAMP CREEK
SHOE TREE LOOP
STROUD
99
EXIT 179
TURNER TURNPIKE (TOLL)
44
OZARK TRAIL OPTION
DAVENPORT
66
18
EXIT 166
CHANDLER
WELLSTON
66B
177
WARWICK
EXIT 157
TO ARCADIA
WELLSTON ---23--- STROUD ---18--- BRISTOW ---23--- SAPULPA ---9--- RED FORK
CHANDLER

WB: From I-244, Take **Southwest Blvd** for 8.4 mi thru **RED FORK** and along the RR thru **OAKHURST** and **BOWDEN** (becomes **Frankhoma Rd**). At the HWY 166 JCT continue **AHEAD** with **Frankhoma Rd**, go under I-44, then turn **RIGHT** on **OK 66 & Alt 75 (Mission St)**, into **SAPULPA**. After almost 1 mi, turn **RIGHT** with **OK 66** on **Dewey Ave**, thru downtown.

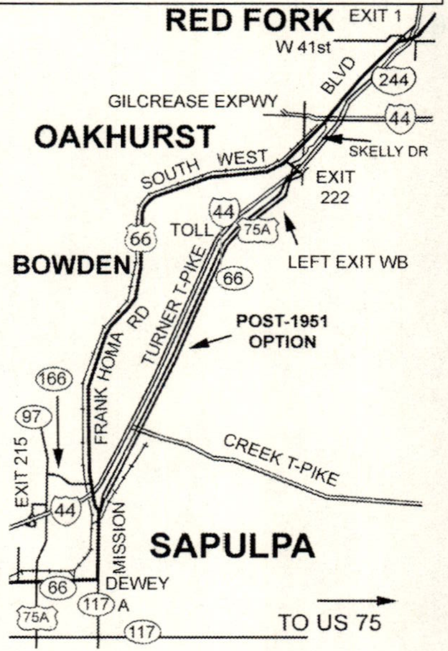

More trains in **RED FORK** at 4070 Southwest Blvd. **Ollie's Station Restaurant** is decorated with a "train" motif, with model trains running along the ceiling. South of the I- 244/I-44 JCT, **Skelly Drive** runs as a service road down to I-44 EXIT 222, past some old motels. **Skelly Drive** was the name of the 1959-era US 66 that bypassed **TULSA** (now buried by I-44 so **IGNORE** the OK 66 signs thru **TULSA**). Old 66 ambles along the tracks thru **OAKHURST** and **BOWDEN**. **Frankhoma Pottery**, makers of fine pottery and collectibles since 1933, and located along this stretch, has closed.

OPTION: POST-'51 US 66 (quick, but dull) follows **OK 66 /ALT 75** south to **SAPULPA**. Join I-44 WB at EXIT 222A (S 49th W Ave), then **QUICKLY** get in the far **LEFT** lane to **EXIT LEFT** onto **OK HWY 66/ALT 75** (**AVOID** the turnpike ahead!). **EB**: Follow **OK 66** north onto I-44, then **QUICKLY** take **EXIT 222A** (S 49th West Ave), cross under I-44 and join **Southwest Blvd** north.

GIANT ALERT! At the "**Tribute to Sapulpa Industry and Workers**" at Frankhoma Rd and OK 66 is a big **COKE BOTTLE** and glass. **Happy Burger** at 215 N Mission is the "oldest hamburger stand in Sapulpa" (since 1957): a great old fashioned burger joint, with some old photos and a large Pepsi collection too. In front of the offices of the **Tulsa-Sapulpa Union Railway Co** on Dewey (a freight line connecting Sapulpa to Tulsa that began in 1917 as an interurban) is a restored **Trolley Car** and caboose. **SAPULPA** INFO: (918) 224-0170.

EB: Follow **OK HWY 66/Dewey Ave** thru **SAPULPA**. Turn **LEFT** at **Mission St** with **OK 66 & Alt 75**. Go 1 mi (cross the tracks), and turn **LEFT** at the light onto **Frankhoma Rd**. Pass under I-44, then stay **AHEAD** with **Frankhoma Rd** at the W HWY 166 JCT. Continue for 8.4 mi thru **BOWDEN** (becomes **Southwest Blvd**) and **OAKHURST** into **RED FORK** and over I-244 towards US 75.

WB: From Mission St, follow **Dewey Ave/OK 66** thru downtown **SAPULPA**, continuing on **OK 66** for 22 mi, passing thru **KELLYVILLE** and across I-44 (no exit), then past **BELLVUE** and under I-44 into **BRISTOW**.

OZARK TRAIL SIDE TRIP: ROCK CREEK BRIDGE WILL BE CLOSED EVENTUALLY EXPECT DETOUR VIA NEW CONNECTION. *ROUGH RD: GO SLOW*

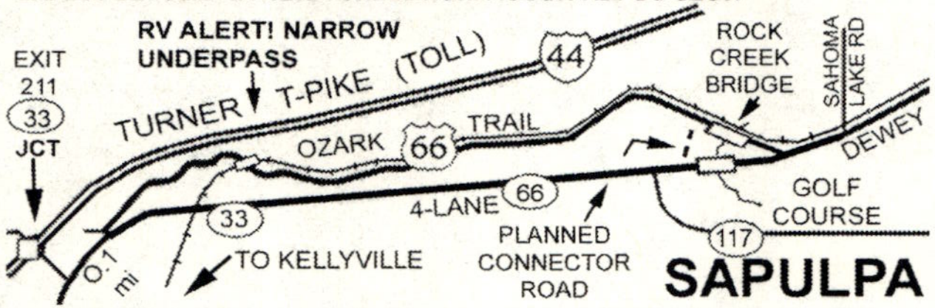

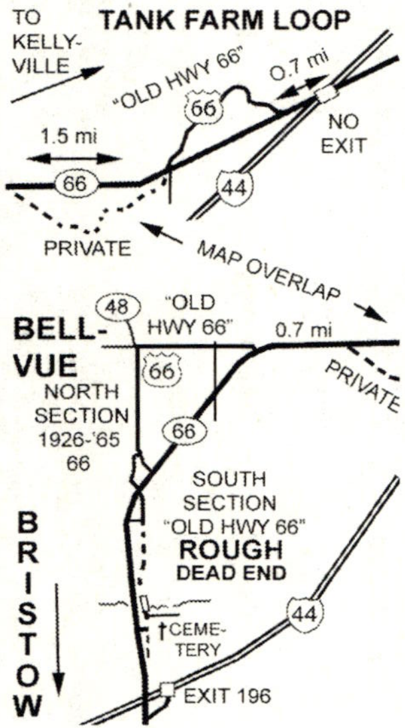

Many "Ghost Signs" (old ads) appear on walls in downtown **SAPULPA** and some sidewalks have US 66 shields in the corners. **SIDE TRIP:** This narrow, twisty and BUMPY **Ozark Trail** section crosses a 1925 iron bridge over **Rock Creek**, slated to be closed in a few years. Use the map to navigate, and expect changes. It then passes a defunct drive-in, and curves thru a narrow RR subway. **SCAVENGER HUNT**! What is the **DATE** on this underpass (watch for cars)? A great 3-mile drive, worth the effort.

In **KELLYVILLE,** an old cotton gin once housed the Gin Diner, while another building has two boats jutting from its front. West is the **TANK FARM LOOP OPTION**: A **BIT** bumpy in places, but worth the drive. The east end is about **0.7 mile** west of I-44. Signed "**Old HWY 66**" this is almost 2 miles of old concrete that winds thru a wooded area of old oil field tanks. Where the old road rejoins **OK 66** on the west end, it once continued across, to loop back in further west. An old motel is used as a residence on this **DEAD END**.

BELLVUE OPTION: Another series of "**Old HWY 66**" loops. See the detail map. The **northern** section makes a dogleg thru **BELLVUE** (a few houses), partly on **HWY 48**. The **southern** section continued south (WB) on the east side of **OK 66** (past the Adobe Wells Bar), but now **DEAD ENDS** at the small iron bridge on the south end. A connection back to 66 exists midway. **ROUGH** and not really recommended.

EB: From **BRISTOW**, stay with **OK 66** as it passes under I-44. Continue with **OK 66** for 22 mi, passing thru **BELLVUE** and across I-44 (no exit) and thru **KELLYVILLE** into downtown **SAPULPA** (becomes **Dewey Ave**).

WB: Continue with **OK 66**, south of I-44, into **<u>BRISTOW</u>** (becomes **Main St**). Go 1.3 mi from I-44, then turn **RIGHT** with **OK 66** on **4th St**. Curve with OK 66 onto Roland, then continue about 17 mi (past the entrance to **<u>DEPEW</u>**-see option) into **<u>STROUD</u>**.

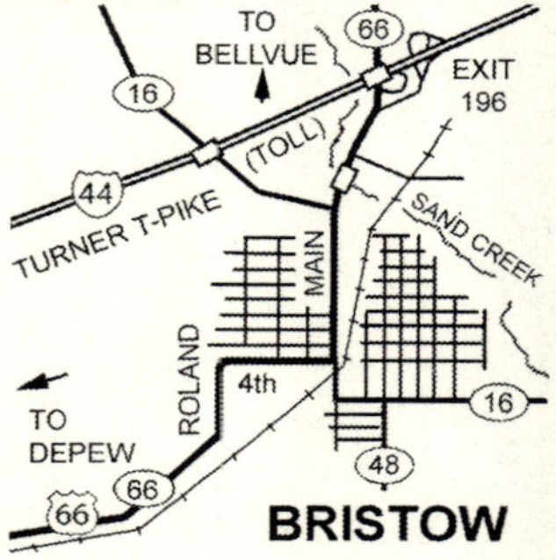

In downtown **<u>BRISTOW</u>**, look for the old **Bristow Motor Co** building, with plaster sculptures of "spoke wheels" on the facade. **SCAVENGER HUNT**! What is the **DATE** on the building? The **Ford** dealer rebuilt from a fire in splendid art deco style. **Bristow Body Shop** sits in a classic recently restored garage. The **Bristow Museum** is at the Railroad Depot on East 7th St. City INFO: www.bristowok.org. Look for the blue-tile roofed former gas station near the corner of Main and 4th. Down the road, at 630 S Roland, the **Anchor Inn** has cooked many a burger since 1950. Nearby is the turnoff sign for the **Wake Island** WW2 memorial.

<u>DEPEW LOOP OPTION</u>: From **1926-28**, US 66 made a curious loop thru downtown **<u>DEPEW</u>**, so be sure to drive the original road thru this small town "time capsule," marked by its "Home of the Hornets" water tower. A remnant of the first bypass 66 lies between OK 66 and the RR tracks, across the mouth of the loop.

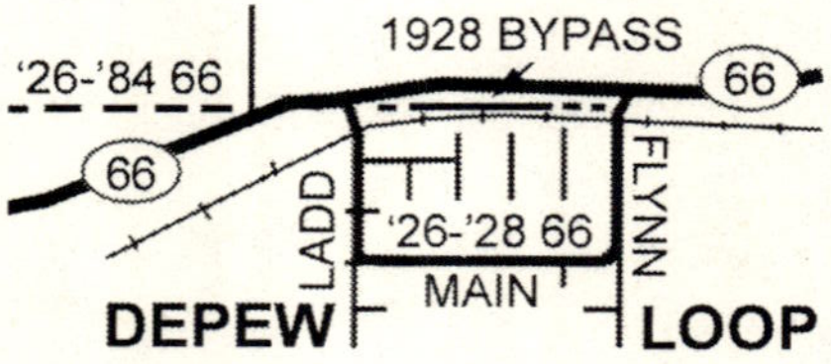

Cast-off remnants of **US 66** lie alongside modern **OK 66** in this area (many bypassed as late as 1984!), some signed as "Old Hwy 66." A few sections are drivable, while others are blocked. **<u>SHOE TREE LOOP</u>**: On private property, but usually kept open (be a good guest). The east entrance to this short stretch of "Old 66 Blvd" ("Shoe Tree Trading Post" sign) is about 6 miles west of **<u>DEPEW</u>**. Here is the famous **OK SHOE TREE**; festooned with funky footwear (recently fallen, a new tree has taken over). Add your own pair of sneakers. If driving east from **<u>STROUD</u>**, the Loop entrance is @ 3.2 mi east of Allied Rd. **<u>STROUD</u>**'s famed **Rock Café** (circa 1939) is back **OPEN** (closes at 3pm weekdays… for sale at this writing). The **Skyliner Motel** has great vintage neon. Check it out. Two other motels are north of OK 66 on Hwy 99.

EB: Follow **OK 66** east from **<u>STROUD</u>** about 17 mi (past the entrance to **<u>DEPEW</u>**-see option) into **<u>BRISTOW</u>**, entering with **Roland St**, then curving onto 4th St. At the HWY 48 JCT, turn **LEFT** onto **Main St** and follow **OK 66** thru downtown. Pass the HWY 16 JCT, then **BEAR LEFT** at the "Y" to **AVOID** the Turnpike entrance (EXIT 196), continue **AHEAD** under I-44 with **OK 66**.

WB: Follow **OK 66** west from **STROUD**, and curve thru **DAVENPORT**. Enter **CHANDLER** on **E 1st St**, then curve with **OK 66** onto **Manvel** at the northside JCT with OK 18 (See **EZ ALERT**). Pass thru downtown. Turn **RIGHT** with **OK 66 (15th St)**, and continue thru **WARWICK**, under the RR and past the JCT of US 177 (**STOP**). Cross under I-44 at EXIT 157, and continue to **WELLSTON**.

NOTE: about 25 miles this page

OZARK TRAIL OPTION: Use the map to drive the 1923-'30 route west of **STROUD** (**ROUGH DIRT** & **GRAVEL**, **AVOID** when muddy). Highlights are two culverts (marked 1909 and 1917) and a graffitied concrete obelisk (Ozark Trail marker). **DAVENPORT**, between **STROUD** and **CHANDLER**, is home to **Gar Wooly's Food-N-Fun** and the **Early Bird Diner** plus a **brick broadway** thru old downtown.

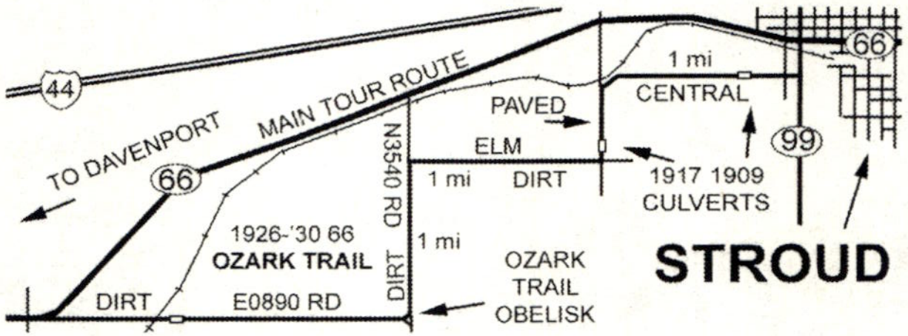

CHANDLER has the classic 1939 **Lincoln Motel,** with its restored neon sign. Check 'em out, and stay if you can. In the massive **1937 Armory** nearby is the impressive **Route 66 Interpretive Center** with cool videos and exhibits.

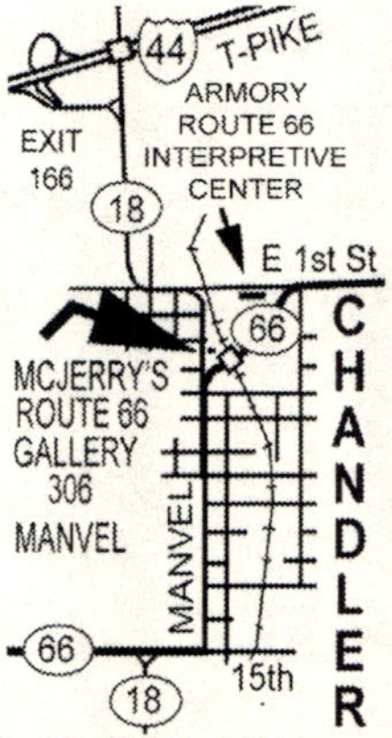

EZ ALERT! **Artist** and **EZ Guide** creator Jerry McClanahan's **McJerry's Route 66 Gallery** at **306 Manvel** (just off Route 66, north of downtown). From OK 66, go north on **OK 18/Manvel Ave** (signs point to I-44) just past the second house on the east (right) side. Get your **EZ Guide autographed**! No set hours: Call or try your luck. Visitors welcome! **Cell: (903) 467-6384 Home: (405) 258-0130** www.mcjerry66.com Downtown, a beautiful **1930 Phillips 66** is being restored by Bill Fernau. Local bed and breakfasts are the **Bungalow Inn** at 523 Manvel and the **Statehood Inn** at 206 W 8th. Phone for both is (405) 258 7569. Downtown is the excellent **Museum of Pioneer History**, plus **Country Kitchen** and **Boom-a-rang Diner**. On 66 about 3.5 miles west of Manvel Ave and 15th is a rare **Meramec Caverns** barn sign (only visible EB). **WARWICK**'s **Seaba Station** is a great antique **motorcycle museum**.

EB: From **WELLSTON**, join **OK 66** east, cross under I-44. **STOP** at US 177, then stay **AHEAD** with **OK 66**. Curve under the RR at **WARWICK**, and continue to **CHANDLER**. Turn north on **Manvel** thru downtown, then curve **RIGHT** with **OK 66** at the northside JCT with OK 18 (see **EZ ALERT**). Join **E 1st St** and follow **OK 66** east, to curve thru **DAVENPORT** on the way into **STROUD**.

(see **MAP # 3 OK page-12)**

OKLAHOMA MAP #4

EL RENO ~ WELLSTON

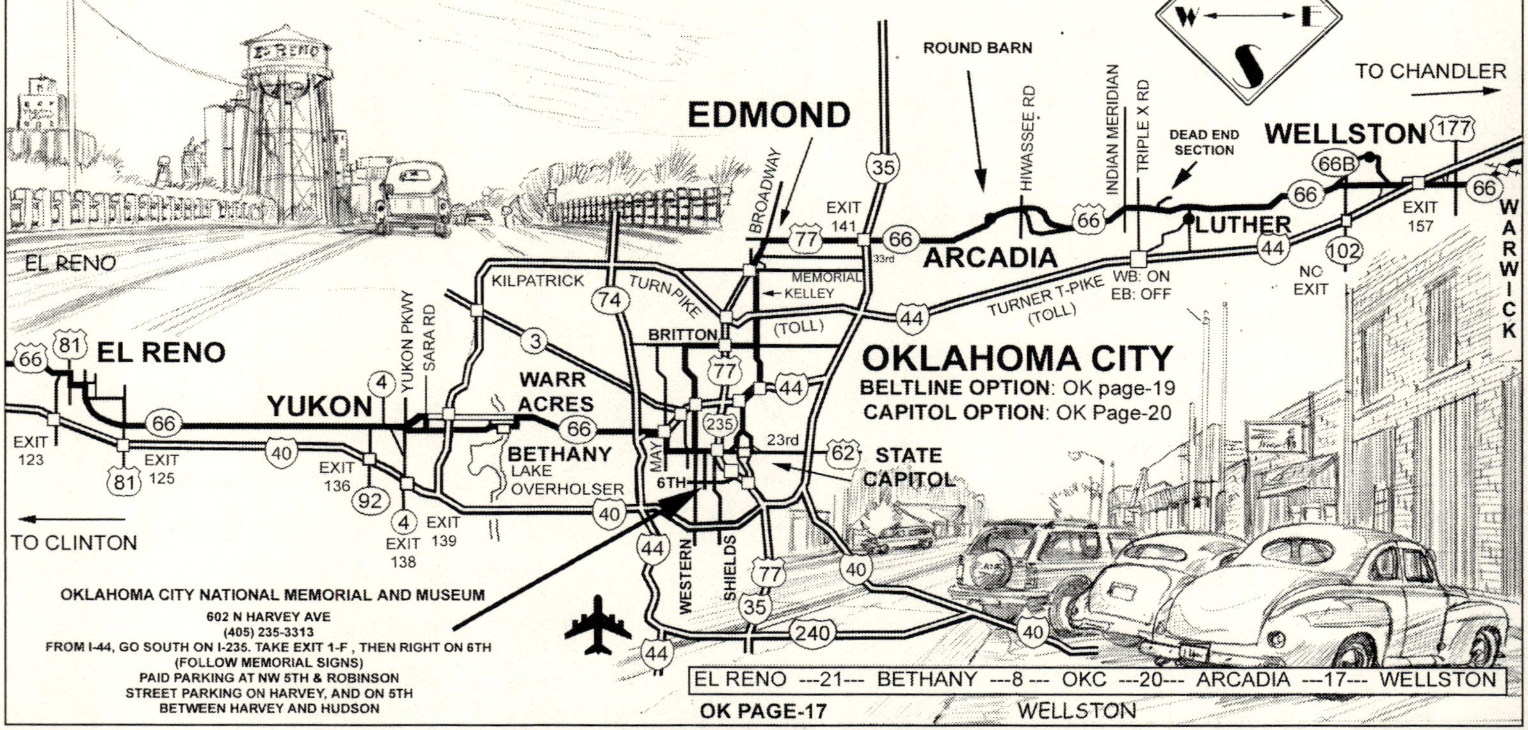

WB: Just west of I-44, bear **RIGHT** onto **HWY 66B** thru **WELLSTON**. 3 miles further, rejoin **OK 66** and continue thru **LUTHER** and **ARCADIA**. **OK 66** ENDS at I-35 EXIT 141, stay **AHEAD** onto **2nd St/US 77** into **EDMOND**. Go 3 mi to Broadway.

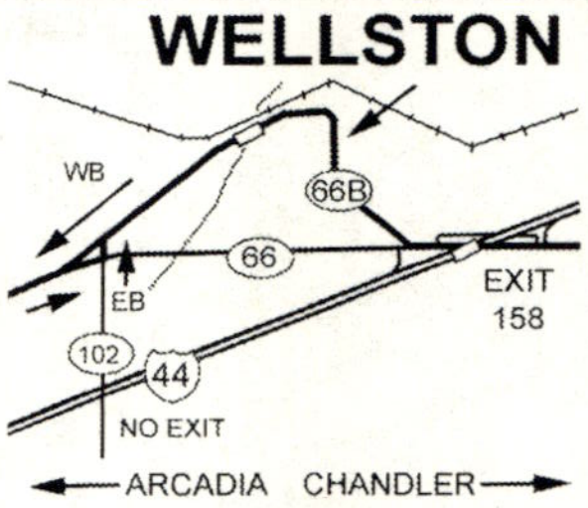

WELLSTON, bypassed since 1933, has a nice little downtown, plus a **1933 iron bridge** over Captain Creek, west on **66B**. **LUTHER** sits a bit south of 66. On the north side of 66 here are former bridge footings that carried US 66 over a railroad and Deep Fork Creek. **SIDE TRIP**: A half-mile **dead end spur** on private property is joined by turning north about one mi west of **LUTHER** (tight turn around at dead end).

West of **LUTHER** try the great Bar-B-Q at **The Boundary**, currently housed in an old gas station on the sharp curve east of Indian Meridian Rd. Between Choctaw Rd and Hiwassee, watch closely on the north for the pull off at the remains of a **stone service station**. **FOLK ART ALERT!** On current OK 66 about 6 mi west of **LUTHER** and about 2 mi east of **ARCADIA**, watch for John Hargrove's fantastic "**Oklahoma County 66 Auto Trim and Mini Museum**." Look for replicas of the Blue Whale, Twin Arrows, and so much more! Stop by and visit if the gate is open. **SIDE TRIP:** Just 0.5 mi west of Hargrove's, at **Hiwassee Rd**, is the west end of a loop of pristine '66 that heads back east, to rejoin current OK 66 after about a mile. Thanks to preservationist and author Jim Ross, this stretch is on the **National Register of Historic Places**. The east portion is 1928 Portland Concrete, the west section, paved in 1929, is blacktop over concrete, with curbs. **CAUTION**: Be careful leaving and joining OK 66. A bit **ROUGH** so go slow.

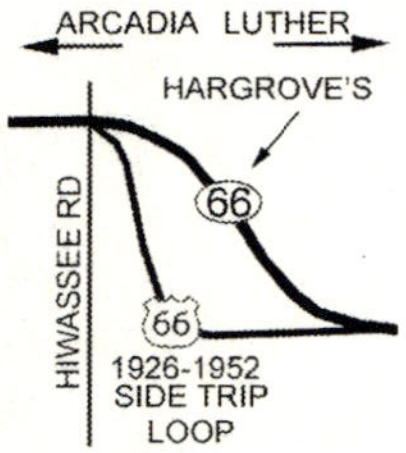

The centerpiece of **ARCADIA** is the restored 1898 **Round Barn**. Downstairs is a **Route 66 Exhibit**, while the loft is rented for dances and events. **GIFT SHOP ALERT**! ADVISORY: **OBEY** the speed limit thru town! **GIANT ALERT! # 1**: After dark, check out the illuminated 66 foot tall **POP BOTTLE** at **POPS**, a great diner and convenience store, with hundreds of soft drink flavors! **GIANT ALERT! # 2:** At the I-35 JCT is a **GIANT CROSS**. Motels are nearby, WB on 66.

EB: Follow **2nd St/US 77** east from **EDMOND**. Cross I-35 at EXIT 141, stay **AHEAD** on **OK HWY 66** thru **ARCADIA** and **LUTHER**. 6 miles further, turn **LEFT** at the HWY 102 JCT, then next **RIGHT** onto **HWY 66B** into **WELLSTON**. About 3 miles further, rejoin **OK 66** eastbound, and pass under I-44

WB: In **EDMOND**, turn **LEFT** on **Broadway / US 77**. Go 3 mi and take the **Memorial Rd/Kelley St EXIT**. Turn **LEFT** on **Kelley Ave**. Take **Kelley** just over 5 mi. **JOIN I-44 WEST** at **EXIT 128B**, but **QUICKLY** take the next ramp for **Lincoln Blvd** at **EXIT 128A**.

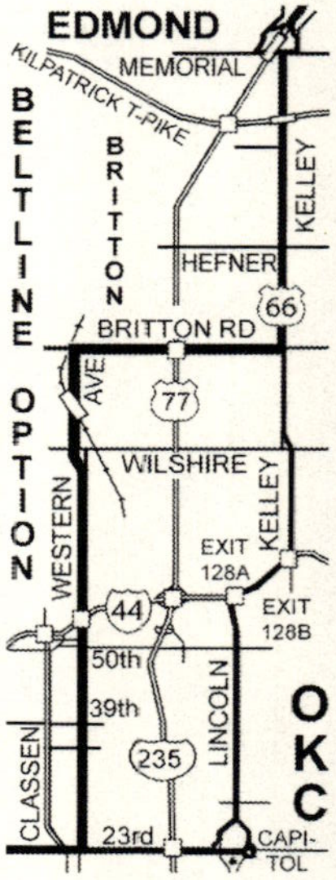

EDMOND outgrew most remnants of old 66. Exhibits honoring what is gone are at the **Edmond Historical Society Museum**, in the old armory at 431 S Boulevard (405) 340-0078. Just west of the corner of 2nd and S Boulevard on the south is the first schoolhouse in the OK Territory (1889). **Non-GIANT ALERT**! At this same corner on the north is a small replica of the **Statue of Liberty**. The **Historic Downtown Shopping District** is located north of the corner of 2nd and Broadway. Park and walk if in a mood to shop for antiques and such.

BELTLINE OPTION (**rest** of this page) In 1931, "Alt 66" detoured much of the US 66 traffic around the northwest of the city until 1953 (Western Ave was bypassed in favor of May Ave in 1947). This option misses the Capitol, but offers some route-flavor with numerous old gas stations and other businesses. **Follow** the **MAP** at right, using **Britton Rd** and **Western Ave** to connect between **Kelley Ave** and **NE 23rd**. Otherwise remain on **Kelley** south to **I-44**.

At **9100 N Western**, the funky **Western Trails Trading Post** has vintage collectibles…call first (405) 842-8306. South on **Western Ave**, past **NICHOLS HILLS**, are more vintage buildings and many restaurants (**Classics Club** has a James Dean mural), plus the **Will Rogers Theatre** near 50th (www.visitwesternavenue.com). The Pre-'47 "Beltline" turned west on **39th St**, but **Western Ave** south of 39th thru **Crown Heights** was US 66 from 1930-'33 (see Jim Ross's book for the tangled tale of '66 in **OKC**). Rejoin the Main Tour route at 23rd and Western. At **23rd St** is the glittering **Gold Geodesic Dome** of a former bank, recently saved from demolition (you'll see this on the Capitol route too).

WB BELTLINE OPTION: REJOIN the **MAIN TOUR ROUTE** via **NE 23rd** on **OK page-20**. **EB**: via **Kelley** at **Britton** (this page).

EB: JOIN **EAST I-44** but EXIT **QUICKLY** at **Kelley Ave**/EXIT 128B. Turn **LEFT** on **Kelley** for 2.2 mi to **Britton Rd**. Continue with **Kelley** for 3 mi. At **Memorial Rd**, turn **RIGHT**, and quick **LEFT** on the marked **Frontage Rd** to join **North US 77** (**Broadway**). Go 3.3 mi into **EDMOND**. Turn **RIGHT** on **2nd St/US 77**.

Follow **Lincoln** 2 mi towards the **Capitol**. Past 28th St, curve to the **RIGHT** with the **WB NE 23rd St EXIT** (right lane), and **JOIN 23rd St** west. Cross under US 77/I-235, and follow **NW 23rd St** for 1 mi, to cross Western Ave (**BELTLINE OPTION** joins here **WB**). Stay on **23rd St** for 2 mi to **May Ave**: turn **RIGHT** on **May Ave** and go 1 mi to I-44. Be in the **left turn lane** crossing I-44, then quickly turn **LEFT** onto **NW 39th ST**. **Quickly** take the **next onramp** and follow the **OK 66** signs onto **NW 39th Expwy** (**AVOID** HWY 74).

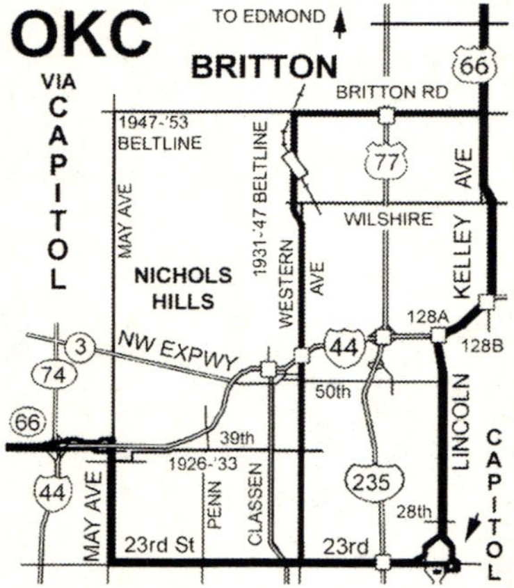

SIDE TRIP: In 1954, US 66 moved to the path of modern I-35 & I-44, passing by **Frontier City Theme Park** (NE 122nd ST EXIT). The **National Cowboy and Western Heritage Museum** at 1700 NE 63D (just north of I-44, east of Kelley) honors the real "old west." (405) 478-2250.

The Capitol route was "mainline" 66 from 1926 to 1954 (with changes over the years). Sadly, most traces of 66 are gone between I-44 and 23rd St, but the view down Lincoln to the Capitol is grand. Aside from its new dome, the **State Capitol** boasts its own oil derricks. For tour info: (405) 521-3356.

SIDE TRIP: North of downtown (see MAP #4) is the **Oklahoma City National Memorial** at NW 5th and Robinson, honoring the 168 victims of the **Alfred P. Murrah Federal Bldg** bombing of 1995 with memorial grounds and a museum (405) 235-3313. City INFO: www.visitokc.com (405) 297-8912.

NW 23rd between **Lincoln** and **May** is full of interest, and worth a detour east if taking the **BELTLINE OPTION** (OK page-19). The **Tower Theatre** on 23rd has a towering neon sign. **GIANT ALERT**! **GIANT MILK BOTTLE** on **Classen** (1926-'30 66) just north of 23rd St. On the south side of this intersection is the glittering **Gold Geodesic Dome** of a former bank, recently saved from demolition. The remaining **Chicken in the Rough** restaurant (once a widespread early franchise based in OKC) is now in a new location at Northwest Expressway and Independence.

EB: Turn **RIGHT** on **May Ave**. Go 1 mi, then **LEFT** on **NW 23rd St**. Take **NW 23rd St** east 2 mi to **Western Ave** (see **BELTLINE OPTION** via **Western** on **OK page-19**). Continue on **NW 23rd** for 1.7 mi (crossing under US 77/I-235). At the **Capitol**, pass thru the "subway," then **EXIT RIGHT** on the curving ramp to **Lincoln Blvd NB**. Follow **Lincoln** for about 2.5 mi to **I-44 EXIT 128A**.

WB: Cross N Portland, and continue on NW 39th for 4.4 miles to the next turn, thru **WARR ACRES** and **BETHANY**. Turn **LEFT** on the third crossover after **N Council Rd**. **CROSS** all lanes, then curve **RIGHT** with **N Overholser Dr.** Cross the iron bridge, continue along the shore of **Lake Overholser**, then curve **RIGHT** at the **"Y"** onto **NW 36th**. Pass under Kilpatrick T-Pike, (no exit) go 0.5 mi, then turn **RIGHT** on **Sara Rd** (to avoid an upcoming tight turn). Turn **LEFT** (west) on 4-Lane **OK 66** into **YUKON**, crossing Yukon Pkwy.

39th Expwy west thru **WARR ACRES** is a typical multi-lane urban strip, but a few refugees from old 66 survive. Sadly, the former **66 Bowl** has split for good. **Jacks BBQ** at 4418 NW 39th Expwy has a good neon sign, while **Ann's Chicken Fry House** (at 4106 NW 39th Expwy since 1971) serves up retro décor along with great meals. See their neon outlined 59 Cadillac! **GIANT ALERT!** Giant **KEY** at A-AAAKey mini storage, north side of street at 4317 NW 39th St (all of the above are between Portland and Meridian).

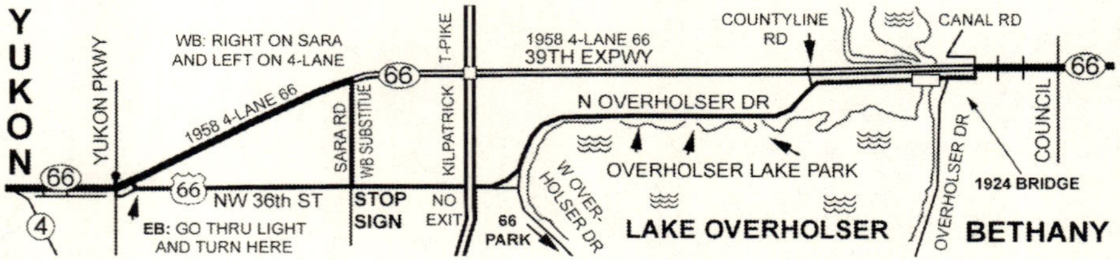

BETHANY is home to **Southern Nazarene University**, as well as **Southern Christian University** (**GIANT ALERT**! for their big **METAL GLOBE**) and some cool antique stores. City INFO: (405) 789-1256. The picturesque, historic Lake Overholser Bridge was restored and reopened to traffic! At last someone gets the fact that these relics are important!

SIDE TRIP: South about a mile on **W Overholser Dr** at **NW 23rd St** (west side of the lake…see map) is **Route 66 Park**, with an 8-state interpretive walk, info signs and a statue of Andy Payne, plus a playground for the kids, who might need to work off energy by now.

EB: Follow **OK 66** from **YUKON**. Just past the Yukon Pkwy stoplight, move to the right lane, then turn **RIGHT** next chance and **QUICK LEFT** onto **NW 36th St**. (Catch it at Sara Rd if you miss) Pass under the Kilpatrick T-pike (no exit), curve **LEFT** at the **"Y"** onto **N Overholser Dr**, along the shore of **Lake Overholser**. Cross the iron bridge, then join **39th Expwy/OK 66** for about 4.4 mi, thru **BETHANY** and **WARR ACRES**. Crossing N Portland Ave, prepare to follow **39th Expwy** as it merges ahead onto **I-44 E** (**"TULSA"**) (OK 66 ends). Prepare to join the right lane, then take I-44 **EXIT 124/May Ave**.

WB: Follow **OK 66** (Main) for 12 mi, thru **YUKON** and into **EL RENO**. Cross the Shepard Ave light (**US 81** & **BL-40** join, OK 66 ends). Continue with **US 81/BL 40** for 2 mi, over the RR and into downtown (on **Rock Island St**). Turn **LEFT** on **Wade** for 2 blocks, then **RIGHT** on **Choctaw** for one block and **LEFT** on **Sunset Dr** (US 81 departs). Take **BL 40** / **Sunset Dr** west for 4.5 mi to next turn.

A massive grain elevator emblazoned with the words **Yukon's Best Flour** (in paint and light) dominates the skyline of **YUKON**. A huge sequentially illuminated sign (bulbs, not neon) shines at the top. Across '66 is **Yukon's Best Railroad Museum**, housed like a hobo in old boxcars. The town is trail-happy, honoring the old cattle-drive days with a **Chisholm Trail Wall Mural** at 4th and Main and the **Chisholm Trail Historic Marker** (at the old watering hole) at 2200 S Holly. Watch for the rare **Standard gasoline sign**. On the west side, halfway between Garth Brooks Blvd and Frisco Rd, friendly A. J. Clements has restored an old gas station on his property into a private hangout "**The Fillin Station**" ("This is NOT a business") just for fun. Visit if you catch him there. Town INFO: www.yukoncc.com

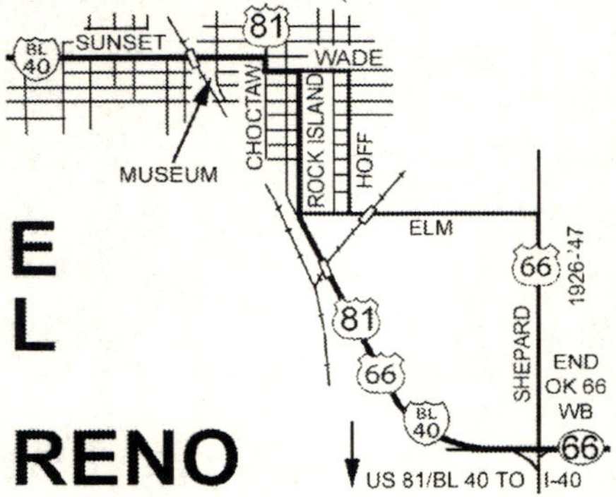

EL RENO

A few miles west of **YUKON** (near Cimarron Rd) is a rusty metal sign with a leering cowpoke and the message "**Watch Your Curves! Eat More BEEF**" **SCAVENGER HUNT!** What **organization** is listed on the bottom of this sign?

EL RENO Pre-1947 OPTION: The early route follows **Shepard Ave** north from **OK 66**. Past the cemetery, it turns west on **Elm**, and crosses under the RR. Before 1932, the route turned north on **Hoff**, then west on **Wade**. After 1932, US 66 continued west on **Elm** to join **Rock Island**. **CURRENT ROUTE**: South of the downtown on BL 40, a rare **twin-engine bomber** from WWII decorates the roadside. It's amazing that US 66 had to endure the tight turns in town up until I-40 came thru. On **Wade**, look for the appliance store that once was a **Chevy dealer** (the "Bow-Tie" above the door gives it away). A Goodyear and two old gas stations (one was a Conoco) round out downtown. For burgers (onion or otherwise), try **Jobe's** on Sunset or **Johnnie's** on Rock Island. (more **EL RENO** on **OK page-24**)

EB: Take **BL 40/ Sunset Dr** to downtown **EL RENO**. Cross under the RR, then turn **RIGHT** on **Choctaw St** with **BL 40** and **US 81**. Get in the left lane, and turn **LEFT** at the next block, onto **Wade St**. After 2 blocks, turn **RIGHT** with **BL 40/US 81** onto **Rock Island** for 2 mi, curving to the JCT of OK 66 and US 81 at the Shepard Ave light: continue **AHEAD** onto **OK 66** for 12 mi thru **YUKON**.

(see **MAP #4 OK page-17**)

OKLAHOMA MAP # 5

CLINTON ~ EL RENO

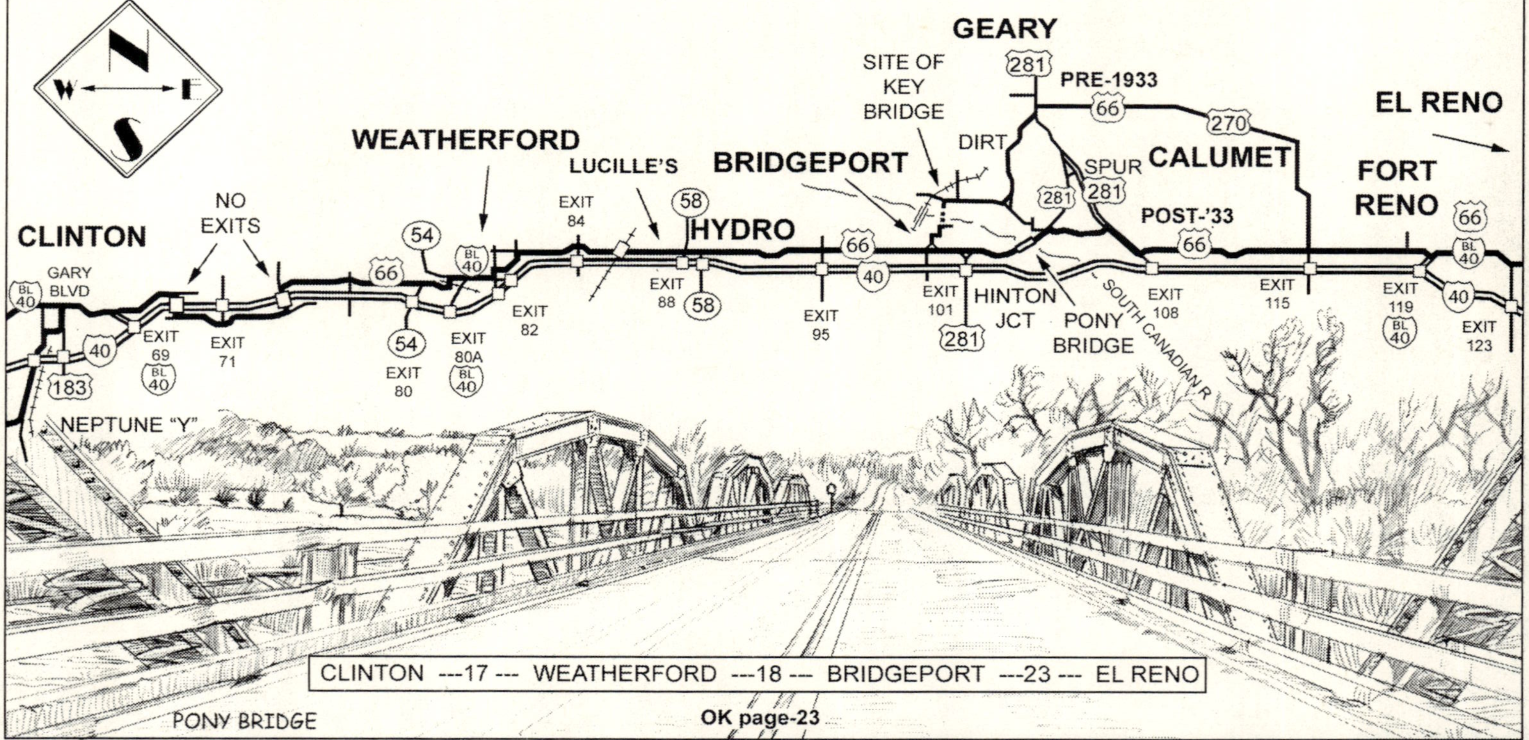

WB: At the curve (4.5 mi from last turn), turn **RIGHT** ("Ft Reno Next Right") onto **2-Lane 66**. Go 4.6 mi, then cross US 270. Continue for 7 mi to **281 SPUR**. Turn **RIGHT**. Go 2.3 mi (uphill past the bridge) & turn **LEFT** (at the house). Descend B**ridgeport Hill**. **LEFT** on **US 281**. Cross the **Pony Bridge**. Continue past **HINTON JCT**. Go 2 mi to the **BRIDGEPORT** turnoff (see **Side Trip** next page).

RV ALERT: Sometimes Old 66 is posted "No Trucks" between Hinton JCT (EXIT 101) and Bethel Rd (EXIT 95) due to washouts. Before leaving **EL RENO**, check out the **Canadian County Historical Museum and Heritage Park** at Wade and Grand (west of Choctaw) for tickets to the **Heritage Express**, a one-mile loop **trolley** that runs thru downtown from Heritage Park, Wed. thru Sunday. (405) 262-5121 for hours. The museum features a replica 1890s town. Out west, '66 passes the entrance to old **Fort Reno** (historic marker).

One of the **BEST** drives on all '66 is the 1930's route from **EL RENO** to **HYDRO.** The curbed-concrete heads arrow-straight for much of the way, interrupted by charming curves (and ugly SPUR 281) as it crosses fields and woods, bridging deep gullies on long concrete-post spans (**SLOW** on asphalt patches). Watch for scattered roadside remnants. The ¾ mi long **Pony Bridge** (1933) uses 38 "pony" (small) trusses to cross the **South Canadian River**.

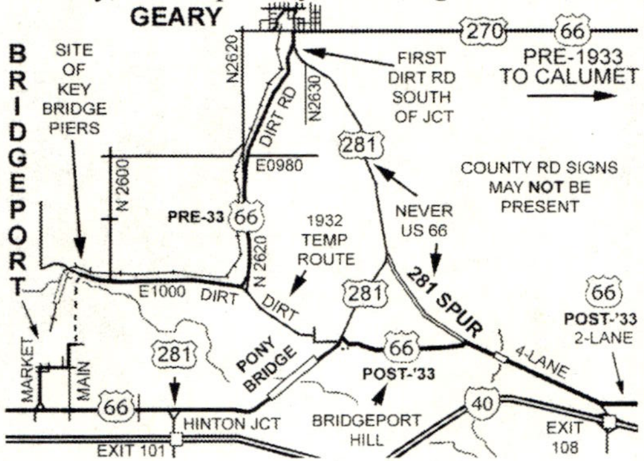

GEARY OPTION: Use **MAP #5** (and this page's detail) to take the lesser-driven **PRE-'33 '66** up **US 270** thru **CALUMET**. Next is **GEARY** (log jail and caboose downtown by the museum on Main St, which 66 bypassed). Then, go south 5.7 mi from the US 270 JCT on 4-lane **US 281 /281 SPUR** and turn **RIGHT** on **POST-33 '66** (reverse **EB**).

SIDE TRIP (DIRT RD): **PRE-'33 66** south from **GEARY** is a dead-end on rough/dusty dirt roads that once led to the 1921 **Key Suspension Bridge** north of **BRIDGEPORT**. Only the anchor piers remain. Turn off 0.2 mi south of the US 270/281 JCT. Use the **detail map** and then retrace your path to pavement. **AVOID** when muddy (or very **HOT**!).

EB: Stay **AHEAD** at **HINTON JCT** (US 281 joins). Cross the **Pony Bridge**, go 0.5 mi then **RIGHT** (first chance) and up **Bridgeport Hill**. Turn **RIGHT** on **281 SPUR**. Go 2.3 mi. Nearing I-40, be in the left-turn lane, and turn **LEFT** onto **2-lane 66 (**before reaching the truck stop). Continue east 11.6 mi (past US 270 & the Fort Reno turnoff). Turn **LEFT** on BL 40 into **EL RENO** (becomes **Sunset**).

WB: Continue past **BRIDGEPORT** for 11 mi to N HWY 58/**HYDRO**. Stay on the **N Frontage Rd** for 5.5 mi into **WEATHERFORD**. At the STOP, continue **AHEAD** onto **E Davis Ave**. Go 1 mi. Turn **LEFT** on **Washington**. Go 0.8 mi, then **RIGHT** onto **Main St/BL 40**. Go 1 mi thru downtown. **AVOID** the BL 40 curve, continue **AHEAD** on **Main**, then **LEFT** on **4th St (HWY 54 S)**. Cross the RR. Continue on the **N Frontage Rd** at the JCT of S HWY 54 (EXIT 80). Go 6.2 mi, **CROSS** I-40 at the "T" (no exit), then turn **RIGHT**. Go 4 mi (pass by EXIT 71) and **CROSS** I-40 (no exit). Turn **LEFT**. Go 1 mi to join **BL 40** (near EXIT 69) to **CLINTON**.

SIDE TRIP BRIDGEPORT Pre-1933 (part **DIRT**-map **OK page-24**): **NORTH** on **Market**, **RIGHT** on **Broadway** and **LEFT** on **Main** to the curve onto **Lonewolf Ave**. After the curve, "Dirt 66" quickly turned north to cross the river. Now **impassable**, so return to paved 66.

Back on "**paved 66**," expect vintage bridges and great views on this hilly section. Go **SLOW** at asphalt patches. **HYDRO**, just north of '66, is worth a detour for its classic downtown. Good barbershop! **Lucille's**, home of **Lucille Harmon** (west of HWY 58), was closed at her passing in 2000, but is preserved by the owner of modern **Lucille's Roadhouse** (at EXIT 84).

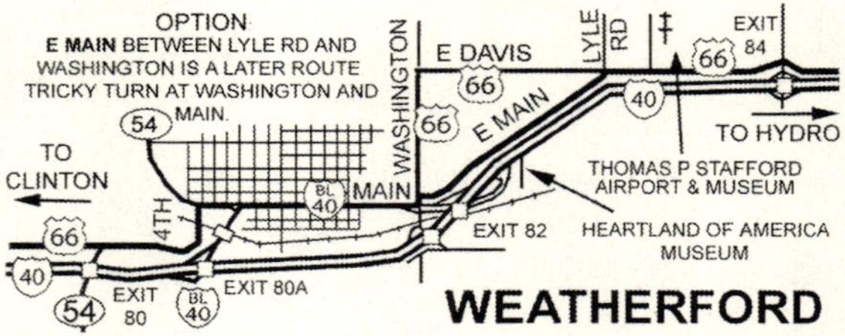

SCAVENGER HUNT! What **jet fighter** is on display east of **WEATHERFORD**? The jet marks the turn to a world class **museum** honoring astronaut **Thomas P Stafford** (planes and rockets, even Moon rocks) (580) 772-5871. The **Heartland Museum** is across I-40 between EXIT 84 and 82. There's an old **Route 66 Diner** that **Elvis** ate at and other relics. (580) 774-2212 In town is the **Mark Motor Hotel and Restaurant** (580) 772-3325. West, at EXIT 71, is **Cherokee Trading Post**. Almost to **CLINTON** near **EXIT 69** (22901 Old 66 Frontage Rd) is the fantastic **White Dog Hill** restaurant (look for the old pickup). Great food and view! (580) 323-0059

EB: Go 1 mi. **CROSS** I-40, then quick **LEFT**. Go 4 mi (pass by EXIT 71). **CROSS** I-40 (no exit), then **RIGHT** on **N Frontage Rd**. Go 6.2 mi to the S HWY 54 JCT (EXIT 80). Continue **AHEAD**, then curve **LEFT** with HWY 54 on **4th St**. Cross the RR. Turn **RIGHT** on **Main**. Go 0.2 mi. Curve **RIGHT** then quick **LEFT** to rejoin Main (**BL 40**) thru **WEATHERFORD**. Go 1 mi, then turn **LEFT** on **Washington**. Go 0.8 mi, then **RIGHT** on **E Davis Ave**. Continue (becomes **N Frontage Rd**) for 6.5 mi (past EXIT 84) to N HWY 58 (**HYDRO**). Continue **AHEAD** for 11 mi to pass the **BRIDGEPORT** turnoff (heading towards the US 281/Hinton JCT).

(see **MAP #5 OK page-23**)

OKLAHOMA MAP # 6

TEXOLA ~ CLINTON

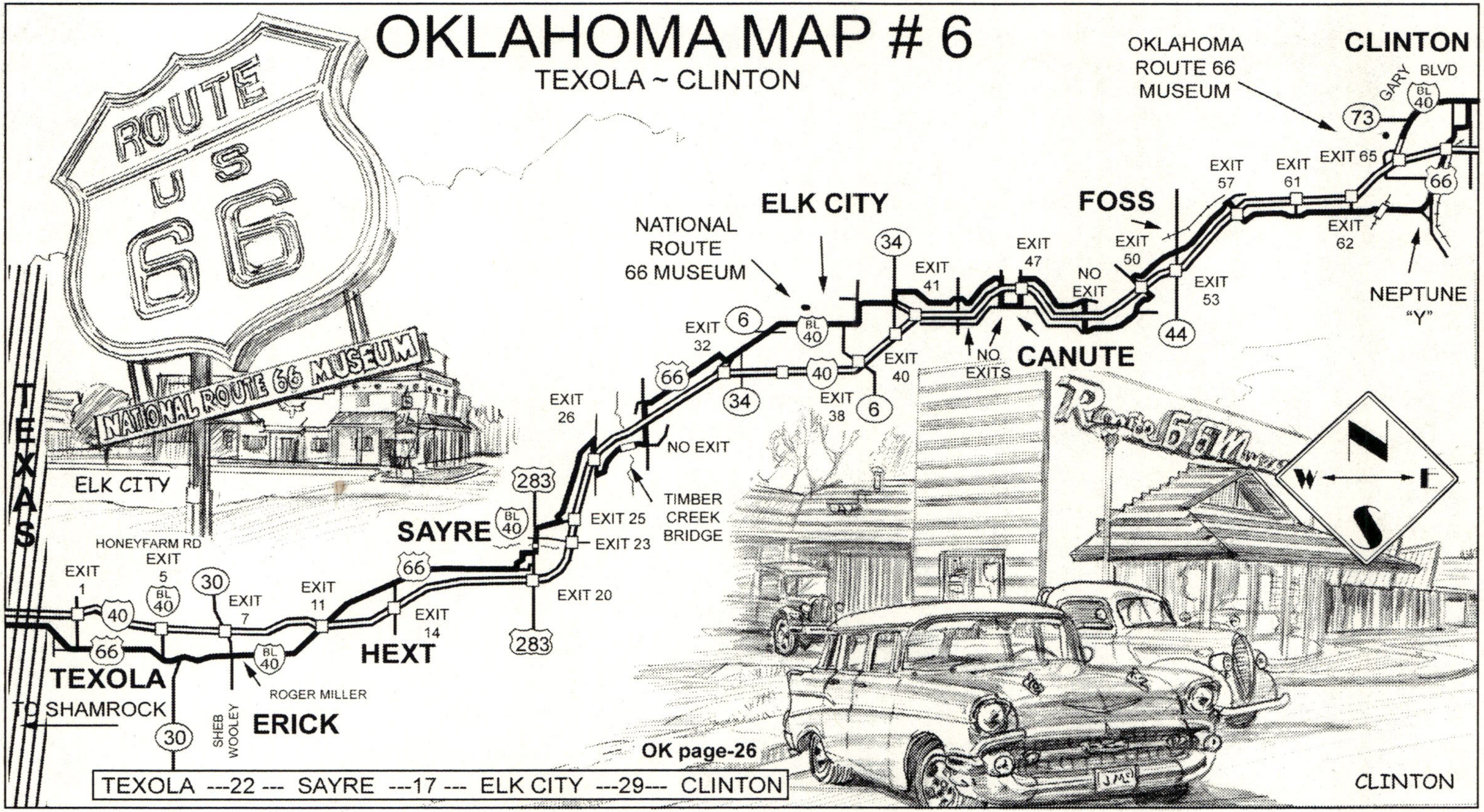

WB: Join **BL 40** (near EXIT 69) east of **CLINTON**, and continue 2.3 mi into town (becomes **Gary Blvd**). (See **MUSEUM Side Trip**) Turn **LEFT** on **4th St (US 183**) one block, then **RIGHT** on **Frisco**. Turn **LEFT** on **10th** and continue for 1 mi thru town, under I-40.

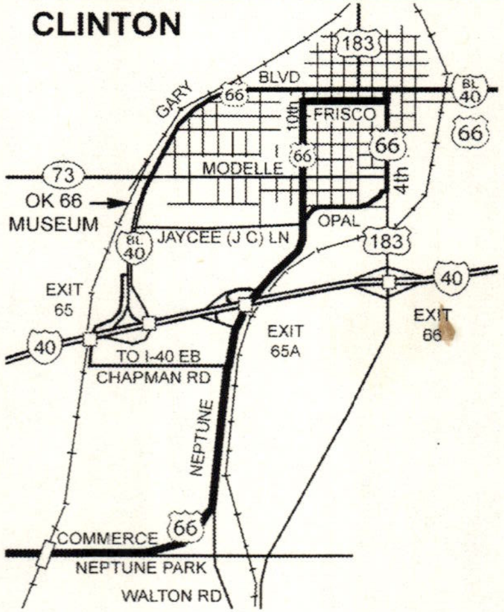

A mile east of downtown **CLINTON** is the first trading post in OK, the **Mohawk Lodge Indian Store** (est. 1892, here since 1940) (580) 323 2360. Nearby is the **Cheyenne Cultural Center** (2250 NE Route 66) with artifacts and gifts (580) 323-6224.

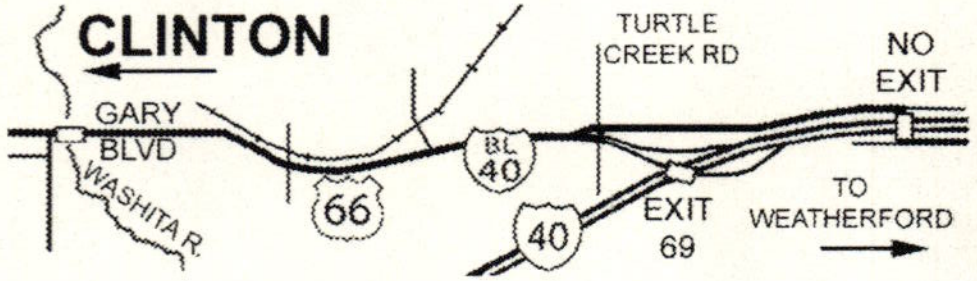

MUSEUM SIDE TRIP: When in **CLINTON**, you **MUST** visit the **Oklahoma Route 66 Museum**, at 2229 W Gary Blvd (between EXIT 65 and HWY 73). Take Gary west, and then return to **Gary** and **4th**. The well-done exhibits feature OK 66, but with a national slant. You'll follow a self-guided narrated tour along the history of 66 from the dirt road days thru the 1960s, incorporating tableaus of antique vehicles, photos and memorabilia, plus a theatre. A restored **Route 66 Diner** sits on the grounds. The museum building itself is an eye-catcher, with glass brick and neon that make for a great night scene. **GIFT SHOP ALERT**! Jaycee (JC) Lane or Modelle Ave are shortcuts from the Museum to 10th. (580) 323-7866. Also on Gary is the old fashioned **Dairy Best** (Broasted Chicken) at 19th St.

South of downtown, at **10th** and **JayCee**, watch for the Art Deco neon gateway to **McLain Rogers Park** and the **Route 66 mini-golf** (let the kids blow off some steam). **Early US 66** used 4th, Frisco and 10th thru downtown. On Frisco is the former **Redland Theatre** (now a gift shop) with a classic marquee. Later 4th to Opal was used. The 1959 route followed Gary Blvd all the way to "4-Lane 66" (now I-40). You can choose among many motels and cafes in town. City INFO: www.clintonok.org or (580) 323-2222.

EB: Stay **AHEAD** with **10th** at the "Y" with **Opal**. Go 7 blocks, then turn **RIGHT** on **Frisco**. At the end of Frisco, turn **LEFT** on **US 183 (4th St**). (See **MUSEUM Side Trip**) Go one block, then turn **RIGHT** and follow **Gary Blvd/BL 40** east for **2.3 miles**. Turn **LEFT** on **Turtle Creek Rd**, (before reaching EXIT 69), then quick **RIGHT** on the **N Frontage Rd**.

WB: Continue **AHEAD** under I-40 at EXIT 65A (becomes **Neptune Dr**). Go 1 mi and curve **RIGHT** at the "Y" (becomes **Commerce Rd** and then **S Frontage Rd**). Stay on the **S Frontage Rd** for 7.4 mi (past EXIT 62 and 61) to **EXIT 57**. Cross under I-40 and turn **LEFT** on the **N Frontage Rd**. Go 6.8 mi (past HWY 44/FOSS) to **EXIT 50**. **CROSS** I-40, and turn **RIGHT** on the **S Frontage Rd**. **CROSS** I-40 at the **next chance** (1.7 mi-no exit). **LEFT** on the **N Frontage Rd** for 2 mi to **EXIT 47**. **CROSS** I-40 into **CANUTE**. Turn **RIGHT** on **"Hwy 66."** Go 1 mi and turn **RIGHT**. Go under I-40, then turn **LEFT** on the **N Frontage Rd** towards **ELK CITY**.

ALERT: **Commerce Rd** west from Neptune Y (**CLINTON**) to EXIT 62 is **BUMPY**.

On the south side of **CLINTON** at the **"Y"** is **Neptune Park,** and an ornate old building that once housed a gas station and roadhouse (see map on **OK page-27**).

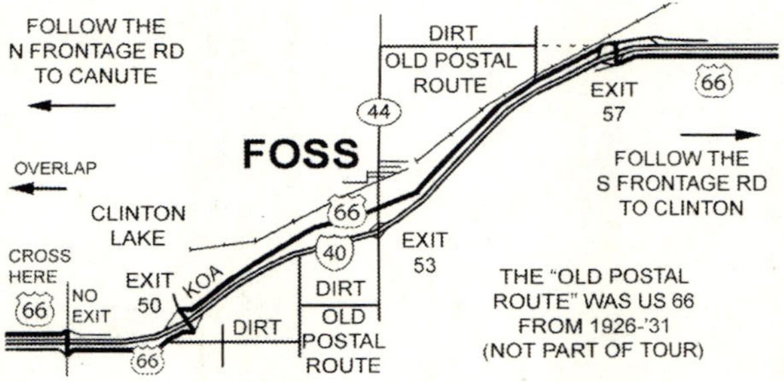

You cross I-40 **many** times west of **CLINTON**, but the pristine sections of original **portland concrete** are well worth the trouble, especially between EXIT 57 and 50, near **FOSS**. At the HWY 44 JCT all that remains are the ruins of **Kobels Place**, but the main town is just north, on a **Pre-1932** dogleg of the Postal Route (not on tour). See **Ross's** book for much more info on the early dirt road routes in Western OK.

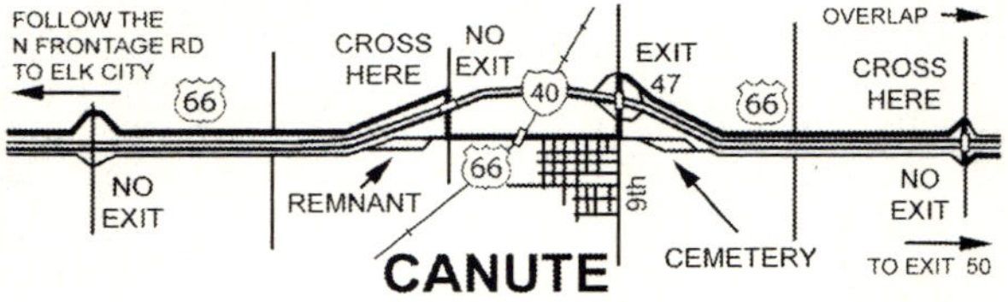

CANUTE is worth the detour, for all the remains of old businesses, including the former **Cotton Boll** and **Washita Motels**, **Uniroyal Tires**, and old cafes and stations. East of town, (on the cut-off approach of 2 and 4-Lane 66) is a 1930s-era WPA park, and the **Holy Family Cemetery**, with a **1928 grotto**.

EB: Go 2.2 mi past first crossover, then **RIGHT** at the **"T."** Go under I-40 and turn **LEFT** on **"Hwy 66"** for 1 mi thru **CANUTE**. At **9th St**, turn **LEFT**, **CROSS** I-40 (EXIT 47) then **RIGHT** on the **N Frontage Rd**. Go 2 miles, **CROSS** I-40 (no exit) then **LEFT** on the S Frontage Rd. At **EXIT 50**, **CROSS** I-40, then curve **RIGHT** on the **N Frontage Rd**. Go 6.8 mi (thru the HWY 44/FOSS JCT) to **EXIT 57**. Go under I-40 and turn **LEFT** on the **S Frontage Rd**. Continue for 7.4 mi (past EXIT 61 and EXIT 62) into **CLINTON** (becomes **Commerce Rd**). Curve **LEFT** at the **"Y,"** then **RIGHT** and quick **LEFT** on **Neptune Dr**. Continue **AHEAD** under I-40 at EXIT 65A.

WB: Follow the **N Frontage Rd** for 4.7 mi, then **LEFT** on **HWY 34**, and quick **RIGHT** on **BL 40** into **ELK CITY** (near EXIT 41). Follow **BL 40** as it curves onto **Van Buren** and then onto **3rd St** thru **downtown**. Continue with **BL 40 west** for almost 9 mi, past HWY 6, towards EXIT 32. Just past the S HWY 34 JCT, and **BEFORE** the exit, turn **RIGHT** and quick **LEFT** onto the **N Frontage Rd**. 4.6 mi further, turn **LEFT** across I-40 (no exit), then **RIGHT** on the **S Frontage Rd**, and cross **Timber Creek Bridge**. Go 1.3 mi, and cross I-40 at **EXIT 26** (Cemetery Rd). Turn **LEFT** on the **N Frontage Rd** for 2 mi to **SAYRE**.

A **T-33 Jet** guards the airport entrance east of **ELK CITY**. **GIANT ALERT**: On the east side of downtown is a **179 foot-tall oil derrick** (one of the world's largest) at the **Anadarko Basin Museum of Natural History** (museum tour by appt only: call (580) 243-0437).
PHOTO OP! Take your picture with a statue of an **Elk** at Washington Ave and 3rd St (tell everyone they named the town after him…not).

ELK CITY's **MUST-SEE** attraction is the **National Route 66 Museum**, on 66 at 3rd and Pioneer in the **Old Town Museum** complex. **GIANT ALERT**! Huge neon **Route 66 Sign** (plus 2 **Giant Kachinas** from the old Queenan's Trading Post). If you're lucky, you'll get to talk to Wanda Queenan herself. Enjoy the stroll thru the many tableaus of life on Old 66, from auto camping in the desert, thru neon tourist courts, diners and gas stations, all realistically depicted with old vehicles, murals and memorabilia. Recorded narration greets you at each scene.
GIFT SHOP ALERT! (580) 225-6266. The complex also houses many old buildings, plus a windmill exhibit outside. There are many motels and cafes in town. City INFO: www.elkcity.com or (580) 225-0207.

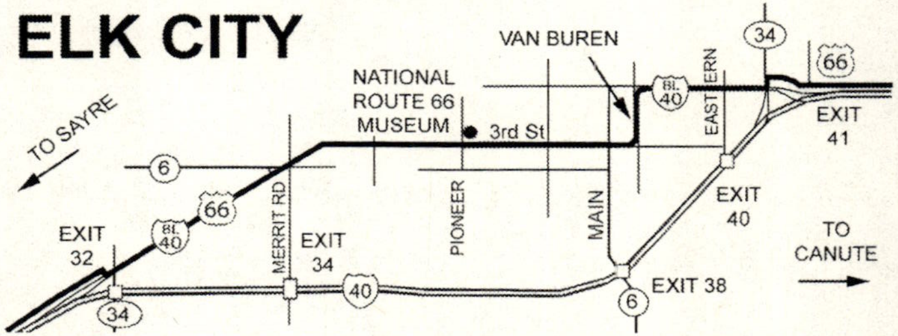

West of **ELK CITY**, be sure to take the short stretch of 66 south of I-40 across endangered **Timber Creek Bridge**, a thru-truss span built in 1928.

EB: Go 2 mi. At **EXIT 26** (Cemetery Rd) cross I-40, then **LEFT** on the **S Frontage Rd**, for 1.3 mi, across **Timber Creek Bridge**, then cross I-40 (no exit) and turn **RIGHT** on the **N Frontage Rd** for 4.6 mi. Curve sharply to a **STOP**, then **LEFT** on **4-Lane 66/BL-40** into **ELK CITY** (near EXIT 32). Follow **BL 40** for 9 mi (onto **3rd St** thru downtown, curving left onto **Van Buren** and then right) to **HWY 34** (near EXIT 41). Turn **LEFT**, then quick **RIGHT** on the **N Frontage Rd**. Go **2.5** mi and curve pass the first crossover (STOP). Continue ahead towards **CANUTE**.

WB: Curve to the JCT of **BL 40** (near EXIT 25) and turn **RIGHT**. Go 1.5 mi and turn **LEFT** with **BL 40** on **4th St (US 283)**. Follow **BL 40** for 1.6 mi, then cross the bridge and take the next **RIGHT** at **Sayre City Park**. Turn **LEFT** at the "**T**." After almost a mile, turn **RIGHT** on the **N Frontage Rd**. Continue for 9 mi (past **HEXT** Rd) to cross under I-40 at **EXIT 11** (becomes **BL 40**). Stay **AHEAD** thru **ERICK** on 4-Lane 66/**Roger Miller**. At Honeyfarm Rd (BL 40 turns), continue **AHEAD** on 4-Lane 66, thru **TEXOLA** into **TEXAS**.

On **SAYRE's** east end, watch for the neon cactus at the **Western Motel**, and the mural on the **Route 66 Bar**. The stately **Beckham Co Courthouse** was (briefly) shown in the movie ***Grapes of Wrath***. The Art Deco **Post Office** at 201 N 4th St has a 1930s "land run" mural. Train buffs will like the **RS and K RR Museum**, with model trains and track galore, at 411 N 6th, so call (580) 928-3525. From **1926-'58**, US 66 crossed the **North Fork of the Red River** via a closed bridge west of US 283, going by **Sayre City Park**'s rock swimming pool. A southern curvy-remnant is shown on the map. INFO: www.sayreok.net (580) 928-3386.

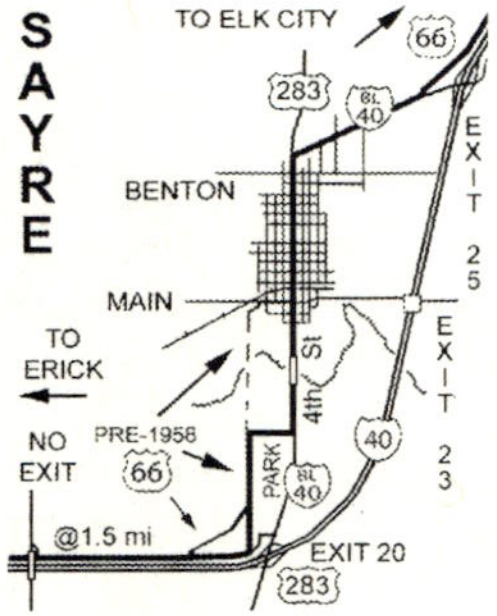

North of **HEXT** the ghostly, abandoned original lanes may become part of a bike trail. **ERICK** birthed much musical talent (mostly in a light-hearted vein). **Roger Miller** (***King of the Road***) was a town native, as was **Sheb Wooley**, infamous for ***Purple People Eater***. Now, the local musical duo is Harley and Annabelle, the "**Mediocre Music Makers**" at the **Sand Hills Curiosity Shop**. You'll get a **non-P.C**. redneck serenade here, just south of '66 on **Sheb Wooley Ave**. No merchandise, just a tip jar. (due to health issues **check ahead**). (580) 526-3738. Also in town is the **100th Meridian Museum** at Roger Miller and Sheb Wooley (by appt: (580) 526-3221) and the **Roger Miller Museum** at the SE corner (580)-526-3833. City INFO: www.rogermiller.com or (580) 526-3505.

Tiny **TEXOLA** 'tis the last town before **TEXAS**. On the east side (a block north on the last street east) is the old **Territorial Jail**. West of town near the State Line is the **Will Rogers Marker**. **PHOTO OP**!

EB: Take 4-Lane 66 thru **TEXOLA**. **BL 40** joins at Honeyfarm Rd: continue **AHEAD** past S HWY 30 to **ERICK** (becomes **Roger Miller Blvd**). Continue thru town, and cross under I-40 at **EXIT 11**. Continue for 9 mi (becomes 2-Lane), then **LEFT** on BK 21 (approaching EXIT 20). Go one mi (passing the park) and turn **RIGHT**. Turn **LEFT** on **BL 40 /US 283** (4th St) for 2 mi, thru **SAYRE**. Curve **RIGHT** with **BL 40**, then go 1.5 mi (towards EXIT 25), but turn **LEFT** (**BEFORE** the off ramp) onto the **N Frontage Rd**.

(see **OK INTRO** on **OK page-1**)

(see **MAP #6 OK page-26**)

TWO LANES ACROSS TEXAS

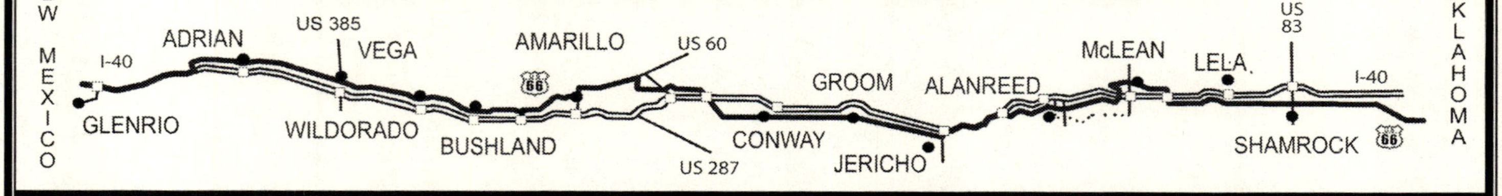

Ironically, the **largest** of the lower 48 States hosts the **second-shortest** alignment of **Route 66**! Only **KANSAS**, with about 13 miles, owns a shorter length of the Mother Road. The generally accepted figure is that there were 178 miles of old 66 across the narrow **Texas "Panhandle**." Of that, about 150 miles remain, more if you count the drivable dirt road. Much of Old 66 is now frontage road, but still rewarding to drive. Hang your elbow out the window and take it EZ.

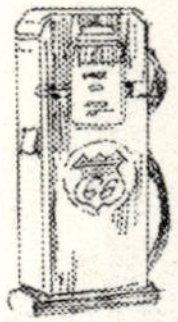

The scene thru the windshield shifts from scrubby trees to eroded gullies to cultivated fields to open rangeland as you travel west. Judging by the accounts on the backs of old postcards ("the flattest places I've ever seen") tourists have traditionally felt that the landscape of the **Texas "Panhandle**" is boring, but there's actually much to see. Small towns such as **SHAMROCK**, **McLEAN** and **ALANREED** still retain their charm, along with numerous roadside remnants. Agricultural icons such as grain elevators and windmills relieve the "flatness" of the terrain, as do water towers and a giant Cross. Views of distant vistas can be had from atop the ridge between **McLEAN** and **GROOM**, or one can commune with nature on **Dirt 66**.

Remnants of another transportation relic, the former **Chicago Rock Island and Pacific Railroad** (also known as the "Cry and Pee" for its initials) cling close to the road across the state, marked by the odd rotting crosstie or bridge timber. **AMARILLO,** Texas 66's big city, is home to a mile of antique stores, plus the **Big Texan** and **Cadillac Ranch**. West of town, the road is hell-bent for **NEW MEXICO**, passing thru **VEGA** and **ADRIAN** along the way. Unfortunately, the last 18 or so miles to **GLENRIO** and the **NM** state line are via I-40, but the view down the sudden drop from the "Caprock" still inspires.

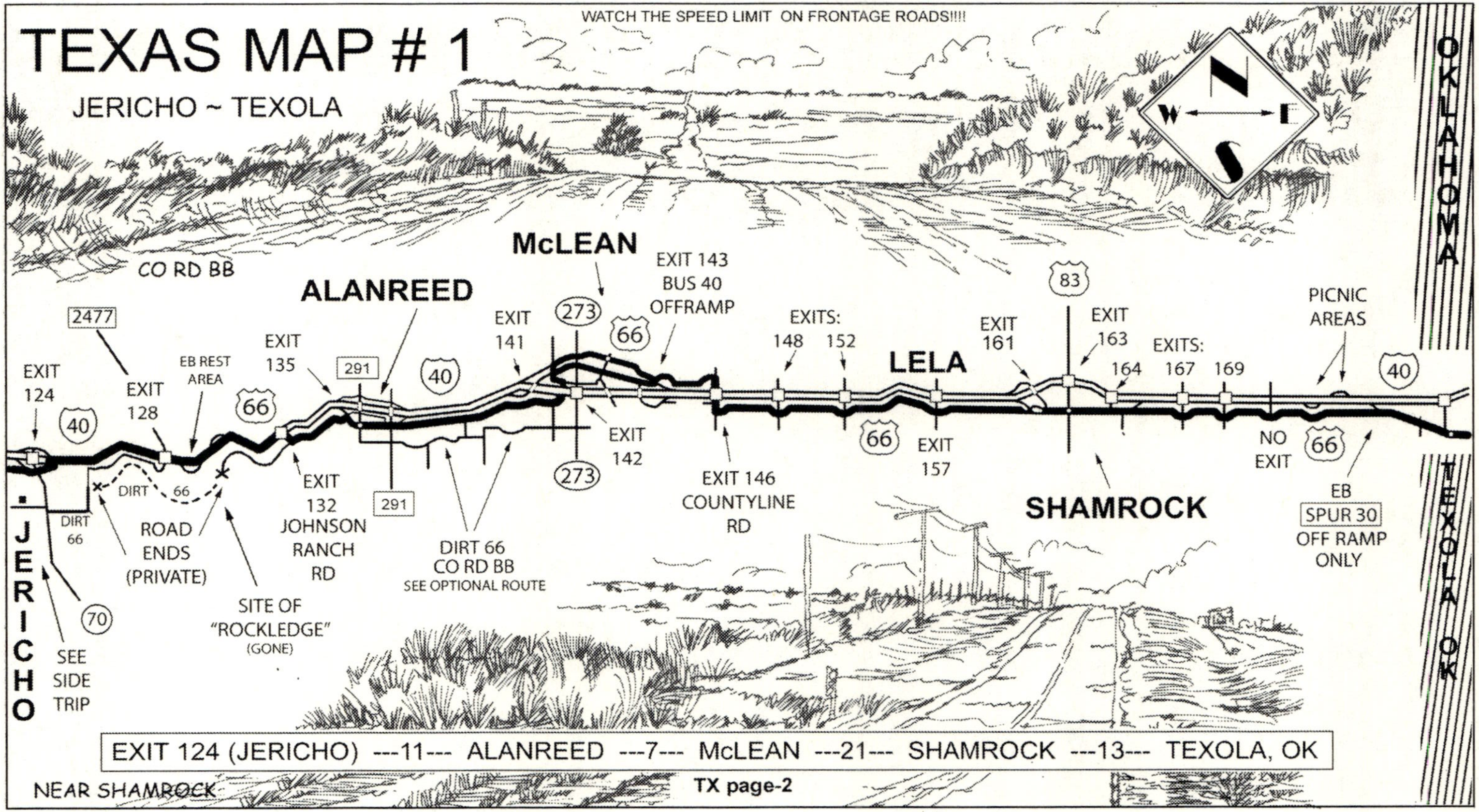
TEXAS MAP # 1
JERICHO ~ TEXOLA
WATCH THE SPEED LIMIT ON FRONTAGE ROADS!!!!
N
W
E
S
OKLAHOMA
CO RD BB
McLEAN
ALANREED
EXIT 143
BUS 40
OFFRAMP
2477
EXIT 124
40
EXIT 128
EB REST AREA
66
EXIT 135
291
40
EXIT 141
273
66
EXITS:
148
152
LELA
EXIT 161
83
EXIT 163
164
EXITS:
167
169
PICNIC AREAS
40
DIRT
66
EXIT 132
JOHNSON
RANCH
RD
291
273
EXIT 142
EXIT 146
COUNTYLINE
RD
66
EXIT 157
SHAMROCK
NO EXIT
66
EB
SPUR 30
OFF RAMP
ONLY
TEXOLA OK
JERICHO
DIRT
66
ROAD
ENDS
(PRIVATE)
SITE OF
"ROCKLEDGE"
(GONE)
DIRT 66
CO RD BB
SEE OPTIONAL ROUTE
70
SEE
SIDE
TRIP
EXIT 124 (JERICHO) ---11--- ALANREED ---7--- McLEAN ---21--- SHAMROCK ---13--- TEXOLA, OK
NEAR SHAMROCK

WB: From **TEXOLA, OK** (south of I-40 EXIT 1) cross into **TEXAS** on **4-Lane 66**, which soon narrows down to become the **South I-40 Frontage Rd**. Continue for 14 mi to the JCT with US 83 in **SHAMROCK** (caution for on-off ramps and STOP signs).

More sections of original circa **1930s concrete pavement** survive east of **SHAMROCK**, rewarding those who shun I-40 here. You'll also see evidence of the oil and gas industry along the way. East of EXIT 169, Old 66 crosses a concrete bridge over the abandoned **CRI&P Railroad**. A few oil wells drilled by the author's Grandpa after WWII are visible (along the south side of 66) 1.5 mi east of EXIT 169

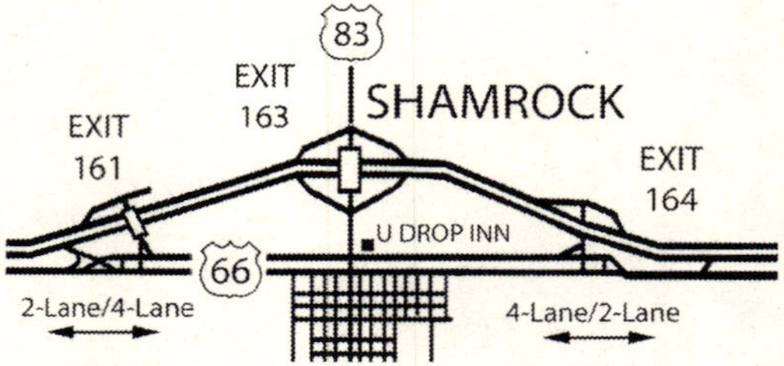

CAR GAME! The **Texas Panhandle** has been called the place "where the wind pumps the water and the cows chop the wood." It might be hard to spot "cow patties" from the car (settlers burned dried cow dung when they had no wood) but **WINDMILLS** are frequent across **TEXAS**. Divide the landscape up into north and south, and see who can spot the **MOST** windmills between exits (only intact windmills with blades count!).

SHAMROCK offers numerous remnants of old motels, cafes and stations. U-can't miss the recently restored **U-Drop Inn/Tower Conoco** at the US 83 junction: an **Art Deco** masterpiece built in 1936, which now houses offices of the Chamber of Commerce. Drop inn during business hours for a visit, and stick around after dark for the dazzling **NEON** which outlines the building's spires (local motels offer "**FREE GOLF**" at the country club with your room). A recent addition across 66 near here is **Big Vern's Steakhouse**.
SIDE TRIP: If you've the time, venture south on US 83 to downtown and visit the **Pioneer West Museum** at 204 N Madden (a block east of US 83) and the restored **Magnolia gas station** nearby. The "Irish City" boasts a piece of the original "**Blarney Stone**" (in Elmore Park east of downtown) and hosts an annual **St Patrick's Day Celebration** in March. INFO: www. shamrocktx.net or (877) Irish TX.

EB: From the JCT of US 83 in **SHAMROCK**, continue **AHEAD** on 66 (becomes **South I-40 Frontage Rd**). Continue for 13 mi (caution for off ramps and STOP signs at exits). Past the SPUR 30 off ramp, continue to follow the **S Frontage Road** away from I-40 as it becomes **4-Lane 66**, crossing into **OKLAHOMA** and on into **TEXOLA** (south of I-40 EXIT 1 if you need to connect from there).

WB: From the JCT with US 83 in **SHAMROCK** follow **4-Lane 66** west (becomes the **South I-40 Frontage Rd** past the offramps). Pass **LELA** (EXIT 157), then go 11 mi to **EXIT 146** (Countyline Rd). **CROSS I-40**, then turn **LEFT** on the **North Frontage Rd**. At the **EXIT 143** WB off ramp, **STOP** and turn **RIGHT** onto **4-Lane 66**. At the "**Y**" follow **First St** (One-Way) past Main in **McLEAN**.

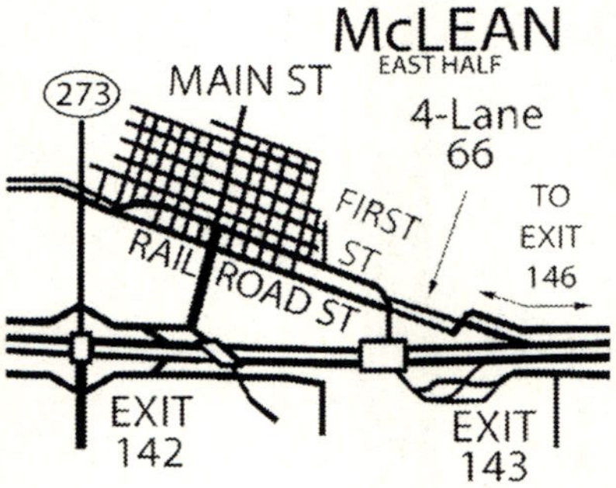

The **South Frontage Road** west of **SHAMROCK** offers another chance to drive original **portland concrete**. West of tiny **LELA** once stood the only remnant of a former roadside reptile empire: the "**RATTLESNAKES EXIT NOW**" sign (now relocated to a park on First in **McLEAN**).

McLEAN was once known as the "**UPLIFT CITY**" for the ladies undergarment factory, which now houses the **Devil's Rope/Old Route 66 Museum.** "Devil's Rope" refers to the museum's huge collection of barbed wire. Also on display is cowboy and ranching history (here's the place to get immersed in western lore). **GIANT ALERT**! The **Route 66 Exhibit** houses a **GIANT COBRA** and a big **BULL** (everything's **BIG** in TEXAS) plus a multitude of memorabilia of the Mother Road. **GIFT SHOP ALERT!** Address: **Kingsley St** between First and Railroad on the east side of town. Check barbwiremuseum.com or 806 779-2225 for seasonal hours of operation.

In 1984, **McLEAN** was the **LAST** town in **TEXAS** bypassed by I-40. Downtown on Main, the **McLean/Alanreed Area Museum** includes info about the WWII prison camp, which housed German POWs nearby. Better housing can be found at the **Cactus Inn Motel** (806 779-2346) which is recommended as a real Mom and Pop. Nearby is the **Red River Steakhouse** (closed Sun-Mon). West of Main on First St is a restored **Phillips 66** gas station, the **FIRST** of that brand in **TEXAS**: a great **PHOTO OP**. Other choice roadside remnants abound throughout town. **SCAVENGER HUNT:** What are the **2 huge balls** on display at the **Devil's Rope Museum** made from (hint…it ain't yarn!)?

EB: From Main St in **McLEAN**, follow **Railroad St** east (One-Way). **AVOID** the right-turn lane for the I-40 EXIT 143 access road: **STOP**, then continue **AHEAD** with **4-Lane 66**. Approaching the WB off ramp, curve **LEFT** to a **STOP**, then cross the WB off ramp lane and curve **RIGHT** onto the **North I-40 Frontage Rd**. At the next overpass (**EXIT 146**/Countyline Rd) **CROSS I-40** and turn **LEFT** on the **South Frontage Rd** for 16.5 mi, continuing past **LELA** to the JCT with US 83 in **SHAMROCK**.

WB DIRT 66 OPTION: In **McLEAN**, take **Hwy 273** south to I-40 EXIT 142. Cross I-40 and continue south for **ONE MILE**, then turn **RIGHT** onto **Gray County Rd "BB"**. About 4 miles on, follow the sharp bend south, then turn **RIGHT** (avoid CO 23) to stay with **CO BB** to the JCT of Hwy 291. **Stay ahead** on **CO BB**, then turn **RIGHT** with **Main St** into **ALANREED**, and rejoin paved 66 at **Third St**.

TO CONTINUE WB from McLEAN on PAVEMENT (MAIN TOUR) see TX page- 6.

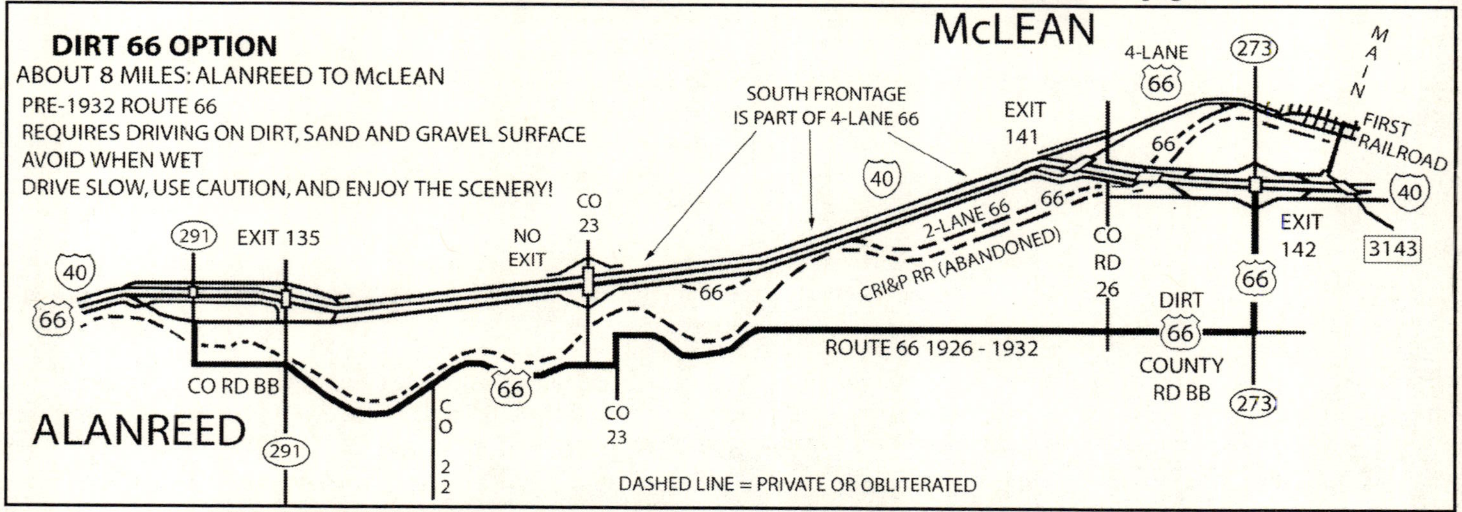

TO CONTINUE EB from ALANREED on PAVEMENT (MAIN TOUR) SEE TX page-6.

EB DIRT 66 OPTION: From **Third St** in **ALANREED**, turn **RIGHT** on **Main**. Follow the sharp bend **LEFT** onto **Gray County Rd "BB"**. At the JCT with Hwy 291, **stay ahead** on **CO BB**. At the **"T"** junction with CO 23 SOUTH, turn **LEFT**, then follow the bend **RIGHT** on **CO BB**. Go about 4 miles to **Hwy 273**. Turn **LEFT**, go one mile, **cross I-40** and rejoin **4-Lane 66** in **MCLEAN**.

WB: From Main St in **McLEAN**, follow **First St** (One-Way WB) as it rejoins the EB lanes, and then cross Hwy 273 on **4-Lane 66**. (**ALSO** See **DIRT 66 OPTION** on **TX page-5**). One mile west, **AVOID** entering I-40 by turning **LEFT** onto **CO RD 26**. Follow the curve **LEFT** onto the **North Frontage Rd** headed back east. At the first opportunity, curve **RIGHT** under I-40, then follow the **South Frontage Rd** 6.5 mi west to **ALANREED**, entering on **Third St** (Loop 271) and continuing past Main St.

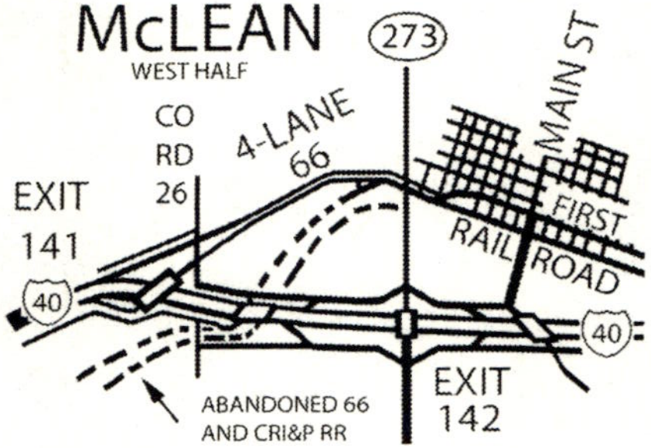

Just west of Hwy 273 in **McLEAN**, the old 2-lane pavement branches off south and dead ends. This section curved along with the defunct **CRI&P RR**; where their path crosses under I-40, east of Co Rd 26, more of the old pavement is visible. The **south frontage road** west from town was a part of **4-Lane 66**, while the **2-Lane** followed the old RR embankment further south. About 2 miles from the I-40 overpass, the 2-Lane comes back in from the south (**private rd**) and the old RR, festooned with rotten crossties, is clearly visible near the road.

West of **McLEAN** the landscape becomes more arid. Spiky plants and prairie grass cover rolling hills cut by eroded gullies, as the road climbs onto the ridge between the drainage of **McClellan Creek** to the north and the **Salt Fork of the Red River**, a historic transportation corridor.

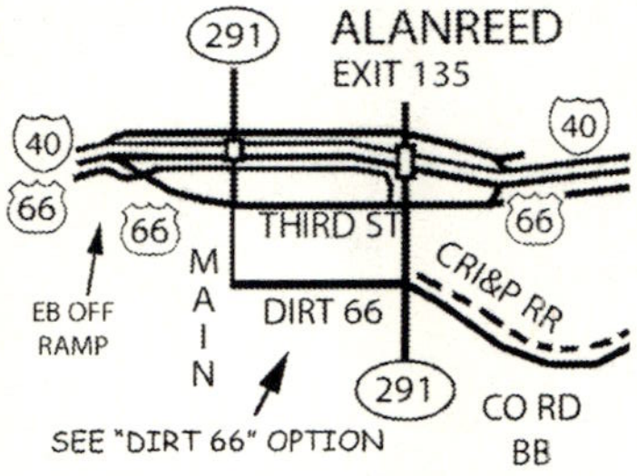

Little **ALANREED** had 3 routings of 66: The original **dirt road** south on **Main**, the paved **2-Lane** on **Third St**, and **4-Lane 66**, which was wiped out by I-40. Along the last route was the **Regal Reptile Ranch**, whose remains were bulldozed in the 1990s. Their **GIANT COBRA** resides now in the Route 66 Exhibit in **McLEAN**. **PHOTO OP**: **66 Super Service Station**, a 1932-era classic restored as a display at Main and Third. **EB Traffic**: See the **DIRT 66 OPTION** to **McLEAN** on **TX page-5**.

EB: From Main St in **ALANREED**, follow **Third St** (Loop 271) across Hwy 291 and onto the **South Frontage Rd**. Go 6 mi, then turn **LEFT** under I-40 and then back **LEFT** on the **North Frontage Rd**. Curve **RIGHT** onto **CO RD 26**, then turn **RIGHT** and follow **4-Lane 66** for 1.6 mi (past Hwy 273…becomes **Railroad** St One-way EB) to cross Main St in **McLEAN**.

WB: From Main St in **<u>ALANREED</u>**, follow **Third St** (Loop 271) west for 0.4 mi. **AVOID** the EB I-40 off ramp ("**DO NOT ENTER**") and turn **LEFT** onto the **South Frontage Rd**. Go 3 mi, to the next overpass (**EXIT 132**) and join **WEST I-40**. Take **EXIT 124** (Hwy 70 South), **CROSS I-40**, then quickly turn **RIGHT** and take the **South Frontage Rd** west towards **<u>GROOM</u>**.

West of **<u>ALANREED</u>,** the terrain offers some great long-distance views from the narrow ridgeline. Old 66 loses its pavement shortly past EXIT 132, then encounters **PRIVATE PROPERTY** at a cattle guard. This marks the beginning of the infamous "**Jericho Gap**," the last 18 miles section of 66 paved in this area in the late 1930s. Much of this section is **ABANDONED** or **PRIVATE**.

EB, be sure to stop (whether you need to "go" or not) at the **EB I-40 "Donley County Texas Route 66 Safety Rest Area."** The neon signs and Art Deco style honor old 66. Inside are exhibits, travel info and a handy tornado shelter. Outside is a playground and **Route 66-history walk**, the sidewalks of which are mini-highways with center stripes leading past brass historic info plaques. The **WB** rest area, resembling an early dugout, honors pioneer history and has a great view.

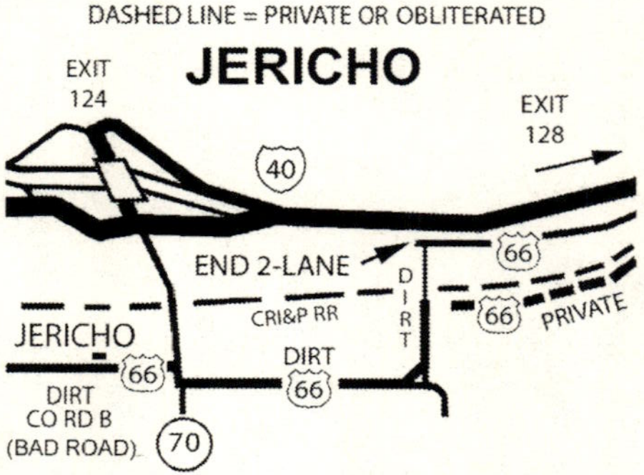

<u>SIDE TRIPS</u>: From **EXIT 128:** About **2 miles** of pavement heads west on the south side, ending at a dirt road. **Return** to **EXIT 128** to stay on asphalt. The dirt road joins **Dirt 66** for a short dogleg to **<u>JERICHO</u>** (**AVOID if WET**).

An easier way to view **<u>JERICHO</u>**, consisting of the (**private property**) ruins of a tourist court and a deserted house or two, is to take **Hwy 70** south **1 mi** from **EXIT 124**, then turn **RIGHT** on **CO RD B** (sign: "**Jericho Cemetery**"). A **historic marker** sits on the east side of Hwy 70). **AVOID when WET!** Farmers made money pulling autos out of the black mud, and this section is still a mudbath after a rain. **Dirt 66** headed west for about 6 mi via CO RD B to Boydston Rd, etc… but this can be rutted and dusty when dry. Instead, **take Hwy 70 back up to EXIT 124.**

EB: Join **EAST I-40** at **EXIT 124** (Hwy 70 S). Take **EXIT 132** (Johnson Ranch Rd) and turn **RIGHT** from the off ramp, then **LEFT** on the **South Frontage Rd** for 3 mi. Nearing **EXIT 135**, turn **RIGHT** onto **LOOP 271** (becomes **Third St**) into **<u>ALANREED</u>**, past Main.

(see MAP # 1 on TX page-2)

TEXAS MAP # 2

EXIT 62 ~ JERICHO

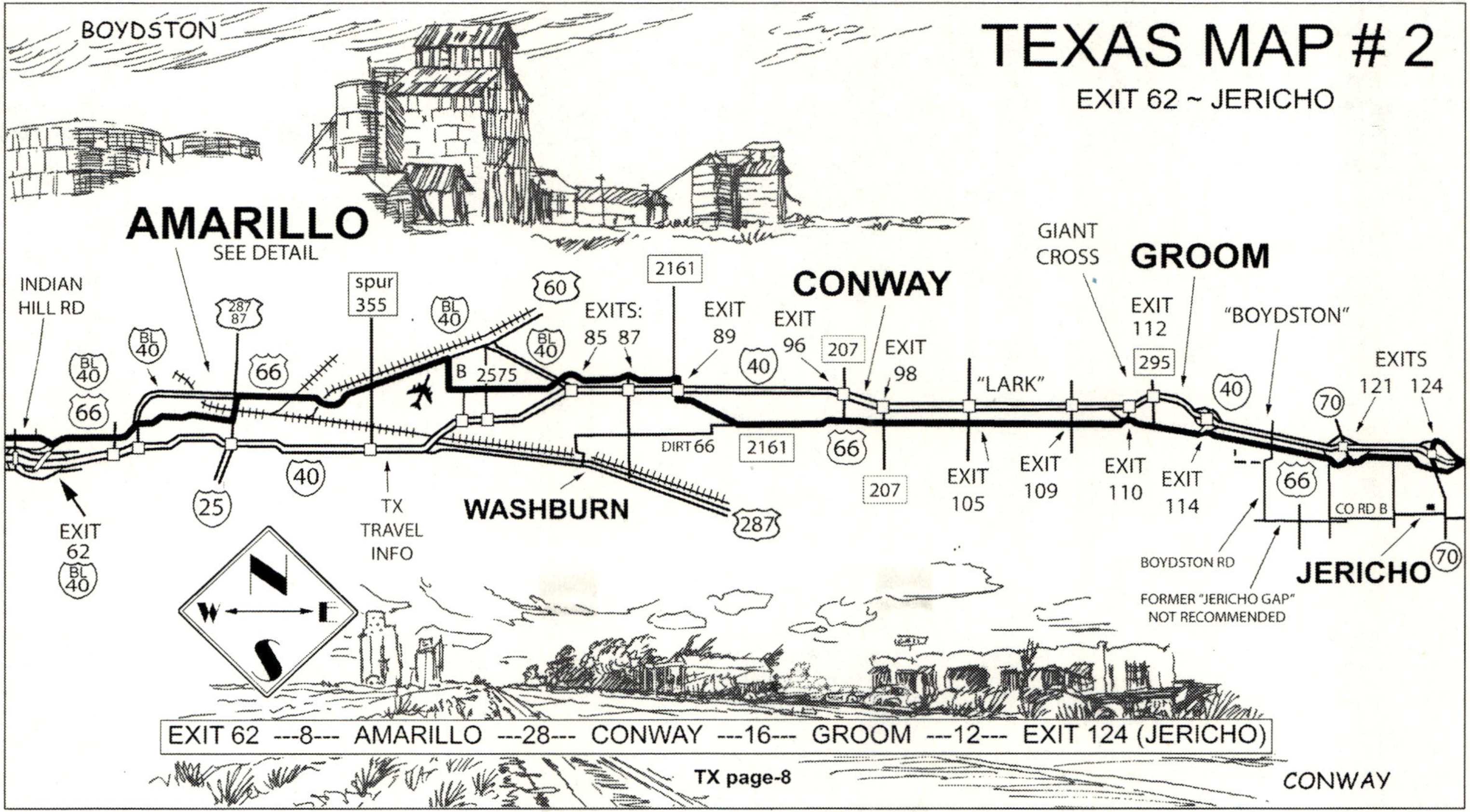

WB: From **EXIT 124** (HWY 70 S) follow the **South Frontage Rd** for 3.5 mi west. At **EXIT 121** (HWY 70 N) turn **LEFT** before curving onto the overpass to continue on the **South Frontage Rd** for 6.5 mi. Approaching **GROOM**, curve sharply right and **yield** to the EB I-40 onramp at EXIT 114, then continue into town with **BL 40**. Continue for 2 mi thru town, past the JCT of Hwy 295.

The narrow ridge that '66 follows starts to widen out into flat tableland west of **JERICHO**. Much of this section's terrain is cultivated land: the same rich dirt that made the "**Jericho Gap**" such a muddy terror is great for crops. Many fields are watered by long, wheeled pivoting sprinklers. West of Exit 121 are two lonely tin silos that are the agricultural remnants of **BOYDSTON**.

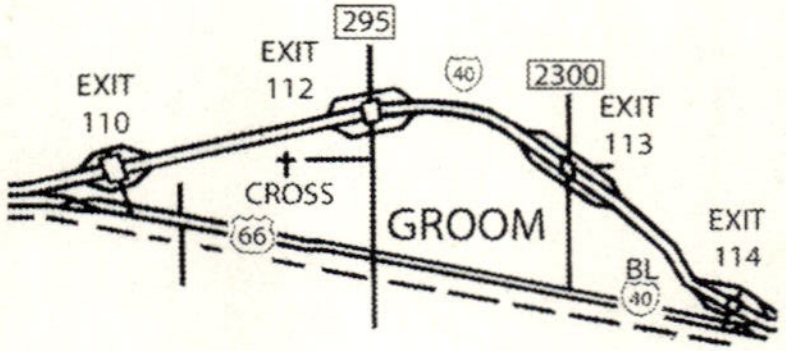

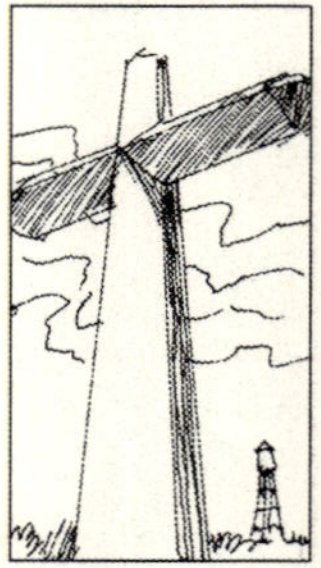

GROOM marks its presence on the plain in several ways. Concrete silos and the town water tower are typical of the Panhandle. A more unusual water tower marks a former truck stop on the north side of I-40 at EXIT 114. This "**leaning tower of Groom**" was built that way, to attract attention. **GIANT ALERT!** The newest and most spectacular vertical attraction is the "**Cross of Our Lord Jesus Christ**" built in 1995. At 190 foot tall (19 stories) this is billed as the "**Largest Cross in the Western Hemisphere**" (Route 66 also boasts a similar religious monument at Edmond, OK, but that one is "only" 100' tall with a 37' base). The giant cross (illuminated at night) stands just south of I-40 EXIT 112 on HWY 295. The complex also includes statues of the "Stations of the Cross." Town INFO: (806) 248-7929.

GROOM was once home to many gas stations, cafes and motels: their remnants remain to remind of the roadside past. The long-abandoned remains of the **66 Courts** and its classic, often photographed sign are now gone. In **1959**, your tour guide stayed here on a trip back east to visit "Gramma." The "McClanahan" suite is now just a memory. Today try the **Chalet Inn**, south of EXIT 113 on Hwy 2300/Eastern Ave. (806) 248 7524. For eats try **The Grill**, on 66 in town. Closed Mon, open late on Thurs-Sat.

Scavenger hunt! What **government office** is in a small former **W Bros gas station** on the west side? __________

EB: From HWY 295, follow **BL 40** for 2 mi thru **GROOM**. At EXIT 114, continue **AHEAD** with the **South Frontage Rd** for 6.5 mi. At EXIT 121 (Hwy 70 N) curve to the **STOP**. Turn **RIGHT** to continue on the **South Frontage Rd** for 3.5 mi to **EXIT 124**.

WB: From Hwy 295, stay **AHEAD** with **BL 40** for 1.5 mi to EXIT 110, then curve to **STOP**, and turn **RIGHT** on the **South Frontage Rd** for 12.6 mi. At the S Hwy 207 JCT (south of EXIT 98), continue straight **AHEAD** into **CONWAY**. Stay with **HWY 2161** for 8.3 mi as it heads west past the JCT of N Hwy 207, then angles north back to I-40. At **next overpass**, cross I-40 & turn **LEFT** on **N Frontage Rd**. Go 4.6 mi west to **EXIT 85** (BL 40/Amarillo Blvd). **AVOID BL 40:** Cross all lanes, **CURVE LEFT** to follow **HWY 2575**.

West of **GROOM** lies more open land, with far horizons dotted by distant silos and windmills, while faint remnants of the old railroad hug the road on the south. East of EXIT 105 a white-painted concrete silo anonymously marks the site of "**LARK**."

At **CONWAY** begins the best section of old 66 in **TEXAS**! The little town once lined the north side of the highway, now only a defunct business or two mark the route's passing. A line of stucco, tile-roofed cabins were recently torn down. Next door was an old wooden building once home to **Buddy's Café**. Further on, a pair of tall, white grain elevators guard the silence of the past. **SIDE TRIP**: Out by EXIT 96 (take Hwy 207 North) is "**BUG RANCH**," an ironic satire of "Cadillac Ranch," with **VWs** buried in the dirt instead of "Detroit's finest."

West from town, the speed limit jumps to **70 mph**, (as of this writing: your MPH may vary) the only place in **TEXAS** you can legally drive that fast on old 66! The feel of the old concrete pavement is evident under a thin layer of blacktop, and I-40 is mostly out of sight on the north. No other stretch in **TEXAS** gives you quite this isolated old-time '66 feel, so savor it while it lasts.

HISTORIC NOTE: Briefly during the late 1920s, US 66 went straight west where HWY 2161 angles to the north, then took a zig-zag of dirt roads down to **WASHBURN**. There it joined the early pavement of what became US 287 into **AMARILLO**. Contrary to some accounts, US 66 **NEVER** went thru Claude, TX.

EB: Follow the **North Frontage Rd** for 4.6 mi to **EXIT 89**. **CROSS** I-40 and turn **LEFT** to follow **HWY 2161** for 8.3 mi to **CONWAY**. At the junction with South HWY 207, continue **AHEAD** and follow the **South Frontage Rd** for 12.6 mi to join **BL 40** (from EXIT 110) into **GROOM**. Continue for 1.5 mi, crossing HWY 295.

WB: Take **HWY 2575** for 4 mi. At the JCT with HWY 1912, continue **AHEAD** with **NE 8th** for 1.7 mi into **AMARILLO**. At the airport fence, turn **RIGHT** onto **AVE B** (to rejoin 66). Go 1.4 mi, pass under the overpass, turn **LEFT** onto **Amarillo Blvd** (BL 40/US 60) for 3.5 mi, crossing LOOP 335. Continue on **Amarillo Blvd** for 5 mi. At the signs for the US 287 JCT, get in the **LEFT LANE**. Continue **AHEAD** across Fillmore St and **TURN LEFT** on **Taylor St** (One-Way). Continue south 1 mi to downtown, turn **RIGHT** on SE **6th Ave**.

NOTE: The final route of US 66 followed **BL 40** (from **EXIT 85**) up to **US 60**. Early **2-Lane 66** is interrupted by the airport (**Triangle Dr** is a remnant).

Many roadside remnants line **E Amarillo Blvd**. Most motels here no longer cater to the tourist trade, but some still have neat signs. The old link to downtown, **Fillmore St**, is now **One-Way** north, requiring **WB** traffic to use **Taylor**. Later, **W Amarillo Blvd** bypassed 6th Ave/"City 66."

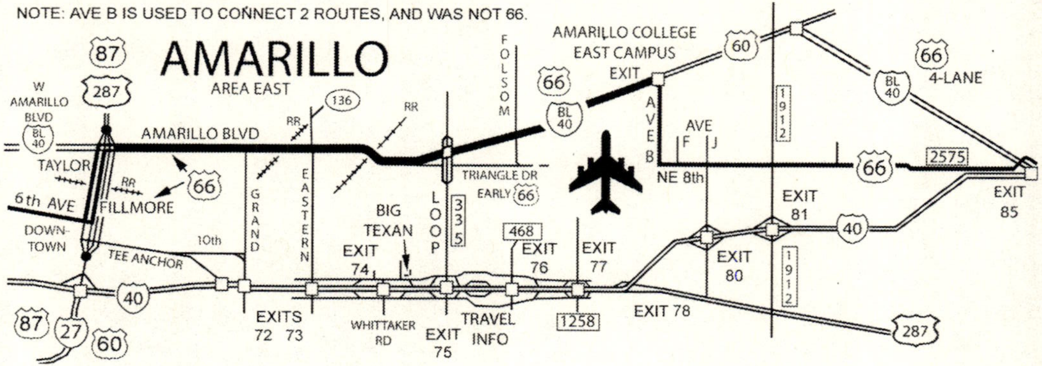

SIDE TRIP: Drop down **Loop 335** from **BL 40** to that **AMARILLO** icon, the **Big Texan**. **GIANT ALERT**! The '**Texan**'s huge **Cowboy** sign had its beefy beginnings on **Amarillo Blvd** in 1959. He moseyed out to I-40 when 66 was bypassed. Home of the "**Free 72 Oz Steak Dinner**" (if eaten in one hour') of billboard fame, the '**Texan** also boasts a motel with a Texas-shaped pool (800-657-7177), and the **Cowboy Palace Theatre**. Your author's painting of the former US 66 location (a "Texas-big" 3 by 5 foot canvas) hangs in the lobby.

EB: Continue on **Amarillo Blvd** for 5 mi, passing LOOP 335. Go 3.4 mi, take the "**Amarillo College East Campus**" EXIT, and curve RIGHT onto **Ave B** south. Go 1.4 mi. **TURN LEFT** on **NE Eight St**. Go 1.7 mi. At the JCT with HWY 1912, continue **AHEAD** onto **HWY 2575** for 4 mi. At **EXIT 85**, cross all 4 lanes of BL 40 and curve to join the **North Frontage Rd** eastbound (avoid ramps).

WB: Follow **SE 6th Ave** (becomes **SW 6th** Ave) for nearly 4 mi, following the wide boulevard as it curves onto **Bushland Blvd** and then onto **9th Ave**. Approaching the JCT of **Amarillo Blvd** at Bell St, **AVOID** the left turn for Bell St, cross under the overpass and **TURN LEFT** onto **West BL 40 (Amarillo Blvd)**. Follow Amarillo Blvd west almost 4 mi (crossing Loop 335 and Helium Rd). When BL 40 curves down to join I-40, **TURN RIGHT** onto **Indian Hill Rd**.

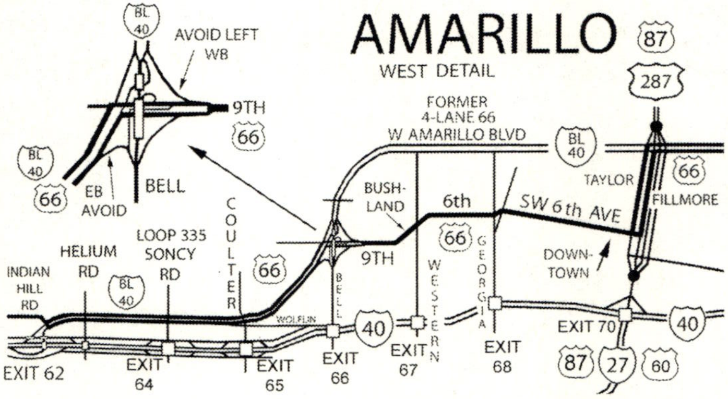

SCAVENGER HUNT! What is the **DATE** on the old **Rock Island Railroad overpass** north of downtown on **Fillmore**? (Sorry, but you **WB** folk will have to double back for this one!) ________________

Look for painted **fiberglass ponies** around downtown. With a population of over 173,000 souls, **AMARILLO** is **"IT"** as far as big cities go on Route 66 in **TEXAS**! The area's many attractions, such as **Palo Duro Canyon**, could keep you busy for days. INFO: www.visitamarillotx.com www.amarillo-chamber.org or 806-373-7800. Make time for **"One Mile Shopping"** in the **Historic Route 66** district along **SW 6th Ave** west of downtown. There are "boo coo" (Texan for "lots") antique stores, galleries and cafes between Western and Georgia Streets in the **San Jacinto Neighborhood**. Look for the **Natatorium**, with its castle-like crenellations, south of the JCT with Georgia. **ART ALERT:** just west of Georgia is **Lile Art Gallery** at 2719 SW 6th (806) 664-3089. "Croc" Lyle is a fellow **Route 66 Artist**. After you've bought some of MY art, buy some of his (or the artists he represents) work too! On the west side a few '66-era motels sit across from the hospital, and then the rangeland opens up again.

See TX page-14 for directions to Cadillac Ranch!

EB: Follow **BL 40 (Amarillo Blvd)** east for 4 mi into **AMARILLO** (passing Loop 335 and Coulter St). **AVOID** the Bell St off ramp, then **TURN RIGHT** onto **9th Ave**. Go almost 4 mi, following the wide blvd as it curves onto **Bushland Blvd** and then onto **SW 6th Ave**. (**AVOID** the **"Turn Only"** lanes at Georgia St and McMasters St). In downtown, cross Taylor, then **TURN LEFT** on **Fillmore St** (One-Way NB). Go 1 mi (passing under the RR overpasses). At **Amarillo Blvd** (BL 40/US 60) **TURN RIGHT.**

(see MAP # 2 on TX-page-8)

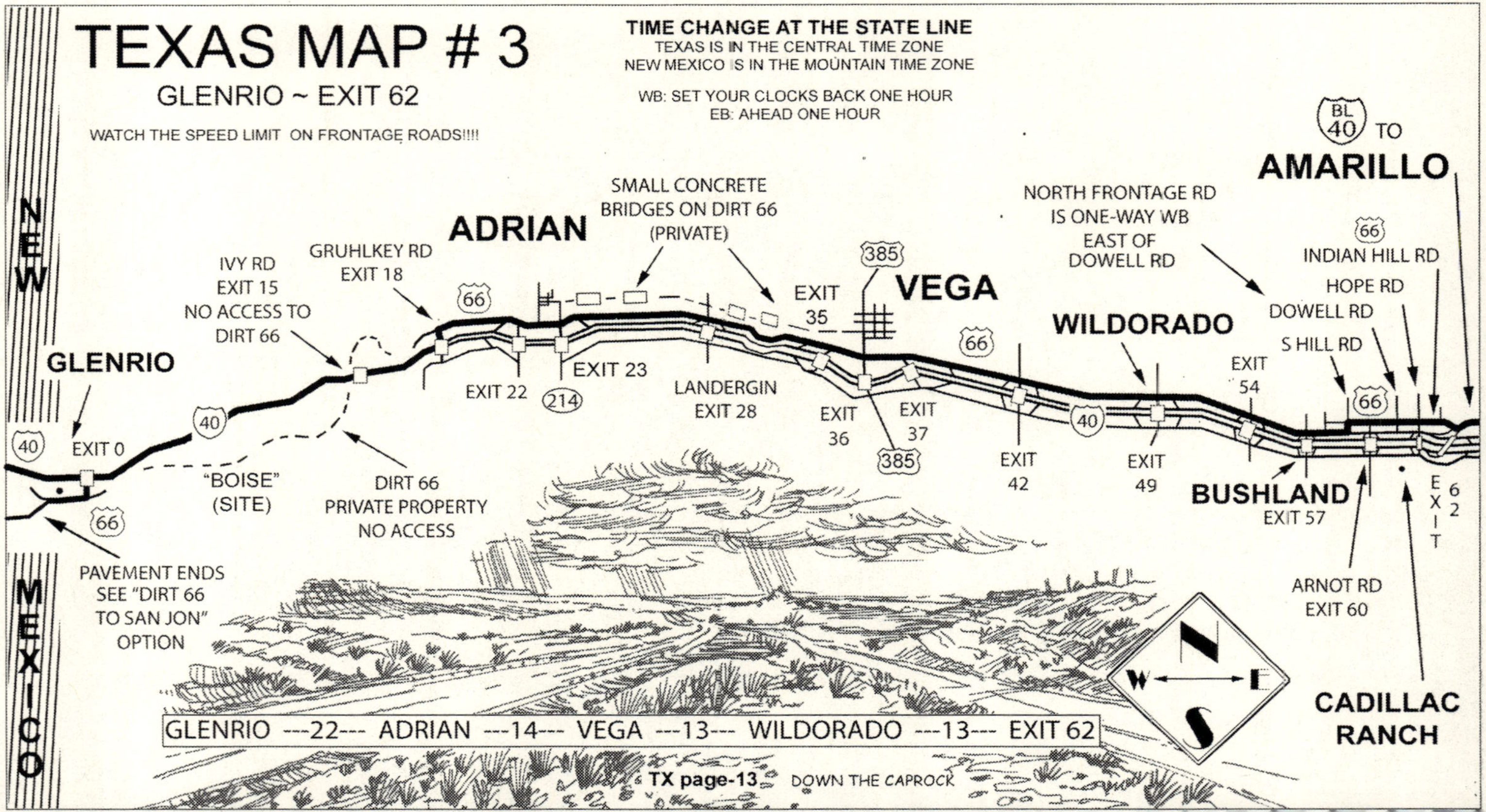

TEXAS MAP # 3
GLENRIO ~ EXIT 62
WATCH THE SPEED LIMIT ON FRONTAGE ROADS!!!!
TIME CHANGE AT THE STATE LINE
TEXAS IS IN THE CENTRAL TIME ZONE
NEW MEXICO IS IN THE MOUNTAIN TIME ZONE
WB: SET YOUR CLOCKS BACK ONE HOUR
EB: AHEAD ONE HOUR
NEW MEXICO
BL 40 TO
AMARILLO
GLENRIO
40
EXIT 0
66
PAVEMENT ENDS SEE "DIRT 66 TO SAN JON" OPTION
"BOISE" (SITE)
40
IVY RD EXIT 15 NO ACCESS TO DIRT 66
DIRT 66 PRIVATE PROPERTY NO ACCESS
GRUHLKEY RD EXIT 18
66
ADRIAN
EXIT 22
214
EXIT 23
SMALL CONCRETE BRIDGES ON DIRT 66 (PRIVATE)
LANDERGIN EXIT 28
EXIT 35
385
VEGA
EXIT 36
EXIT 37
385
66
EXIT 42
40
WILDORADO
EXIT 49
NORTH FRONTAGE RD IS ONE-WAY WB EAST OF DOWELL RD
EXIT 54
BUSHLAND
EXIT 57
66
INDIAN HILL RD
HOPE RD
DOWELL RD
S HILL RD
66
ARNOT RD EXIT 60
EXIT 62
CADILLAC RANCH
N
W
E
S
GLENRIO ---22--- ADRIAN ---14--- VEGA ---13--- WILDORADO ---13--- EXIT 62
DOWN THE CAPROCK

WB: Follow **Indian Hill Rd** for 3.5 mi past Hope Rd, Dowell Rd and Arnot Rd (EXIT 60) to **S Hill Dr**: **TURN LEFT**, then a quick **RIGHT** onto the **North Frontage Rd**. Continue for 22 mi, passing en route **BUSHLAND** (EXIT 57), **WILDORADO** (EXIT 49). and EXIT 37 (**VEGA**). **BL 40** joins from this exit, stay **AHEAD** into **VEGA**, crossing HWY 385.

SIDE TRIP: Despite **MANY** reports, the outdoor artwork titled "**Cadillac Ranch**" was **NEVER** located on Route 66 (even before the cars were uprooted and moved to the current location in 1997)! Still, it is a road icon not to be missed. The 10 luxury-barges, planted nose down in the fertile soil, are located on the **South Frontage Rd** between **Arnot Rd** (EXIT 60) and **Hope Rd**, either of which can be used to rejoin Route 66. Although occasionally repainted for special events, fresh coats of graffiti soon cover the "Caddies" (also see "**Bug Ranch**" in **CONWAY** on TX page 10).

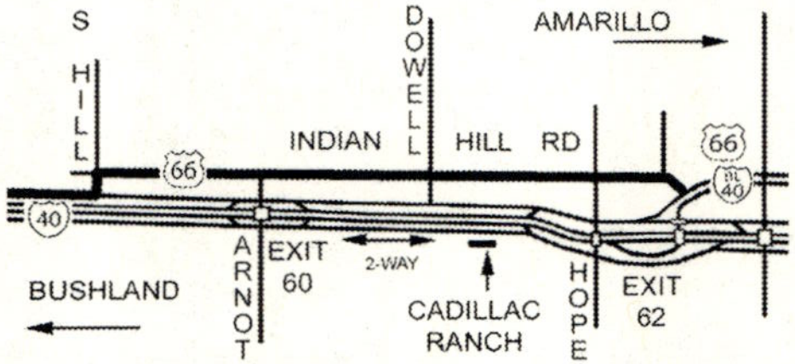

N FRONTAGE RD IS ONE-WAY WB BETWEEN EXIT 62 AND DOWELL RD

A Texas millionaire who commissioned the artist group "**Ant Farm**" to install Cadillac Ranch in 1974, was also responsible for those whacky signs you may have noticed in the area: diamond-shaped signs with puzzling messages such as "**Crock of Gin**" and "**Hot Pink**." In a similar vein (pun intended), keep an eye out for the "**Bates Motel**" sign at the corner of Hope Rd and the N Frontage Rd ("Each room with a shower, knives sharpened").

After the thrill of roadside art, the frontage-road ride past **BUSHLAND**, marked by white concrete silos, is more sedate (drive 55-the friendly cop gave me a warning!). Watch for rounded "quonset huts," refugees from old military bases, along the way. The vanished **CRI&P Railroad** exhibits ghostly traces along the north side of 66. **WILDORADO** may be (in)famous for the odiferous cattle feed lot just east of town (roll up the window and hold your nose). Notice that many trees seem to have a perpetual "lean" into the wind. Wind and cattle rule the range, and there are many windmills to count on the way to **VEGA**.

EB: Take **BL 40** past **VEGA'**s east exit (EXIT 37). Continue on **North Frontage Rd** for 20 mi, passing **WILDORADO** (EXIT 49) and **BUSHLAND** (EXIT 57). **2 miles** east, **TURN LEFT** on **S Hill Rd**, then a quick **RIGHT** onto **Indian Hill Rd**. Go 3.5 mi (passing Arnot Rd (EXIT 60) and Dowell Rd). East of Hope Rd, curve right to the **STOP**, then **TURN LEFT** on **BL 40** towards **AMARILLO**.

WB: Take **BL 40** thru **VEGA**, remaining on **North Frontage Rd** for 13 mi, past EXIT 28 (**LANDERGIN**), to **ADRIAN**. Stay on **North Frontage Rd** for 5 mi to **EXIT 18/Gruhlkey Rd**. **JOIN WEST I-40** here for 18 miles to **EXIT 0** in **GLENRIO**. (see **SIDE TRIP**).

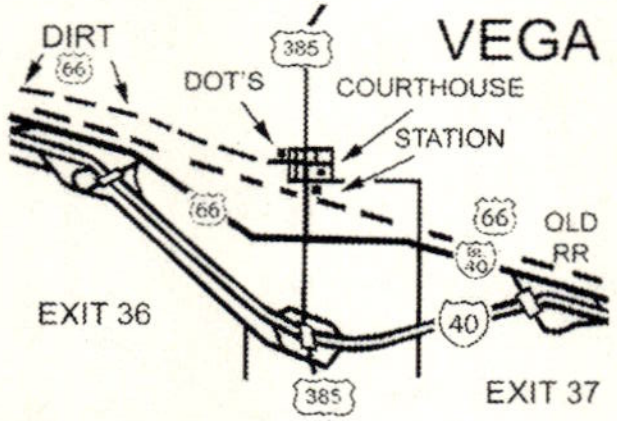

VEGA is a great stop in this remote country. Take HWY 385 (North Main) north a couple of blocks for the restored **1920s Magnolia Gas Station** on older 66 near the courthouse. A few blocks west of the courthouse on dead-end early 66 (**WEST** Main at 12th), **Dot's Mini Museum** houses the late Dot Leavitt's personal collection of artifacts. At 66 and Hwy 385 is the **Boot Hill Saloon and Grill**. The vintage **Vega Motel** is now a strip mall. City INFO: 806 267-2828.

Watch for some small concrete culverts on the north between **VEGA** and **ADRIAN**: remnants of "Dirt 66." Little is left of **LANDERGIN**, where the **Federation** staged the first **John Steinbeck Award Banquet** in a circus tent on October 11, 1997. **ADRIAN**, billed as Route 66's geographical midpoint, may be small, but has lots to offer at the **Mid Point Café and Gift Shop**. New owner Dennis offers fine vittles, plus a new **MIDPOINT Marker** across 66. www.route66midpointcafe.com (806) 538-6379. Famed former-owner Fran has opened her new western gift shop, **Sunflower Station**, in the old gas station next door. Sign her pickup (if you can find room!). (806) 538-6380

A classic **Stuckeys** has long stuck to the EB off-ramp at **EXIT 18 (Gruhlkey Rd)**, sticking tourists with pecan logs and rubber tomahawks. Old 66 **dead-ends** just to the west of this exit (north side), where the remote **Cap Rock Texaco** (long closed) was the last bit o'civilization before the route plunged down the escarpment on its way to **NEW MEXICO**. The early dirt-66 pathway thru "**BOISE**" is inaccessible.

GLENRIO SIDE TRIP Beaten by the bypass, this former bustling road-town, astraddle the **Texas/New Mexico State Line**, is now home to picturesque ruins and barking dogs (respect private property). The forlorn **Texas Longhorn Motel** once boasted of being the "First/Last Motel in Texas." After your 1 mile trip to end of pavement from **EXIT 0**, **WB** drivers can either join the "**Dirt 66" OPTION** to **SAN JON**, NM (see **NM page-3**) or go back and rejoin **I-40** to continue west on pavement. **EB:** get ready for the great state of **TEXAS**.

EB: From **EXIT 0 in GLENRIO**, follow **EAST I-40** for 18 miles to take **EXIT 18 (Gruhlkey Rd)**. **CROSS I-40**, and turn **RIGHT** to follow the **North Frontage Rd** for 17 mi, thru **ADRIAN** and past EXIT 28 (**LANDERGIN**), to join **BL 40 AHEAD** thru **VEGA**.

(see Texas INTRO on TX page-1)

(see MAP # 3 on TX page-13)

Navigating New Mexico

Since the days of **Coronado**, **NEW MEXICO** has been a popular destination for its beauty, history and people. Offering extremes between peaceful isolation to busy city strips, and from small Spanish communities with rustic chapels, to majestic adobe missions, **Route 66** encounters distant peaks, craggy cliffs, multi-hued mesas and tree covered mountain slopes in its nearly 400 mile traverse across the state. That mileage figure is purposely vague, for the mileage you drive depends on which version of 66 you take. **Before 1937**, Route 66 zigged up to **SANTA FE** before plunging down thru the heart of **ALBUQUERQUE** to **LOS LUNAS**, to join the **POST-1937** route at **CORREO**.

Thus, the modern tourist must make a choice: **PRE or POST 1937 66**. Both have plusses: Sadly, **Post 37 US 66** from **SANTA ROSA** to **MORIARTY** is all I-40, but this does make for a quick drive, and Old 66 west of **MORIARTY** thru **Tijeras Canyon** and on **Central Ave** into **ALBUQUERQUE** is rewarding. The **SANTA FE LOOP**, on the other hand, requires much less interstate travel, and offers vistas of magnificent scenery and history. This leg will take much longer but the time is well spent. Let your schedule be your guide (if your trip is bi-directional, do both ways!). See **NM page 23-30** for the **PRE-1937 OPTION**.

Portions of **Route 66**, and its ancestors across the state, have known many names: **El Camino Real, Old Santa Fe Trail, Ozark Trail, National Old Trails** and now the **Route 66 Scenic Byway**. **NEW MEXICO** lays claim to many of the records for **"OLDEST"** in the nation, and much of that history is right on the route, including many **Native American Pueblos**. Inquire at their visitor centers about regulations, especially before photographing, as these are not "theme parks" but people's homes and places of worship. Be a good guest, and you'll find the people of **NEW MEXICO** to be as warm and friendly as the ever-present Zia "sun symbol" that graces the state.

NEW MEXICO MAP # 1

CUERVO ~ GLENRIO

DASHED LINE = ROUGH, PRIVATE OR IMPASSABLE

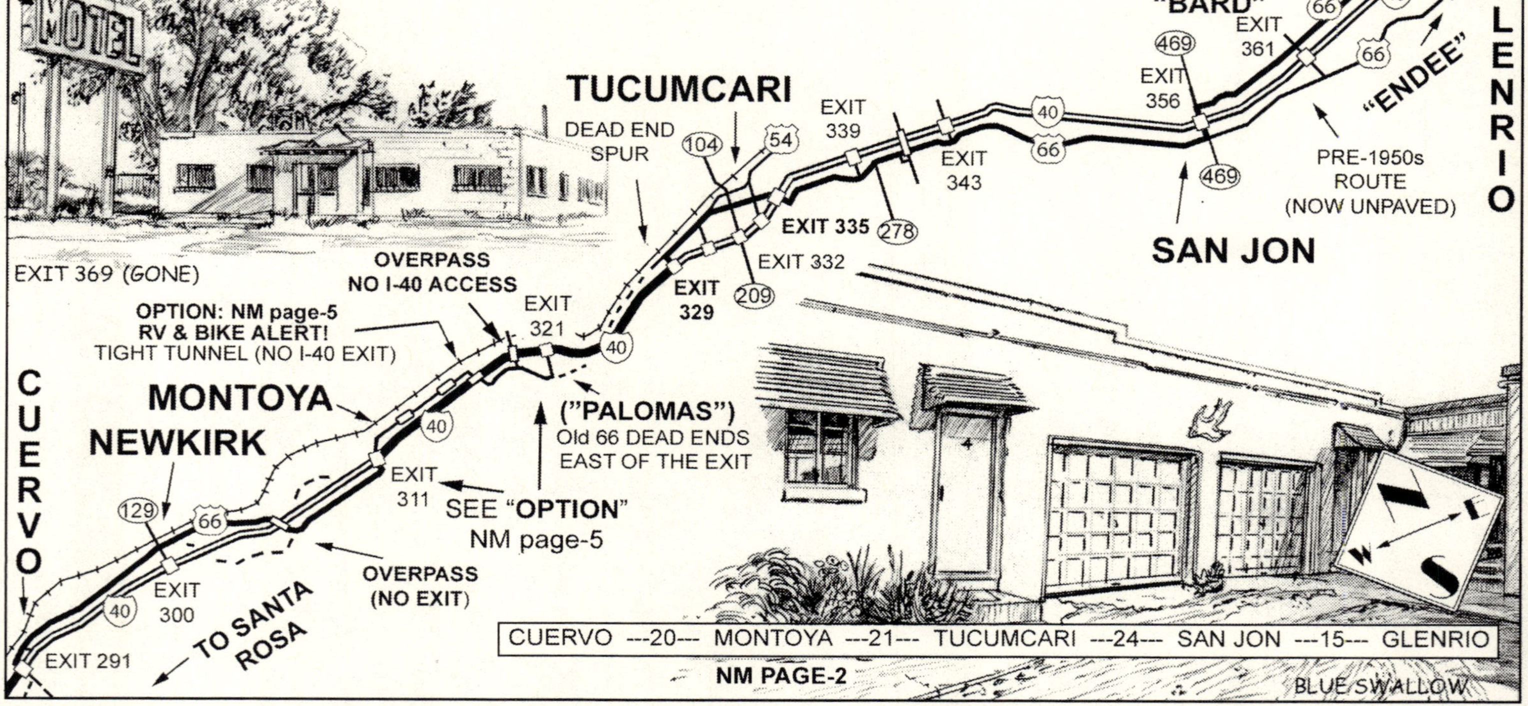

WB: From **EXIT 0** at **GLENRIO**, follow **I-40** across the State Line into **NM**. Take **EXIT 369**, turn **RIGHT** from the off ramp, then **LEFT** on the **N Frontage Rd**. Pass EXIT 361 (**"BARD"**) and then curve around the Truck Inspection Station. At **EXIT 356**, turn **LEFT** on **Hwy 469**, and cross under I-40 into **SAN JON**. After 0.5 mi, turn **RIGHT** on the wide blvd (becomes **South Frontage Rd**).

OPTIONAL "DIRT 66"

GLENRIO TO SAN JON

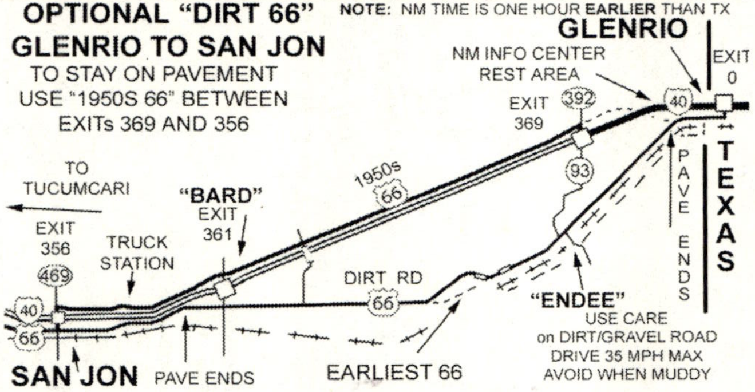

If you've made the **SIDE TRIP** from **EXIT 0** into **GLENRIO**, (or if headed **EB** from **SAN JON**) you have a CHOICE. The **tour route** is via the **1950s pavement** north of I-40. **OR:** follow the **"DIRT 66" OPTION**:

About 18 scenic miles of formerly paved '66 (now good dirt and gravel) exist from **GLENRIO** thru **"ENDEE"** to **SAN JON**. Enjoy this quiet and peaceful drive away from I-40, across a few quaint wooden-post bridges and beside visible remnants of the abandoned **CRI&P RR**. **WB**: follow the dirt road past where the pavement dead ends west of **GLENRIO** (the abandoned pavement crosses a long concrete bridge). **EB**: follow 66 thru **SAN JON**, and then along the south side of I-40 onto the dirt road. Hold the speed to 35 MPH and **AVOID** if muddy. In the middle, lonely **ENDEE** consists of the ruins of a few old motel cabins and a "two-holer" privy shack, emblazoned with the boast "**MODERN RESTROOMS**" (they DID flush). This is actually the **SECOND** route of US 66 along here. The **FIRST** route ran along the south side of the RR until west of **ENDEE**, where it rejoined the later route on a tangent to a curve. Little trace of the early path is visible. **EB**: rejoin the main tour at EXIT 0 (**GLENRIO**).

At **EXIT 369** on the 1950s road is the new **Russell's Travel Center**, with an extensive old car and toy display. (575) 576-8700.

SAN JON (say "HONE") **SIDE TRIP**: This town was devastated by a one-exit bypass. Now mostly empty ruins haunt the broad main drag. Double back east on 66 from NM 469 to see what's left of town (unless doing the **DIRT OPTION**). The **San Jon Motel** is just about the only remaining business here on 66.

EB: In **SAN JON**, turn **LEFT** on **Hwy 469**. Pass under I-40 at **EXIT 356**. Turn **RIGHT** on the **N Frontage Rd** (Quay Co Rd 58.5). Pass the Truck Inspection Station. Pass by EXIT 361 ("**BARD**"). At **EXIT 369**, join **EAST I-40** to **EXIT 0** (**GLENRIO**) in **TEXAS**.

WB: Follow the **South Frontage Rd** for 21 mi, past EXIT 343 and 339. At **EXIT 335**, curve around, cross under I-40 and curve with **BL 40**/Tucumcari Blvd into **TUCUMCARI**. Continue for 6.6 mi, then rejoin **I-40 WEST** at **EXIT 329**. (see SIDE TRIP NM page-5)

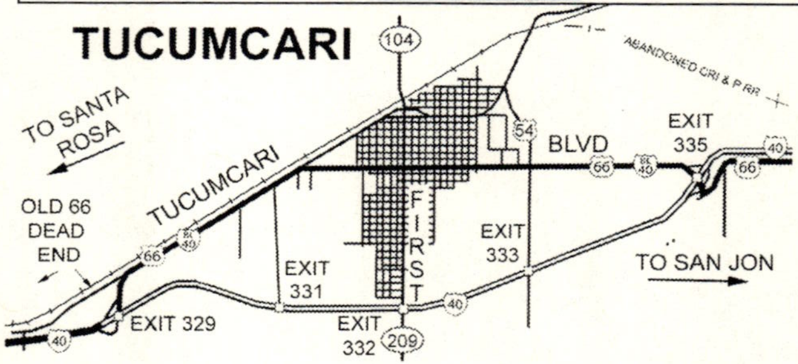

West of **SAN JON**, '66 briefly cuts away from I-40 as it drops down thru red hills. An old gas station ruin below the ridge (private) once had a canopy roofed with flattened oilcans. Flat-topped **Tucumcari Mountain** looms ahead.

TUCUMCARI still clings to a variety of precious neon, although many signs have gone dim. Fortunately, the blazing neon at the famed 1939 **Blue Swallow Motel** at 815 E 66 is in good hands. Longtime home to the late Lillian Redman, enthusiastic new owners are keeping up the tradition, having restored the walls to their pink glory. (575) 461-9849 A well liked and recently renovated (by equally proud owners) alternate is the nearby **Motel Safari** with its cool camel sign. (575) 461-1048 Also located here is **Quarles Art Gallery**, featuring work of the prolific mural artist.

Curious for curios? Enter **Tee Pee Curios** thru their big teepee. The neon sign was recently restored with federal grant money, as have been many New Mexico signs. For eats, try **Del's Restaurant** (with the bovine-topped sign) at 1202 E Tucumcari Blvd or **Cornerstone Deli** at 711 E Tucumcari Blvd. **GIANT ALERT**: Sombrero atop **La Cita**, at the NM 104 JCT (plus a revolving neon sign). The restaurant at the **Pow Wow** is also good. **Route 66 Inn** has an espresso bar. For an educational experience, try the **Mesalands Community College Dinosaur Museum**, at 211 E Laughlin St (north of 66 on First, right on Laughlin) for the "Largest collection of life sized bronze skeletons in the world" (505) 461 DINO. Nearby at 416 Adams is the **Tucumcari Historical Museum**. Many old gas stations feature bright murals, such as **The Trade Station** with its Texaco homage. The **Convention Center** (west side of town) has a tail-finned **Route 66 Sculpture** and houses a photo exhibit and an upcoming (summer 2013) **Route 66 Museum**. A bit further west is the colorful **Tucumcari Trading Post**.

EB: Take **EXIT 329**, and follow **BL 40/Tucumcari Blvd** thru **TUCUMCARI** for 6.6 mi. On the east side, cross under **I-40** at **EXIT 335** (AVOID the EB onramp) and turn **LEFT** onto the **South Frontage Rd**. Continue 21 mi, past EXIT 339 and 343, to **SAN JON**.

WB: Join **WEST I-40** at **EXIT 329**. Take **EXIT 311 (MONTOYA)**. Turn **LEFT**, cross I-40, and follow the **S Frontage Rd** for 6 mi. Cross I-40 again (no exit) and continue for 14 mi, alongside the RR thru **NEWKIRK**, to **CUERVO**. Join **WEST I-40** here at **EXIT 291**.

ALERT! Many "dips" (**low water xings**) exist on some sections. **DON'T** drive into deep or running water! Bikes go slow on **cattleguards**.

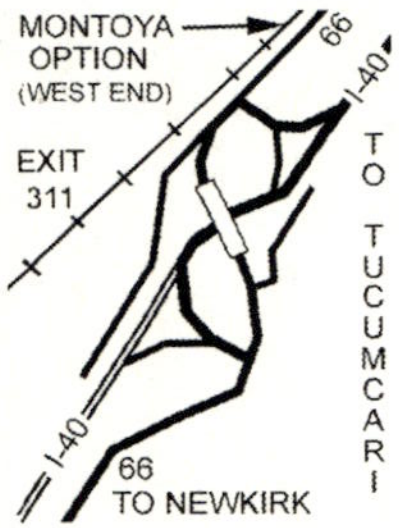

SIDE TRIP: Where **Tucumcari Blvd** turns towards **EXIT 329**, a **dead end** spur of 66 veers off **RIGHT**, and can be followed a short ways along the tracks before the turn-around. Close to the big RR trestle is an older approach to a long gone bridge. Nearby, a hand-painted TEXACO advertisement fades on west-facing boulders. The squat towers that dot the area house well pumps.

West of **TUCUMCARI** road and railroad soon travel a wide-open valley, rimmed with steep bluffs of various hues. On a mesa to the south, light colored streaks of mining tailings give evidence to something desirable hidden in one layer of strata. Another **Stuckey's** is at EXIT 321.

MONTOYA OPTION (**RV& BIKE ALERT**!) Use the map on **NM page-2** (and this page's detail) to follow 66 from "**Palomas**"/EXIT 321 to **MONTOYA**/EXIT 311. The tight tunnel under I-40 midway can be **ROUGH** and filled with water/mud. **AVOID** when wet. Look for several concrete bridges east of **MONTOYA**. **SCAVENGER HUNT**! What is the **DATE** on these bridges? (all the same…watch for cars!) **OR** visit the **west portion** (on the north side of I-40, headed east from EXIT 311), thru **MONTOYA**, then double back (tricky for RVs…**NO** turn-around at the eastern tunnel entry.) **MONTOYA** has weathered down to just a few old remnants.

NEWKIRK has decaying ruins of an old motel and gas stations. There are extensive stretches of an earlier 66 east of town, but all are inaccessible. If you happen to be at the **EB Rest Area** (shame for not being on 66!) you can see the old road and a former bar and old house from across the fence. **NOTE**: The frontage road from **NEWKIRK** to **CUERVO** becomes a **bit rough**. Some of the eastern portion is an I-40-era replacement. I-40 chopped poor **CUERVO** in two. The single line of mostly empty businesses hint at past commerce, while to the south, an attractive stone chapel, and a boxcar turned abode, abut the ruddy slopes of **Cuervo Mesa**.

EB: Take the **N Frontage Rd** for 14 mi, thru **NEWKIRK**. Cross over I-40 (no exit) and follow the **S Frontage Rd** for 6 mi to **EXIT 311**. (SEE **MONTOYA OPTION**) Turn **LEFT** at the onramp (before the overpass) to join **EAST I-40**. Take **EXIT 329** into **TUCUMCARI**.

(see **MAP # 1** NM page-2)

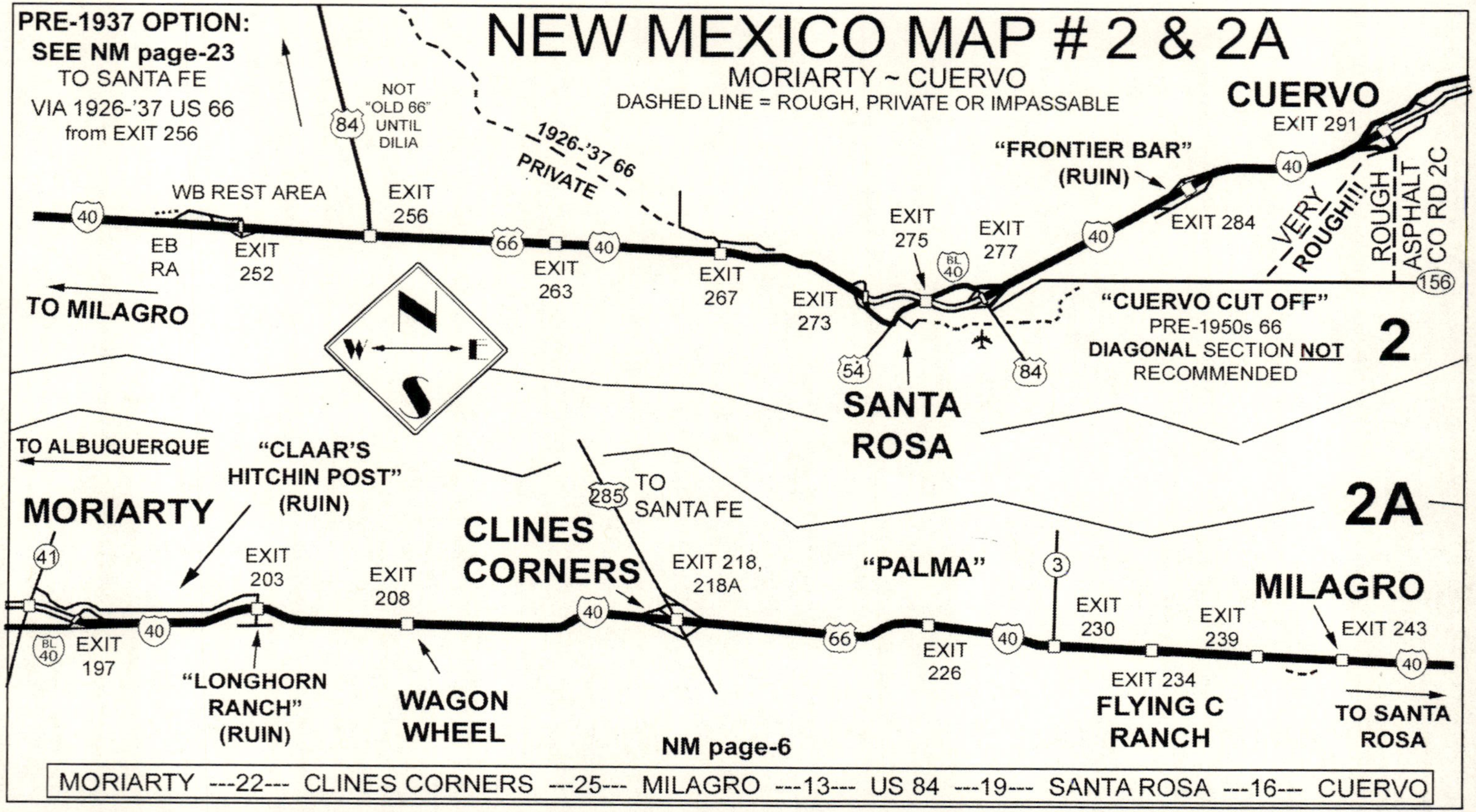
NEW MEXICO MAP # 2 & 2A
MORIARTY ~ CUERVO
DASHED LINE = ROUGH, PRIVATE OR IMPASSABLE
PRE-1937 OPTION:
SEE NM page-23
TO SANTA FE
VIA 1926-'37 US 66
from EXIT 256
84
NOT "OLD 66" UNTIL DILIA
1926-'37 66
PRIVATE
CUERVO
EXIT 291
"FRONTIER BAR" (RUIN)
EXIT 284
VERY ROUGH!!!
ROUGH
ASPHALT
CO RD 2C
156
40
WB REST AREA
EB RA
EXIT 252
EXIT 256
66
EXIT 263
EXIT 267
EXIT 273
EXIT 275
BL 40
EXIT 277
TO MILAGRO
N
W
E
S
54
84
SANTA ROSA
"CUERVO CUT OFF"
PRE-1950s 66
DIAGONAL SECTION NOT RECOMMENDED
2
2A
TO ALBUQUERQUE
"CLAAR'S HITCHIN POST" (RUIN)
MORIARTY
41
EXIT 197
EXIT 203
"LONGHORN RANCH" (RUIN)
EXIT 208
WAGON WHEEL
CLINES CORNERS
285
TO SANTA FE
EXIT 218, 218A
"PALMA"
EXIT 226
3
EXIT 230
EXIT 234
FLYING C RANCH
EXIT 239
MILAGRO
EXIT 243
TO SANTA ROSA
MORIARTY ---22--- CLINES CORNERS ---25--- MILAGRO ---13--- US 84 ---19--- SANTA ROSA ---16--- CUERVO

WB: Take I-40 for 14 mi to **EXIT 277**. Exit, turn **RIGHT** and follow **BL 40/ Will Rogers Dr** into **SANTA ROSA**. After 1.5 mi, cross under I-40 at EXIT 275, and continue on **BL 40** (becomes **Parker Ave)** thru downtown. Follow **BL 40** across the Pecos River.

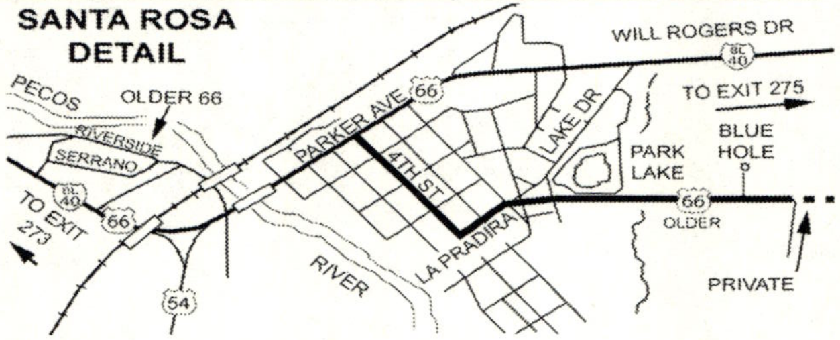

HISTORIC NOTE: Pre-early 1950s, US 66 west of **CUERVO** followed the "**CUERVO CUT OFF**," which cut the corner on a former dirt "dog-leg" (see map on NM page-6). The cut-off is in **VERY BAD** shape, with many washouts and plenty of potholes and bumps. It is signed "**DEAD END**." I really do **NOT** recommend this road to the casual vacationer (it shows up with no warnings on some maps, which is why I mention it)! The dog-leg, **ROUGHLY-paved CO RD 2C**, drops down for 5 mi to Hwy 156, then west 13 mi to EXIT 277. Near US 84, oldest 66 (private) dropped down the mesa, then thru the airport.

I-40 overlays the final route of '66, passing the ruins of the **Frontier Bar and Museum** at EXIT 284. Perched on a long downhill slope leading to the Pecos River, this defunct business began its slide to oblivion years ago, and not much is left.

On the east side of **SANTA ROSA** is the **Route 66 Auto Museum** where, for a small fee, you can see a collection of customs, hot rods and restored vintage cars (some for sale). You can't miss the yellow street rod on the tall pole in front! **GIFT SHOP ALERT**! A few motels in town still cling to their neon tubes, as does the **Comet II Restaurant** on Parker. Less fortunate was the famous **Club Café**, closed for years. Their "Fat Man's" friendly face still grins from **Joseph's Bar & Grill**. Old storefronts line 4th St Downtown, where the original route joins Parker Ave. INFO: (800) 450-7084.

SIDE TRIP: Follow **4th St** from Parker thru downtown. Turn **LEFT** on **La Pradira**, then angle **RIGHT** at 6th St, before Lake Dr, to the **Blue Hole**, a deep, clear blue sinkhole favored by landlocked divers. Old 66 enters private property as it runs east towards the airport.

EB: Follow **BL 40/Parker Ave** from downtown **SANTA ROSA**, uphill under I-40 at EXIT 275. Continue on **BL 40/Will Rogers Dr** for 1.5 mi to **EXIT 277**. Join **EAST I-40** for 14 mi, take **EXIT 291**, cross under I-40 and then **RIGHT** on **N Frontage Rd** thru **CUERVO**.

WB: Just across the bridge, curve **RIGHT** with **BL 40** at the US 53 JCT, and under the **RR** tracks to **EXIT 273** (less than 1 mi). Join **WEST I-40** for 76 mi (see **NM page-23** for **SANTA FE OPTION at EXIT 256**). At **EXIT 197**, take **BL 40** into **MORIARTY**.

On the way west from **SANTA ROSA**, 66 crosses the **Pecos River**, then curves under the railroad. You won't see the iron rails for many a mile. **Riverside Drive**, which curves along under the west side of the RR bridge close to the river, is a bit of older 66. One last section of old businesses line '66 before the evil necessity of superslab travel rears its limited access head.

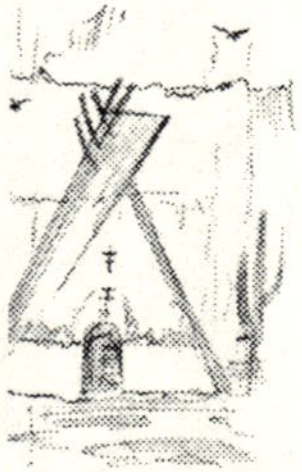

US 66 to **MORIARTY** is almost totally buried under I-40. The good news is this makes for fast driving (your chance to make up time) but watch the weather closely when **snow** is predicted! EXIT 267 marks the point where **Pre-1937 "Dirt 66"** headed towards **DILIA** (impassable today). **US 84** (**EXIT 256**) is the **WB** starting point for the **SANTA FE LOOP OPTION** (see **NM page-23** if you chose to drive this option).

A rare fragment of **Post-1937 66** survives at the **WB Rest Area** (EXIT 252), running a short distance west past the WB I-40 on-ramp (undriveable). An old blacktop curve is visible on the south side, just west of **MILAGRO**, one of the few outposts of civilization along this long, empty stretch. They have a long Route 66 pedigree, as does **FLYING C RANCH** (their "**Running Indian**" mascot still pauses to catch his breath on their billboards). Watch for slow trucks crawling up steep **Palma Hill**.

Been wondering if it's "**Worth Waiting For?**" Check out **CLINES CORNERS**. Begun in 1934 (before 66 came this way), Cline's is the biggest gift shop in this area (someone had a sense of humor in these land-locked plains, naming the street in front of the store "Yacht Club Dr"). Next stop is little "**WAGON WHEEL**," a name harking back to the old west, as do the few ruins of **LONGHORN RANCH**, lying scattered across old 66 from a topless joint and the Longhorn Motel at EXIT 203. **HISTORIC NOTE**: **WB** on I-40, watch along the north-side frontage rd for a glimpse of an abandoned complex between EXITS 203 & 197. Claar's **Hitchin Post** rests here in quietude, a far cry from the days of the free museum, roadside zoo, and "**Den of Death**." Requires backtracking, or detour from NM 41 to reach. Respect ruins.

EB: From **MORIARTY**, join **EAST I-40** at EXIT 197 for 76 mi. (the **EB Pre-'37 OPTION** rejoins at EXIT 256) At **EXIT 273**, take **BL 40** into **SANTA ROSA**. Cross under the RR, then curve **LEFT** at the US 54 JCT with **BL 40** onto **Parker Ave**, thru downtown.

(see **MAP # 2/2A** NM page-6)

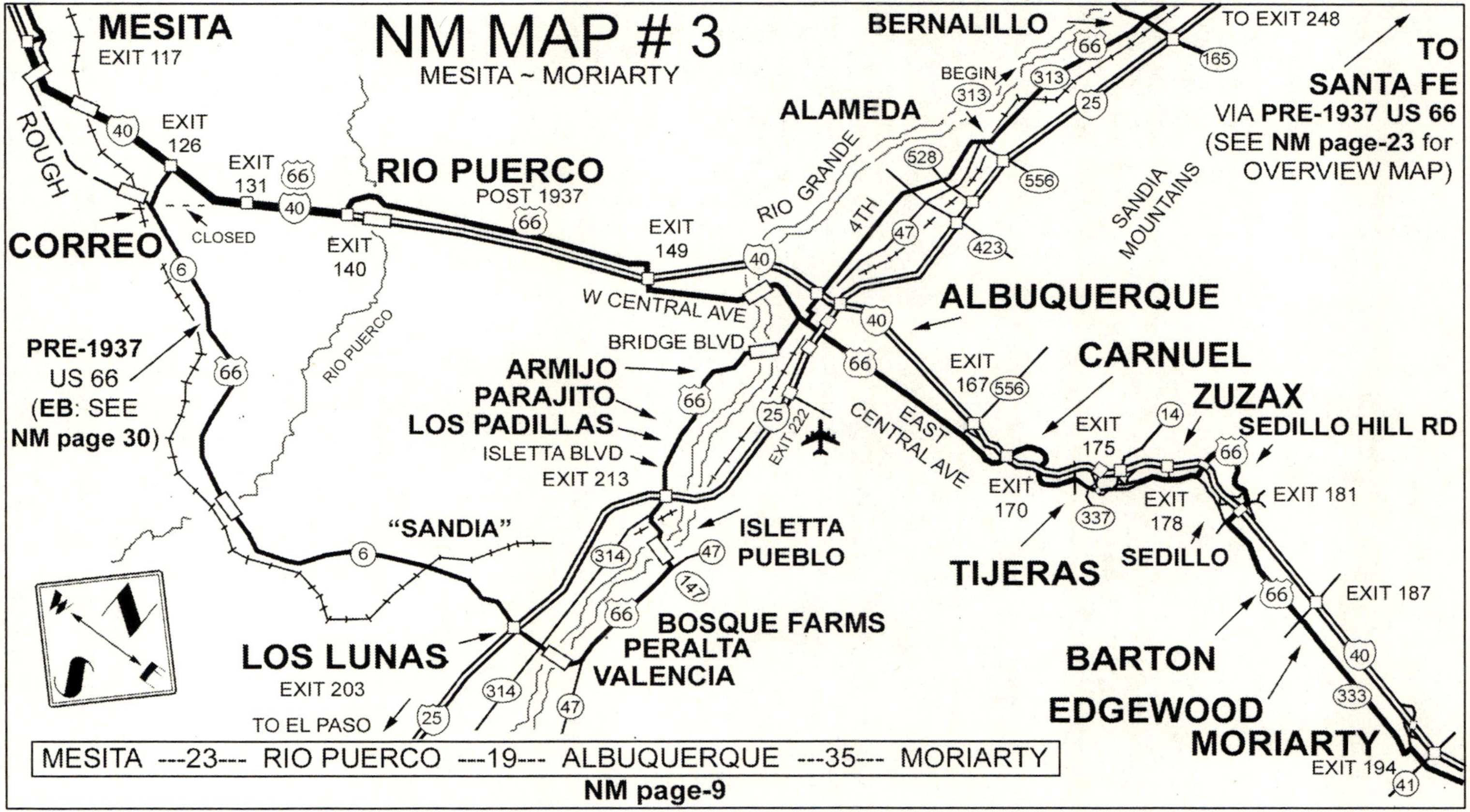
NM MAP # 3
MESITA ~ MORIARTY
MESITA
EXIT 117
ROUGH
EXIT 126
EXIT 131
CLOSED
CORREO
RIO PUERCO
POST 1937
EXIT 140
RIO PUERCO
PRE-1937
US 66
(EB: SEE
NM page 30)
EXIT 149
W CENTRAL AVE
BRIDGE BLVD
ARMIJO
PARAJITO
LOS PADILLAS
ISLETTA BLVD
EXIT 213
"SANDIA"
LOS LUNAS
EXIT 203
TO EL PASO
ISLETTA
PUEBLO
BOSQUE FARMS
PERALTA
VALENCIA
RIO GRANDE
4TH
ALAMEDA
BEGIN
BERNALILLO
TO EXIT 248
TO
SANTA FE
VIA PRE-1937 US 66
(SEE NM page-23 for
OVERVIEW MAP)
SANDIA
MOUNTAINS
ALBUQUERQUE
EXIT 222
EAST
CENTRAL AVE
EXIT
167
CARNUEL
EXIT
170
TIJERAS
EXIT
175
ZUZAX
SEDILLO HILL RD
EXIT
178
SEDILLO
EXIT 181
EXIT 187
BARTON
EDGEWOOD
MORIARTY
EXIT 194
MESITA ---23--- RIO PUERCO ---19--- ALBUQUERQUE ---35--- MORIARTY
NM page-9

WB: Take **BL 40** thru **MORIARTY**. 1.2 mi past the HWY 41 JCT **AVOID** entering I-40 at EXIT 194 by turning **LEFT** (just before the curve to the exit ramps), then quick **RIGHT** with **HWY 333**. Continue 13.8 mi, thru **EDGEWOOD** and **BARTON**, to **EXIT 181**. Cross I-40 and curve **LEFT** with **Sedillo Hill Rd** (AVOID the WB I-40 on ramp). Go 2 mi. At Meadow Dr bear **LEFT** with **Sedillo Hill Rd** for 1.3 mi as it curves, to cross under I-40. Turn **RIGHT** on **Hwy 333**, and continue 4 mi, past **ZUZAX**, to the HWY 14 JCT in **TIJERAS**.

MORIARTY maintains many memories of the Mother Road. The last **Whiting Bros** station to pump gas under the yellow and red "WB" signs is here (no gas now). **Whiting Bros** began in 1917, and established a chain of cut-price stations across 66 from Shamrock, TX to west of Barstow, CA. The east-side **Sunset Motel** is a great mom and pop! I heartily recommend it. (505) 832 4234. On Route 66 is the **Moriarty Historical Museum**. Just west of HWY 41, **Crossley Park** has four statues depicting area history, including the surveying of US 66.

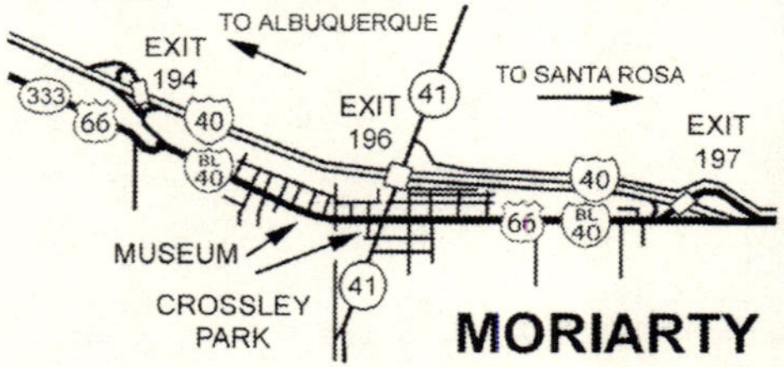

The road slowly climbs as it passes thru **EDGEWOOD** and then **BARTON** (home of the late 66 booster **Bob Audette**). Just east of **EDGEWOOD** look for the colorful (but non-operating) **Red Top Diner** in front of the **Route 66 RV Park**. At the summit, before the long steep drop thru **Tijeras Canyon**, is **Sedillo Hill Rd** (1937-1949 era 66). Although not currently marked as Historic 66, it is definitely the route of choice. One mile longer (but miles better) than staying on 1950s era HWY 333, this is an enchanting descent (or climb) along a twisty but well maintained road thru verdant forest, with awesome vistas of a valley rimmed by surrounding peaks. There are few places to pull off (drive carefully on the narrow **2-lane**) but the drive is satisfying (**WB** drivers, IGNORE the "Mountainous Unimproved Road" sign, which refers to a side road). Back on HWY 333, **ZUZAX** has a strange name (and once had a small aerial tram), but now is not much more than a gas station/RV Park.

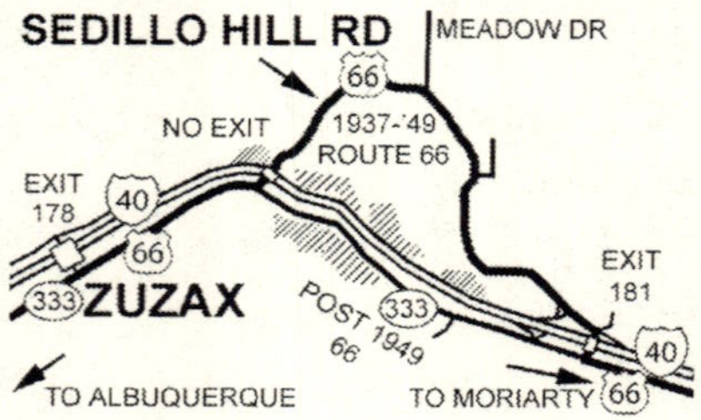

EB: From the HWY 14 JCT, follow **HWY 333** uphill for 4 mi. Turn **LEFT** (1.3 mi past EXIT 178/**ZUZAX**) and cross under I-40 on **Sedillo Hill Rd**. After about 3.3 mi, curve **RIGHT** to cross I-40 (first, **AVOID** the I-40 on ramp), then turn **LEFT** on **HWY 333**, for 13.8 mi, thru **BARTON** and **EDGEWOOD**. Nearing **MORIARTY** (EXIT 194), curve **LEFT**, then **RIGHT** on **BL 40** thru town for 2.6 mi.

WB: At the HWY 14 JCT stoplight, turn **LEFT** with **HWY 333**, along the south side of I-40 thru **TIJERAS** (AVOID all "turn ONLY" lanes and on ramps). Pass under the next overpass (no access), then **STOP** at the **HWY 337** JCT. Continue **AHEAD** with **HWY 333** (curve under I-40 and continue thru **CARNUEL**). About 4.6 mi from HWY 337, be ready to bear **LEFT** to cross **OVER** I-40 and continue with **HWY 333** for 1.6 mi. Stay **AHEAD** onto **Central Ave (**at Tramway Blvd near EXIT 167) into **ALBUQUERQUE.**

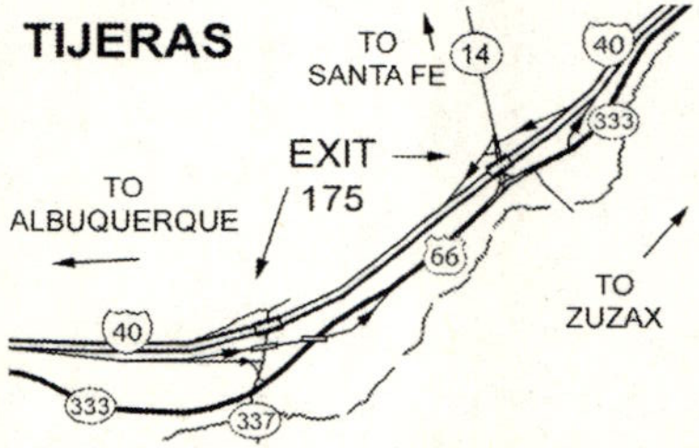

SIDE TRIP: NM HWY 14, the "**Turquoise Trail Scenic Byway**," boasts many attractions, including **HWY 536**, the road that climbs thru the **Sandia Mountains** to 10,678 foot **Sandia Crest**. On the way, **Sandia Crest Rd** passes **Tinkertown Museum** (**FOLK ART ALERT**!) a 40-year collection of carved figures, animated scenes, and odd collections, housed in a 22-room museum (some walls are built from 50,000 bottles) (505) 281-5233. Up **HWY 14** towards **SANTA FE** are the former ghost towns of **Madrid** and **Cerrillos,** now cultural extensions of the capitol city. Another way to reach the mountaintop is via the **Sandia Peak Tramway** (the "worlds longest"), from off Tramway Blvd, north of EXIT 167.

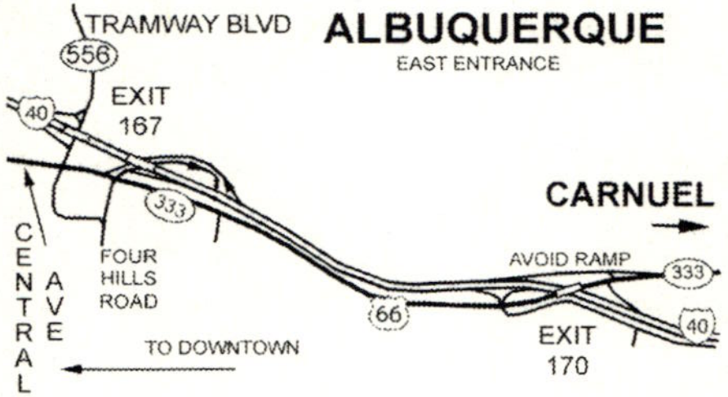

Back on 66, the mountains tightly confine the path thru **Tijeras Canyon**. East of **CARNUEL**, a road cut for older 66 scars the hillside above. Watch for the (defunct) **Mountain Lodge** neon sign, a stereotypical "senor" astride a burro. Finally, the road escapes the boulder-strewn slopes to continue its downhill dash into **ALBUQUERQUE**. **East Central Ave** once traversed a mostly empty land, now packed to the foothills with homes and commerce. Many old motels (mostly of the mission/pueblo style) and businesses hang on (some on the National Register) along with a colorful variety of neon signs. There's almost TOO much to absorb amongst the hustle and bustle (this is a gritty urban area so DO use discretion). Stay in the inside lane to avoid turns.

EB: Continue **AHEAD** thru the intersection with Tramway (near EXIT 167) onto **HWY 333** (AVOID all "turn ONLY" lanes and on ramps). Follow **HWY 333** OVER I-40 (At EXIT **170)** to **CARNUEL**. Follow the curve under I-40, then climb with **HWY 333** into **TIJERAS**. **STOP** at the HWY 337 JCT (5 mi total from EXIT 170): stay **AHEAD** with **HWY 333**. When HWY 14 branches off left, stay in the **RIGHT** lane, and bear **RIGHT** with **HWY 333**.

WB: From Tramway Blvd (near EXIT 167), follow **Central Ave** downhill for 8 mi, then under I-25 into downtown **ALBUQUERQUE**.

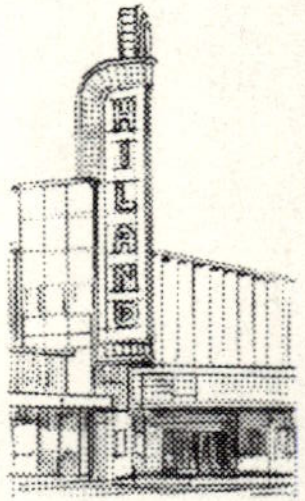

GIANT ALERT! Another "lumberjack" style axe-man perches on the **May Café** sign just south of '66 at Louisiana Blvd. Nearby, Central Ave passes the **State Fair Grounds**. NOTE: If you're in town during the September Fair, you'll have trouble getting a room (unless you've reserved ahead!). Same deal with the annual **International Balloon Festival** in October. These are "plan ahead" events. www.NMStateFair.com www.balloonfiesta.com

Nob Hill is an early strip-mall from 1947, with stylish "streamline modern" architecture punctuated by stepped towers. A mile east is **Hiland Theatre** and **Shopping Center**, dating to 1952. More "streamline" style, complete with stubby tower, is found at **Kelley's Pub and Restaurant**, housed at 3222 Central in a 1939-era Ford Dealer. More towers sprout from former gas stations along Central. Across '66 is the 1936 **Monte Vista Fire Station**, a "Pueblo Revival" structure where only appetites are extinguished today. **Central Avenue** must surely be the **Neon Sign Capitol** of NM, with dozens of vintage and modern beauties blazing away along its 17-mile length! After dark, check out the dazzling show windows of **Absolutely Neon** at 3903 Central near Nob Hill.

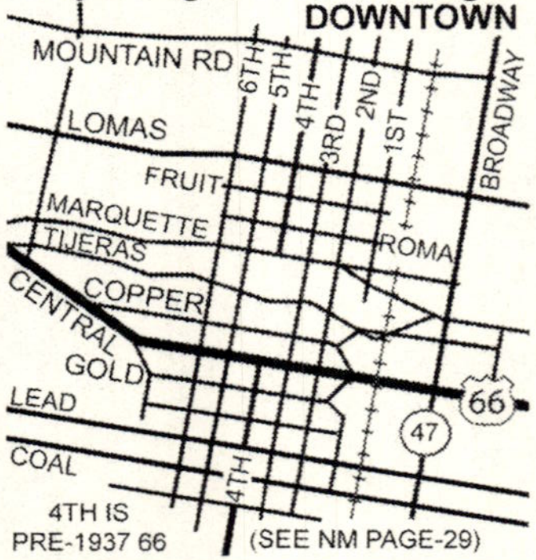

Just east of the **University Of NM** campus, in the triangle of Central and Monte Vista Blvd, look for the former "Little House" Diner, now a police substation. Another flashy stop is the neon draped **Route 66 Diner** at 1405 Central NE, with excellent food and vintage "roadside Americana" décor (including the front of an old car "stuck" into a dining room). Lots of interesting stores are in the area.

West of the colorful, former "Santa Fe" RR underpass is colorful downtown. The city center can be congested (**RV ALERT**), but there's much to enjoy. The old Hotel Alvarado is gone (a replica serves as a transport center) but the Hotel Andaluz (formerly La Posada De Albuquerque) reopened as a "boutique hotel" with 107 rooms and suites at 125 2nd St. (505) 242-9090 Park and walk the downtown streets (see **NM page-13**). City INFO: (505) 842-9918 (also see **NM page-29** for **PRE-1937 66**).

EB: Follow **Central Ave** from downtown **ALBUQUERQUE**, under I-25, for 8 mi to the Tramway Blvd intersection (near EXIT 167).
NM page-12

WB: From downtown, follow **West Central Ave** thru the traffic circle and then across the Rio Grande. **RV ALERT**: tight streets at circle

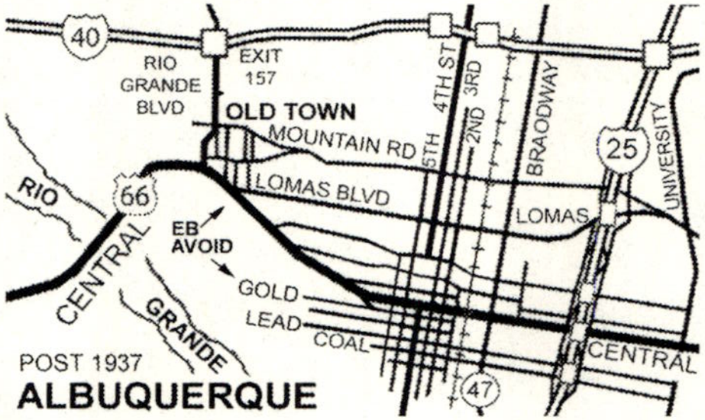

While downtown, be sure to see the restored **KiMo Theatre** at 423 Central. Built in 1927, this showplace embodies "**Pueblo Deco**" style, a mix of Southwestern and Art Deco style with Indian motifs, plus cow skulls, murals and even "Swastikas" (they pre-dated WW II). Self-guided tours of the fantastic interior are available on weekdays, guided tours by appt. Check at http://www.cabq.gov/kimo/ for a virtual tour and info on performances, or call (505) 768-3522. **SCAVENGER HUNT**! Who's **NAME** on the **KiMo** Building plaque out front?________

Across from the **KiMo** in the next block west is **Maisel's Indian Jewelry** (circa 1939), a most authentic place to shop for turquoise and silver goodies. Down the street, a rope-twirling neon cowpoke leans languidly on the **Avalon Restaurant** sign. Headed west, another rope-wielding cowboy spurs his neon stallion from atop the recently restored **El Don Motel** sign. "***Route 66** New Mexico*" (Fall, 2003) gave them a good review, so you might check 'em out before deciding. Yet more neon action is at the **Dog House** (1216 central), where a wiener dog happily wags his neon tail while scarfing hot dogs.

Old Town (north on Rio Grande Blvd) is the site of "**Villa De Albuquerque,**" founded in 1706 and grown into a classic Spanish plaza with over 150 shops and restaurants, plus several museums, including the **American International Rattlesnake Museum**. **GIFT SHOP ALERT**: "skins and fangs!"(www.rattlesnakes.com). Check out **The National Museum of Nuclear Science & History**, at 601 Eubank Blvd. SE and Southern Blvd, six blocks south of Central Ave, for the "Story of the Atomic Age" from Madam Curie thru the Cold War. **GIFT SHOP ALERT**! The museum store once offered mushroom cloud t -shirts! nuclearmuseum.org/ The **Dining and Lodging Guide** lists many motels in town, but the only one I stay at is the great **Monterrey Non Smokers Motel** at 2402 Central (near Old Town). Clean, quiet and attractive rooms plus a vintage neon sign, too! (shortcut: use EXIT 157(A) south from I-40, then right) (505) 243-3554. Closer to the Rio, the currently vacant 1937 **El Vado Motel** was endangered, but is being saved. The beautiful neon sign will be restored.

(see NM page-29 for Pre-1937 66)

EB: Cross the river on **Central Ave**. Stay in the right lane to **AVOID** Lomas. Follow **Central Ave** thru the traffic circle to downtown. **RV ALERT:** tight streets at circle

WB: Take **Central** for 6 mi from the river. At **EXIT 149 (Paseo del Volcan)**, turn **RIGHT** with the sign "East Santa Rosa" but **AVOID** the on ramp: cross I-40 ("To Frontage Rd"). Turn **LEFT** on the **N Frontage Rd**, then join **I-40 WEST** at **EXIT 140** (**RIO PUERCO**). Go past **EXIT 126** (ignore H-66 sign…**PRE-37 rejoins**). Take **EXIT 117** at **MESITA**. Turn **RIGHT** from the ramp, then first **LEFT**.

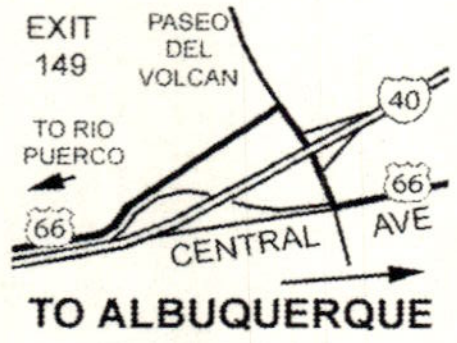

Across the river, **ALBUQUERQUE** struggles westward for a ways, finally petering out on the sandy slope of "**Nine Mile Hill**," another gritty urban area. Many old motels on this faded section of Central Ave lost the struggle and were demolished, but a few soldier on. Notable visually is the **Westward Ho Motel** at 7500 Central, with its brilliant green saguaro cactus sign. I stayed here as a kid, and will always have a soft spot for this place. **Mac's La Sierra Coffee Shop** has a cute sign depicting a bull sitting in a basket of French fries and biscuits, hawking their specialty "Steak in the Rough." The high ground west of town offers a grand view, as twilight fades to night and the city lights fill the valley below, with the **Sandia Mountains** forming a glowing backdrop. **Enchanted Trails RV Park & Trading Post**, on the tour west of EXIT 149 on the north side, is a great RV stop (or stay in a vintage trailer). enchantedtrails.com

At **RIO PUERCO**, stop and walk across the preserved **1933 Rio Puerco Bridge**. **SCAVENGER HUNT**! Who ERECTED this "**Parker Through-truss**" bridge?" Multiple **GIANT ALERT**: Across I-40 waits Laguna Pueblo's Giant **Route 66 Casino**, behind the huge "**neon gas pump sign**" and the **giant arrows** in the parking lot. Inside, the faux '66 theme continues, with **Johnny Rockets Diner** (that evokes **TEXAS'** U Drop Inn), **Kicks Café**, and more. Also inside (where he's safe from giant arrowheads) is **BIG TEX**, in front of the **Hungry Cowboy Café**. Like, totally Hollywood.

HWY 6, the **Pre-1937 OPTION**, connects to/from **LOS LUNAS** at EXIT 126 (**EB**: **DECIDE NOW**!) South of this exit, older 66 crossed the RR overpass near **CORREO**. This old road continues west across **Laguna Pueblo** lands to **MESITA** (crossing over I-40 east of EXIT 117) but is **ROUGH** and partly unpaved, so it's NOT a part of the tour (respect Pueblo rules, and don't trespass when driving across their land). The tour route follows **I-40** along the path of the **1950s 4-lane 66**.

EB: From **MESITA**, join **EAST I-40** past **EXIT 126** (see **Pre-1937 OPTION** NM page-30). Take **EXIT 140** (**RIO PUERCO**), and join the **N Frontage Rd** to **EXIT 149**. Cross I-40, then turn **LEFT** onto **Central Ave**, for 6 mi to the Rio Grande in **ALBUQUERQUE**.

(see MAP # 3 NM page-9)

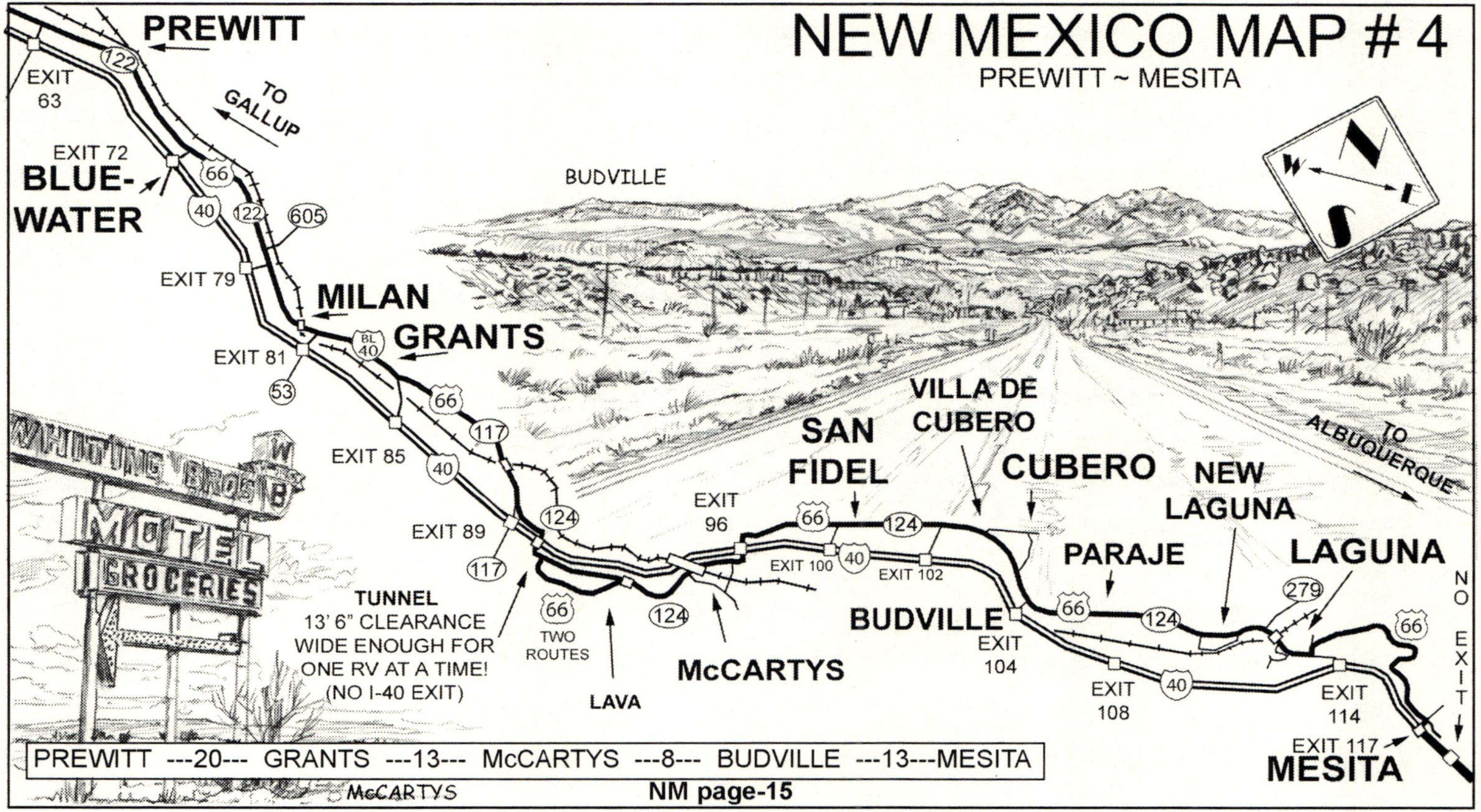
NEW MEXICO MAP # 4
PREWITT ~ MESITA
PREWITT
TO GALLUP
EXIT 63
EXIT 72
BLUE-WATER
EXIT 79
BUDVILLE
MILAN
GRANTS
EXIT 81
EXIT 85
EXIT 89
TUNNEL
13' 6" CLEARANCE
WIDE ENOUGH FOR
ONE RV AT A TIME!
(NO I-40 EXIT)
TWO ROUTES
LAVA
McCARTYS
EXIT 96
SAN FIDEL
EXIT 100
EXIT 102
VILLA DE CUBERO
CUBERO
BUDVILLE
EXIT 104
PARAJE
NEW LAGUNA
EXIT 108
LAGUNA
EXIT 114
EXIT 117
MESITA
NO EXIT
TO ALBUQUERQUE
WHITING BROS
MOTEL
GROCERIES
McCARTYS
PREWITT ---20--- GRANTS ---13--- McCARTYS ---8--- BUDVILLE ---13---MESITA
NM page-15

WB: From **MESITA**, take the **Frontage Rd** (**"Old Rte 66"**) for 5 mi to **LAGUNA** (follow the curves away from I-40, and around "Dead Man's Curve.") Nearing town, follow the sharp **LEFT** turn, then **RIGHT** onto **HWY 124**, thru **LAGUNA**. Stay with **HWY 124**, past **NEW LAGUNA**, **PARAJE**, and **BUDVILLE** (near EXIT 104), then continue past **VILLA CUBERO** (about 11 mi from **LAGUNA**).

From **MESITA**, the route still traverses **Laguna Pueblo Land**, so be a good guest and obey posted rules about cameras, trespassing, etc. This quality drive takes you off I-40 for over 20 miles. West of MESITA, the road curves past a mesa that I-40 (and 4-lane 66) blasted thru. **GIANT ALERT**! Suddenly, up looms the large lava outcrop known as "**Owl Rock.**" Next is notorious "**Dead Man's Curve**," a looong tight loop around a narrow point of rock that SURELY deserved the name.

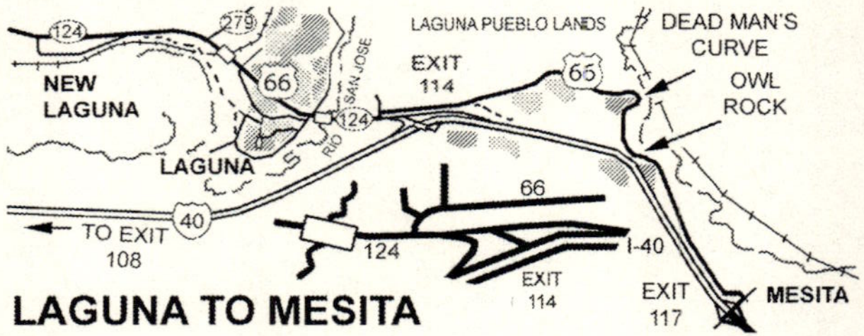

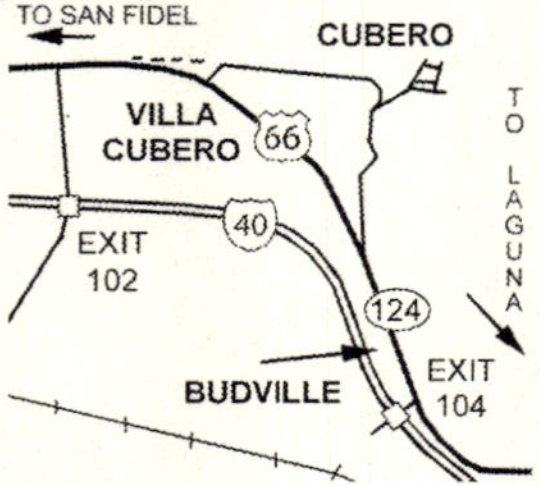

More curves await uphill (**WB**), before the drop into old **LAGUNA**. Topping the ancient village is **San Jose Mission**; built in 1699 (a pullout from I-40 south of town offers an excellent view). "DIRT" 66 followed an abandoned **AT&SF RR** grade around the base of the hill (now a paved street), while the paved 2-lane ran above town. For info on annual events: (505) 552-6654. Santa Fe Blvd ("L 50") carried earlier 66 along RR tracks thru neighboring **NEW LAGUNA**. Current **HWY 124** is a nice, peaceful drive thru the rocky hills, among rock buildings scattered around the Pueblo. Just west of Encinal Rd, an ancient concrete bridge is visible to the north, in the deep gully.

Outside the Pueblo is **BUDVILLE**, home of the **Budville Trading Co** (since 1928). Beyond the boulder-strewn hills, mighty **Mt Taylor** dominates the horizon. US 66 bypassed the small village of **CUBERO** in 1937, while the current road curves past **Villa Cubero Trading Post,** a 1937 "Mediterranean Revival" structure still selling groceries and gas (listen to the "ding-ding" of the driveway bell). It's reported that **Hemingway** (maybe) wrote "***The Old Man and the Sea***" in the old cafe. Or, maybe not. Another Route 66 mystery.

EB: From **VILLA CUBERO**, follow **HWY 124** past **BUDVILLE** (near EXIT 104), **PARAJE** and **NEW LAGUNA**, then over the RR tracks. Continue 1.2 mi, thru **LAGUNA** (crossing Rio San Jose bridge) then turn **LEFT** (signs: "Laguna School/Historic 66"): **AVOID** joining I-40. Follow "**Old Rte 66**" for 5 mi as it curves around "Dead Man's Curve," then join **EAST I-40** at **EXIT 117** in **MESITA**.

WB: Take **HWY 124** thru **SAN FIDEL**. Cross **OVER** I-40 at **EXIT 96 (**sign: "TO EAST I-40") but stay with **HWY 124** on the south side, past **McCARTYS** and under the RR. Curve sharply **UNDER** I-40 (**RV ALERT**-narrow tunnel-but passable) then sharply out on the north. Turn **RIGHT** onto **HWY 117** (at EXIT 89... about 7.4 mi from EXIT 96)

Many local drivers give friendly waves here on the **Acoma Reservation**. This is a quiet stretch of lonely road, past the remains of the **Mt Taylor Motel** (now a stable) towards **SAN FIDEL**. Quite charming is **St Josephs' Church**, a small stucco chapel with two blue, horn-tooting cherubs flanking the door. The ramshackle **White Arrow Garage** is a remnant. West of town, near EXIT 96, the ruins of a former **Whiting Bros** gas station continue to decay.

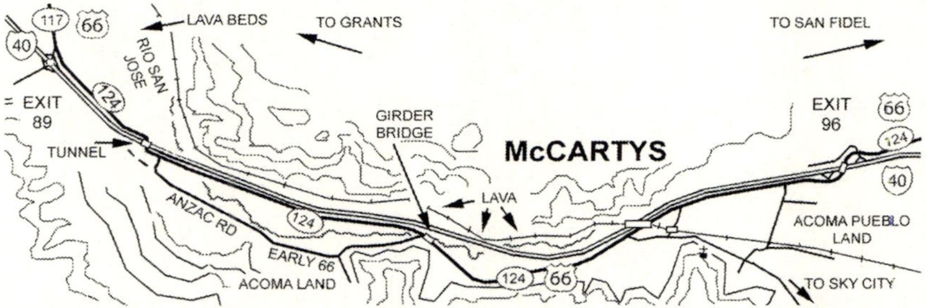

SIDE TRIP: At **McCARTYS**, "Route 38" runs south to **Acoma Mesa** and "**Sky City**," termed the oldest continuously inhabited city in the country, perched hundreds of feet above the valley floor and site of the **San Esteban Del Rey Mission**, built between 1629-1640. Also accessed south from EXIT 102 or EXIT 108. Call (800) 747-0181 for tour info (including a one hour guided walking-tour). **NOTE:** Photo permits are needed on the **Acoma** lands (sccc.acomaskycity.org/guidelines)

Back in **McCARTYS**, the stone **Santa Maria de Acoma Church**, perched on the hillside above the RR tracks, resembles Acoma's mission. HWY 124 gives a good view. The rough lava flows along here ("**malpais**") hinderéd early travel thru this narrow valley.
OPTION: **Early 66** skirted the south side of the lava beds, running alongside a small working aquaduct on **Anzac Rd** (not a water park, so don't trespass). This road veers southwest from just west of the **small girder bridge** over **Rio San Jose**, then reconnects just east of the I-40 tunnel. See the map for details.

EB: From **HWY 117**, turn **LEFT**, just **BEFORE** EXIT 89, onto **HWY 124**, and continue along the north side of I-40. Curve sharply **UNDER** I-40 (**RV ALERT**-narrow tunnel-but passable) and curve **LEFT** on the south side. Stay with **HWY 124**, under the RR and past **McCARTYS**. At **EXIT 96**, cross I-40, and stay with **HWY 124** thru **SAN FIDEL** and **VILLA CUBERO** (6.6 mi from EXIT 96)

WB: Follow **HWY 117** across the RR to **GRANTS** (5 mi). Merge **AHEAD** onto **BL 40** on the east side, and continue thru town 2.7 mi, thru the HWY 53 light (near EXIT 81). Continue ahead on **HWY 122** for 18.6 mi, thru **MILAN** and **BLUEWATER** to **PREWITT.**

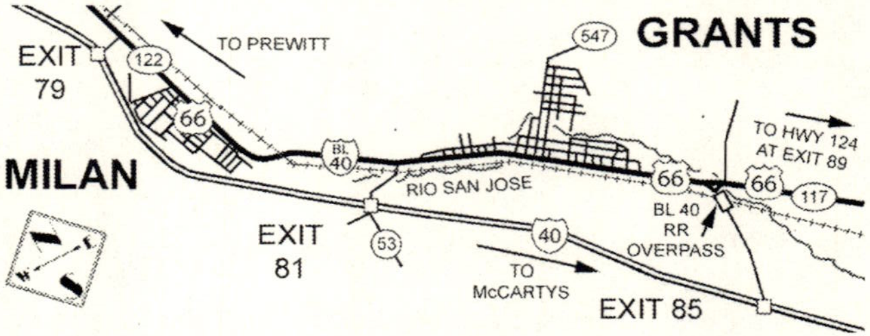

GRANTS offers you the chance to "Go Underground," at the **New Mexico Mining Museum**. Cold war era uranium mining was big in the region, and this facility recreates a typical mine (one story underground) plus fossil and Route 66 exhibits 800-748 2142. On the other extreme, the railroad tracks run **higher** than most of the motel roofs along '66. Radioactive lore was honored in the name of the **Uranium Café**, now the **Badland Burgers**.
There's still some good neon in town, while some are now dark, like the recently restored **Grants Café** sign (now closed). Among the signs to look for (bright or busted): Franciscan Lodge, the West and Lux Theatres, and **Pat's Bar** (which will be restored!). For vintage lodging try the **Sands Motel** (Elvis stayed here) (505) 287 2996 or the nearby **South West Motel** (505) 287 7901. Both have nice neon signs.

The **Northwest New Mexico Visitor Center**, just south of I-40 at EXIT 85, provides info on area attractions. **SIDE TRIP**: 25 miles southwest of EXIT 81 on HWY 53 is **Bandera Volcano and Ice cave**, where blue-green ice survives year round in a lava cave. (888) ICE-CAVE www.icecaves.com

MILAN is usually a good place to fill up your tank. Numerous remnants of old motels, garages and trading posts line the west side of old 66 (4-lane for much of the way) thru **BLUEWATER** to **PREWITT**. Faded murals of Indian life still decorate the former Bowlins "Old Crater" Trading Post (their "Running Indian" mascot barely clings to cracked stucco).

EB: From **PREWITT**, take **HWY 122** for 18.6 mi, thru **BLUEWATER** and **MILAN**, into **GRANTS**. Go 2.7 mi past the HWY 53 light, then, just **BEFORE** reaching the BL 40 railroad overpass, turn **LEFT** and curve onto **HWY 117**(Historic 66). Follow **HWY 117** for 5 mi towards EXIT 89.

see MAP 4 NM page-15)

NEW MEXICO MAP # 5 & 5A

LUPTON, AZ ~ PREWITT

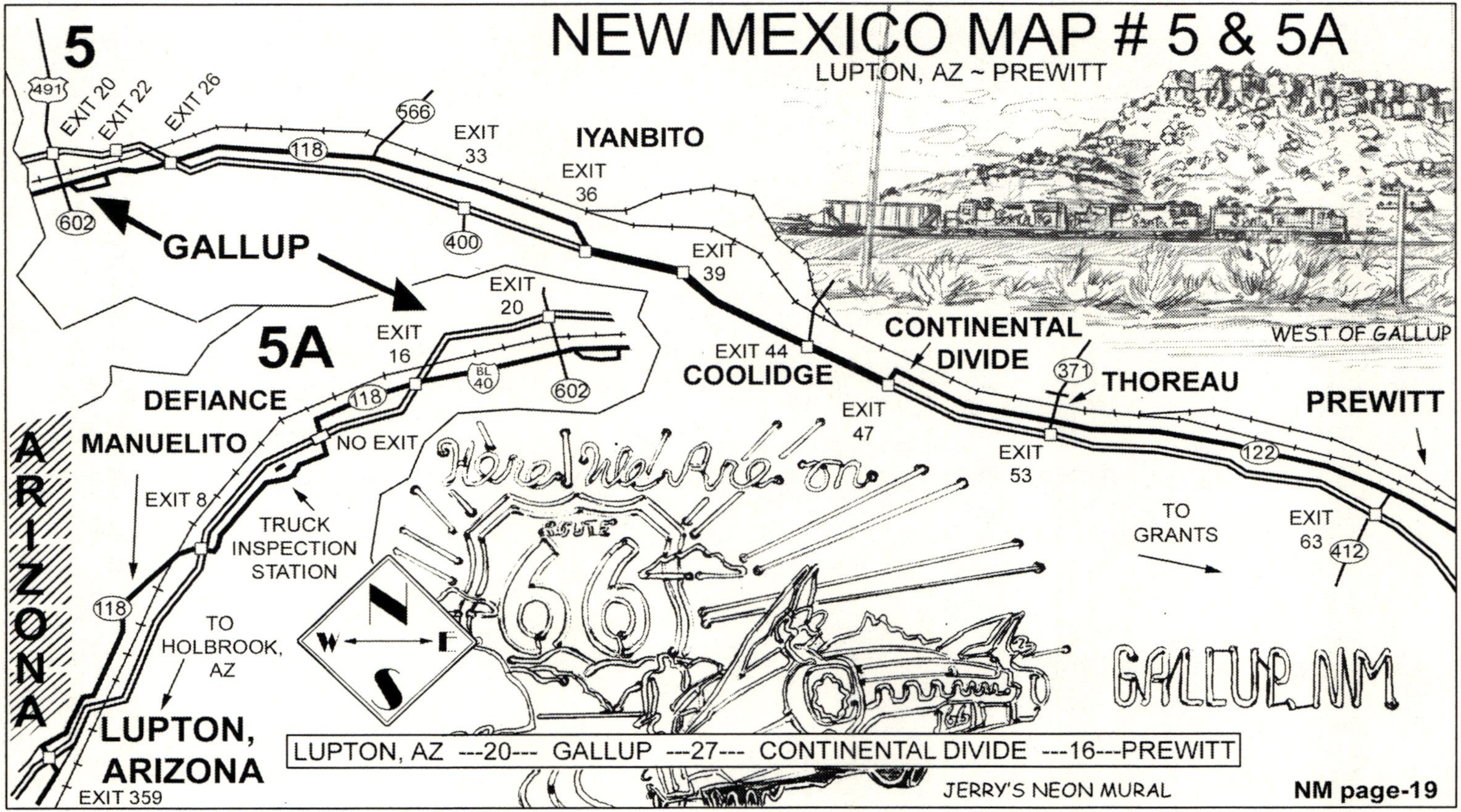

LUPTON, AZ ---20--- GALLUP ---27--- CONTINENTAL DIVIDE ---16---PREWITT

WB: Stay with **HWY 122** for 15 mi from **PREWITT**, past **THOREAU** to **CONTINENTAL DIVIDE**. Here, join **WEST I-40** at **EXIT 47**. Take **EXIT 36** (**IYANBITO**) and follow **HWY 118** along the north side of I-40, then under **EXIT 26** into **GALLUP** with **BL 40**.

East of **PREWITT**, a small building covered in hubcaps was once home to "**Swap Meet 66**". On the west end of town, near EXIT 63 is the hot pink facade of the Quonset hut that is **Tomahawk Bar**. To the west, peek carefully thru each railroad trestle for several glimpses of old bridges along abandoned "**Dirt 66**" north of the tracks (don't trespass). Along here is where Route 66 begins to parallel a long row of pink-tinged cliffs and hills. These provide a majestic backdrop all the way thru **LUPTON**, **ARIZONA.**

At the side road to **THOREAU** (HWY 371), sits the **Red Mountain Market and Deli**. Just west is **Herman's Garage**, a pre-fab steel service station (now stuck to a stucco garage) first erected in 1931 in **GALLUP** and moved to **THOREAU** later. A mile west are the remains of an old trading post, notable for its mural of a flying hawk and pink cliffs. Next up is the **Thunderbird Bar**, then comes confusing **CONTINENTAL DIVIDE**. Confusing, because the elevation is variously given from 7263 to 7,275 feet, and because it is often claimed to be the highest point on 66. Points in AZ and NM are higher! Anyway, a marker here (**PHOTO OP**!) marks the divide separating the water drainage to the **Pacific** from that which drains into the **Gulf of Mexico**. Trading posts have long balanced here on the backbone of the land, to divide tourists from their wampum (you've been seeing the classic billboards for miles). A "Historic 66" sign atop a "**DEAD END**" marker made a poignant juxtaposition. Along this spur is a former **Whiting Bros** motel and station.

An old "**Dirt 66**" route existed between the RR tracks from **COOLIDGE** to **IYANBITO** (continuing the early road from **PREWITT**). Stick to I-40 past the huge travel center, to EXIT 36. The final run into **GALLUP** provides a nice panorama of colorful rock cliffs and spires, including **Church Rock**, and **Red Rock State Park and Museum**, north on HWY 566 and host to the **Inter Tribal Indian Ceremonial**, an annual celebration of Native Americans. www.theceremonial.com

EB: On **GALLUP**'s east side, follow **HWY 118** under I-40 (**EXIT 26**), and continue to **EXIT 36** (**IYANBITO**). Here, join **EAST I-40** to take **EXIT 47** (**CONTINENTAL DIVIDE**). Cross over, then **RIGHT** on **HWY 122** for 15 mi, past **THOREAU**, to **PREWITT**.

WB: Follow **BL 40 (Route 66)** thru **GALLUP** for about 9 mi. On the west side, cross under I-40 at EXIT 16. Continue with **HWY 118**.

The sharp, slanted ridge of the **Hogback** slashes across east **GALLUP**. The narrow breach in this barrier made the city a target for nukes during the heat of the **Cold War** (one bomb could take out US 66, the RR, pipelines and communications).

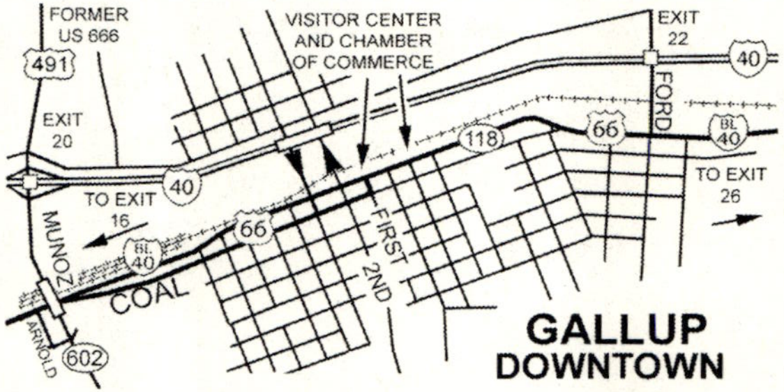

Despite the cold war's passing, there remains much evidence of old 66, including many old motels (some with nice neon) like the Blue Spruce and Lariat. Many hotel and café signs also survive. An oldie but goodie is historic 1937 **El Rancho Hotel** with its impressive lobby and rooms named after movie star guests (800) 543-6351.

GALLUP has a profusion of trading posts and galleries and public art, including the **neon mural** designed by the author: "**Here We are On Route 66, Gallup NM**" depicting a pink '59 Caddy headed into a Route 66 neon sunset, atop the **Chamber of Commerce Bldg** on **BL 40** downtown. (Hard to see from the road-park in the free lot and walk). Nearby is the **Gallup Cultural Center** in the Amtrak station, with a "Welcome" Hogan (Navajo house) and FREE parking (convenient for a stroll downtown). The rail action at the train yard is still visible, but the scene is framed and screened by decorative red fences. On the west side of downtown, the **Rex Museum** (great neon sign) offers local history, including the coal mining days, the WWII saga of the Navajo code talkers, and Rte 66 of course. City INFO: www.GallupNM.org

OPTION: Old 66 turned south on **First St,** then followed **Coal St** thru downtown (see the map). This narrow street later carried "one way" traffic WB, but is 2-way again, past cafes, shops and the **El Morrow Theatre**. Double back and drive both sections thru downtown.

GIANT ALERTS! Days past, postcards promoted the town with images of a **GIANT YELLOW KACHINA** on the east side (a smaller one said "Hurry Back", on the west). A similar (if not identical) giant now stands north of I-40 at 827 J M Montoya Blvd, just west of Miyamura (EXIT 22). Also, at Coal and 5th St. a **GIANT MUFFLER-MAN COWBOY** stands proud at John's Used Cars.

EB: Follow **HWY 118/Route 66** under I-40, joining **BL 40** into **GALLUP** for about 9 mi.

WB: Follow **Hwy 118** for 3.5 miles. Turn **LEFT** (in **<u>DEFIANCE</u>**) with the **HWY 118** sign. Cross under I-40 and quick-turn **RIGHT** with **HWY 118**. Continue for 4.3 mi. Curve under I-40 at **EXIT 8** (AVOID on ramps), and stay with **HWY 118** thru **<u>MANUELITO</u>**, to the **<u>ARIZONA</u>** state line and **EXIT 359** at **<u>LUPTON</u>** (about 9 mi from EXIT 8). (see **AZ page-1 to <u>continue</u> WB**)

<u>RV ADVISORY</u>: the HWY 118 "underpass tunnel" at EXIT 8 is a bit tight, so use care. **BIKES**: watch for cattleguards.

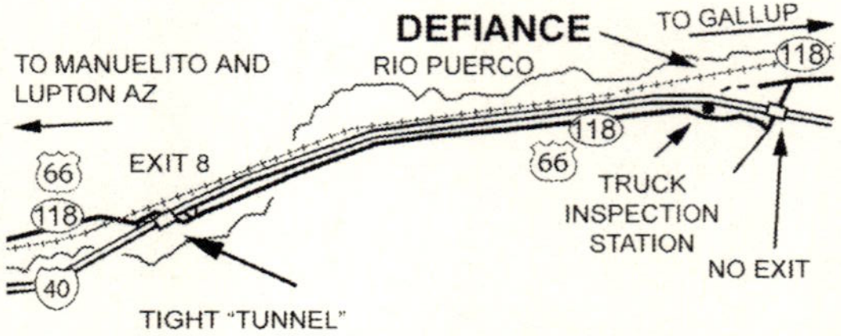

Route 66 makes one last scenic break from I-40 before hitting the state line, passing thru **<u>MANUELITO</u>**, which is marked by the ruins of **Mike Kirk Trading Post**. Headed west, the road climbs and clings to the sheer side of **Devil's Cliff**, beneath boulders balanced precariously above (a mesh fence offers protection). Ahead is a grand view of '66, the RR and the Rio Puerco as they squeeze between rugged mesas into **ARIZONA**.

Near milepost 4 are faded remnants of various old-time advertisements painted on the rock walls by canny businessmen, including "**Rocky Point Trading Post Navajo Rugs Homemade Jewelry**," one of the many old enterprises that formerly lined this stretch (no <u>new</u> graffiti, please). Another, the **Cliff Dwelling Trading Post** (as it was last known), was located a bit further west, in front of a big hollow in the rock face. Fake cliff dwellings were an attraction, built for the 1951 movie, "***Ace in the Hole***" starring **Kirk Douglas**, that was filmed here.

The true path of old 66 is lost just before reaching **<u>ARIZONA</u>**, buried where **HWY 118** curves to avoid I-40, but the faux fort at **Chief Yellowhorse's** is the latest in a long line of tourist enterprises at what has been variously called "**Cave of the Seven Devils**" or "**Millers Cave**." Yet another "cliff dwelling" waits within the cave-like opening in the ruddy cliff. Excited signs hawk **WILD BUFFALO**, along with blankets and sand paintings.

<u>TO CONTINUE WB</u>: see **AZ page-1** (SKIP the **<u>Pre-1937 "Santa Fe Loop</u>**" section that follows).

NOTE: **<u>ARIZONA</u>** doesn't follow Daylight Savings Time (check your watches locally).

EB: From **EXIT 359** at **<u>LUPTON</u>**, **<u>ARIZONA</u>**, follow **HWY 118** for 9 mi (thru **<u>MANUELITO</u>**). Curve under I-40 at **EXIT 8** (AVOID onramps), and continue with **HWY 118** for 4.3 mi (past the truck inspection station). At **Salt Water Wash Rd**, turn **LEFT**. Cross under I-40, then turn **RIGHT** with **HWY 118**, for 3.5 mi, to cross under I-40 at **EXIT 16** on the west side of **<u>GALLUP</u>**.
(see **NM INTRO NM page-1.**)

(see **MAP 5&5A NM page-19**)

OVERVIEW

PRE-1937 ROUTE 66

NM pages-24 thru 30

DASHED LINES = IMPASSABLE, ROUGH OR PRIVATE

"SANTA FE LOOP"

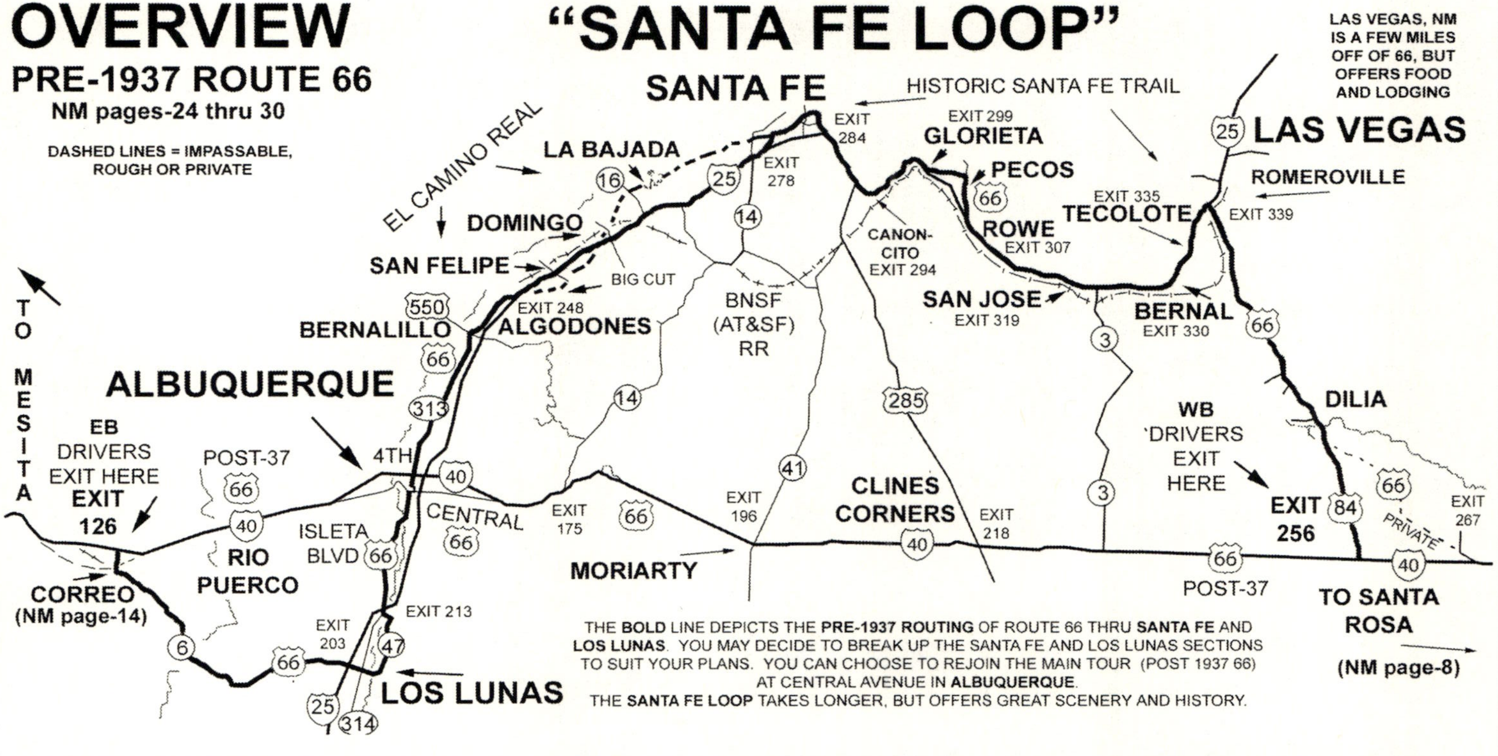

THE **BOLD** LINE DEPICTS THE **PRE-1937 ROUTING** OF ROUTE 66 THRU **SANTA FE** AND **LOS LUNAS**. YOU MAY DECIDE TO BREAK UP THE SANTA FE AND LOS LUNAS SECTIONS TO SUIT YOUR PLANS. YOU CAN CHOOSE TO REJOIN THE MAIN TOUR (POST 1937 66) AT CENTRAL AVENUE IN **ALBUQUERQUE**.
THE **SANTA FE LOOP** TAKES LONGER, BUT OFFERS GREAT SCENERY AND HISTORY.

CORREO ---36-- LOS LUNAS ---23--- ALBUQUERQUE ---59--- SANTA FE ---57--- ROMEOVILLE ---41---EXIT 256

Take **I-40 WB** from **SANTA ROSA**. At **EXIT 256**, follow **US 84** north 41.5 mi (thru **DILIA**) to I-25/**EXIT 339** (**ROMEROVILLE**). Cross, then **LEFT** on **Frontage Rd** for 19.4 mi (past **TECOLOTE**, **BERNAL** & **SAN JOSE**). Cross I-25 at **EXIT 319**.

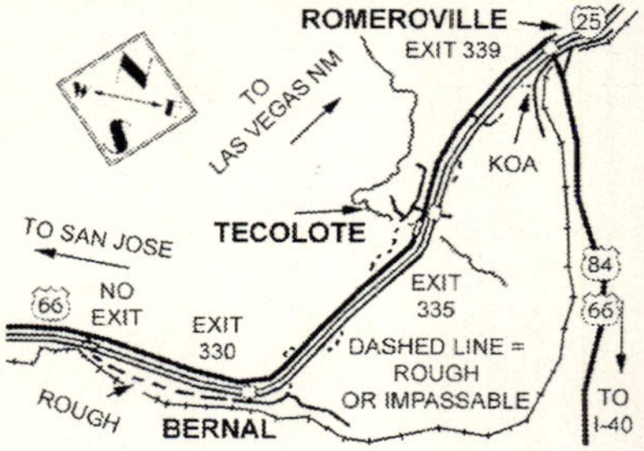

"**Dirt 66**" lies stranded off the current route along **US 84** between I-40 and **DILIA**. North of town, **US 84** overlays old 66: a peaceful, scenic drive. At I-25/**EXIT 339**, old **US 85** (frontage road) takes over.
SIDE TRIP 1: From **US 84**, @ 0.7 mi south from I-25 EXIT 339, **ROUGH** "Dirt 66" veers right, to cross the RR at grade in **ROMEROVILLE** (avoid if muddy). Head back west to EXIT 339.
SIDE TRIP 2: The old road (now blacktop) continues west from the south side of EXIT 339 as **Sheridan Rd** (some potholes). From the **KOA** (a nice setting for camping), a rough dirt road heads west a short way, to end at a charming **concrete post bridge** in a quiet canyon (**PRIVATE PROPERTY**, so ask at the **KOA** beforehand). (505) 454 0180

There's a trace or two of old 66 on the way to **TECOLOTE** (EXIT 335). **Historic NOTE**: A **DEAD END** section (POSTED **NO TRESSPASSING**) curves thru the plaza, past a tin-roofed adobe church and **Santa Fe Trail Marker**, to END at a defunct bridge, whose supports can be seen from the 1940-era US 85 bridge west of town. Old 66 consists mostly of inaccessible fragments west to **BERNAL**.

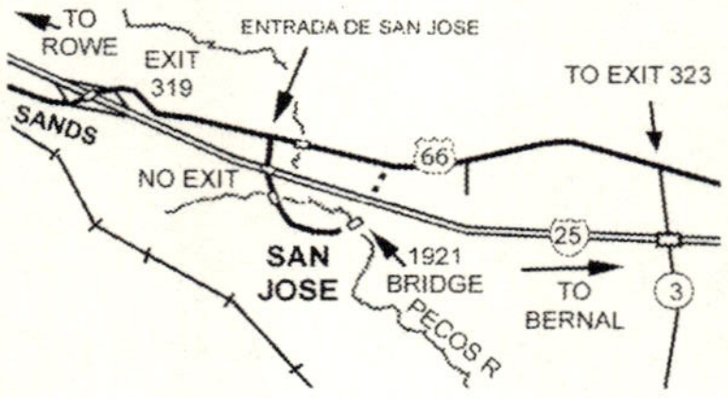

SIDE TRIP 3: Here, south from **EXIT 330**, a short, dead-end paved section heads LEFT, past an old store and a 1916-era church. **Starvation Peak**, a tragic **Santa Fe Trail** landmark, haunts the skyline.
SIDE TRIP 4: **West** from **EXIT 330**, on the **south** side, the pavement on **B 26A** turns to **ROUGH** dirt along the RR for about 4 miles, then squeezes thru a tunnel under I-25 to rejoin the **N Frontage Rd (**for die-hard Route-Buffs ONLY…avoid when muddy).
SAN JOSE SIDE TRIP: 1.8 mi **WEST** of **HWY 3** and 0.8 mi **EAST** of **EXIT 319**: On the west side of the **Pecos River**, turn south on **Entrada de San Jose**, and pass under I-25 (mixed dirt/pave). Curve thru town, past the 1826 plaza church, to the closed **1921 thru-truss bridge**, then retrace your path.

EB: Cross I-25 at **EXIT 319**, and follow the **N Frontage Road** for 19.4 mi (past **SAN JOSE**, **BERNAL** and **TECOLOTE**). At **EXIT 339** (**ROMEROVILLE**) cross I-25. Take **US 84** for 41.5 mi (thru **DILIA**) to I-40 **EXIT 256**. Join **EAST I-40** to **SANTA ROSA**. (**END** of **PRE-1937 OPTION**: to continue **EB** see **NM page-8**)

WB: From **EXIT 319**, continue 12.5 mi on **South Frontage Rd**, past **SANDS** and **ILFIELD** to **ROWE**. Turn **RIGHT**, cross under I-25(**EXIT 307**), and follow **HWY 63** for 5.6 mi north to **PECOS**. At **HWY 50**, turn **LEFT**. Go 6 mi to **GLORIETA**. Join **WEST I-25 (EXIT 299)**. Take **EXIT 294/CANONCITO**. **RIGHT**, then **LEFT** on **Old Las Vegas Hwy**, for 10 mi (past US 285) to **SANTA FE**.

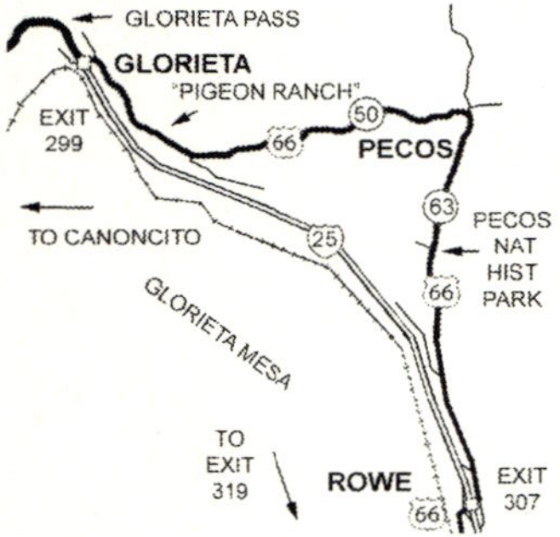

This is another scenic stretch, backstopped by long, tree-covered **Glorieta Mesa**. There's not much to the quiet towns here. **ILFIELD** has just a gas/grocery, while in **ROWE** is long shuttered E.T. Padilla's Grocery and Victory Bar, mainly notable for the faded painting of a beer bottle and foaming glass. South of **PECOS** is **Pecos National Historic Park**, home to the ruins of a pueblo and mission church. This area saw some heavy **Civil War** action. On **Hwy 50**, about a mile east of **GLORIETA**, the **Pigeon Ranch** ruins crowd the east side of the road. Inside (peek but don't enter) are old brands written on walls of this old stage stop, site of a battle between Union and Confederate troops in 1862.

Northwest of **GLORIETA** (famous for the Baptist Conference) is **Glorieta Pass**, at over 7,500 feet the **highest point on '66** (Pre-1937).

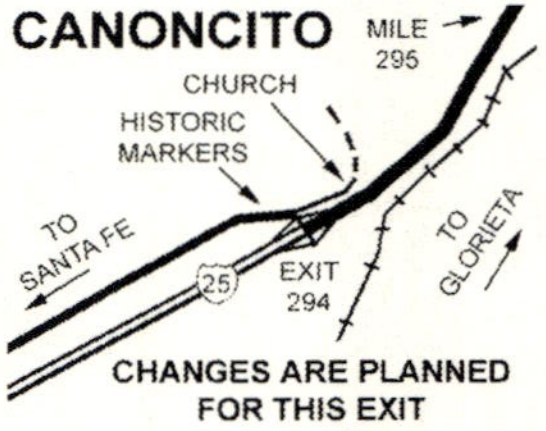

For **EB travelers**: just east of milepost 295 at a wide spot on the south shoulder (**CAUTION**: **NOT** an official pull-off…stop at own risk) is "**Glorieta, Gettysburg of the West**." **FOLK ART ALERT**! This sincere assemblage pays homage to the victims of the battle of March 26, 1862, when Union forces wiped out a Confederate supply train. Included are a mock burial (with feet sticking out) and an improvised canon, plus many, many signs. West, the road and railroad squeeze thru **Apache Canyon** to **CANONCITO**, site of another classic chapel (on the dead end east). **SCAVENGER HUNT!** At the turn to **EXIT 294** is a small **Santa Fe Trail Marker**. What **YEAR** was the marker dedicated? The current drive up towards **SANTA FE** parallels I-25, past **Bobcat Bite** and **Harry's Roadhouse**, longtime popular roadside stops.

WB and EB NOTE: Changes are planned for EXIT 294 at CANONCITO.

EB: Take **Old Las Vegas Hwy** for 10 mi (past US 285). At **CANONCITO**, join **EAST I-25** at **EXIT 294**. Take **EXIT 299 (GLORIETA)**, cross I-25 & turn **RIGHT** on **HWY 50**. Go 6 mi (ignore CO RD 63), then **RIGHT** on **NM HWY 63** thru **PECOS**. Go 5.6 mi, cross under I-25 (EXIT 307) & **LEFT** on the **S Frontage Rd** thru **ROWE**. Go 12.5 mi, past **ILFIELD** and **SANDS** to EXIT 319.

WB: Turn **RIGHT** on **Old Pecos Trail/HWY 466** (near EXIT 284). Go 1.2 mi, then bear **RIGHT** with **Old Pecos Trail**. After 1.6 mi, merge **AHEAD** onto **Old Santa Fe Trail**. Go 0.6 mi to **Alameda St**. <u>NOTE</u>: **<u>Before</u>** reaching **Alameda**, **<u>READ the OPTION</u>** or **<u>park and walk.</u>** See **<u>parking info below</u>**. Afterward, take **Alameda** back west to **Galisteo**. Turn **LEFT** (southwest) to leave **SANTA FE**.

<u>RV ALERT</u>! Streets downtown are very narrow and crowded: turns are tight. Park and walk. Busses go to area attractions (check locally). **<u>EVERYONE</u>**: **Paid-Parking lots** are on **Water St**, east of Don Gaspar and on **Alameda**, just east of **Cathedral Pl** (**<u>RV parking here</u>**). Metered street parking if you are lucky. The one-way streets are confusing, <u>expect</u> to get lost! **More INFO: see NM page-27**.

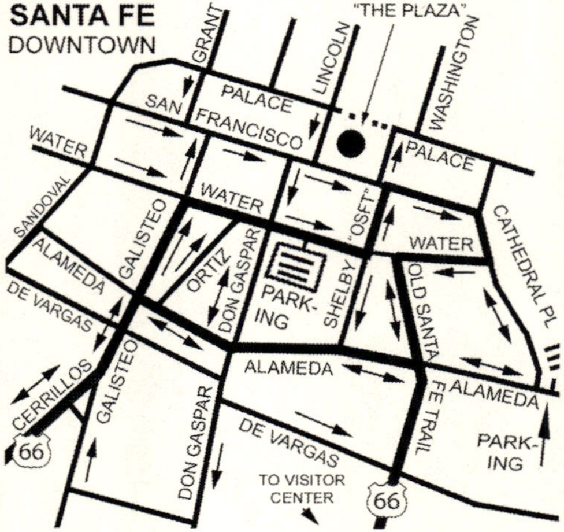

<u>Driving OPTION</u>: (see **MAP** on left) **EB**: continue on **Galisteo** across Alameda. **WB: LEFT** on **Alameda,** then **RIGHT** on **Galisteo**. Then **<u>BOTH</u>** turn **RIGHT** on **Water St**. **LEFT** on **Old Santa Fe Trail** (OSFT). **RIGHT** onto **San Francisco**. **RIGHT** on **Cathedral Pl**. **RIGHT** on **Water**. **LEFT** on **Old Santa Fe Trail** back to **Alameda**. Rejoin WB or EB tour.

<u>HISTORIC NOTE</u>: An **Early route** (EB) used **Galisteo** to **De Vargas** to **Don Gaspar** to **San Francisco** (but **Don Gaspar** is **One-Way** above **Water** now). Past the Plaza it turned south on **Old Santa Fe Trail** (now also **One-Way**). By **1931**, 66 bypassed the Plaza on **Water St**.

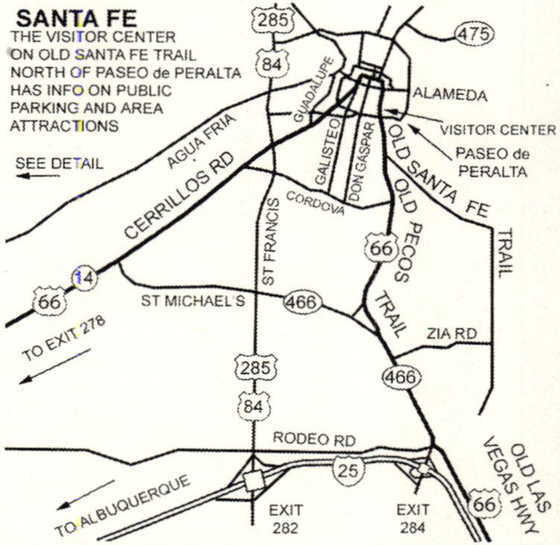

EB: Follow **Galisteo** across De Vargas St to **Alameda St**. **<u>NOTE</u>**: **<u>Before</u>** reaching **Alameda**, **<u>READ the OPTION</u>** or **<u>park and walk.</u>** See **<u>parking info above</u>**. Afterward, follow **Old Santa Fe Trail** south from **Alameda** for 0.6 mi. At the "Y", **BEAR RIGHT** onto **Old Pecos Trail**. Go 1.6 mi. At the stoplight for HWY 466/St Michaels, turn **LEFT** onto **HWY 466/Old Pecos Tr**. Go 1.2 mi (get in the left turn lane after 1.1 mi) to the Rodeo Rd stoplight **BUT** turn **LEFT** onto **Old Las Vegas Hwy** (**BEFORE** reaching I-25 EXIT 284).

WB: Go 2 blocks on **Galisteo**. At the "**Y**" veer **RIGHT** onto **Cerrillos Rd**. Go 0.2 mi. At the **STOP**, **RIGHT** on **Manhattan**, then quick **LEFT** back on **Cerrillos**. Continue 0.5 mi, then stay in the right lanes ("Cerrillos Rd Thru Traffic") thru the St Francis/US 84/285 intersection. **Cerrillos** becomes **HWY 14**. Go 7 more mi, then cross under I-25 (**EXIT 278)** with **HWY 14**. Go almost 2 mi, then **RIGHT** on **HWY 599** (towards EXIT 276) **BUT** quickly turn **LEFT** (next light) onto **Frontage Rd**, and follow it about 9 mi to **EXIT 267**.

NOTE: The Cerrillos Rd/I-25 JCT may change in the future.

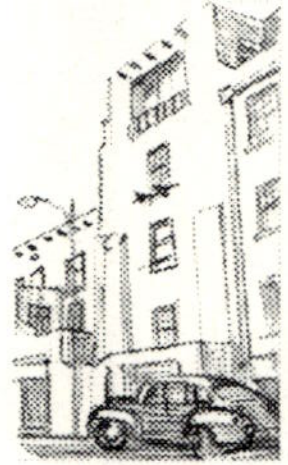

You could spend a lot of time (and cash) in **SANTA FE**, "The City Different" (**SEE**: **Plaza** Directions and city maps on **NM page-26**). The whole city is a "**GIFT SHOP ALERT**!" with numerous shops and galleries, plus a heaping' helping of history. City **INFO**: Visitors Bureau: (505) 955-6200. http://www.santafe.org/ Lodging is more costly on average than in **ALBUQUERQUE**, but the **EL Rey Inn** (1862 Cerrillos) is a good value that dates back to 1936, expanded over the years into a 4.5 acre mini-village with unique atmosphere. (800) 521-1349. The most historic lodging (but pricier) is the **La Fonda Hotel** at 100 E San Francisco (just off the Plaza). Called "The Inn at the End of the Trail," the La Fonda has amazing multi-story adobe-style architecture. Check the **Federation Guide** for more.

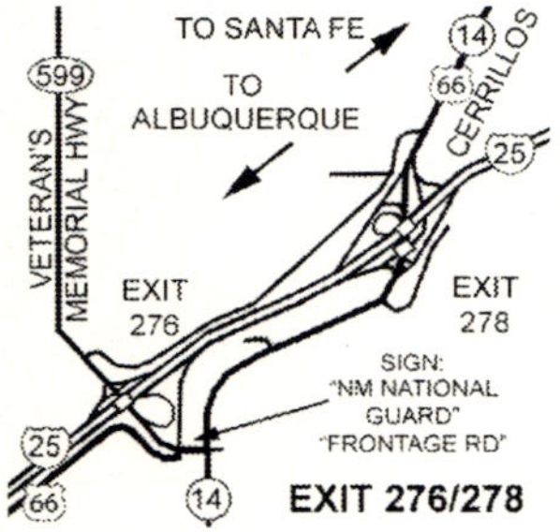

Plaza streets are tight and crowded, so I suggest taking a **Walking Tour** (guided or not) of this compact area. **NOTE**: **SEE RV ALERT** NM page-26. Get brochures and parking info at the **NM Dept of Tourism Visitor Center**, north of Paseo de Peralta at 491 Old Santa Fe Trail, **OR** (if EB) at the **Chamber of Commerce Office and Visitors Center** located in the **Santa Fe Premium Outlets** (Cerrillos Road and I-25). **SANTA FE** brags on its antiquity, with the **OLDEST CHURCH**, **BELL** and **HOUSE** in the United States, all located conveniently near Old 66. Also, see the ornate and mysterious "**miraculous staircase**" at **Loretto Chapel**. "**The Palace of the Governors,**" on the north side of the **Plaza** since 1610, now holds a museum.

EB: Follow the **Frontage Rd** as it curves to stop at **HWY 599**: turn **RIGHT**, then **LEFT** on **HWY 14**. After 2 mi, cross under I-25 at **EXIT 278**, and follow **Cerrillos Rd/HWY 14** into **SANTA FE**. Go almost 7 mi, then stay in the right lane thru the St Francis/ US 84/285 JCT ("Historic Plaza"). Continue 0.5 mi on **Cerrillos**. Be in the RIGHT lane, and continue with **Cerrillos** when Sandoval veers left (at Manhattan). Merge **AHEAD** onto **Galisteo**, towards the plaza. **NOTE**: **see the INFO on OPTION and parking on NM page-26**

WB: At **EXIT 267**/Waldo, you must join **I-25 SOUTH** to **EXIT 248**. Exit here, and go **RIGHT** briefly to **HWY 313**: turn **LEFT**. Continue with **HWY 313** for 14.5 mi, thru **ALGODONES** and **BERNALILLO**. Curve with **4th St** thru the **traffic CIRCLE** at the HWY 566 JCT. Stay on **4th St** when 2nd St branches off. Go about 7.5 miles from here and cross under I-40 into **ALBUQUERQUE**.

THE BASE of LA BAJADA HILL

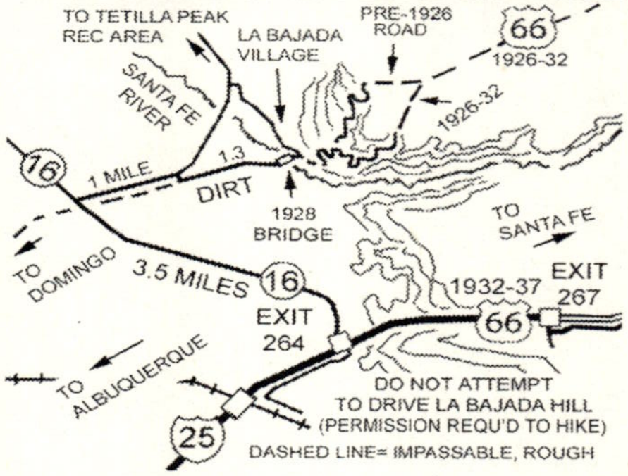

SIDE TRIP: **La Bajada Hill**. Too **treacherous** to drive sans an "experienced" **4WD!** To visit the **foot** of this road-building feat, follow **HWY 16** for 3.5 miles west from **EXIT 264**, then **RIGHT** 1 mile. Jog **RIGHT** to join a **rub-board dirt road** for 1.3 miles, over the **1928 Santa Fe River Bridge**. The road bends left to **La Bajada Village**, but the faint path of **1926-'32 '66** curves right, to zigzag drunkenly up steep **La Bajada Mesa**. A **Pre-'66** road carved a long gash across the slope to the left. Some folks hike the hill, but contact the Cochiti Pueblo Natural Resources Manager at (505) 465-2244 (mon-fri 8-4) for **permission** first (if you're lucky) (don't leave valuables exposed, and park/hike at your own risk). On top, **"Dirt 66"** ran to **SANTA FE**, joining Airport Rd over to Cerrillos; but you must return to **EXIT 264**.

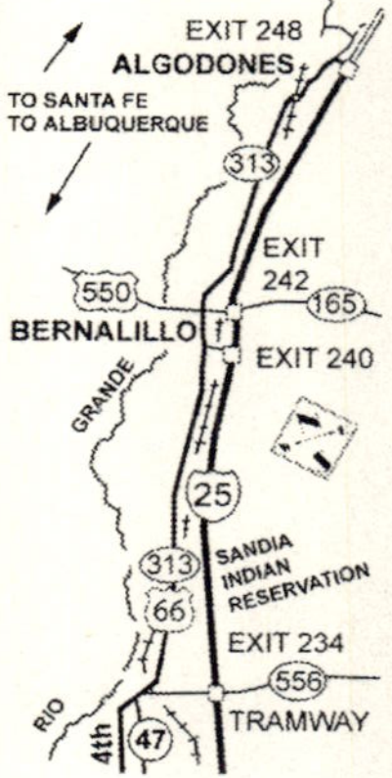

Headed west, the impassable path (no trespassing) of **Pre-32 '66** enters the **Santo Domingo Reservation**, to cross the RR at **Domingo (**off HWY 22, west of EXIT 259**)**, where the old trading post recently burned. Restoration is well underway. Then the faint trace jumps I-25 (west of EXIT 257), to cross a high ridge thru "**BIG CUT**," a notch in the hill visible to the southeast from just **north** of **EXIT 252** (behind the **San Felipe Casino**). **No** access. From **ALGODONES** thru **BERNALILLO**, **HWY 313** is a nice, scenic drive along the RR, also signed "**El Camino Real**." (see **MAP # 3** on **NM page-9** for an overview). South of **HWY 566**, urbanization crowds in as you approach **ALBUQUERQUE**. Some roadside relics look old enough to date back to old '66. **Visually**, the **El Camino Motor Hotel** is the coolest-looking remnant of tourist days.

EB: Take **4th St** north for about 8 mi. At the HWY 556 JCT **CIRCLE**, curve to join **HWY 313** (AVOID "TO I-25"). Follow **HWY 313** north 13.3 mi (thru **BERNALILLO** and under the railroad) into **ALGODONES**. Just past town, turn **RIGHT** (1.2 mi from RR) to **EXIT 248 (**follow signs). Join **I-25 NORTH ("Santa Fe")**. Take **EXIT 267/Waldo**, go **RIGHT** then **LEFT** on the **Frontage Rd** for 8.8 mi.

WB: Take **4th St** south 1 mi to downtown **ALBUQUERQUE**. **LEFT** on **Roma**, then **RIGHT** on **3rd St**. Turn **RIGHT** on **Central**, and **LEFT** onto **4th St.** At **Bridge Blvd** (1 mi); turn **RIGHT**, go 0.7 mi, then **LEFT** at the light on **Isleta Blvd**. Go 1.4 mi. At the Goff/Arenal Rd light, turn **LEFT** to stay with **Isleta Blvd** for 7.5 mi thru **ARMIJO**, **PARAJITO** and **LOS PADILLAS**. Cross I-25

RV ALERT! 4th to Central Ave to 3rd are tight turns with heavy traffic. **ALT:** Coal to Broadway to Lomas, then back on 4th.

SEE **NM pages-12 and 13** for more **ALBUQUERQUE** (Post-1937 route)

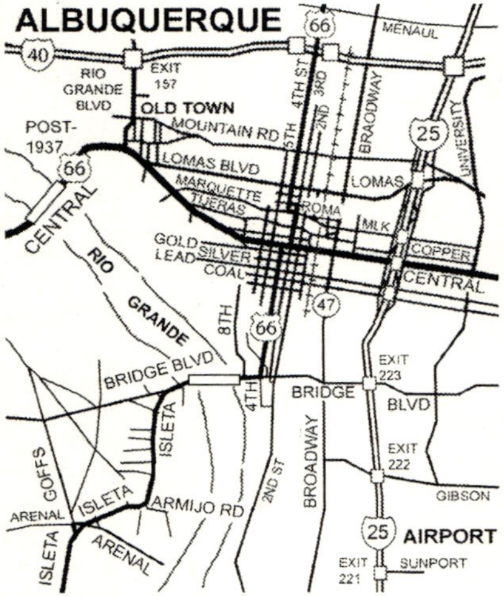

GIANT ALERT #1: At 4th and Marble (north of Lomas) is the 18 foot tall "**Madonna of the Trail"** monument, dedicated in 1928 to "Pioneer Mothers," one of 12 installed along the National Old Trails, and a twin to one in **UPLAND CA**. The Civic Plaza blocks 4th south of Marquette, requiring a short detour to reach Central Ave.

Earliest 66 **briefly** took 2nd St south. But **classic Pre-'37 '66**, south of **Central Ave**, follows **4th St**, past the **Red Ball Café**: "Home of the **Original Wimpy Burger** Since 1922." On **Bridge Blvd**, don't be fooled: 4th and 8th Streets are separated by only ONE block!

GIANT ALERT #2: On Isleta Blvd (south of Arenal Rd) look west for the **GIANT ROADRUNNER** between Blake and Ferris Streets. The towns south of the city blend together once you leave the urban area, a succession of walled adobe houses hidden among the trees, small farms, and a few old roadside remnants.

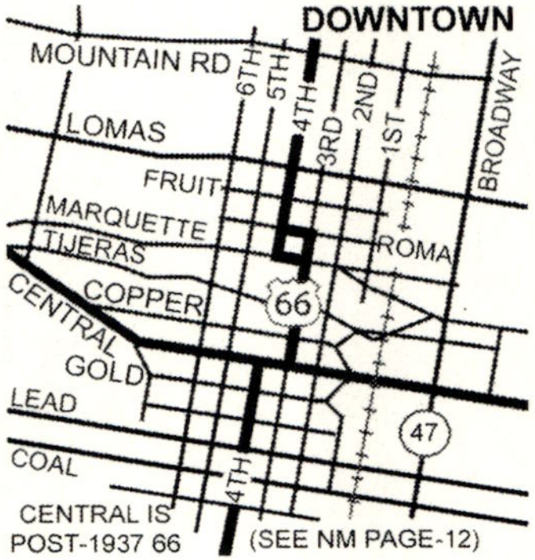

EB: From I-25, follow **Isleta Blvd** for 7.5 mi thru **LOS PADILLAS**, **PARAJITO** and **ARMIJO**. At the **Arenal Rd** light, curve **RIGHT** with **Isleta Blvd**. Stay on **Isleta** for 1.4 mi, then curve **RIGHT** onto **Bridge Blvd** and cross the **Rio Grande**. Past 8th St, prepare for a **QUICK LEFT** onto **4th St** (next light). Go 1 mi, turn **RIGHT** on **Central Ave** in downtown **ALBUQUERQUE**. Turn **LEFT** on **3rd St**. Turn **LEFT** onto **Marquette St** (One-Way), then **RIGHT** on **4th St**, and continue north for 1 mi to pass under I-40.

WB: South of I-25, stay **AHEAD** with **Isleta Blvd/HWY 314**. After 2 mi, veer **LEFT** on **HWY 147**, go across the RR and past **ISLETA PUEBLO**. Cross the river and turn **RIGHT** on **HWY 47**. Go 7 mi, thru **BOSQUE FARMS**, **PERALTA**, and **VALENCIA**. When HWY 47 branches left, continue **AHEAD** onto **HWY 6** (Main St), and cross the **Rio Grande** again into **LOS LUNAS**. Follow **HWY 6** across HWY 314, then continue for 34 mi, passing I-25 and then **CORREO**, to join **WEST I-40** at **EXIT 126.**

(This is the western **END** of the **PRE-1937 OPTION**: Turn to **NM page-14** to continue **WB** to **MESITA**, and on to **ARIZONA**)

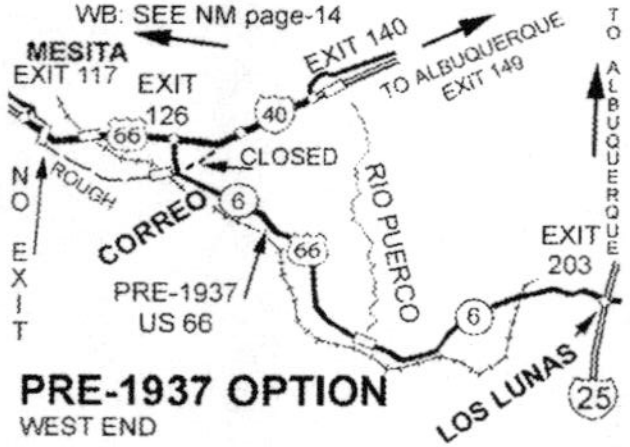

Ancient **ISLETA PUEBLO**, with its enchanting mission church and plaza, is accessed by several side roads from **HWY 147**. Visitors are welcome, but don't trespass, and DO obey all Pueblo rules concerning photos, etc. Old 66 passes thru a mix of residences and farms before briefly urbanizing in **LOS LUNAS**. The **Luna Mansion** at HWY 6 and HWY 314, offers dining in a historic 1881 mansion. Before 1937, '66 **briefly** followed **HWY 314** from **ISLETA** to **LOS LUNAS**.

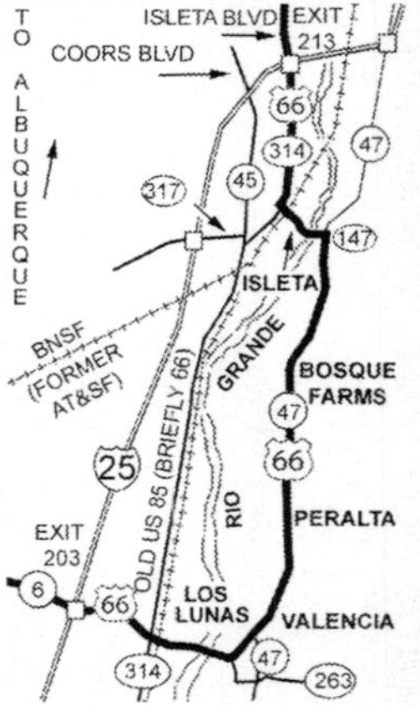

West of I-25, the climb up the sandy slope was easier for early road and railroad builders, than at **ALBUQUERQUE**. Portions of **PRE-1937** 66 follow an abandoned RR alignment. Watch for traces alongside current **HWY 6**, especially where red rock bridge abutments are visible: these are left over from the **AT&SF RR**. West of the **Rio Puerco**, watch closely, between MM 18 and MM 13, for more undriveable road fragments (don't trespass on Laguna lands). **Historic NOTE**: At **CORREO**, the old road turns off and crosses over the tracks, thru **Laguna Pueblo** land (**rough**, unpaved sections). The **WB tour** joins **I-40** (former 4-lane 66) west to **MESITA**.

EB FROM AZ: **TURN** to **NM page-22** to **CONTINUE** into **NM**. Return to this page **IF** you choose the **Pre-1937 Option** at **NM page 14**.

PRE-1937 OPTION EB: From **I-40 EXIT 126**, follow **HWY 6** for 34 mi, past **CORREO** and across I-25 into **LOS LUNAS**. Stay with **HWY 6** (Main St) across HWY 314, and cross the **Rio Grande**. **AVOID** HWY 263: stay with **HWY 6**. At the **HWY 47 stoplight**, merge **AHEAD** onto **North HWY 47**. Go 7 mi, thru **VALENCIA**, **PERALTA** and **BOSQUE FARMS**. Turn **LEFT** on **HWY 147**, cross the river, then curve past **ISLETA PUEBLO**. Cross the RR tracks, then bear **RIGHT** on **HWY 314**. After 2 mi, cross under I-25 at EXIT 213, and stay **AHEAD** onto **Isleta Blvd** towards **ALBUQUERQUE**.

(see **NM INTRO NM page-1**) (see **Pre-1937 OVERVIEW MAP** on **NM page-23**)

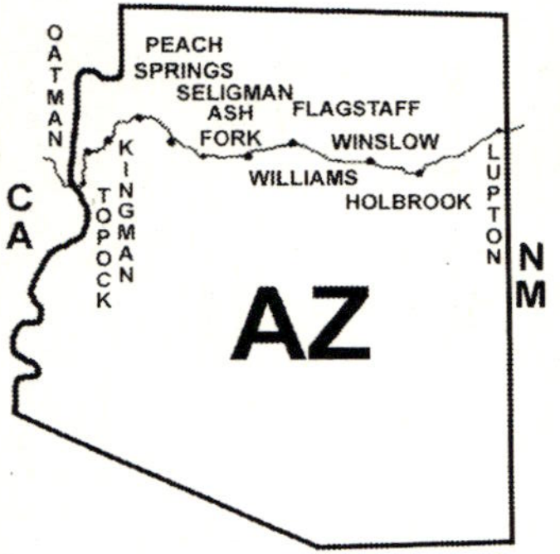

Praising Arizona

Route 66 thru Northern **ARIZONA** plays "connects the dots" with history-filled towns across this little-peopled region. This is the place to breathe easy and enjoy the wide-open spaces. **ARIZONA** is famous for scenic beauty, and some rather big holes accessed by 66: **Meteor Crater**, **Grand Canyon**, and even **Grand Canyon Caverns**. The rocky landscape of **ARIZONA** is fascinating, especially at famous **Petrified Forest**, while even the bare soil itself possesses a brilliant palate at colorful **Painted Desert**.

ARIZONA offers much first-class driving along Route 66.While there are many abandoned or extremely rough alignments in the eastern portion, gems of old road are scattered along the interstate. Western **ARIZONA** has plenty of terrific '66 to drive, including infamous but not to be missed **Oatman Hwy**. Look for **Arizona Byways** signs marking old '66. **US 66** generally followed the path of the 1857 **Beale Wagon Road** across Arizona, as evidenced by numerous markers along the way. **LUPTON** gives the state a grand start with majestic red cliffs, which quickly peter out in favor of red dirt and distant hills thru **HOLBROOK** and **WINSLOW**. Ahead, the **San Francisco Peaks** loom ever larger as you climb to **FLAGSTAFF** (don't forget **WINONA**). You enter the **Coconino National Forest** at **Canyon Padre**, and ride the tall timber thru **WILLIAMS** and the **Kaibab National Forest**. The route drops in elevation passing thru **ASH FORK**, and enters the well-preserved **159 miles** of pristine 2-lane west of EXIT 139, thru **SELIGMAN** and **PEACH SPRINGS**, to **KINGMAN**. The most ruggedly scenic section is **Oatman Hwy**, a roller-coaster ride thru the craggy **Black Mountains** and **OATMAN** (40-foot vehicle limit). **NOTE**: Mountain and desert driving requires **CARE**. Go **SLOWER** on steep mountain grades. Use lower gears downhill to save on brakes, watch your speed and do not hog the centerline. Park well off the road. In low desert areas, be aware of the **flash flood** danger in low washes, and **DO NOT** drive into water. Just take it EZ, and take the time to savor **ARIZONA**. You too will sing its praises.

ARIZONA MAP # 1

HOLBROOK ~ LUPTON

DASHED LINES = OBLITERATED, ROUGH OR PRIVATE

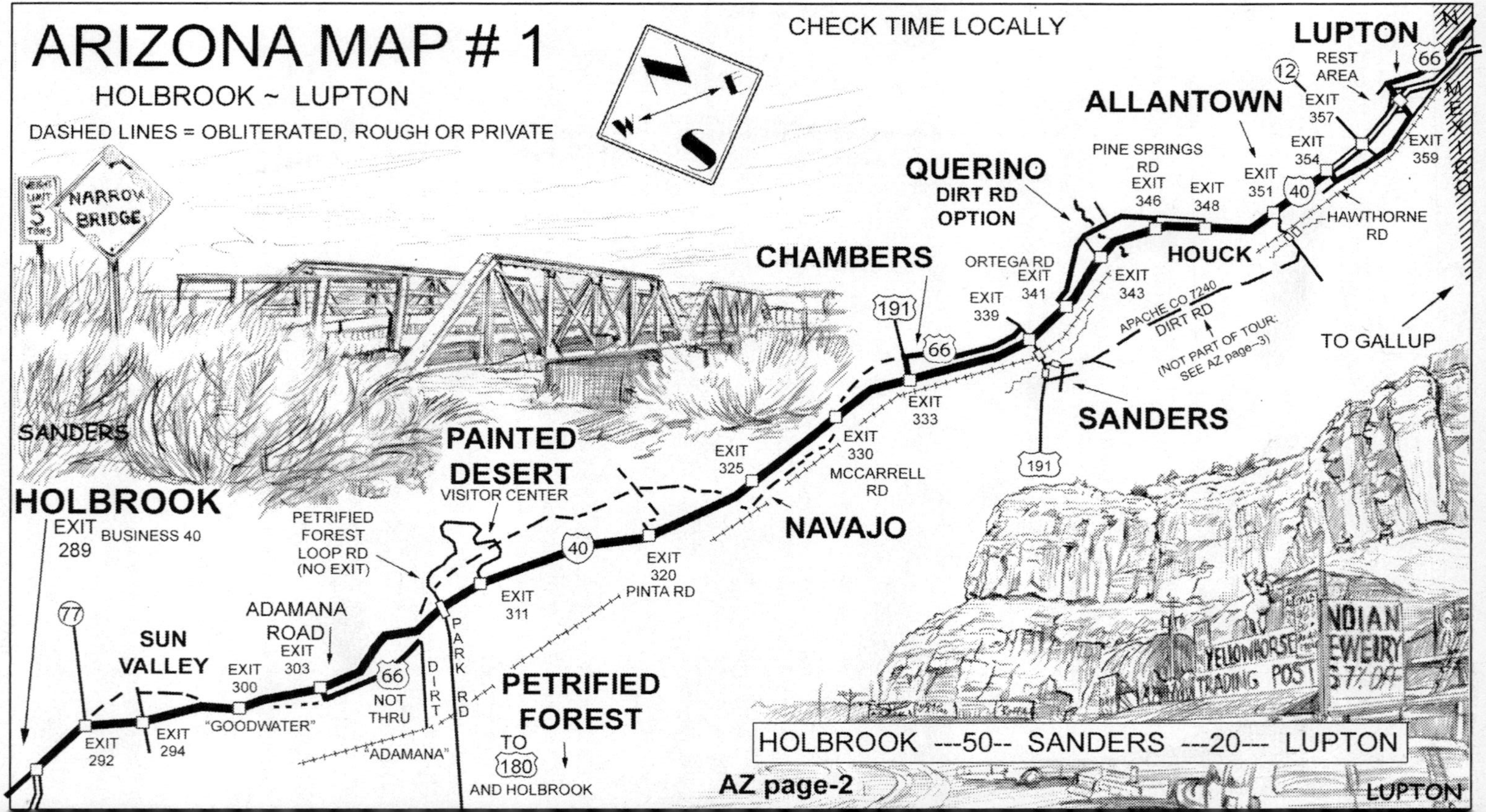

WB: Cross the state line into **ARIZONA**. At **EXIT 359 (**first left), cross under I-40, then **RIGHT** on the **South Frontage Rd** thru **LUPTON** (avoid offramp). Go 4.6 mi (pass by EXIT 357) and turn **RIGHT** (Hawthorne Rd) at **EXIT 354**, cross under I-40, then **LEFT** onto **WEST I-40**. Pass EXIT 351 (**ALLANTOWN)** and EXIT 348 (**HOUCK**). (See the "**DIRT 66**" **OPTION** at **EXIT 346/**Pine Springs Rd) Continue on **I-40** past EXIT 341. Take **EXIT 339** in **SANDERS.**

RESPECT PRIVATE PROPERTY on the reservation

At the **State Line**, colorful gift shops huddle at the base of majestic brown cliffs, while a painted mural and plenty of plastic animals perch precariously (and incongruously) on bare rock faces above. **GIANT ALERT**! See the Giant Tee Pee! **LUPTON** once had many old businesses along 66, but now note the closed **Geodesic Dome**: a recurring theme in the state. Here begins the **Navajo Indian Reservation** (thru **SANDERS**). MOST of the twisty frontage roads here are **NOT** remnants of '66, but all are lined with flashy billboards for area trading posts, just like the good old pre "roadside beautification" days.

SIDE TRIP: Just south of the RR tracks from **EXIT 351** (part gravel) is the closed **1923 bridge** that carried 1926-'31 US 66 over the **Rio Puerco**. A dusty/muddy and bumpy dirt road (**NOT** part of the "OFFICIAL" tour) turns west and continues along Apache Co 7240 for 12.5 corrugated miles to **SANDERS** (and a smaller 1923 bridge there). Best just to view the historic bridges from either end.

Fort Courage, at **HOUCK**, has long been advertised as "**Home of F Troop**," due to claims that part of the campy 1960s TV show's set was utilized in this faux frontier fort ("Take Pictures of the Past!"). If you pull off here, you might as well drive the North Frontage Rd to EXIT 346, but only the last half mile is really 66.

DIRT OPTION: between **EXIT 346** and **EXIT 341** is the dusty, bumpy, formerly paved **POST-1931** route via Co Rd 7250. This is a rough but drivable dirt stretch that crosses the 269-foot **Querino Canyon Bridge** (built in 1930). See the detail map, take it slow (some rub board sections) and avoid when wet.

EB: Take **EAST I-40** past EXIT 341 (see **DIRT 66 OPTION**) and EXIT 346. Continue on **I-40** past EXIT 348 (**HOUCK**) and EXIT 351 (**ALLANTOWN**). Take **EXIT 354** (Hawthorne Rd), turn **RIGHT** then **LEFT** to follow **South Frontage Rd** for 4.6 mi, past EXIT 357 and thru **LUPTON**, to **EXIT 359**. Cross under I-40 and turn **RIGHT** on **North Frontage Rd** (becomes **NM 118**) into **NEW MEXICO**.

WB: At **EXIT 339** in **SANDERS**, turn **RIGHT** then **LEFT** to take **North Frontage Rd** west to **CHAMBERS**. Go 6 mi, then **LEFT** on **US 191**. Join **WEST I-40 at EXIT 333**. Stay with **I-40** past **NAVAJO** (EXIT 325) and EXIT 311 (**Painted Desert/Petrified Forest**).

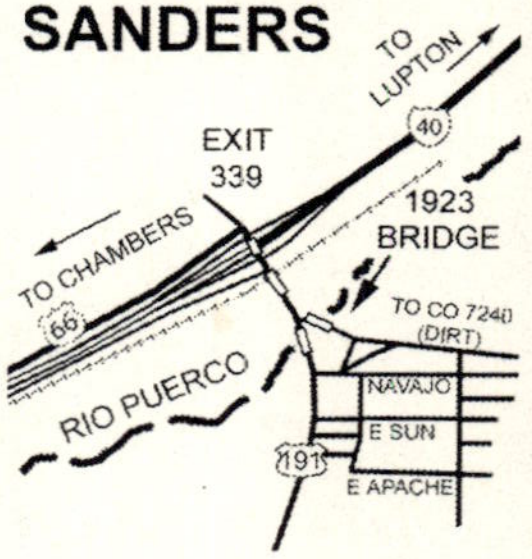

SIDE TRIP: Take **US 191** south across the RR tracks into **SANDERS**. Just across, to the east, is the **1923 bridge** (closed) that first carried '66 over the **Rio Puerco**, then onto current CO Rd 7240 (see **AZ page-3** and **MAP #1**: **NOT** part of TOUR). **SCAVENGER HUNT!** What **COLOR** are the bridge girders painted?_______ Just south of the current Rio Puerco Bridge, turn **LEFT** on **Navajo** for one block, then **RIGHT** to the charming pink/white **66 Diner**. A classic **Valentine Diner**, relocated from **HOLBROOK**, was combined with a house trailer and ingenuity to create a unique café. Also in town is historic **R B Burnham Trading Post** on US 191.

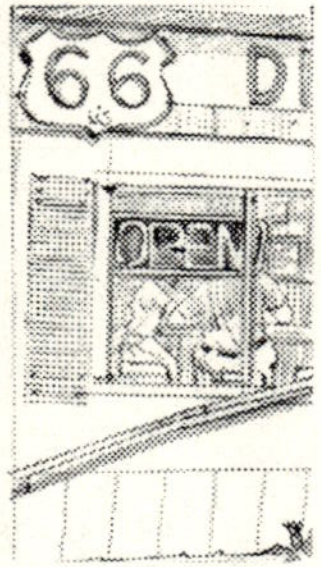

Remains of old businesses pepper the road to **CHAMBERS,** where an old **Chevron Station** sits on the dead end north frontage road west of the exit. Most of the abundant abandoned old 66 sections west of here to **WINONA** are inaccessible or unadvisable, due to roughness and washouts or are private property. **Historic NOTE**: NOT included on this tour, partly due to its fragility and unfortunate exposure to vandalism (and now a locked gate), is the haunting, crumbling ruin of the former **Painted Desert Trading Post** on the banks of **Dead Wash**.

SIDE TRIP (fee): An abandoned section of '66 runs thru the **Painted Desert** area of the **Petrified Forest National Park**. Two miles north on the Loop Road is the restored 1924 **Painted Desert Inn**. The park road continues south thru the **Petrified Forest**. **DON'T** pick up petrified wood in the Park. If you have some from outside, let the ranger mark it.

US 180 OPTION: **WB**: Use **US 180** from the Park's **South** entrance (28 miles south of I-40) to rejoin 66 at **HOLBROOK**. **EB**: Take **US 180** from **HOLBROOK** to the park, then north to I-40. But either way you'll miss cool stuff…unless you return to **EXIT 311** to continue.

CAR GAME! "**Billboard FREE for all**!" First person to see the word "**FREE**" on a billboard yells "**FREE**." First to yell 5 times wins!

EB: Follow **EAST I-40** past **NAVAJO** (EXIT 325). At **EXIT 333**, take **US 191 NORTH** in **CHAMBERS**. Turn **RIGHT** after a half-mile onto **Apache Co 7060**, which becomes the **North Frontage Rd**. Continue 6 mi to **SANDERS**. JOIN **EAST I-40** at **EXIT 339**.

WB: Continue on **WEST I-40** to take **EXIT 289**. Join **BL-40/Navajo Blvd** (**RIGHT** from ramp) into **<u>HOLBROOK</u>**.

<u>SIDE TRIP</u>: At **EXIT 303** is **Adamana Rd**, a **10-mile** round-trip drive along a **paved** spur of Route 66 that ends at the site of **Rocky's Pony Express Station** (private). On the south side of this exit, go east along **Adamana Rd** for 5 miles, to where it bends south and turns dirt. **Return** to EXIT 303. A nice view of the **Painted Desert** is had along the way.

Back at **EXIT 303** are a couple of rock shops and the **Painted Desert Indian Center**, a gift shop decorated in the traditional roadside style with Indian cutouts, corrals and old wagons. Their colorful statues of dinosaurs in combat evidently came from a defunct attraction once located nearer to **<u>HOLBROOK</u>**.

GIANT ALERT! Stewarts Rock Shop, on the northeast side of the exit, has colorful and crazy folk-art style statues, including a T-Rex eating a woman (female manikins in peril abound), plus a caveman riding an animated dinosaur, among others. The two-headed Dimetrodon east of the exit is theirs, too, as are many colorful billboards worthy of the old days, hawking fossils, meteorites, ostriches and **FREE** petrified wood. **GIFT SHOP ALERT!** This is the type of cool place where my Dad wouldn't stop!

The only thing left these days at nearby **<u>GOODWATER</u>** is the restored 420-foot timber bridge over "Little Lithodendron Wash," a twin to the decrepit structure over not-so-little "Lithodendron Wash," west of EXIT 303.
<u>SUN VALLEY</u> is a mostly empty housing development platted on the sand east of **<u>HOLBROOK</u>**. At the exit is a former Stuckey's (now a knife shop), and an old motel or two plus the **Root 66 RV Park**.

One can see for quite a ways from atop the mesa east of **<u>HOLBROOK</u>**, unless the ever-present wind has raised the dust! Look for the nearby strange purple hills, and far off buttes. A few dinosaur statue refugees also ended up at **Hopi Travel Plaza**, EXIT 292. **<u>HOLBROOK</u>** was long the headquarters of the extinct **Whiting Bros** chain of discount gas stations. See an online gallery of my photos of locations that still existed in the 80s/90s at: **route66.atwebpages.com/wbros/mcjerry.html**

EB: From **<u>HOLBROOK</u>**, follow **EAST I-40** past EXIT 311 (**Painted Desert/Petrified Forest**) towards **<u>NAVAJO</u>**.

(see MAP AZ page-2)

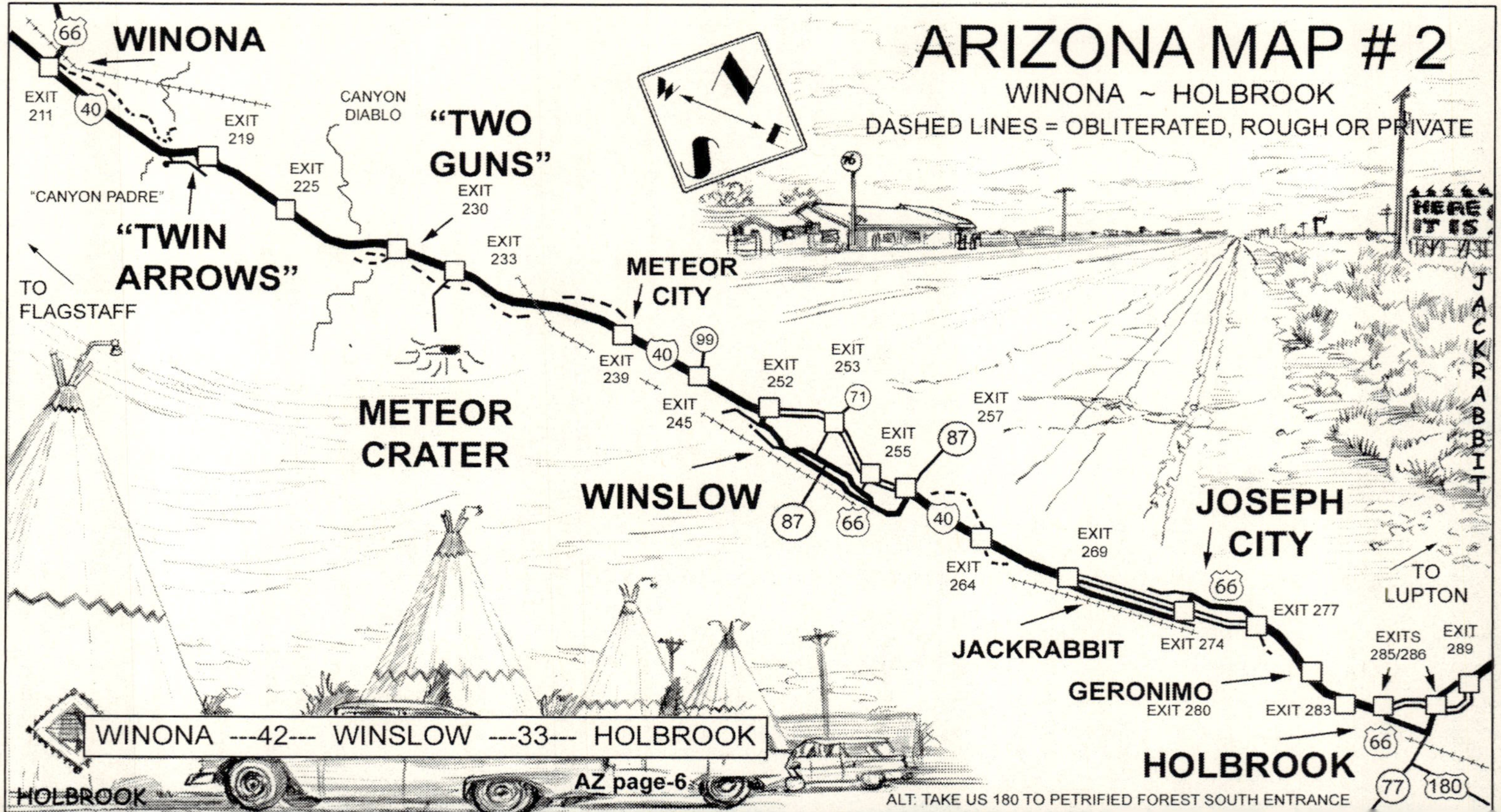
ARIZONA MAP # 2
WINONA ~ HOLBROOK
DASHED LINES = OBLITERATED, ROUGH OR PRIVATE
WINONA
EXIT 211
EXIT 219
"CANYON PADRE"
"TWIN ARROWS"
TO FLAGSTAFF
EXIT 225
CANYON DIABLO
"TWO GUNS"
EXIT 230
EXIT 233
METEOR CRATER
METEOR CITY
EXIT 239
EXIT 245
EXIT 252
EXIT 253
EXIT 255
EXIT 257
WINSLOW
EXIT 264
EXIT 269
JACKRABBIT
EXIT 274
EXIT 277
JOSEPH CITY
GERONIMO
EXIT 280
EXIT 283
EXITS 285/286
EXIT 289
TO LUPTON
HOLBROOK
HERE IT IS
JACKRABBIT
WINONA ---42--- WINSLOW ---33--- HOLBROOK
HOLBROOK
ALT: TAKE US 180 TO PETRIFIED FOREST SOUTH ENTRANCE

WB: Follow **BL 40/Navajo Blvd** into **HOLBROOK**. Go 3 mi (passing under I-40 EXIT 286 en route) to downtown, then **RIGHT** on **Hopi Dr BL/40**. Continue for 1.6 mi, cross under I-40 then **LEFT** on the ramp to join **WEST I-40 (EXIT 285)**. Take **EXIT 277** and turn **RIGHT** to join **BL 40** into **JOSEPH CITY** for 2.5 mi.

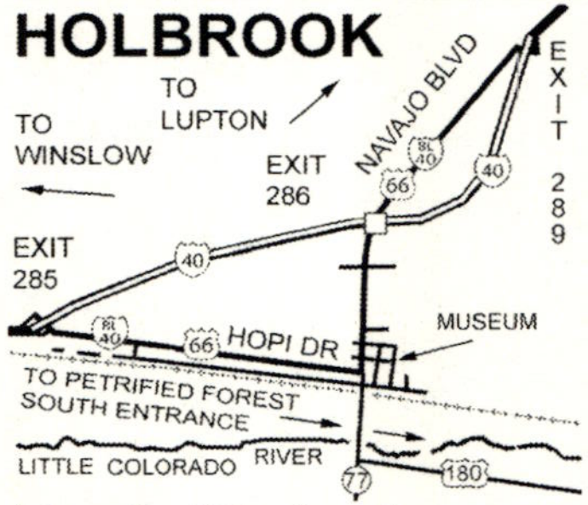

The most historic place to overnite in town is the **Wigwam Motel** at 811 W Hopi Dr, owned by the original family since they built the concrete teepees in 1950. The rooms are basic (and a bit quirky), but bigger on the inside than they look and feature the original highly polished wood furnishings. Many old vehicles repose on the grounds for a great **PHOTO OP**. For reservations (recommended) call (until you get thru) (928) 524 3048 from 4-9 MST. The office is not open other hours. This is the penultimate in a chain of seven built from 1933 to 1950. **SAN BERNARDINO**'s Wigwams, the last built, were recently restored, so now you've TWO chances to "Sleep in a Wigwam." Or try the nearby and much recommended (by EZ Guide users) **Globetrotter Motel** (902 W Hopi) with its homey feel and clean rooms. (928) 297 0158.

GIANT ALERT! If you haven't seen enough **DINOSAURS** yet, still more live on Navajo Blvd (south of Hopi) at the **Rainbow Rock Shop**. Nearby at 109 Hopi Dr, **Julien's Roadrunner** offers tin signs, roadside and railroad memorabilia and "Route 66 Stuff" from a mural-decorated store. "Looking is FREE!" For good grub, try **Jo and Aggie's** Café at 120 W Hopi, or **Romo's Restaurant** across the street. Both have great neon. Those of a historic bent can explore the **Holbrook Visitor Center and Museum** in the former **1898 Navajo County Courthouse** at Arizona and Navajo, with its funky and graffitied pre-fab jail cell (shipped here ages ago by rail). **Local INFO**: 928-524-6558 (Museum) or (800) 524-2459 (C of C).

West of town at EXIT 280, the **Geronimo Trading Post** huddles at the base of a rocky brown bluff. Signs boast "**World's Largest Petrified Tree.**" At 80 tons, I guess that qualifies for a **GIANT ALERT**! Cliffs crowd I-40 to **JOSEPH CITY**.

EB: Take **EXIT 285**, turn **RIGHT** to follow **BL 40/Hopi Dr** for about 1.6 mi into **HOLBROOK**. Downtown, turn **LEFT** on **Navajo Blvd**. Go 3 mi (passing under EXIT 286 en route). At **EXIT 289**, cross under I-40 then **LEFT** on the ramp to join **EAST I-40**.

WB: Take **BL 40/Main St thru JOSEPH CITY**. At the access road to **EXIT 274** ("TO I-40") turn **LEFT** and cross over I-40. Turn **RIGHT** and follow the **South Frontage Rd** (a bit rough) past the **JACKRABBIT** to **EXIT 269**. Cross under to join **I-40 WEST**. Take **EXIT 257/AZ Hwy 87**. Cross I-40, turn **RIGHT** with **"Hwy 87 South"/ Historic 66**." Continue into **WINSLOW**.

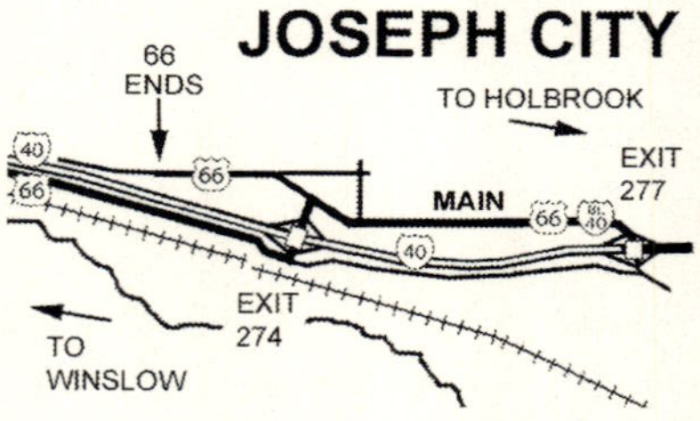

JOSEPH CITY, once home to many lively tourist stops like Apache Fort, now hosts little more than private residences. On east side of town is a **Historic Marker** made of polished petrified wood, bearing a plaque dedicated to the Mormon colonists that settled here in 1876. **SCAVENGER HUNT**! What was **JOSEPH CITY FIRST** known as?__________

SIDE TRIP: For that lonely old Route 66 feeling, be sure to take the dead end section west from the EXIT 274 turnoff (see MAP). This heads west on the north of I-40, past a feed store which over the years was home to **Hopi Village, Howdy Hanks and Sitting Bull's Indian Store**. The tourist Teepee is still in front, and old **Howdy Hank** himself has been restored and repainted on the west wall (may be hard to see). Further west are the sad remains of "one of the Oldest Trading Posts on 66". Those red log walls last served as **Ella's Frontier**. Earlier, this was **San Diego Rawson's Frontier Days Trading Post**. Most of the old signs and symbols that once graced this structure are gone, but a few remain to tease the memory. Respect private property.

"If you haven't been to the **Jackrabbit**, you haven't been in the southwest," reads the old postcards. The **Jackrabbit Trading Post** is still a hopping happening alongside 66, but those yellow and black signs that once taunted literally hundreds of miles of Route 66 with the mileage countdown to the place are mostly gone. A large billboard with a black jackrabbit, topped by little rabbit silhouettes, stands proudly across the road, loudly exclaiming "HERE IT IS!" **GIANT ALERT!** Where else can you sit on a giant jackrabbit (besides Rabbit Ranch in Illinois, which pays loving homage)! **PHOTO OP**! Be sure to check out the **GIFT SHOP** for a variety of roadside souvenirs.

EB: Cross the Little Colorado River, then turn **LEFT** with **NORTH Hwy 87** to **EXIT 257**. Here join **EAST I-40** to **EXIT 269/ JACKRABBIT**. Take **South Frontage Road** for about 5 mi to **EXIT 274** (a bit rough). Cross I-40 to the "**T**" JCT. Turn **RIGHT** to follow **BL 40/Main St** for 2.6 mi thru **JOSEPH CITY** to **EXIT 277**. Join **I-40 EAST** & take **HOLBROOK** EXIT 285.

WB: Continue into **<u>WINSLOW</u>** past Transcon Ln (**BL 40** joins from EXIT 255), then continue thru downtown (becomes **Third St** One-Way WB) for about 3 mi. On the west side of town, turn **RIGHT** on **Hipkoe Dr**, cross over and JOIN **I-40 WEST** (at **EXIT 252**).

WINSLOW

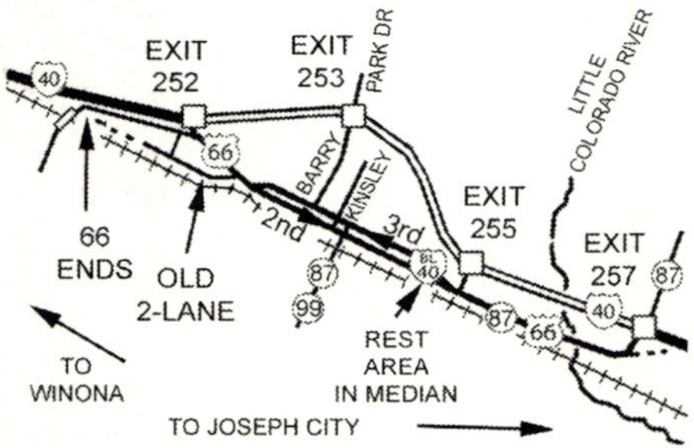

In **<u>WINSLOW</u>**, follow the signs to the **Old Trails Museum** on Kinsley between 2nd and 3rd, which is currently open Tues thru Sat from 10-4 pm, featuring old west, road and railroad history.

PHOTO OP! At Kinsley and 2nd is the "**Standing on the Corner**" statue, dedicated to the classic Eagles song "Take it Easy." A mural painted on the building behind the statue depicts a girl in a flat bed Ford, as if reflected in a shop window, while a HUGE painted 66 sign fills the intersection. Across the street is Dominique's "On the Corner" gifts. Local INFO: 928-289-2434

2nd St is the older route, so you should drive both directions, as either street has plenty of relics of roadside 66. Old gas stations, cafes, and motels abound. A former **Whiting Bros** gas station is located near the east "Y." At 512 E Third is **Earl's Motor Court**, with its beautiful neon. I haven't been able to try them yet but they do seem worth checking out.

<u>WINSLOW</u> is justifiably proud of the beautifully restored **La Posada Hotel** at 303 E Second, an ornate former **Harvey House** built in 1928. Check out the southwestern style lobby, with fine dining at the **Turquoise Room**, or try one of their charming rooms for the night (928) 289-4366. The unique art of **Tina Mion** fills the public areas, and her own museum. A **Route 66 Art Museum** will occupy the restored **Depot** next door. An old **Valentine diner** sits across on Second St: the former "**Highway Diner**" is currently for sale and stripped of paint. You CAN eat today at the **Falcon Restaurant** at 1113 E 2nd. **Berry St**, which goes north to I-40 EXIT 253, is also signed as "**Beale Wagon Route**," commemorating the ancestor of the roads and railroad across northern Arizona. Route 66 dead ends on the west end of town, past EXIT 252. An older 2–lane remnant runs along closer to the RR nearby.

EB: From **EXIT 252** in **WINSLOW**, turn **RIGHT** then **LEFT** to follow **BL 40**/"**Historic 66**" east into town. Continue with **Second St/BL 40** (One-Way EB) thru downtown, and continue with **NORTH Hwy 87**/"**Historic 66**"(no turn) past EXIT 255 towards EXIT 257.

WB: Follow **I-40** from **WINSLOW**. Continue past EXIT 245 (Hwy 99), EXIT 239 (**METEOR CITY**) EXIT 233 (**METEOR CRATER**) EXIT 230 (**TWO GUNS**) and EXIT 219 (**TWIN ARROWS**) to take **EXIT 211** at **WINONA**. Turn right from the offramp.

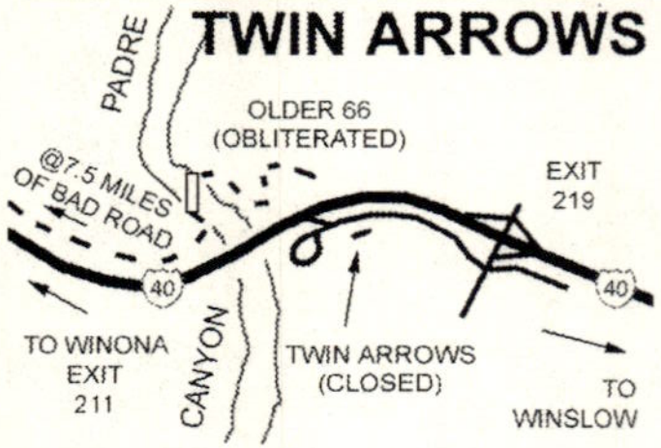

Still another geodesic dome has housed **Meteor City** off Exit 239 (closed down as of 12-23-2012). Here is (was?) the (reputed) "**World's Longest Map of Route 66**." Hope it reopens. Off **EXIT 233**, the actual **METEOR CRATER** is the site of a tremendous meteor impact, which left a **HUGE** hole in the desert, well worth a look. **GIFT SHOP ALERT**. Near the exit, yet another DOME at the Mobil Station was featured in the movie ***STARMAN***. http://www.meteorcrater.com/

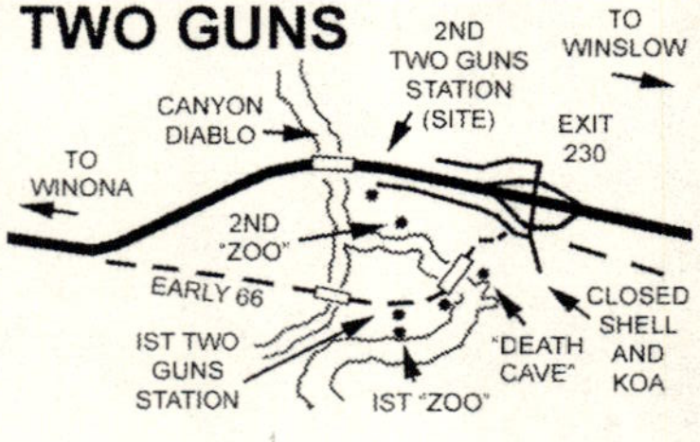

TWO GUNS was a storied tourist town on the edge of **Canyon Diablo**. Past an old concrete arch bridge lie crumbling rock ruins of gas stations, two roadside zoos (hence the oft photographed sign: "**Mountain Lions**") and infamous **Apache Death Cave** (I toured the cave years ago when **TWO GUNS** enjoyed a brief resurgence...dangerous and NOT recommended now!). Once you could get guided tours of the area, but all of this, including the KOA and Shell station, is now **closed** and on **PRIVATE PROPERTY**. The old ruins can be hazardous, and there are nails scattered about (one reader reported getting a flat tire!), so please play it **safe** and just view the ruins from the exit.

GIANT ALERT! TWIN ARROWS was once an attractive establishment, with its red/white Valentine diner, and namesake gigantic arrows thrust into the soil. Now boarded up, the remains, now owned by the Hopi Tribe, are easiest reached for photo purposes by **EB** travelers: just take the off ramp for **EXIT 219** and there you are. **WB**, take the **EXIT 219** overpass to the South Frontage Rd, then go west. You'll have to circle back (the place may be restored someday…but a casino is now on the NE side of the exit). **Historic Note**: A **1914 concrete bridge** arches over **Canyon Padre**, out-of-sight north of I-40. **Unfortunately**, the only public access is via a 15-mile round-trip on a **VERY ROUGH** stretch of old 66 (a **BAD** cattleguard near end), east from EXIT 211. **NOT** your casual vacation side trip. **NOT advised**.

EB: From **EXIT 211** at **WINONA**, follow I-40 past EXIT 219 (**TWIN ARROWS**), EXIT 230 (**TWO GUNS**), EXIT 233 (**METEOR CRATER**), EXIT 239 (**METEOR CITY**) and EXIT 245 (HWY 99), then take **EXIT 252** on the west side of **WINSLOW**.

(see MAP 2 AZ page-6)

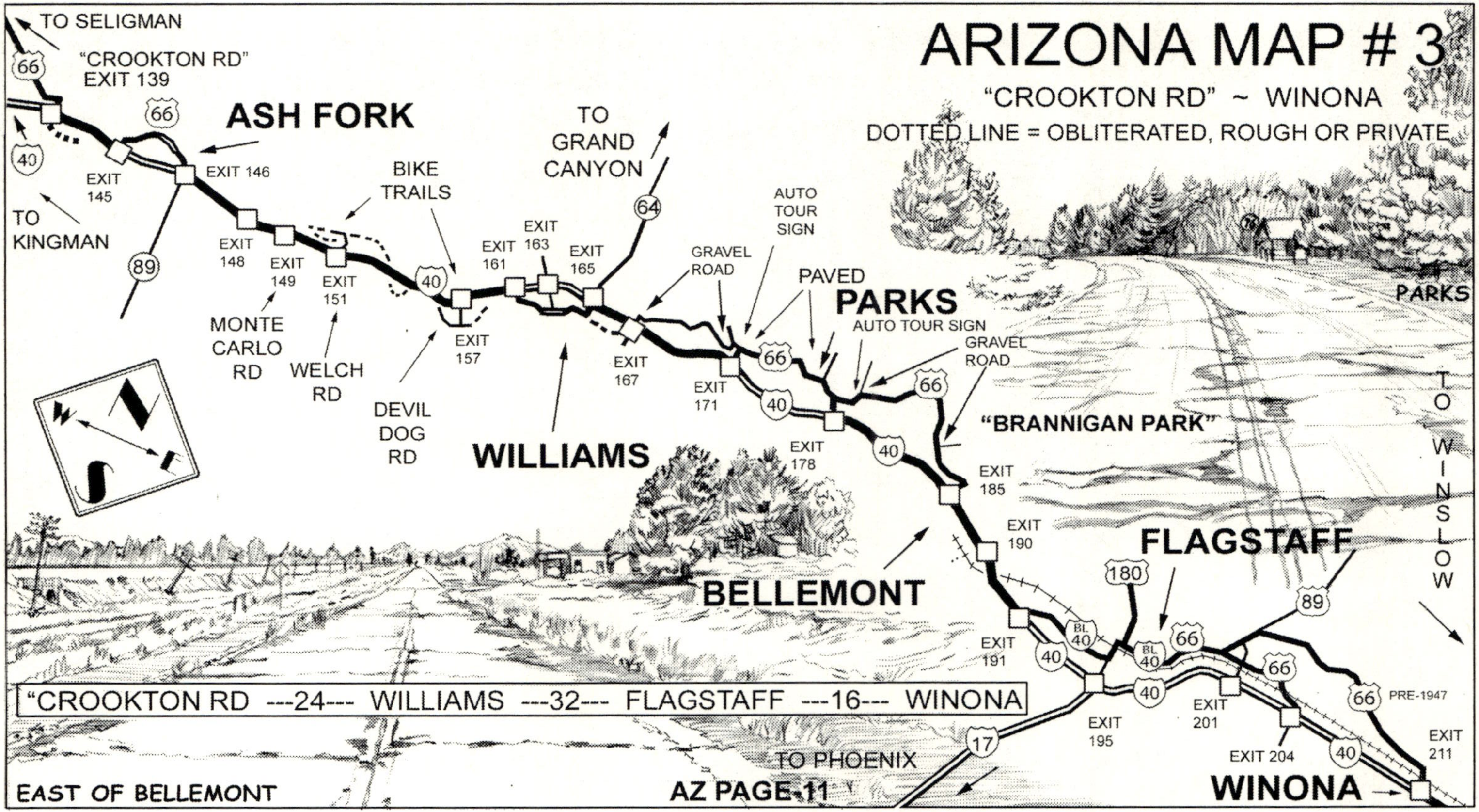
ARIZONA MAP # 3
"CROOKTON RD" ~ WINONA
DOTTED LINE = OBLITERATED, ROUGH OR PRIVATE
TO SELIGMAN
"CROOKTON RD"
EXIT 139
ASH FORK
EXIT 145
EXIT 146
TO KINGMAN
EXIT 148
EXIT 149
EXIT 151
MONTE CARLO RD
WELCH RD
BIKE TRAILS
DEVIL DOG RD
EXIT 157
EXIT 161
EXIT 163
EXIT 165
TO GRAND CANYON
WILLIAMS
EXIT 167
GRAVEL ROAD
AUTO TOUR SIGN
PAVED
PARKS
AUTO TOUR SIGN
GRAVEL ROAD
EXIT 171
EXIT 178
"BRANNIGAN PARK"
EXIT 185
EXIT 190
EXIT 191
BELLEMONT
FLAGSTAFF
EXIT 195
EXIT 201
EXIT 204
EXIT 211
PRE-1947
TO WINSLOW
TO PHOENIX
WINONA
PARKS
"CROOKTON RD ---24--- WILLIAMS ---32--- FLAGSTAFF ---16--- WINONA
EAST OF BELLEMONT

WB: Cross the RR tracks, and follow **Townsend-Winona Rd** for about 10 mi to the JCT of **US 89**. Turn **LEFT** and follow **US 89** into **FLAGSTAFF**. About 2 mi on, at the Country Club Dr stoplight ("To I-40"), continue (NO TURN) with **US 180 (BL 40** joins) and **"Route 66"** into downtown, along the north side of the RR tracks. US 180 turns just past downtown, stay with **BL 40**.

WINONA kinda forgot itself: there's not much here besides the old **Winona Trading Post** just west of EXIT 211. Most photogenic is the old (closed, but walkable) **iron bridge** on the early route.

OPTION: POST 1947 66 between EXIT 204 and US 180 (just west of Country Club Rd). See detail Map. This was my favored route, until they covered much of the original concrete pavement with asphalt. Still a nice (if BUMPY) drive along the RR, but it involves using I-40 between EXIT 204 and **WINONA**.

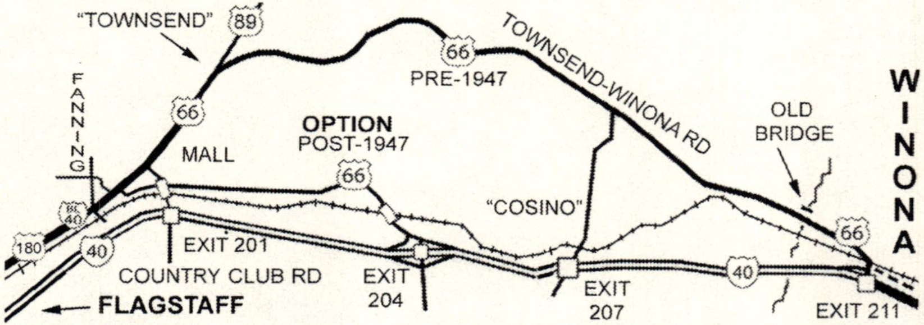

FLAGSTAFF, nestled at the foot of the **San Francisco Peaks**, is the gateway to many tourist areas, including the Arizona Snowbowl and Grand Canyon. Roadside goodies on the EAST side include **Miz Zips** for good roadfood and the **Museum Club**, reportedly housed in the southwest's **LARGEST LOG CABIN**, built in 1931 as a museum of native artifacts and taxidermy, now a roadhouse offering live music. **GIANT ALERT!** The fork of a **huge TREE stump** frames the entry, while a **BIG NEON GUITAR** shines out front. Speaking of neon, some of the old motels like the **Western Hills** (with its newly restored neon sign) still light up the roadside. Also neon-noteworthy is the **Route 66 Motel** nearby. **Downtown FLAGSTAFF** has a variety of old buildings housing interesting shops and cafes. Towering over all is the **Hotel Monte Vista** neon sign. South side of 66 between San Francisco and Beaver is the **Visitor Center** in the Amtrak Depot.

EB: Take **US180/BL 40 (AKA "Route 66")** east from downtown **FLAGSTAFF**. Follow **US 180** as it curves away from the RR tracks, and thru the Country Club Dr stoplight (BL 40 ends). The street becomes **US 89**: continue about 2 mi to the stoplight at **Townsend-Winona Rd**: Turn **RIGHT**, and continue about 10 mi east to **WINONA**. Cross the RR Tracks, and join **I-40 EAST** at **EXIT 211**.

WB: West of downtown **FLAGSTAFF**, curve under the RR tracks with **BL 40/Route 66**. Go 0.5 mi, then turn **RIGHT** with **W Route 66/BL 40** ("TO I-40"). Continue about 4 mi to **EXIT 191**, and join **I-40 WEST**, continuing past **BELLEMONT**/EXIT 185.

WB: see **GRAVEL OPTION #1** on **AZ page-14** (accessed by **EXIT 185)**.

SIDE TRIP: Before 1934, one version of '66 crossed the RR (WB) from downtown on **Beaver**, then turned **RIGHT** on **Phoenix** and **LEFT** on **Mikes Pike** to **Milton Rd**. Beaver is **ONE-WAY** now, so take Phoenix east to **San Francisco** to loop back across the tracks. Some fascinating motel relics survive along here, including the Downtowner apartments, and the **DuBeau Hostel**, both with a great neon signs. Local INFO: (928) 779-7611.

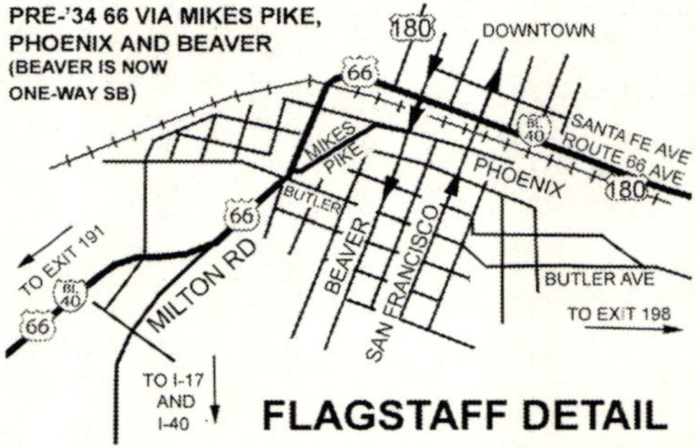

FLAGSTAFF DETAIL

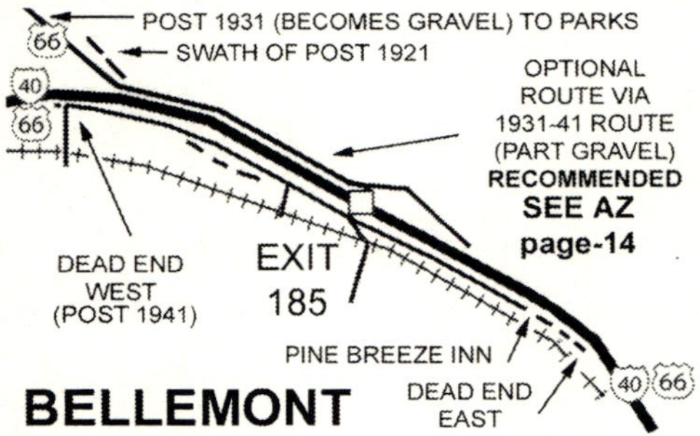

BELLEMONT

GIANT ALERT! **Granny's Closet,** a nice restaurant on Milton, is the site of the former **Lumberjack Café**. This was home to the very **FIRST** of the **GIANT** so-called "**Muffler Men**," an axe-wielding **Paul Bunyan** installed circa 1962, ancestor to the three Illinois giants. Granny's currently displays their own smaller rendition of Tall Paul, but whither the original? **Northern AZ University** has TWO identical giants (honoring their "Lumberjacks" team). Perhaps Paul didn't venture very far?

BELLEMONT, at EXIT 185, sat idle for years, but new building has eroded much '66 feel. **DEAD END SIDE TRIPS:** On the south of I-40, Old 66 runs for about 2 miles to the west (before getting ROUGH). To the east, the road (now paved over in blacktop) heads to the old **Pine Breeze Inn**, filmed for the movie "**Easy Rider**." The old concrete emerges here, to dead end after a bumpy 0.7 of a mile. **Route 66 Roadhouse** and a **Harley Davidson** dealer are near the EXIT.

EB: Follow **EAST I-40** past **BELLEMONT** (EXIT 185). Take **EXIT 191,** curve under I-40, then **RIGHT** on "**W Route 66"/BL 40** into **FLAGSTAFF**. After 4 mi, turn **LEFT on Milton Rd (BL40/Route 66)**. Go under the RR tracks, then curve to pass thru downtown (US 180 joins).

WB: Past **BELLEMONT** (see **GRAVEL OPTION** #1), take **I-40 EXIT 178**, go **RIGHT** to the JCT with **CO RD 146**: Turn **LEFT**. Go about 6.4 mi (thru **PARKS**). At the access road for **EXIT 171**, turn **LEFT** then join **I-40 WB**. Pass EXIT 167, and take **EXIT 165**.

GRAVEL OPTION #1 (Scenic and **very** recommended) **WB**: from **EXIT 185** in **BELLEMONT**, take the **North Frontage Rd** west, then curve away from I-40. As the pavement ends, stay **AHEAD** onto the good **GRAVEL** road (go **SLOW**) thru **BRANNIGAN PARK** (15 mph), then over **Fortynine Hill** (highest point of '66 in **AZ…**not marked) and down. Pavement resumes at JCT Co 107: (no turn) continue to **PARKS** (but first stop at the **Auto Tour Sign** (IF there) for a pleasant **hiking trail** on old 66). **EB:** East of **PARKS**, stay **AHEAD** on **CO 146** past the I-40 JCT and curve past the **Auto Tour Sign**, then stay **AHEAD** onto the **gravel** past the JCT of CO 107 (**SLOW**). Past **BRANNIGAN PARK** (15 mph), pavement resumes, and becomes the **N Frontage Rd** to **EXIT 185**. Join **I-40 EAST** here (on **AZ page-13**).

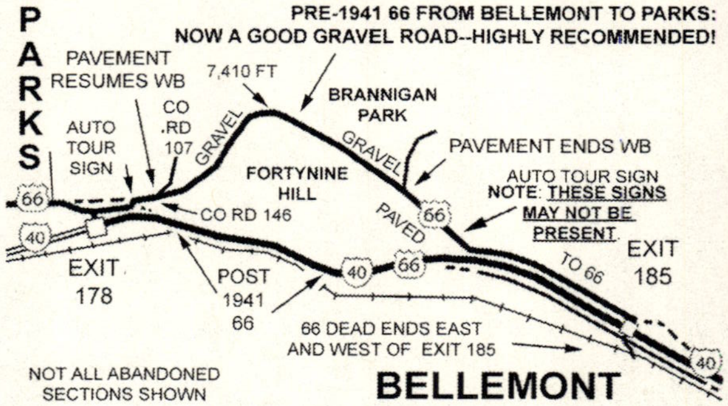

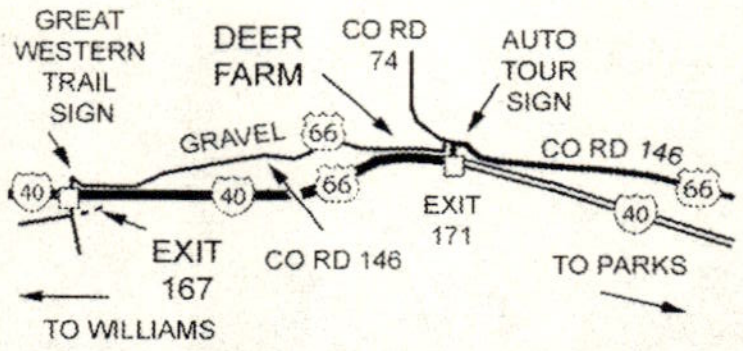

GRAVEL OPTION 2

"**PARKS in the Pines**" consists mainly of the picturesque **Parks Store / Union 76**. Bits of 1921 and '31 '66 remain, but much of the picturesque 1939 concrete road, visible from **Garland Prairie Vista** as it drops east thru the dark forest towards majestic peaks, is now smeared with ugly blacktop. Past the old Wagon Wheel Lodge (a residence) is (hopefully) an **Auto Tour Sign (**maps and info**)**, near EXIT 71.

GRAVEL OPTION 2: Paved until just west of **Deer Farm**, a unique **petting zoo**. **WB**, turn sharply **LEFT** just past the road to EXIT 171 (Avoid CO Rd 74) and follow "**Deer Farm Rd**" (still Co Rd 146). Continue on the good **gravel road**, along Davenport (mostly dry) Lake. Near **EXIT 167** the blacktop resumes. Join **I-40 WB** here. **EB:** Do the reverse from **EXIT 167**, then follow **Co Rd 146 EB** to **PARKS** (see map).

EB: Continue on **I-40 EAST**. Pass EXIT 167, (see **GRAVEL OPTIONS** # 2 and #1) then take **EXIT 171**. Cross I-40, and then turn **RIGHT** on **CO RD 146**. Go about 6.4 mi. Just east of **PARKS**, turn **RIGHT** with signs "To I-40" to join **EAST I-40** at **EXIT 178**.

WB: At **EXIT 165**, turn **LEFT** and pass under I-40. Follow **BL 40** into **WILLIAMS** (becomes **Railroad Ave** … ONE-WAY…double back to drive **BOTH** streets). Continue to **I-40 EXIT 161**, and join **I-40 WEST** (almost 4 mi total this page).

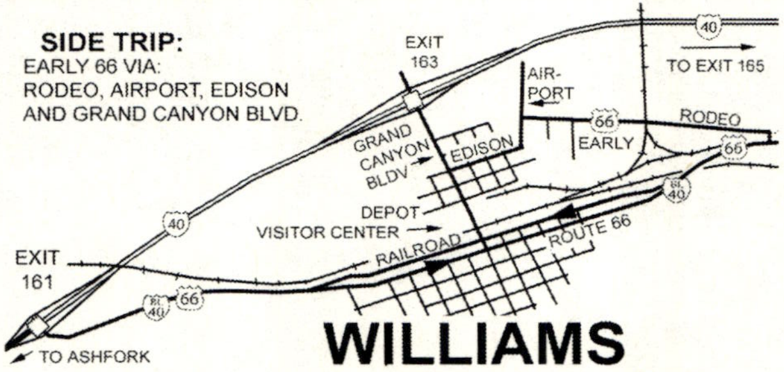

WILLIAMS has the distinction of being the **LAST** US 66 town bypassed, on Oct 13, 1984. **Bearizona** drive-thru animal park is at 1500 E Route 66, near EXIT 165. **SIDE TRIP**: East from their entrance, Mountain Man Trail/Forest Rd 51A is an old gravel section that ends at EXIT 167. **Main Route**: **Scavenger Hunt!** What is the "fun" slogan painted on the RR overpass above BL 40/ Route 66 just west of EXIT 165? (barely visible). Of the one-way streets thru town, the earlier route ran via "**Route 66**." The **WB** route, **Railroad Ave**, came along in 1955. The town is so compact you should drive **BOTH**. It's traditional for overnighters to stroll downtown in the evening, but you may need a coat, even in summer! At 101 E Route 66, check out **Pete's Gas Station Museum**, with his father's 1950 Ford in front, and gas collection inside. **GIFT SHOP ALERT**!

For eats, try **Rods Steakhouse** (look for the big **Neon Bull**) or **Twisters 50's Soda Fountain** or the many other places (reviews vary widely). Plenty of motels to choose-check the Federation Guide or go online for info and reviews. Two of the most unusual are the **Red Garter Bed and Bakery** at 137 W Railroad in an 1897 bordello (look for the "manikin of the evening" leaning out a window), and the **Drover's Inn** at "**Wild West JCT**," an old motel remodeled into a "false-front" frontier town at 321 E Route 66 with a saloon and restaurant too. See the MAP for another early 66 **SIDE TRIP**.

WILLIAMS' major attraction is the **Grand Canyon Railway**, which offers train rides in restored 1880s coaches (pulled by a vintage engine) to the canyon for day visits, or overnight (they advise getting room reservations for the Rim 6 months in advance!). Headquartered at the **Williams Depot** at 233 N Grand Canyon Blvd (just north of the RR tracks). Nearby is the **Grand Canyon Railway Hotel**. INFO: (800) THE TRAIN. www.thetrain.com

EB: From **EXIT 161**, take **BL 40** into **WILLIAMS**. Follow "**Route 66**" ONE-WAY thru downtown (double back to drive **BOTH** streets). Continue east with **BL 40** to **EXIT 165**, and join **I-40 EAST** ("to Flagstaff")…(almost 4 mi total this page).

WB: Take **I-40 WB** from **WILLIAMS**. Use **EXIT 146** (AZ Hwy 89 S) but turn **RIGHT** with **BL 40** into **ASH FORK**. Follow **BL 40** thru town ONE-WAY WB on **Lewis**, then re-join **I-40 WB** at **EXIT 144**. Take **EXIT 139**, and follow "**Crookton Rd**" to **SELIGMAN**.

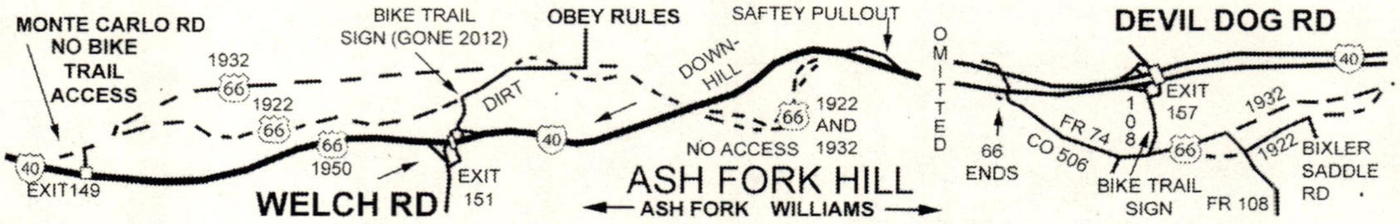

SIDE TRIP: If you've brought your **mountain bike** along (or rent one in Flagstaff), two sites in the **Kaibab National Forest** offer **BIKE TRAILS** on sections of abandoned '66!

Devil Dog Loop: South of EXIT 157 should (I hope) be a **Bike Trail sign**, directing you along the **1922 & '32 Routes**, thru thick woods. **Ash Fork Hill Loop**: From I-40, down the steep escarpment of infamous **Ash Fork Hill**, (smell the overheated brakes!) take **EXIT 151 (Welch Rd)** north for 0.2 mi and park. Sadly, this bike trail sign is currently gone. This tour follows the precariously perched **1922 unpaved road** along a steep hillside, before returning by the **1932 road**, from near **EXIT 149** (**Monte Carlo Rd**). (**DO NOT** attempt entry/egress via **this** exit: respect private property). **Safeguard any valuables in your vehicle**. Due to the missing sign and possible changes, I'd advise you to check at the **Williams Ranger District**, 742 S Clover Rd in **WILLIAMS** for latest info/rules before using either loop. (928) 635-5600.

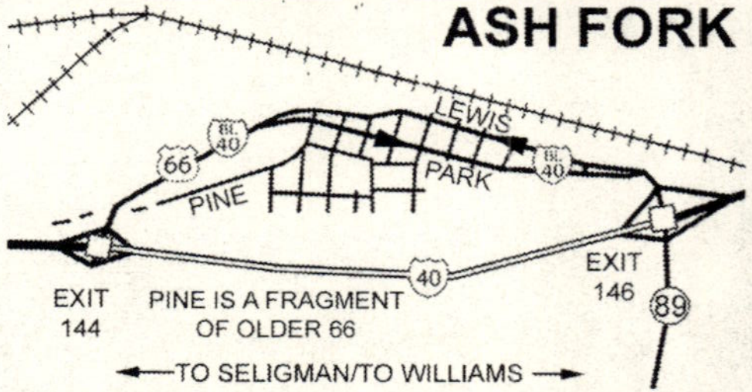

The I-40 bypass wasn't kind to **ASH FORK** (famous for flagstones) as few businesses still line its pair of ONE-WAY streets. The WB street, **Lewis**, is the oldest. **PHOTO OP!** Among the points of interest in town is a cool **1958 Desoto** perched on the roof of an old gas station which housed **Desoto's Beauty and Barber Shop** (for sale). A couple of architecturally interesting old motels (one with cobblestone walls) rest alongside Lewis Street. Other relics line the street. For eats, the **Ranch House Café** at 111 E Park is recommended. An abandoned railroad runs alongside I-40 west from town.

EB: Take **EXIT 144**, cross under I-40, then **LEFT** on **BL 40** thru **ASH FORK** . At the Y continue ONE-WAY EB on **Park** (double back to drive **Lewis** too) then re-join **I-40 EAST** at **EXIT 146**. Take **EXIT 161**, and turn **RIGHT** to follow **BL 40 EB** into **WILLIAMS**.

(see MAP #3 AZ page-11)

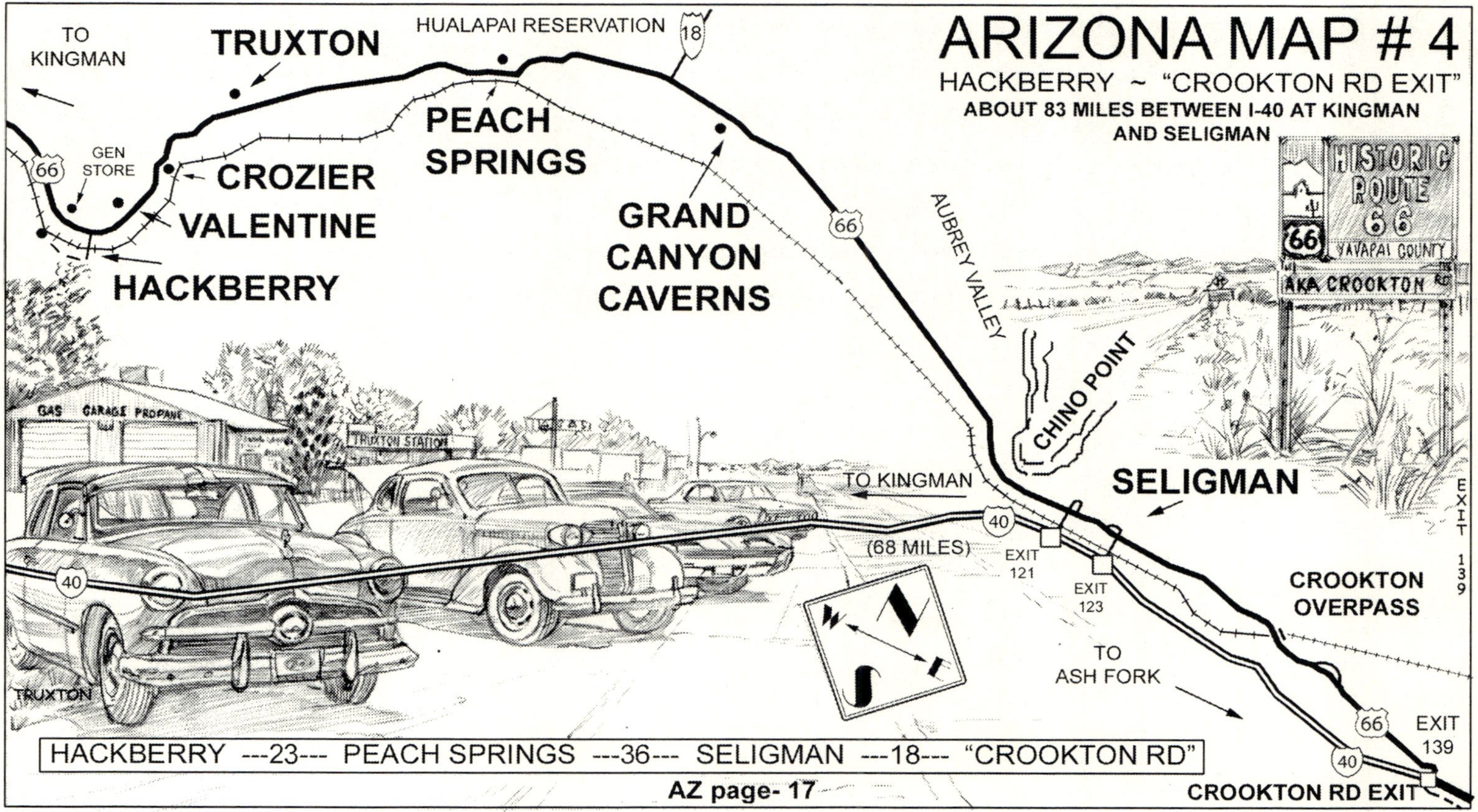
ARIZONA MAP # 4
HACKBERRY ~ "CROOKTON RD EXIT"
ABOUT 83 MILES BETWEEN I-40 AT KINGMAN AND SELIGMAN
TO KINGMAN
TRUXTON
HUALAPAI RESERVATION
18
GEN STORE
66
CROZIER
VALENTINE
HACKBERRY
PEACH SPRINGS
GRAND CANYON CAVERNS
AUBREY VALLEY
HISTORIC ROUTE 66
YAVAPAI COUNTY
AKA CROOKTON
CHINO POINT
SELIGMAN
EXIT 139
GAS GARAGE PROPANE
TRUXTON STATION
TO KINGMAN
40
(68 MILES)
EXIT 121
EXIT 123
CROOKTON OVERPASS
TO ASH FORK
TRUXTON
EXIT 139
CROOKTON RD EXIT
HACKBERRY ---23--- PEACH SPRINGS ---36--- SELIGMAN ---18--- "CROOKTON RD"

WB: Follow **"Crookton Rd"/ "Historic 66"** for about 17 mi from **EXIT 139**. At the east side of **SELIGMAN**, follow the **WB lane** as it curves **RIGHT**, then STOP, and **LEFT** into town. Continue 1.2 mi on **Historic 66**, passing by the I-40 EXIT 121 access rd turnoff.

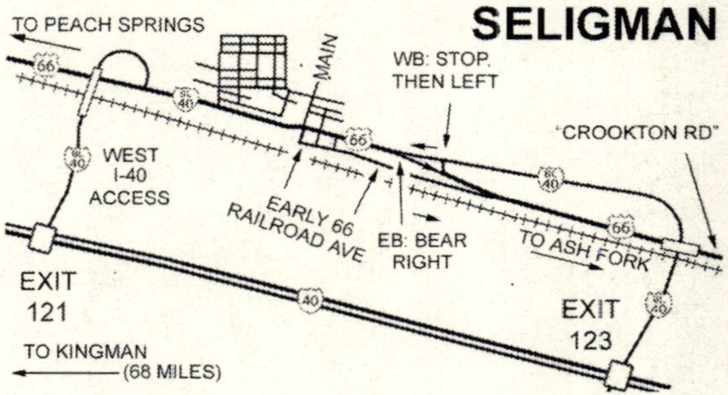

EXIT 139 is the **eastern gateway** to a golden stretch of about 159 almost uninterrupted miles of pristine, EZ-driving Route 66. "Go WEST, young man," and you'll reach **TOPOCK** on the Colorado River **WITHOUT** setting tires on I-40 (you DO have to cross under it a couple of times). Recently rebuilt "**Crookton Rd**" follows alongside a bygone railroad alignment as it climbs steadily into the hills.

OPTION: About **6 miles** west of **EXIT 139** you can elect to turn **RIGHT** (just before the guard rails) onto a short loop of **ROUGH older 66** that curves below a hillside (which the newer road carves thru). **EB**: turn **LEFT** almost **2 miles** east of the RR.

At "**Crookton Crossing**" is a pair of railroad overpasses. The **unused** span makes a good platform for train spotting. Look for abandoned **1920s and '30s roadbed** alongside current **66** from here to **SELIGMAN**.

Enjoy replica **Burma Shave** signs on both sides of **SELIGMAN**, birthplace of the **Historic Route 66 Association of Arizona** and home of the **Annual Fun Run**. Each spring hundreds of cars cruise town, then head to **TOPOCK** (or visa versa). If lucky, you might meet association founder **Angel Delgadillo** (as seen on TV) at his barbershop, now the **Route 66 Visitor Center**. **GIFT SHOP ALERT**! Nearby is the world's famous **Snow Cap**. This has long been the funniest food spot on '66, as the late **Juan Delgadillo** (Angel's brother) played a gamut of jokes and tricks on his customers, including false doorknobs, "squirting" catsup bottles and "slightly used napkins." Each visit to his outlandishly decorated diner was a colorful experience, including a sign proclaiming "**Dead Chicken**" and a customized, flamboyant parade car parked out front. Despite Juan's untimely passing in 2004, his family keeps up the comical tradition and the good food.

(**SELIGMAN** continues on **AZ page-19**)

EB: Continue with **BL 40/Historic 66** thru **SELIGMAN**. On the east side (1.2 mi from the BL 40 overpass), bear **RIGHT** from BL 40 (left is "To I-40") with the sign "**Crookton Rd/ Historic 66**." Go about 17 mi. At **EXIT 139**, join **I-40 EAST** to **ASH FORK**.

WB: Cross under the west side I-40 EXIT 121 access road, and continue on "**Historic 66**" west about 36 mi thru **PEACH SPRINGS**.

SELIGMAN part 2: There are many places to spend the night, such as the **Route 66 Motel** (928) 422-3204, the **Deluxe Inn (928)** 422-3244 and the super **Supai Motel** (928) 422-4153 with its lovely neon sign (motels fill during the **Fun Run** (first weekend in May) so reserve ahead). Choices for road food (not literally, one hopes) include the **Roadkill Café**, or the **Copper Cart Restaurant**. An old-time place for liquid refreshment is **Black Cat Cocktails**. Eye-catching **Seligman Sundries** is a way cool and friendly stop for coffee, shakes or gifts. Check out their collection of old advertising that came with the store! **SELIGMAN** is best early am, before tour buses block the view.

SIDE TRIP: The **early route** thru town came in from the east on **Railroad Ave** (past the still-standing Delgadillo Pool Hall and the nearby site of a couple of old-time brothels), then turned north on **Main St**. (see map AZ Page-18)

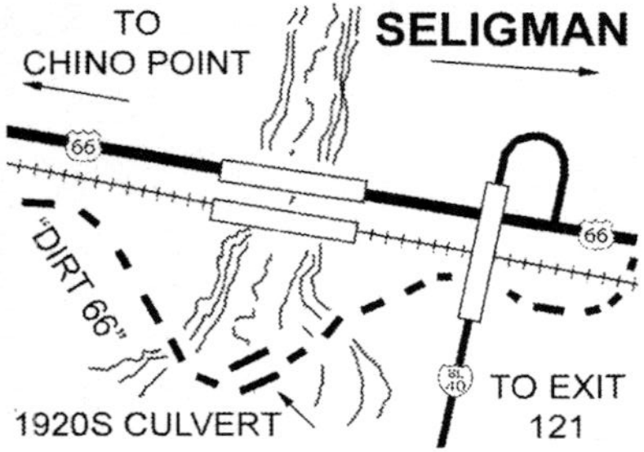

As for the abandoned route (private) west of **SELIGMAN**: from 66, look under the RR trestle west of town to peek at a **1920s rock culvert**. This faint dirt route (edged with rocks and the remains of an old flivver) can also be seen (caution) from atop the west side **BL 40** overpass. Back on 66, at **Chino Point** the road and RR squeeze around the sharp "point" of the **Aubrey Cliffs** before entering **Aubrey Valley**. Just west of the base of the hills, the 1930s route is visible as it veers off for a few miles on the north. Further on are the buildings of an old motel on the south side.

Grand Canyon Caverns (formerly **Dinosaur Caverns**) was another place my Dad would not stop at (We **ALMOST** did in 1969, 'till he found it was situated a whole MILE off of 66)! The slight detour for the cave tour (and restaurant) is worth the time (I **MADE** Dad stop on a 1981 trip). **GIANT ALERT**! The great green **Allosaurus (?...**can't be a **T-REX** with three fingers!) still poses out front for obligatory snapshots. **GIFT SHOP ALERT!** On isolated **66** here is the **Caverns Inn** (mixed reviews) (928) 422-4565.

SCAVENGER HUNT! What **COLOR** is the big Cavern dinosaur's **BELLY**?

EB: Continue on 66 for about 36 mi. Approaching **SELIGMAN**, follow "**Historic 66**" under the west-side I-40 EXIT 121 access road.

 (see MAP 4 AZ page-17)

WB: Follow WEST **AZ 66** from **PEACH SPRINGS**, thru **TRUXTON** and **VALENTINE** to **HACKBERRY** (about 23 mi this page)

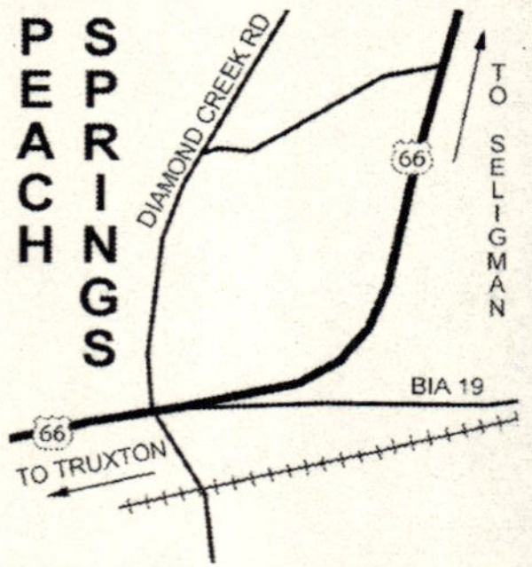

The steep hill east of **PEACH SPRINGS** offers a quick view of the distant **Grand Canyon**. This town is the headquarters of the **Hualapai Indian Reservation**. The Hualapai Tribal Forestry Dept is housed in a cobblestone former trading post (that predates 66) on the north side of the road, while a picturesque old gas station/garage (Osterman's Shell from 1932) remains on the south. Modern **Hualapai Lodge** offers lodging and the **River Runner's Resort** restaurant (928) 769-2230. Arrange for tours of the **Lower Grand Canyon** here.

Wooden markers welcome you to tiny **TRUXTON**, (est. 1951) home to the old **Frontier Motel and Café**. Their neon sign had been restored circa 2002, but when asked to turn it on in August 2012 they told me it did not work. Sic transit neon. There's a cool painting of a chef on the (currently closed) café front wall.

Further west, 66 drops down into **Crozier Canyon**, where the wide-open spaces surrender to craggy slopes. Just west of mile post 89, old 66 veers off across a concrete bridge (PRIVATE) before passing by a row of tin roofed tourist cabins visible in the floodplain of **Crozier Creek** below. The LAST paving on US 66 in **ARIZONA** occurred along here circa 1937, shortly after workers blasted big bites from out of the hills above the RR tracks for the improved path of Route 66.

Near **VALENTINE** is "**Keepers of the Wild Nature Park**." Old 66 always had dubious roadside "zoos" but this non profit attraction is dedicated to the care of "abused, neglected, abandoned and retired captive wildlife." www.keepersofthewild.org The old **VALENTINE** Post Office (famous for Valentine's Day postmarks) is long gone, but the **Valentine Indian School** although long disused, is still standing. The "Non-Indian" school, a one-room bldg, is nearby across the tracks (private).

A few roadside remnants cling to the flanks of 66, including former Chief's Motel and an old Union 76 station. The boulder strewn slopes of some area hillsides were scarred by an unfortunate mining effort, but the rugged beauty endures.

EB: Follow **EAST AZ 66** from **HACKBERRY**, thru **VALENTINE**, **TRUXTON** and **PEACH SPRINGS** (about 23 mi this page)

(see MAP 4 AZ page-17)

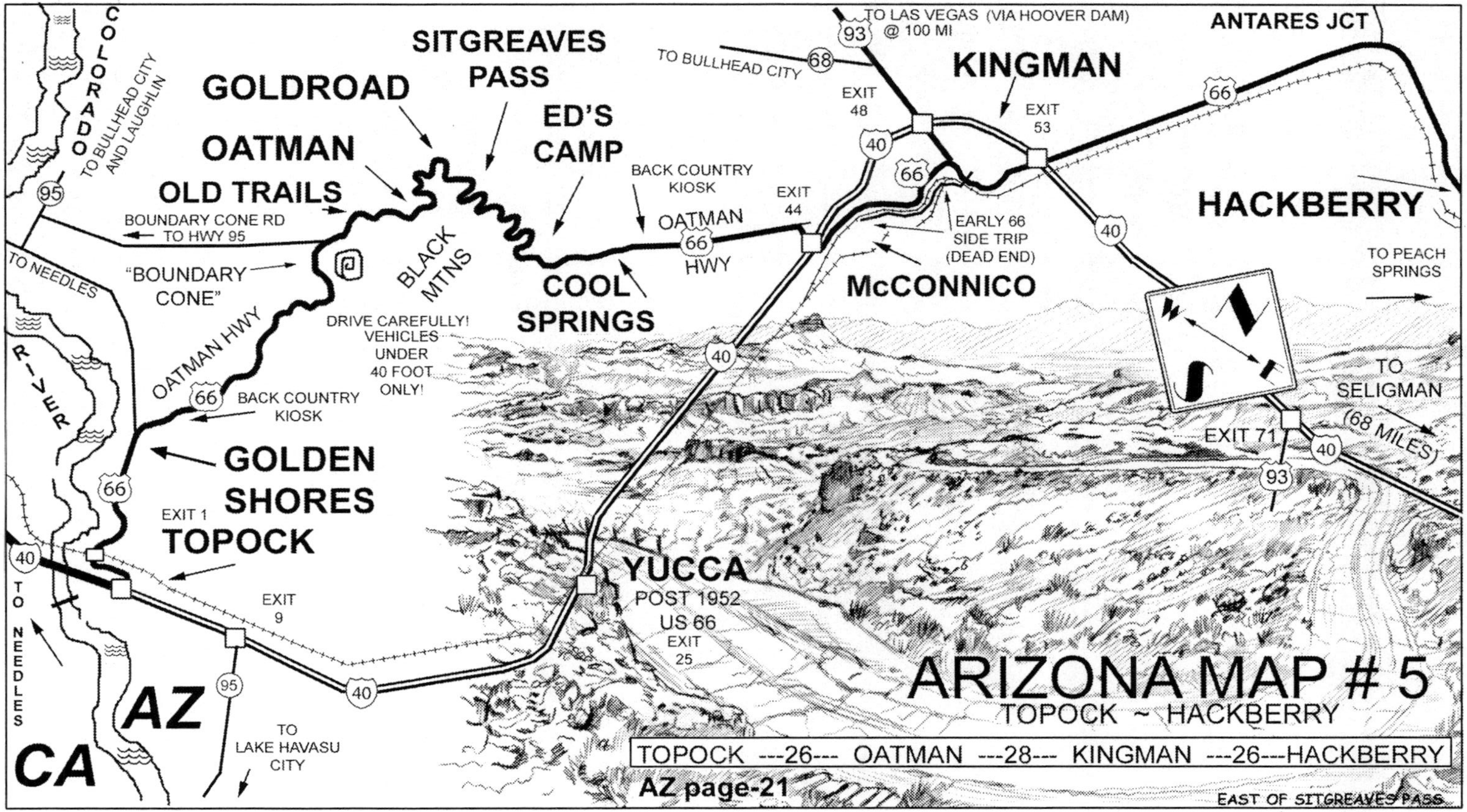
ARIZONA MAP # 5
TOPOCK ~ HACKBERRY
TOPOCK ---26--- OATMAN ---28--- KINGMAN ---26---HACKBERRY
COLORADO
RIVER
TO BULLHEAD CITY AND LAUGHLIN
95
GOLDROAD
SITGREAVES PASS
ED'S CAMP
OATMAN
OLD TRAILS
BOUNDARY CONE RD TO HWY 95
"BOUNDARY CONE"
TO NEEDLES
BLACK MTNS
DRIVE CAREFULLY! VEHICLES UNDER 40 FOOT ONLY!
OATMAN HWY
66
BACK COUNTRY KIOSK
GOLDEN SHORES
EXIT 1
TOPOCK
40
TO NEEDLES
EXIT 9
95
TO LAKE HAVASU CITY
AZ
CA
BACK COUNTRY KIOSK
OATMAN 66 HWY
COOL SPRINGS
EXIT 44
TO BULLHEAD CITY
68
93
TO LAS VEGAS (VIA HOOVER DAM) @ 100 MI
EXIT 48
KINGMAN
EXIT 53
EARLY 66 SIDE TRIP (DEAD END)
McCONNICO
ANTARES JCT
HACKBERRY
TO PEACH SPRINGS
TO SELIGMAN (68 MILES)
EXIT 71
YUCCA
POST 1952 US 66
EXIT 25
EAST OF SITGREAVES PASS

WB: Take **AZ 66** from **HACKBERRY** for about 24 mi, and cross under EXIT 53 into **KINGMAN** on **BL 40/Route 66/Andy Devine**.

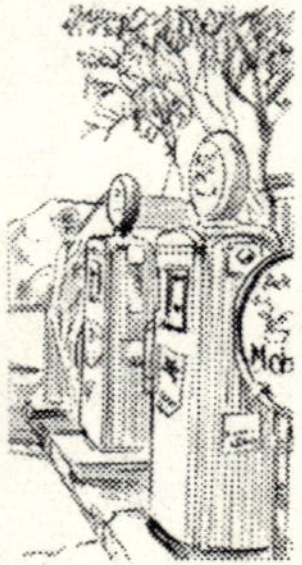

Old **HACKBERRY** rests south of the railroad on "**Dirt 66**," but the **Hackberry Gen Store** offers a great stop on **AZ 66**. This was the former haunt of the late Route artist **Bob Waldmire**, now operated by the **Pritchards**, who have kept up the tradition to make this a place that makes the brake lights glow. **PHOTO OP!** There is a passel of cool old stuff to see outside, including rusty old sedans, vintage gas pumps and signs, and a bright red '56 Corvette. **GIFT SHOP ALERT**! Plenty to see on the inside, too. **Guys**, check out the "tasteful" men's room decor! hackberrygeneralstore.com

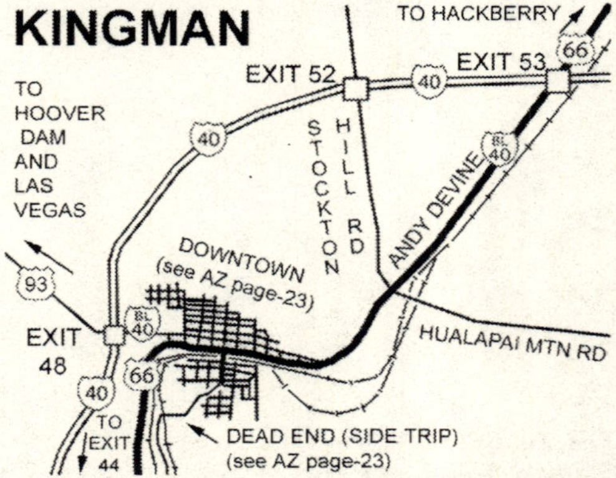

West of **HACKBERRY**, 66 and the RR negotiate long "**Antares Curve**," centered on the junction with Antares Rd. Here, near the Kozy Corner Trailer Court and an A-Frame structure that once housed a popular restaurant, is a **GIANT ALERT!** Delightfully out of place is "Headacus," a 14 foot tall "**Tiki**" (or Easter Island) **Idol** head! Why? Why not.

The way west is fast and straight into **KINGMAN,** where you encounter I-40 for the first time in miles. **ADVISORY**: Going either WB or EB, this is a good location to top off your **gas tank** (shop for best price). Old 66 thru town is variously signed as "**Route 66**" and "**Andy Devine**" (to honor an old-time actor). Many chain motels cluster near the exits, while classic Route 66 lodging remains along the route, some with neon signs. For a vintage motel with great neon try the **Hill Top Motel**, on the hill east of downtown, at 1901 E Andy Devine. (928) 753-2198 I stayed there in 2012 and liked it. Haven't tried the nearby, recently renovated **El Trovatore Motel**, but they get points for restoring their neon (including a "towering" sign), and feature theme rooms. (928) 753-6520. The downtown **Hotel Brunswick** may reopen in 2013. A water tower with a huge "**Historic Route 66**" shield welcomes you to a downtown full of photogenic architecture, dominated by the tall "Hotel Beale" signs. (more **KINGMAN** on **AZ page-23**).

EB: From EXIT 53 in **KINGMAN** continue with **EAST AZ 66** (sign: "Peach Springs") for about 24 mi to **HACKBERRY**.

WB: Take **Andy Devine/Route 66/BL 40** for 3.8 mi thru downtown. Past **Locomotive Park**, prepare for LEFT turn. At the "**Y**," turn **LEFT** with **Historic 66/Andy Devine** (follow sign "**To OATMAN**" and **AVOID** BL 40/US 93 as they continue to EXIT 48/"Vegas"). Take **Historic 66** for 5 mi down the canyon, thru McCONNICO. At **EXIT 44**/Oatman Rd (next exit), turn **RIGHT**, crossing under I-40.

WB NOTE: If using US 93 to **Las Vegas**, PLEASE come back here to finish Route 66! Or take US 95 north from **NEEDLES**.

KINGMAN DETAIL

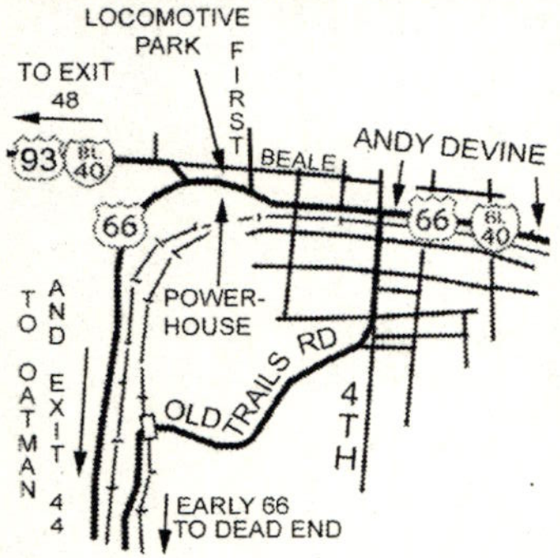

On the west side of downtown, in a historic 1907 building, is the **Powerhouse Visitor Center**, the head-quarters of the **Historic Route 66 Association of AZ.** Make time for the fantastic **Route 66 Museum** upstairs, open 7 days a week. It's worth the small charge to view the quality displays, including dioramas of a **dustbowl family** and earlier sojourners in a prairie schooner, plus murals, wall-sized quotes from ***The Grapes of Wrath***, large maps of old 66, scrapbooks, and a bullet-nose Studebaker. **GIFT SHOP ALERT!** (928)753-9889. Also noteworthy is the nearby **Mohave Museum** for regional history.

Across from the Powerhouse is **Locomotive Park**, featuring a majestic black **Santa Fe steam locomotive** and **a red caboose**. **PHOTO OP**! My family posed here in 1961…you should too. At the west end of the park is a monument dedicated to the **Beale Wagon Route**, with wagons and camels on top (camels were used in experiments with desert travel). **SCAVENGER HUNT**! According to the marker, what **YEAR** did the railroad come to **KINGMAN**?

SIDE TRIP: This paved **round trip** of almost **6 miles** provides an enjoyable, scenic drive down OLD 66 towards McCONNICO. From downtown KINGMAN, cross the tracks on **4th St**. A few streets south (about 0.2 mi), follow the **main road** as it curves **RIGHT** onto **Old Trails Rd**. Follow the **SHARP** turn **LEFT** under the **RR trestle**, then **SLOW** and watch out for the **NARROW** squeeze between blocks of boulders on a blind curve. Imagine meeting a truck here on some dark night in the 1930s. After a pleasant drive of about 2.8 mi between the two branches of the RR tracks, along **Perfume Canyon** (named for the sewage treatment plant?), the road curves away from the RR. **Turn around** next chance to rejoin current Route 66 (which descends the canyon on the opposite side) at 4th St in **KINGMAN**.

EB: From **EXIT 44**, follow the **Frontage Rd/ Historic 66** for 5 mi (thru McCONNICO and up the canyon) into **KINGMAN**, curving **RIGHT** on **Andy Devine/Route 66**/BL **40**. Then continue past downtown 3.8 mi to cross under I-40 at EXIT 53.

WB: From I-40 at **EXIT 44**, stay **AHEAD** for 0.3 mi (follow the "**Historic 66 Oatman Hwy**" sign). Turn **LEFT** to follow **Oatman Hwy** (see text **ALERT**). Climb the twisty mountain grades past **COOL SPRINGS** to **SITGREAVES PASS** (about 18.7 mi from I-40).

NOTE: It is about 48 miles from EXIT 44 (**McCONNICO**) to EXIT 1 (**TOPOCK**) via **Oatman Hwy**-at least 1.5 hours straight driving. **ALERT (RV's take note): Oatman Hwy/Back Country Byway** is **HIGHLY** recommended, but **VERY** steep/crooked (and a bit **rough** at **patches**), with scary drops! **No vehicles over 40 feet**. **RV**'s should take **I-40**, the **POST-1952** route. Cars can drive back up to **OATMAN** from **TOPOCK** if desired (best for those who hate heights). PARKING is LIMITED. See **AZ page-1** for mountain driving tips.

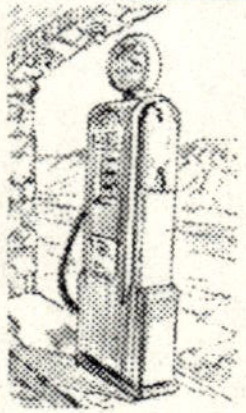

The drive across the drainage of **Sacramento Wash** is one of the most laid back on 66. No turns, no stops, just ease along at 45mph and watch the ragged ramparts of the **Black Mountains** loom ever closer. **WB**, stop at the pullout (milepost 34) to read the **Back Country Byway sign** for history and tips ("…lookout for **wild burros** and **bighorn sheep** in the road."). The first sign of life on the mountain is recently rebuilt **COOL SPRINGS**. This 1926 store and camp had reverted to stone rubble, before being rebuilt the first time for the movie "***Universal Soldier***." Not much was left of the set after Van Damme was thru. Fortunately, Ned Leuchtner had a vision (and Dennis Dechenne had the skills) to restore this "cool" place to life, basing the restoration on old photos. Those old Mobilgas pumps look fine under the rock canopy. **GIFT SHOP ALERT**.

Up the hill resides another old-time place, intact but closed and forbidden to tourists. Ed Edgerton, an old prospector who forsook the "Mother Lode" to mine "the Mother Road," started **ED'S CAMP**. **NO TRESSPASSING (obey all such signs)**! The road **REALLY** gets hairy west of Ed's, with hairpin curves and sheer drops coming hot and heavy. Note the interesting variety of stone or cable guardrails (or the LACK thereof) that offer faint comfort. **PHOTO OP**! Just east of **Milepost 30**, (0.7 mi east of the summit, 4.3 mi w of **COOL SPRINGS**) a wide spot on the inside shoulder offers a place to park, and over 30 rock steps lead up to **Shaffer's Fish Bowl Springs**, a man-made basin that collects water from a seep. Flowers appear in season (as do bees). Please respect the fragile beauty of this area (and use **CAUTION** for falls and snakes!). The view of the switchbacks downhill is tremendous (and often photographed). Next (**WB**) is the final push to the summit!

EB: Descend from **SITGREAVES PASS** (about 18.7 mi to I-40). Pass **COOL SPRINGS** on **Oatman Hwy**. Nearing I-40, **STOP**, then turn **RIGHT** ("To I-40"). Cross under I-40 at **EXIT 44**. **LEFT** on the **Frontage Rd** towards **KINGMAN**.

WB: Descend from **SITGREAVES PASS** for about 4.4 twisty mi, curving thru **GOLDROAD** to **OATMAN**. Continue for 2.4 miles from the Oatman Hotel, then bear **LEFT** at the **"Y,"** and follow **Oatman Hwy** for 17.6 mi to **GOLDEN SHORES** (the **HWY** from Bullhead City joins). Continue for 4.5 mi, curve under the RR Tracks, then join **I-40 WEST ("Needles")** at **EXIT 1** in **TOPOCK**

Don't waste a "sigh of relief" on reaching 3550 foot high **SITGREAVES PASS**," for now's the time for the dizzying drop **DOWNHILL** either way (watch those brakes…use lower gear!). On the east side of the pass are a foundation and a few pipe guardrails belonging to on old ice cream stand (yes, roadside enterprise conquered even this remote pass). A new pipeline scar degrades the view somewhat. To the west, another wide spot offers a grand view of crags, cliffs and remnants of old mining days. A bit further, a gravel road takes off along a spur of rock. You can walk this out to see a great vista of **three states** (**AZ, CA** and **NV**), IF it isn't too hazy. Watch for snakes (and bad cell reception)! Obey **no trespass** signs.

WB, a series of tight hairpins take you down to the level of old **GOLDROAD**, a long-gone gold mining town (the mine tour is closed). Bare rocky peaks provide a rugged backdrop for rustic **OATMAN**, which once mined for gold, but now digs for tourist dollars with shops and cafes, staged gunfights and live music all crammed into its one burro-lined street. Feed the wild (protected) burros carefully, as they bite (what they do to the sidewalks is worse)! The circa 1902 **Oatman Hotel and Café** is the most authentic place in town, with great atmosphere (but likely NO rooms). During the May Fun Run, old 66 is jammed bumper to nerf bar with all sorts of colorful street rods and hot rods. Park and walk a while. Your brake-foot needs rest. INFO: (928) 768-6222.

Thankfully, the road between **OATMAN** and **GOLDEN SHORES** was repaved, after neglect had rendered it nearly defunct. Today's drive is pleasant at **45 mph! ALERT**: Many tight curves on the low ridges can fool you at higher speeds. Shaggy trees offer a temporary green respite in the last stretch before **TOPOCK**, and the bridges over the **Colorado River** into **CALIFORNIA**. Relief is short lived, as the desert resumes on the other side of the river. **Topock 66 Spa & Resort** is due in 2013.

EB DRIVERS: See the **ALERT** (especially **RVs**) and **NOTE** on AZ page-24 **BEFORE** driving to **OATMAN** and stop at the **Back Country Byway** kiosk at milepost 3 (north of **GOLDEN SHORES**).

EB: Take **EXIT 1** (**TOPOCK**), cross I-40, go **LEFT** and curve thru the RR underpass (see text for cautions and **RV ALERT**). Follow **Oatman Hwy** for 4.5 mi, thru **GOLDEN SHORES**. At the "Y" JCT ("Bullhead City"), **BEAR RIGHT** with **Oatman Hwy** for 20 mi to **OATMAN**. Continue, climbing for about 4.4 twisty mi, past **GOLDROAD**, to the crest of **SITGREAVES PASS.**

(SEE INTRO, **AZ page-1**) (see Map 5, **AZ page-21**)

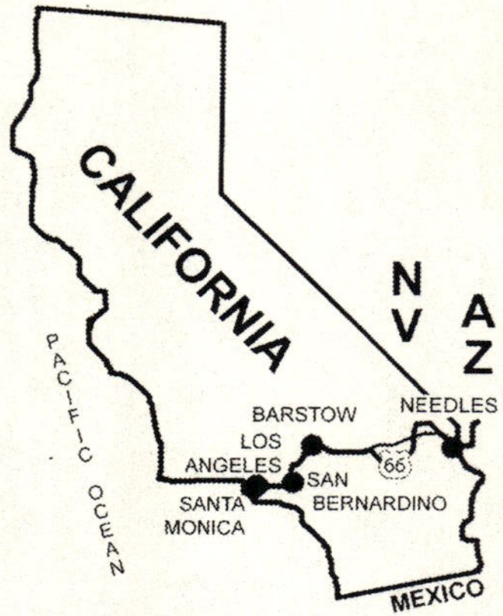

CALIFORNIA OR BUST!

This was the **Battle Cry** for generations of westward bound travelers, starting with the Gold Rush days, and stretching into the 21st Century. Dirt-poor **Dust Bowl Okies**, with hopes and belongings tied to a beat up jalopy. Wanna-be celebrities with movie stars in their eyes, bound for **HOLLYWOOD** with only a bus token and their dreams. Vacationing families heck-bent for **Disneyland,** with a backseat full of whining kids. **Route 66** was their road of choice.

The Mother Road's swath across **SOUTHERN CALIFORNIA** offers a stark contrast between the vast, wide-open spaces of the arid **Mojave Desert** and the tightly packed humanity of the **LA Basin**. Spindly palm trees add a vertical dimension, and a bit of exotica, to most towns along the way, while sagebrush, broom weed, tamarisk and spiky Joshua Trees decorate the desert. Separating these extremes is the "tear on the dotted line" fracture of the San Andreas Fault. Look for new blue and gold "**San Bernardino County 66**" signs between **NEEDLES** and **CLAREMONT** (it's a BIG county). **ALERT:** The replacement of 135 timber bridges between EXIT 115/Mountain Springs Rd and **DAGGETT** is planned for sometime in the future. Check www.mcjerry66.com for updates.

SAN BERNARDINO is the gateway to the metro **LOS ANGELES** area. **Foothill Blvd** was once lined with orange groves and vineyards, now strip malls and houses spring from the rich soil. This corridor still has remnants of Old 66 to enjoy, with the **San Gabriel Mountains** a continuous backdrop. **LA** was an early adopter of the freeway culture. The infamous **Arroyo Seco Parkway** was the first such east of the Mississippi, and much of the "Drive-In, Thru and Around" culture was birthed on or near the Twin Sixes. California driving requires attention, whether in deserted desert or crowded, unfamiliar urban areas. Watch for tailgaters impatient with out of state slowpokes, and **perpetual** traffic jams in the **LA** area. In desert climes, beware of **flash floods** and heat. Carry water and watch your **gas gauge**! Either starting or ending your trip here, may you find **YOUR** Route 66 dreams in sunny **CALIFORNIA.**

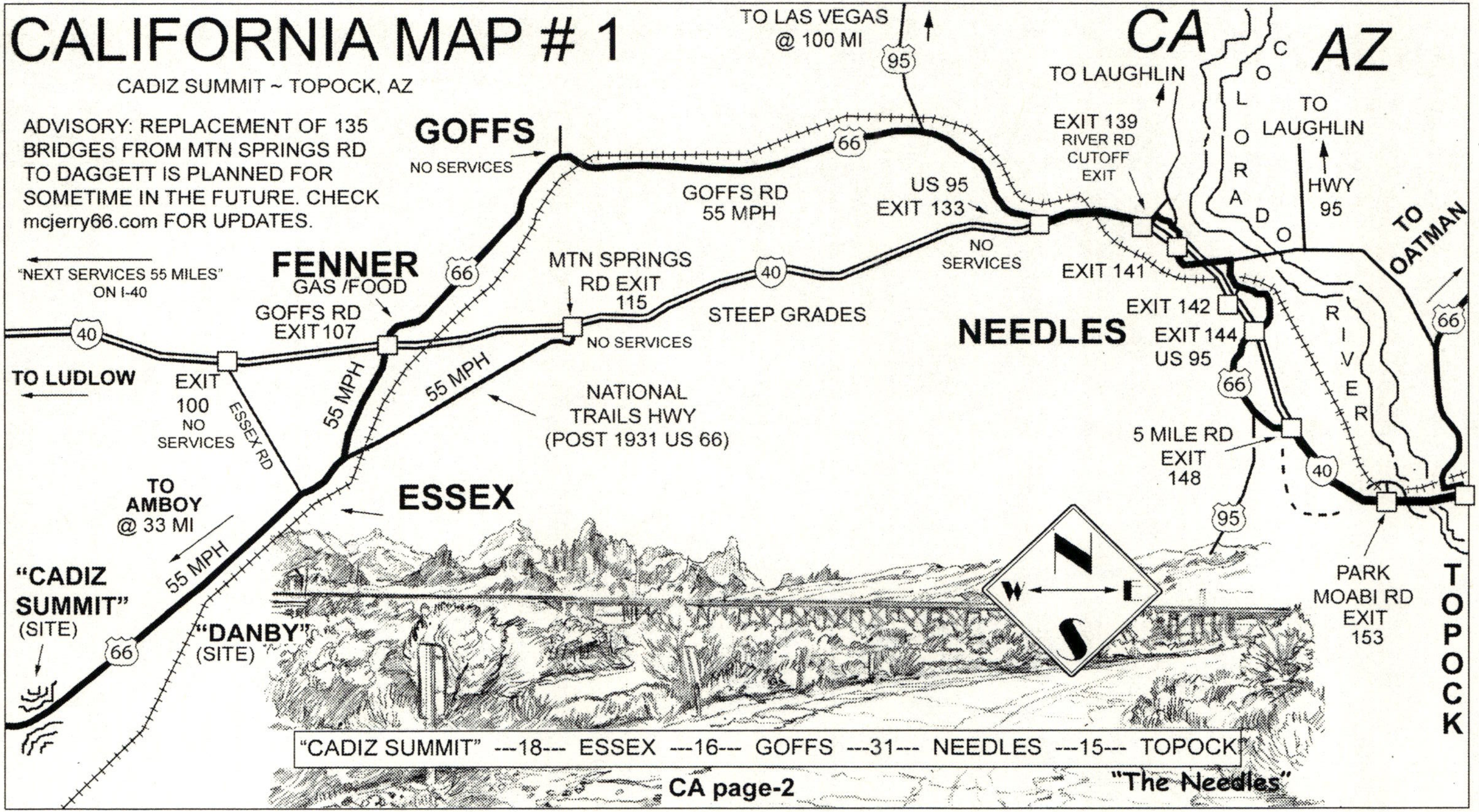
CALIFORNIA MAP # 1
CADIZ SUMMIT ~ TOPOCK, AZ
ADVISORY: REPLACEMENT OF 135 BRIDGES FROM MTN SPRINGS RD TO DAGGETT IS PLANNED FOR SOMETIME IN THE FUTURE. CHECK mcjerry66.com FOR UPDATES.
"NEXT SERVICES 55 MILES" ON I-40
TO LAS VEGAS @ 100 MI
95
CA
AZ
TO LAUGHLIN
COLORADO RIVER
TO LAUGHLIN
HWY 95
TO OATMAN
66
GOFFS
NO SERVICES
66
GOFFS RD 55 MPH
US 95 EXIT 133
EXIT 139 RIVER RD CUTOFF EXIT
NO SERVICES
EXIT 141
EXIT 142
EXIT 144 US 95
NEEDLES
66
5 MILE RD EXIT 148
40
95
PARK MOABI RD EXIT 153
TOPOCK
FENNER
GAS /FOOD
GOFFS RD EXIT 107
66
MTN SPRINGS RD EXIT 115
NO SERVICES
40
STEEP GRADES
40
TO LUDLOW
EXIT 100 NO SERVICES
ESSEX RD
55 MPH
55 MPH
NATIONAL TRAILS HWY (POST 1931 US 66)
TO AMBOY @ 33 MI
ESSEX
55 MPH
"CADIZ SUMMIT" (SITE)
66
"DANBY" (SITE)
N
W
E
S
"CADIZ SUMMIT" ---18--- ESSEX ---16--- GOFFS ---31--- NEEDLES ---15--- TOPOCK
CA page-2
"The Needles"

WB: Cross the **Colorado River** into **CA**. Pass Park Moabi Rd/EXIT 153 and the inspection station. Take **EXIT 148/Five Mile Rd**. Cross over (“**TO US 95**”) Go 1.5 mi, then turn **RIGHT** on **US 95**. Continue 4 mi, under I-40/EXIT 144 and onto Broadway in **NEEDLES**.

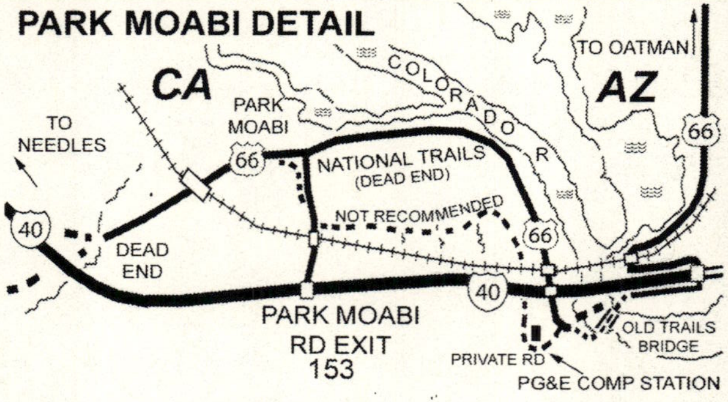

SIDE TRIP (entire page): **Park Moabi Road EXIT 153**: Just like in “Easy Rider” take **Park Rd** north, across the tracks, down to **National Trails/Route 66**. Ahead is **Mohave Regional Park**. (760) 326-3831 **LEFT**, 66 passes thru a **1942 RR overpass** before ending after a mile in a pile of rubble at a now bridge-less gully. **Historic NOTE**: The cut path of early 66 veered off left across the impassable sandy wash and under I-40, resuming again as a much washed-out road that runs south from the Five Mile Rd Exit (this latter is **BAD Road: NOT recommended**).

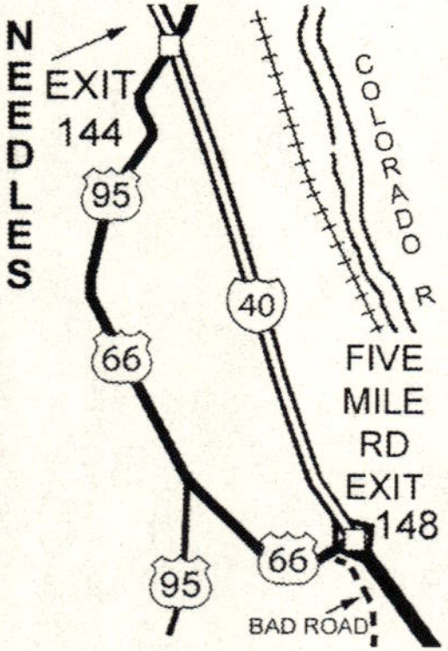

Following **National Trails RIGHT** (EAST) from Park Rd, you’ll curve along the foot of the bluff that marks the edge of the **Colorado River**, and under both the RR and I-40. **PHOTO OP!** Stand in front of the ancient stone billboard welcoming you to Historic 66. Visible are the first and current automobile bridges over the **Colorado River**. To the left is **I-40**; to the right is the graceful **Old Trails Arch Bridge** (seen in “Grapes of Wrath”), built in 1916 for auto traffic, but now supporting a pipeline. In between was the **Red Rock Bridge**, originally built for trains, but taken over by Route 66 in 1947. Bypassed in 1966, this was demolished later. The early road from the arch curves along the bluff, then climbs to the top of the ridge where the **PG&E Compressor Station** sits. All this road is **PRIVATE**, so return to I-40. **Historic NOTE**: the early route came down from the compressor ridge, and dipped in and out of washes as indicated on the detail map. This dead end road is washed out in several places and is **NOT recommended**. Obey current and posted park rules about off road travel (not allowed here at this writing).

EB: Follow **US 95** from I-40. After 4 mi, **BEAR LEFT** at the “Y” onto **Five Mile Road** (“**TO I-40**”). Go 1.5 mi, then join **I-40 EAST** and continue past Park Moabi Rd/EXIT 153. Cross the **Colorado River** into **AZ** (be prepared to take the first exit at **TOPOCK**).

WB: Follow **Broadway** into <u>**NEEDLES**</u> for 0.9 mi. At the **Y** (with Front St), bear **LEFT** with **Broadway** thru downtown. Past J St, curve with **Broadway**, cross the RR tracks, then **LEFT** on **Needles Hwy** (0.6 mi from J St). Pass under I-40, go 0.6 mi and cross I-40 again. Go 0.7 mi. At the "**Y**," bear **LEFT** with **Historic 66**. Go 1.3 mi. **LEFT** on **Park Rd/River Road Cutoff**. Join **I-40 WEST**.

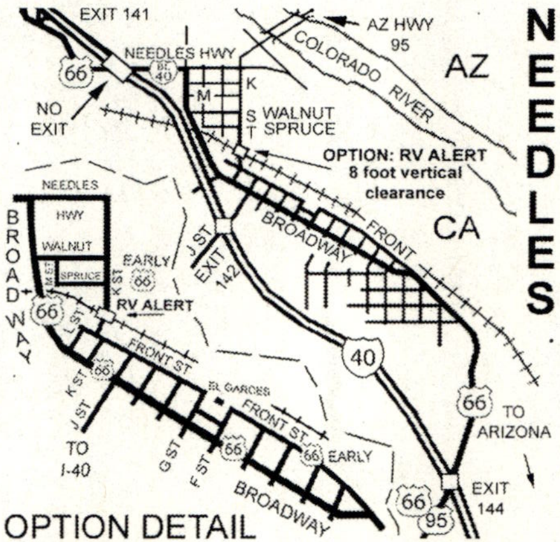

PHOTO OP! On <u>**NEEDLES**</u>' east side is the restored "**66 Motel" NEON SIGN**. Nearby's the official "**Welcome Wagon**," an old freight wagon bearing the town name. The former **Masonic Temple** (with three Moroccan-arch doorways) at Broadway and F St dates to 1929.

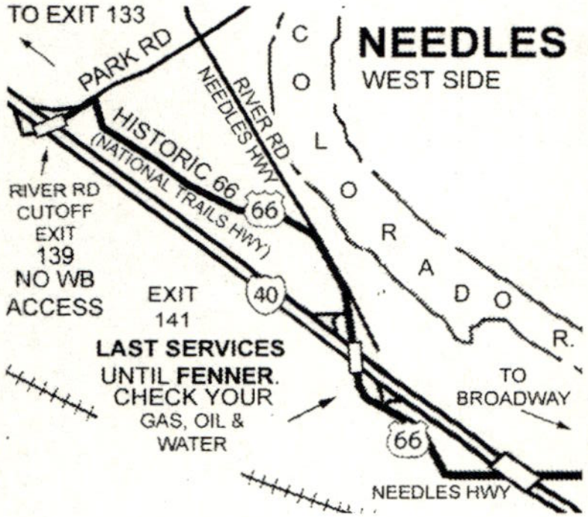

<u>**OPTION (RV ALERT)**</u>: **Front St** (from the Y with Broadway on the east side) carried **early 66** by the tracks, then jogged around the **El Garces**, the huge Harvey House being restored. <u>**NEEDLES**</u> has long been a railroad town. Train spotters will enjoy the view of the railroad yard. West of downtown on **Front St**, a small park features a few old railroad boxcars and a **Santa Fe caboose**. Early 66 then crossed under the railroad on **K St**, thru a <u>**low**</u>, <u>**narrow**</u> underpass (**8-foot vertical clearance**-go back to Broadway if higher). It turned on **Spruce** to N St (now Broadway) but you must go up to **Walnut** or **Needles Hwy** to reconnect.

For eats, try **Burger Hut** at Broadway and D. Reviews vary on the many motels. You might check out **Fender's River Road Resort** at 3396 Needles Hwy (a small riverside motel/camp with a nice neon sign and a "license-plate tree") or the **Budget Inn**, 2104 Needles Hwy.

EB: Take **River Rd Cutoff/Exit 139**, cross I-40, then quickly turn **RIGHT** onto **Historic 66**. Go 1.3 mi, then merge **AHEAD** onto **River Rd/Needles Hwy** and cross I-40, then curve with **BL 40** and cross back under I-40. Go <u>0.2 mi</u>, then curve **RIGHT** on **Broadway**. Follow **Broadway** 2 mi (past J St and thru downtown <u>**NEEDLES**</u>), to the JCT with I-40. Cross I-40 and follow **US 95** from town.

WB: Follow **I-40 WEST** from **NEEDLES** for 6 mi. Take **EXIT 133** ("To Las Vegas") and go 6 mi on **US 95 NORTH**. Just before the RR XING, turn **LEFT** on **Goffs Rd.** Go 14 mi. Cross the RR tracks into **GOFFS**. Continue with **Goffs Rd** (along the RR) for 10 mi to **FENNER**. Pass under I-40, and continue 5 mi to the STOP at **National Trails Hwy**. Turn **RIGHT**, go 2 mi to **ESSEX**, then continue (no turn) on **National Trails Hwy** for 18 mi (passing "**DANBY**") to the mountain pass at "**CADIZ SUMMIT**"

CAR GAME! Don't get lost in the vast **Mojave Desert**! Thankfully, there are **Route 66 Shields** painted on the pavement. Tell the kids to watch carefully for them, lest ye go astray! **First** to spot **each sign** gets 10 points…50 points wins!

OPTION: US 66 took two routes west of **NEEDLES.** The **Post-1931** road, covered by **I-40**, **(see CA map #1)** charges boldly over the **South Pass** of the **Sacramento Mountains**. An 11-mile stretch connects **Mountain Springs Rd/Exit 115** with **ESSEX**. The **Pre-1931** EZ TOUR follows the railroad over an easy-driving no-grade route bypassing the mountains.

SIDE TRIP: Just north of old 66 on **Lanfair Rd** in **GOFFS** is the restored 1914-era **Goffs Schoolhouse**. Inside the one-room school are exhibits of the cultural history of the **Mojave Desert**. Outside are displays of road and mining machinery, vehicles, and a windmill. Open by appointment only (2 to 3 days notice) but outside areas and a historical marker can be seen from the drive. www.mdhca.org (760) 733-4482 **SCAVENGER HUNT!** Who was the architect for the Goffs school?

FENNER (I-40/EXIT 107) has the only (pricey) gas/food for miles. **ESSEX** has the remains of the **Wayside Market**, but the well that once provided "**FREE WATER**" to thirsty drivers is dry. West of town is what might be called an unofficial "**Route 66 Public Art Corridor**." From here to **AMBOY** hundreds of travelers have written their names with rocks on the dirt berm along the north side of 66. Legal? Illegal? Be careful of heat stroke and snakes if you choose to add your own-at your own risk! ("McClanahan" is too darn long). "**DANBY**" is the fenced-off site of an old station/cabins complex dating to the 1930s. On the south side of 66 (15.5 mi from **ESSEX**, 2.3 mi from "**CADIZ SUMMIT**") is a restored roadside "rest area" pullout. Tablets describe the history and geology of the area.

EB: From "**CADIZ SUMMIT**" pass, go 18 mi on **National Trails Hwy** (past "**DANBY**") to **ESSEX**. 2 miles further, turn **LEFT** on **Goffs Rd** (BEFORE reaching the RR overpass). Pass I-40, continuing past **FENNER** to **GOFFS** (10 mi). Curve to cross the RR tracks, then go 14 mi on **Goffs Rd** to **US 95**. Turn **RIGHT**, continue 6 mi to **I-40**. Join **I-40 EAST** for 6 mi to **NEEDLES**.

(see **MAP # 1** on **CA page-2**)

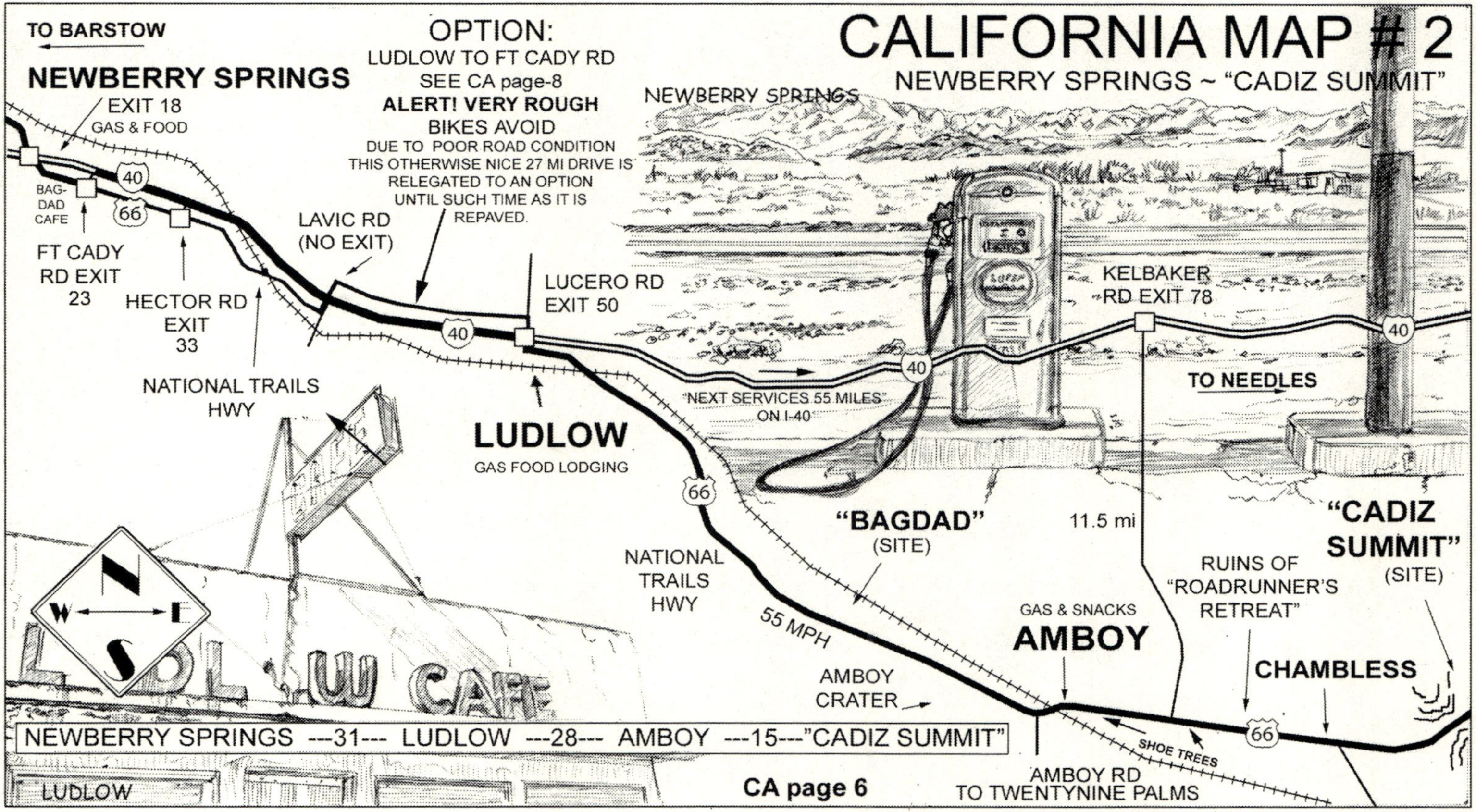

CALIFORNIA MAP # 2
NEWBERRY SPRINGS ~ "CADIZ SUMMIT"
TO BARSTOW
NEWBERRY SPRINGS
EXIT 18
GAS & FOOD
OPTION:
LUDLOW TO FT CADY RD
SEE CA page-8
ALERT! VERY ROUGH
BIKES AVOID
DUE TO POOR ROAD CONDITION
THIS OTHERWISE NICE 27 MI DRIVE IS
RELEGATED TO AN OPTION
UNTIL SUCH TIME AS IT IS
REPAVED.
NEWBERRY SPRINGS
40
66
BAG-DAD CAFE
FT CADY RD EXIT 23
HECTOR RD EXIT 33
LAVIC RD (NO EXIT)
LUCERO RD EXIT 50
NATIONAL TRAILS HWY
LUDLOW
GAS FOOD LODGING
"NEXT SERVICES 55 MILES" ON I-40
KELBAKER RD EXIT 78
TO NEEDLES
"BAGDAD" (SITE)
11.5 mi
"CADIZ SUMMIT" (SITE)
NATIONAL TRAILS HWY
55 MPH
RUINS OF "ROADRUNNER'S RETREAT"
GAS & SNACKS
AMBOY
CHAMBLESS
AMBOY CRATER
SHOE TREES
AMBOY RD TO TWENTYNINE PALMS
W
E
N
S
LUDLOW CAFE
NEWBERRY SPRINGS ---31--- LUDLOW ---28--- AMBOY ---15---"CADIZ SUMMIT"
LUDLOW

WB: Descend the pass at "**CADIZ SUMMIT**." Go 15 mi (passing **CHAMBLESS** and the Kelbaker Rd JCT) to and thru **AMBOY**.

"**CADIZ SUMMIT**" was the site of a café/station/garage and cabins complex, perched just before the pass thru the **Marble Mountains**. Only low walls, foundations and the cinder-block ruin of the garage remain, all heavily encrusted with more "**public art**." I **don't** encourage graffiti, but this has been the tradition here for many years. This is an eerie place, feeling like a set for one of those post-apocalyptic movies, (the coming of I-40 WAS doomsday for businesses like these) with remains of old autos, campfires, assorted unidentifiable junk, evidence of "parties" and a lonely, pink cross on a nearby peak. Down the hill, the now-shuttered **Chambless Market** once shaded its gas pumps with a huge awning, under which the temperature was still a balmy 122 degrees when my Dad had a tire fixed once.

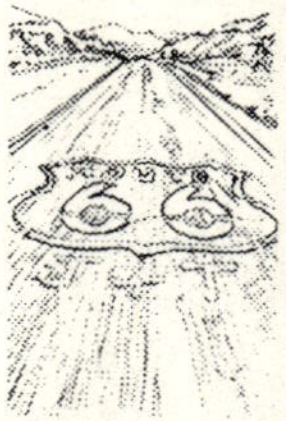

WB ALERT (bikers take note): The road ahead between **AMBOY** and **LUDLOW** is currently a bit harsh and choppy in places (especially at bridges), but this section is a "must-drive" and **NOT** bad enough yet to skip, so just drive with care. Some repaving has been done near Ludlow and Amboy. IF necessary (road construction, etc) take **Kelbaker Rd** (JCT 6 mi east of **AMBOY**) for 11.5 mi north to I-40, then west to **LUDLOW** (see map on CA page-6). I-40 can be pretty rough too!

GIANT ALERT! Between **CHAMBLESS** and **AMBOY**, in so-called "**East Amboy**," are the ruins of the **Roadrunner's Retreat Café and Station**, with its immense neon sign depicting a (recently headless) **GIANT ROADRUNNER**. Between **Roadrunner** and **AMBOY** look for more "**Public Art**:" two "**SHOE TREES**" (bushes?) festooned with cast-off footwear (if not gone-see MAP 2). No littering!

Dodge filmed a commercial at the "Retreat" in 1988, but for the Route 66 place that must hold the record for appearances in commercials, videos, and movies, check out **Roy's Café and Motel** in **AMBOY**, begun in 1927 by Roy Crowl and run by the late **Buster Burris** for decades since 1938. In the spring of 2005, Albert Okura, (of Juan Pollo restaurant fame) bought Roy's, and is restoring the place to its glory. Gasoline, snacks and restrooms are currently available.

EB: Curve with **National Trails Hwy** to cross the tracks into **AMBOY** (avoid the turn onto "Amboy Rd"/"29 Palms"). Go 15 mi, (passing the JCT of Kelbaker Rd and then past **CHAMBLESS**), climbing the pass to the ruins of "**CADIZ SUMMIT**."

WB: In AMBOY, cross the tracks and take **National Trails Hwy** 28 mi to **LUDLOW**. At **Lucero Rd,** turn **RIGHT**, then join **I-40 WEST** ("Barstow"). Go 26 mi and take **EXIT 23/Ft Cady Rd**. Cross I-40, then **RIGHT** (past ramp) to **NEWBERRY SPRINGS**.

Visible for miles near **AMBOY** is the cone of **Amboy Crater**, a US Dept of the Interior **National Landmark**, whose lava flow crosses Route 66 a bit west. A lone, scraggly tree north of '66 (7.4 mi w of **AMBOY**) marks the site of "**Bagdad**," a vanished "ghost town" once host to the "real" **Bagdad Café**, the inspiration for the cult-movie filmed in **NEWBERRY SPRINGS** (home of the current café).

Picturesque roadside ruins reside in **LUDLOW**, including the former "Ludlow Café." Recommended is the **Ludlow Café/Coffee Shop**, with its genuine "Googie"-style coffee shop architecture. Check out the angled stained glass window, and the display of old mining carts out front. **SCAVENGER HUNT!** What is the date on the "**Ludlow Mining Co**" cart? A marker here commemorates a wonderfully whacky 1963 plan to use **23 nuclear bombs** to BLAST a path for I-40 thru the nearby mountains! Next door is the small **Ludlow Motel** (the Federation Guide said "no frills but very clean"). Check in at the Chevron (760) 733-4338.

OPTION (VERY ROUGH) LUDLOW to **Ft Cady Rd-**about 27 miles: (see map **CA page-9)** Motorbikes should avoid. **WB**: At **Lucero Rd in Ludlow,** cross under I-40. Turn **LEFT** on the North Frontage Rd **(National Trails Hwy**). At **Lavic Road,** turn **LEFT** across I-40 (no exit) then **RIGHT** back on **National Trails Hwy**. Cross the RR tracks, then pass **Hector Rd** and **Ft Cady Rd**: rejoin the tour. **EB**: reverse.

66 passes thru the **Pisgah Crater** lava field and along the edge of the white expanse of **Troy Dry Lake**. There is actually water in **NEWBERRY SPRINGS**, named for the springs at the foot of the mountain that crowd '66 on the south. Also in town is a relic of the former **Whiting Bros Gas Station** chain (AKA "Dry Creek Station") preserved, complete with pumps, behind a fence. Another spot on your "must-stop" list (2 mi west of Ft Cady Rd. 3 mi east of EXIT 18) the current **Bagdad Café** of movie fame (formerly the Sidewinder Café) draws a worldwide clientele for eats and stories: the defunct motel from the film is right next door. (760) 257-3101

EB ALERT (bikes take note): The road between **LUDLOW** and **AMBOY** is a bit rough in places (especially at bridges), but this is a "must-drive" and **NOT** bad enough yet to skip, so drive carefully. If needed, an ALT is **Kelbaker Rd** south from I-40 EXIT 78 (CA page-6)

EB: Take **National Trails Hwy** for 5 mi to **Ft Cady Rd**. Turn **LEFT**, then **RIGHT** to join **I-40** for 26 mi. Take **LUDLOW EXIT 50**. **RIGHT on Crucero Rd**, then **LEFT** on **National Trails Hwy**. Cross the tracks east of town and continue 28 mi to **AMBOY**.

(see **MAP # 2 CA page 6)**

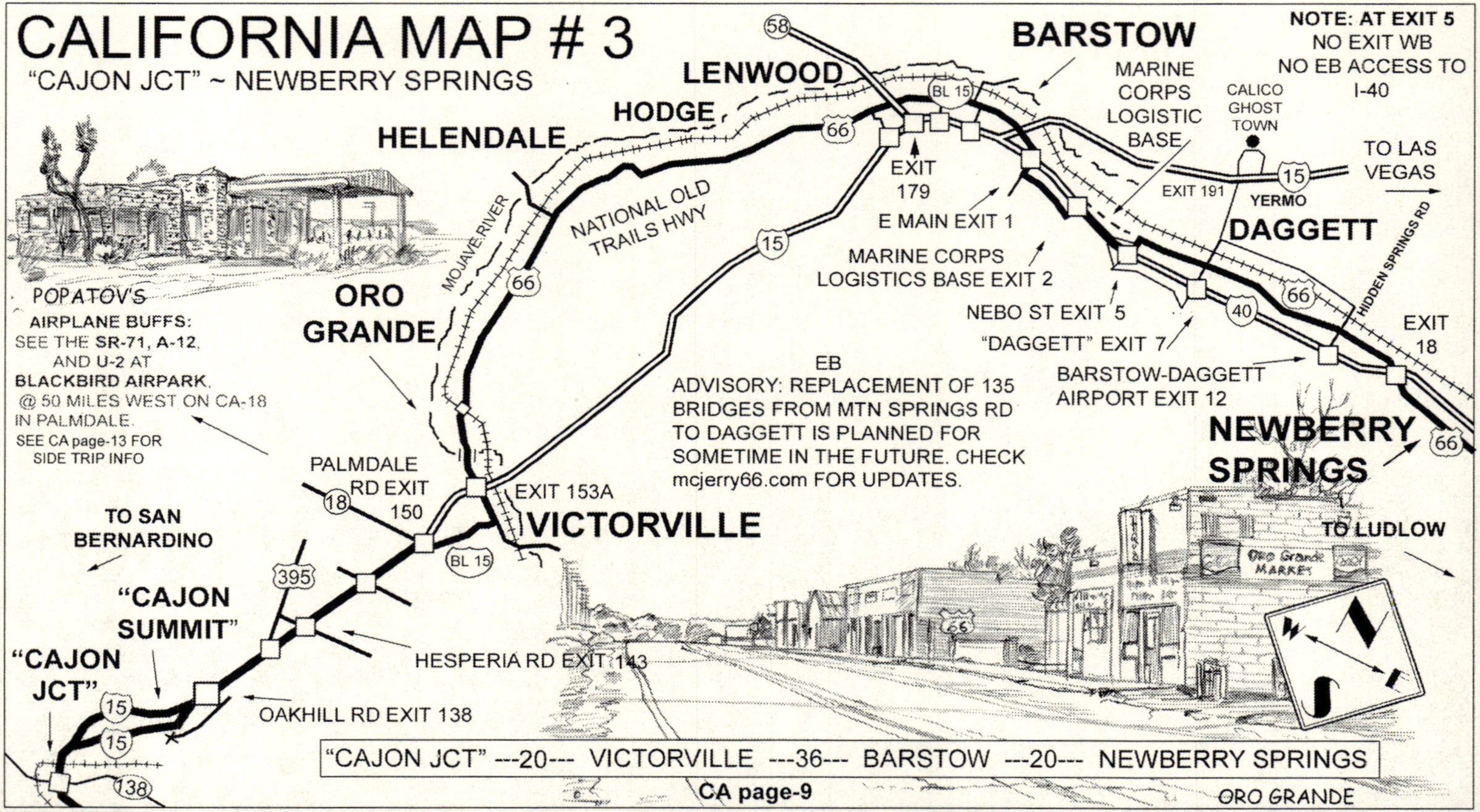
CALIFORNIA MAP # 3
"CAJON JCT" ~ NEWBERRY SPRINGS
BARSTOW
LENWOOD
HODGE
HELENDALE
NOTE: AT EXIT 5
NO EXIT WB
NO EB ACCESS TO
I-40
MARINE
CORPS
LOGISTIC
BASE
CALICO
GHOST
TOWN
TO LAS
VEGAS
EXIT 191
YERMO
DAGGETT
HIDDEN SPRINGS RD
EXIT
179
E MAIN EXIT 1
MARINE CORPS
LOGISTICS BASE EXIT 2
NEBO ST EXIT 5
"DAGGETT" EXIT 7
EXIT
18
BARSTOW-DAGGETT
AIRPORT EXIT 12
NATIONAL OLD
TRAILS HWY
MOJAVE RIVER
ORO
GRANDE
POPATOV'S
AIRPLANE BUFFS:
SEE THE SR-71, A-12,
AND U-2 AT
BLACKBIRD AIRPARK,
@ 50 MILES WEST ON CA-18
IN PALMDALE.
SEE CA page-13 FOR
SIDE TRIP INFO
EB
ADVISORY: REPLACEMENT OF 135
BRIDGES FROM MTN SPRINGS RD
TO DAGGETT IS PLANNED FOR
SOMETIME IN THE FUTURE. CHECK
mcjerry66.com FOR UPDATES.
NEWBERRY
SPRINGS
PALMDALE
RD EXIT
150
EXIT 153A
VICTORVILLE
TO SAN
BERNARDINO
TO LUDLOW
"CAJON
SUMMIT"
"CAJON
JCT"
HESPERIA RD EXIT 143
OAKHILL RD EXIT 138
Oro Grande MARKET
"CAJON JCT" ---20--- VICTORVILLE ---36--- BARSTOW ---20--- NEWBERRY SPRINGS
ORO GRANDE

WB: Take **National Trails Hwy** for 5 mi thru **NEWBERRY SPRINGS** and cross under I-40. Go 11 mi to **DAGGETT**, then continue for 2.4 mi (no turns). Follow the curve **LEFT** onto **NEBO St (AVOID** the turn onto Nat Trails Hwy), and join **I-40 WEST (**at EXIT 5**)**. Take **EXIT 2** ("Marine Corps Logistic Base"). Turn **LEFT**, go under I-40, then **RIGHT** on the **South Frontage Rd (E Main**). At **Montara Rd**, turn **RIGHT**, cross under I-40 at EXIT 1 (avoid left lane) and follow **BL 15/Main St** into **BARSTOW**.

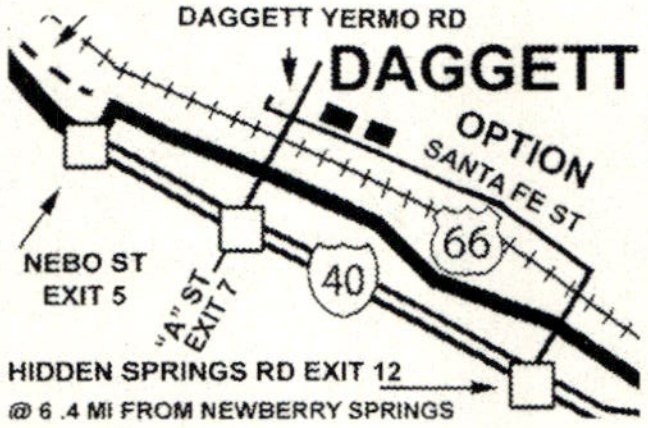

SIDE TRIP: 6 mi north of **DAGGETT** on Daggett/Yermo Rd (becomes Ghost Town Rd across I-15) is **Calico Ghost Town Regional Park**. Mine tour & **MYSTERY SHACK**! calicotown.com 800-86-calico

OPTION: **Santa Fe St** (the older route) runs north of the railroad for about 5 mi between **Hidden Springs Rd** and **DAGGETT**. Just east of **Daggett/Yermo Rd** are several photogenic old buildings, including the still-open **Desert Market**, an empty hotel, and the **Daggett Garage**, dating back to the 1880s. **Scavenger Hunt**! What date is on the front of the Desert Market?

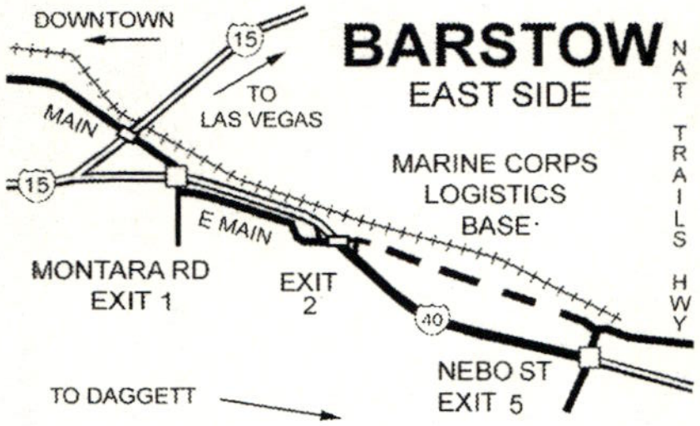

Back on the **main tour route** in **DAGGETT** is an odd little building with a sharply peaked triangular roof and lower sides that curve out and tuck under, once a café. I remember eating at the now closed **Daggett Café** as a kid, and innocently taking the waitresses' tip! **NOTE**: the town was NOT named for the cute robot dog in the original (1970s) ***Battlestar Galactica***!

Old 66 bounces up and down thru a series of dips west of **DAGGETT**, but soon runs into an obstacle: the **Marine Corps Logistics Base** sitting astride the old route. A stub of National Trails Hwy continues for just 0.3 mi before reaching the east gate, which security concerns have closed, enforcing a brief return to I-40 at Nebo Rd, before following old 66 into **BARSTOW**.

EB drivers: It's a **VERY GOOD IDEA** to gas up before leaving **BARSTOW**.

EB: Cross under I-40 with **Montara Rd** (in the LEFT LANE): turn **LEFT** at the stoplight onto **E Main St (South Frontage Rd)**. At the **NEXT EXIT** (**"NEEDLES"**), join **I-40 EAST**. Take **EXIT 5**. Turn **LEFT** under I-40 on **Nebo St**. Go 0.3 mi and curve **RIGHT** onto **National Trails Hwy**. Go 2.4 mi to **DAGGETT**, then continue (no turns) for 11 mi, under I-40 into **NEWBERRY SPRINGS**.

WB: Follow **Main St/BL 15** across I-15 and thru downtown **BARSTOW**. Continue with **Main St** when BL 15 turns off at L St (3 mi from I-15). 2 mi further, pass under Hwy 58. Continue with **Main St** (AKA **National Old Trails Hwy)** thru **LENWOOD**.

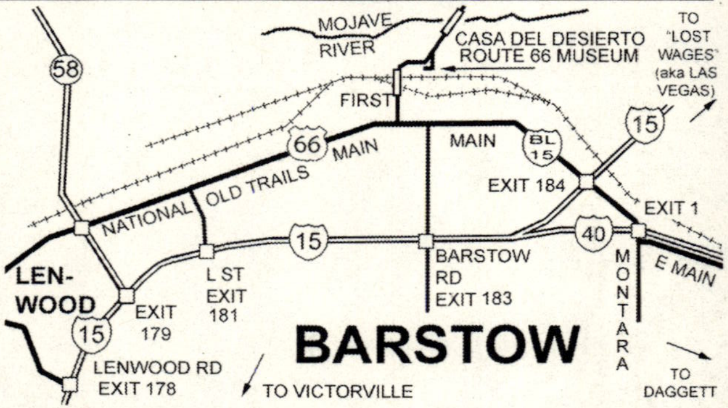

BARSTOW owes its existence to the railroads. In fact, the current location of downtown was dictated by the **Santa Fe** in 1925, when the whole town had to be moved to current Main St, so the railroad yards could be expanded. Left behind, north of the railroad yards, was the 1910-era **Casa Del Desierto**, a former **Harvey House**. Here are the **Western America Railroad Museum** and the **Route 66 Mother Road Museum**, a truly first class collection of displays and artifacts. Fri-Sun 10-4 or appt: www.route66museum.org or (760) 255-1890.
MUSEUM SIDE TRIP: From Main, follow **First St** north over the railroad yard, then curve down and turn off **RIGHT** to the museums. **GIFT SHOP ALERT**!

A variety of vintage motels line Main. The architecturally notable **El Rancho** was built from railroad ties salvaged from the defunct Tonopah and Tidewater RR (across the street is a neat mural honoring the 1857 **Beale camel caravan**). My favorite is the **Route 66 Motel**, (195 W Main) with its great **NEON SIGN** and courtyard display of old cars. Conditions in the remodeled 1920s-era stucco cabins are simple (no phone), but usually clean and quiet (and affordable). ROUND beds! The office is full of road-related clippings, photos and goodies (the owner is a Route 66 booster). Their guest book lists lots of Europeans, who enjoy the old-road ambiance. (760) 256-7866 www.route66motelbarstow.com. The **Palm Café** has a nifty neon sign, plus a palm tree or two. On downtown's east side at Barstow Rd is a replica of the Roy's Café sign at **Juan Pollo** (good chicken). West of town, the Rte 66 Apartments in **LENWOOD** are an "adaptive reuse" of a former motel. Rustic remnants of roadside businesses abound all along the way west to **VICTORVILLE**. I-15 was once 4-lane 66, but the 2-lane rules!

EB: From **LENWOOD**, follow **Main St** (AKA **National Old Trails Hwy)** under Hwy 58. Pass L St into **BARSTOW** (BL 15 joins). Follow **Main St/BL 15** thru downtown for 3 mi. Continue w **Main** over I-15, then curve to the **Montara Rd** underpass at I-40 EXIT 1.

WB: From **LENWOOD**, follow **National (Old) Trails Hwy** thru **HODGE**, **HELENDALE** and **ORO GRANDE**.

The directions are **EZ** on this stretch of '66, so is the driving: most of the 'Vegas-bound traffic stays on I-15. Enjoy the slower pace here, and if someone's in a hurry, just let them fly by. Enjoy the many relics of Route 66 while cruising sandy, sagebrush dotted hills, beside the **Santa Fe Railroad** and the tree-lined, mostly-dry course of the **Mojave River**.

It's easy to miss **HODGE**. Marking the town of **HELENDALE** is the **Helendale Market**. **GIANT ALERT!** Just west is a sign for **Newton's Towing**, bearing a ponderous **PARROT,** the mascot for the old **"Polly"** gasoline brand. The vintage gas prices shown (**REG: 18.9 ETHYL 21.9**) will make you cry for the good old days when "Polly" was "cheep!" (groan)

Among the numerous roadside remains is a stone residence adapted from the old **Sage Brush Inn**, about 1.5 miles west of **HELENDALE**. Here **Sagebrush Annie** ran a roadhouse that reportedly raised eyebrows and rumors. **FOLK ART ALERT!** Almost 3 miles west of **HELENDALE** (between **Citation St** and **Turner Rd**) a fenced desert lot is now home to "**Bottle Tree Ranch**." Elmer Long's artistic creation, composed of countless colorful bottles arrayed on "trees," is intermixed with '66 signs and other artifacts in the tradition of the late Miles Mahan (about 6.5 mi east of **ORO GRANDE**). **SAD NEWS**: "**Popatov's Service Station**," yet another picturesque stone business that stood abandoned for decades along 66, is gone. Between **HELENDALE** and **ORO GRANDE** bikers (and adventurous 4-wheelers) might enjoy a stop at **Iron Hog Saloon**.

East of **ORO GRANDE** 66 squeezes thru a narrow **1925-era RR underpass** and then past the Riverside Cement Plant (which explains all the parked cars coated with white dust). The old storefronts of "downtown" **ORO GRANDE** line one side of 66. The Mohawk Mini Mart is closed, as is "Club 66," which offered "happy hour" from a bright yellow building with an expressive rounded facade. Looking for antiques? Check out the false-fronted **Route 66 Antique Station,** complete with old fire truck and caboose.

WB & EB: ABOUT 23 miles of travel on THIS PAGE

EB: Follow **National (Old) Trails Hwy** thru **ORO GRANDE, HELENDALE**, **HODGE** and **LENWOOD** towards **BARSTOW**.

WB: Follow **National (Old) Trails Hwy** for 4 mi from **ORO GRANDE**. Continue under I-15 and enter **VICTORVILLE** on **D St** (BL 15). Go about 0.7 mi. At the stoplight for **7th St**/BL 55 turn **RIGHT**. Go 2.5 mi. At the Mariposa Rd stoplight, follow the "**San Bernardino**" signs, cross the overpass (**HWY 18/Palmdale Rd** EXIT 150) and curve off **RIGHT** to join **I-15 SOUTH**.

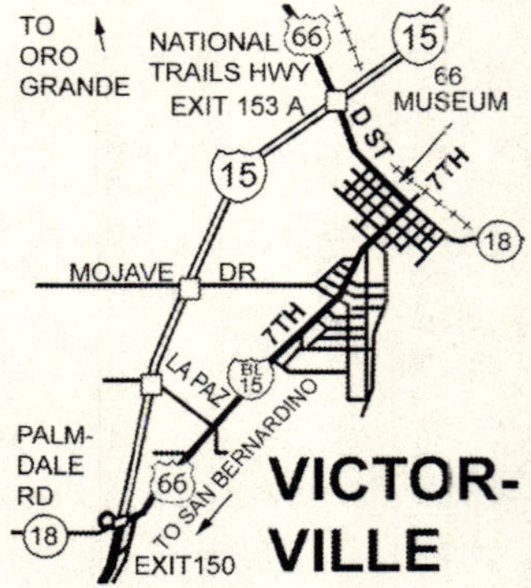

A majestic 1930 "**Modified Baltimore Truss" Bridge** (you bridge fans know what that means, right?) carries '66 over the **Mojave River** (which actually shows some water here at times). Especially ornamental are those ornate guardrails along the curved approach to the steel bridge. Before you reach I-15, be sure to slow down for **Emma Jean's Holland Burger**, a well preserved (both inside and out) vintage truckstop café. Friendly staff (only a stranger once) and fine roadfood, PLUS: a scene from "Kill Bill" was filmed here. (760) 243-9938 (Hmmmmm…pancakes!)

VICTORVILLE is home to many relics of 66. You'll sure want to spend some time in the great **California Route 66 Museum** on D St between 5th and 6th St. On hand are many exhibits, a gallery, research library and travel info. **GIANTESS ALERT!** The museum has carefully preserved relics from the late **Miles Mahan's "Hulaville" Museum"** (AKA Mahan's Half Acre), a long-gone open air folk-art exhibit of artfully arranged bottles, strange and humorous signs, and a **15 foot tall Hula Dancer** (rescued from a restaurant). She now shimmies her grass skirt inside the museum, along with a model of Hulaville itself. Too bad for the **Illinois Giants** that she is clear on the other end of 66. If they met, giant romance could bloom. **GIFT SHOP ALERT!** Use the alley behind the museum and between 5th and 6th St to reach the parking lot. Http://www.califrt66museum.org or (760) 951-0436.

SIDE TRIP: If you like fast jets, before grabbing the superslab towards SAN BERNARDINO, consider visiting the **Blackbird Airpark** (and adjoining **Joe Davies Airpark**) in **Palmdale**. Not on 66, but 50 miles is an eyeblink in an **SR-71** at Mach 3 (also a YF-12A, U-2, D-21 drone and F-117A)! 2503 East Avenue P, Palmdale (661) 274-0884 Usually open thurs-sun 11-4 pm (for both), but check beforehand.

EB: Curve with the EXIT 150 off-ramp (middle left-turn lane) then **LEFT** at the light (follow the **BL 15** signs). Before the NEXT light, get in the **RIGHT LANE**, then **RIGHT** with **BL 15/ 7th St** into **VICTORVILLE**. Follow **7th St** for 2.5 mi (thru downtown). Turn **LEFT** on **D St (BL 15)**. Go 0.7 mi, then continue AHEAD, under I-15 on **National (Old) Trails Hwy** for about 4 mi into **ORO GRANDE**.

WB: From EXIT 150, follow **I-15** south, past the US 395 JCT and down "**CAJON SUMMIT**" to pass by EXIT 131/"**CAJON JCT**."

UPPER CAJON PASS

6% GRADE FOR 4 MILES

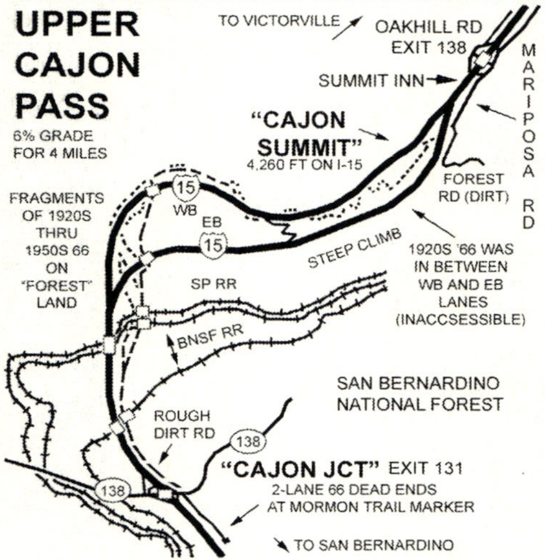

Parts of the frontage roads in this section (especially Mariposa Rd) may be bits of old 66. I-15 is easier here, and overlaps the path of **4-Lane 66** between **BARSTOW** and **CAJON PASS**.

At the JCT of US 395, the **Old Outpost Café** is an old-timer, as is the **Summit Inn,** just off the **Oakhill Rd Exit** at the top of **Cajon Pass**. Besides "**Ostrich Burgers**," the Summit has lots of cool "stuff" to admire. An earlier incarnation of the **Summit Inn** was located on the original **Cajon Summit** of Route 66, which was higher than I-15, in between the WB and EB lanes. Intact sections of **1920s** and **'30s era pavement** survive near the summit (unreachable).

SIDE TRIP (part unpaved): Follow **Mariposa Rd** (indeed part of old 66 here) south from the **Summit Inn** to its end, where a sandy **Forest Rd** turns left uphill. If you **cautiously** drive this a short way to a turnout, you will be able to see the **1930s pavement** on the other side of the EB lanes, and a nice view of the railroad far below in the valley. Note: a **Forest Adventure Pass,** available at Circle K Stores, is required to park and hike anywhere in the forest.

BACK on I-15, EB tourists can catch a glimpse of the **circa 1915 road** that became 66 as a faint shelf that curves in and out along the hills above. This early route, narrowly paved with chunks of rocks embedded in asphalt, was a terror, with sharp, blind curves, sheer drops and no shoulders. The higher **1930s 2-lane** that followed was in turn covered up by **1950s 4-Lane 66**, and then **I-15's WB lanes**. Today the white knuckles are found on truckers careening downhill (or on drivers stuck behind slow trucks crawling up). Note the "**Runaway Truck Ramps**" on the downhill stretch, and watch your speed. **Scattered fragments** of **1920s-1950s '66** lie on "Forest" land, as shown on the detail map. The dirt road in is rough. Hours are required to scout all these bits thru the brush (**NOT advised**).

EB: Continue on **I-15** NORTH over "**CAJON SUMMIT**" for 17 mi. Then take **EXIT 150** (HWY 18/ BL-15) in **VICTORVILLE**.

(see **MAP # 3 CA page-9**)

CALIFORNIA MAP # 4

PASADENA ~ "CAJON JCT"

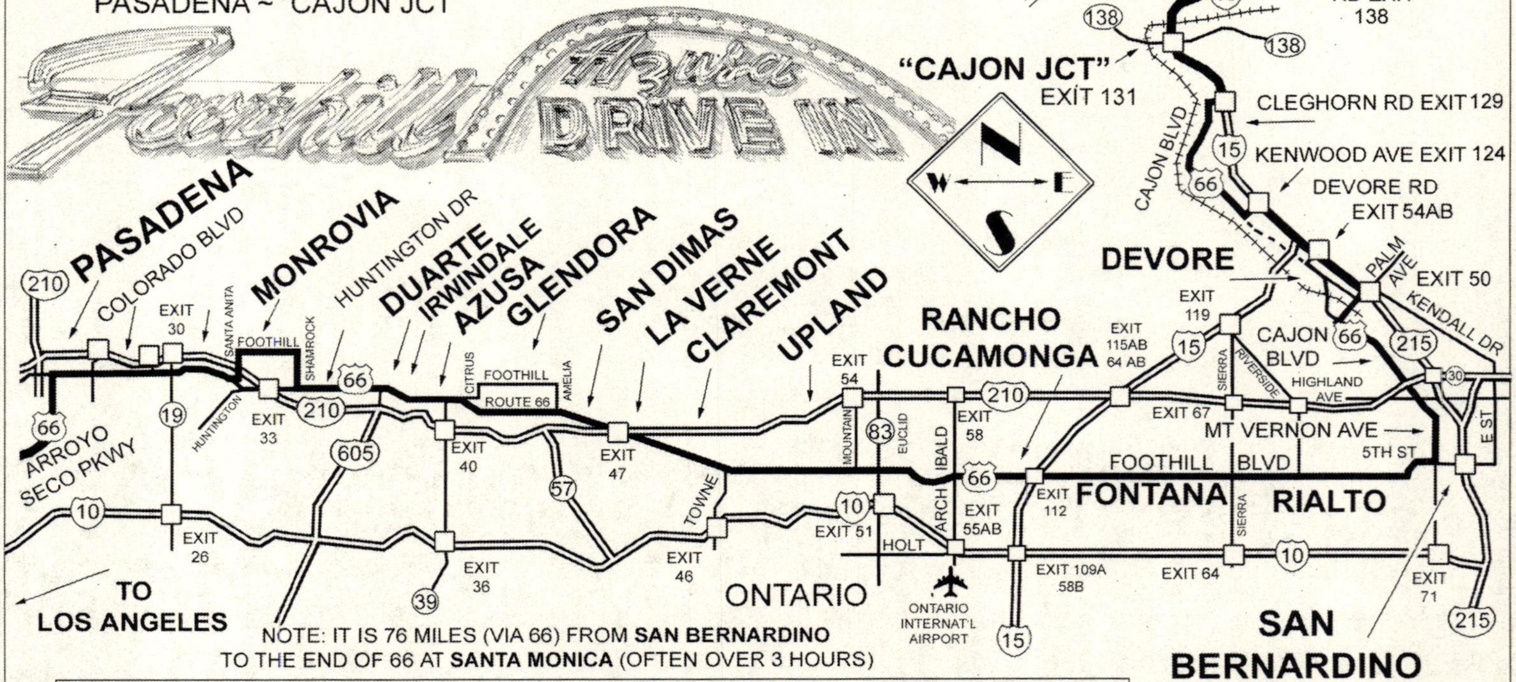

NOTE: IT IS 76 MILES (VIA 66) FROM **SAN BERNARDINO** TO THE END OF 66 AT **SANTA MONICA** (OFTEN OVER 3 HOURS)

PASADENA ---22--- LA VERNE ---28--- SAN BERNARDINO ---18--- "CAJON JCT"

WB: Pass EXIT 131. Continue on **I-15** to take **EXIT 129/Cleghorn Rd**. At the foot of the off ramp, turn **RIGHT** and curve **LEFT** onto **Cajon Blvd** southbound. 6 mi further, at the barricades, turn **LEFT** onto **Kenwood Ave**. Join **I-15 SOUTH**. (see **NOTE** CA page-17)

EXIT 131 SIDE TRIP: Long before paved roads and railroads, this pass was an important corridor, including an early toll road and the **Mormon Trail**. On the east side of EXIT 131 turn south on **Wagon Train Rd**. This short stretch of old 66 dead ends at the **Mormon Trail Marker** (it crossed near here).

The **Cleghorn Rd EXIT** leads to a great stretch of 66. **Cajon Blvd** ends just to the north, but south, the former 2 and 4-Lane winds along **Cajon Creek**, thru the rugged topography created by the infamous **San Andreas Fault**. Some classic old bridges cross normally dry gulches along the way. **SCAVENGER HUNT!** What is the **DATE** on the old bridge just south of **Cleghorn Rd?** ________

Swarthout Canyon Rd was the site of an old **Migrant Workers Camp** during the **Depression**. Further along, the **Blue Cut** is named for the blue-gray colored rock that Cajon Creek cuts thru. The immediate area of **Blue Cut** includes a wide, tree-shaded spot on the creek bank, with a historical marker. This was **ONCE** a great place to picnic or watch trains. Unfortunately, it is now at times a haven for "illicit activity." I wouldn't worry, but I do suggest just admiring the rugged scenery as you drive past this **short** stretch. Just south, along the curve, a stone wall guards the drop to the creek, while the former EB lanes of 4-Lane 66 crowd the rock-strewn hillsides. Many remnants of 1920s and '30s roadway lie in the flats, long abandoned due to floods. Some are on private property, others are buried or hard to get to (or out of....I got stuck once). Enjoy Ma Nature while you can, before joining the freeway towards **SAN BERNARDINO**.

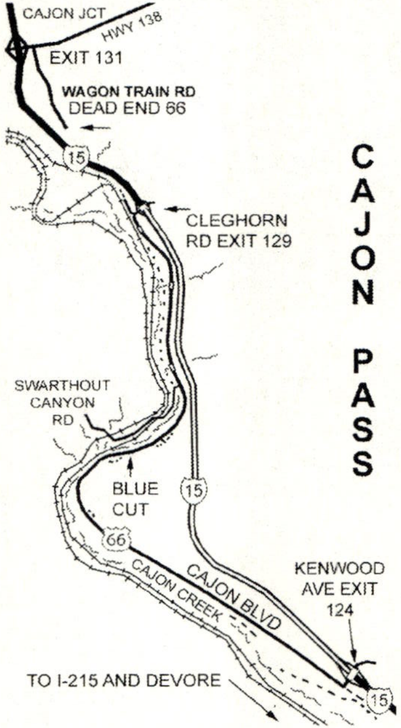

EB: Take the **Kenwood Ave EXIT** from **I-15**. Turn **LEFT**, cross under **I-15**, then turn **RIGHT** on **Cajon Blvd**. After about 6 mi, veer **RIGHT** from Cajon Blvd to pass under I-15 at **Cleghorn Rd/ EXIT 129**, and join **I-15 North** past "**CAJON JCT**"/EXIT 131.

WB: From EXIT 124/Kenwood Ave, join **I-15 SOUTH**. **QUICKLY** move to the **middle/left lanes** ("Riverside/San Bernardino I-215"). **I-15** splits right: **BEAR LEFT** with **I-215**, then take **EXIT 50**/Kendal Dr/Palm Ave (5 mi from Kenwood Dr Exit)**.** Circle around onto **Kendal**, then **LEFT** on **Palm**. Cross the tracks, then **LEFT** on **Cajon Blvd**. Go 4.5 mi. Curve away from the RR tracks, then **STOP** at 21st St. Turn **RIGHT**, then **QUICK LEFT** on **Mt Vernon** (at the stoplight) into **SAN BERNARDINO** (about 1.8 mi to next turn).

NOTE: The interchange of I-15, I-215 and Cajon Blvd will be rebuilt circa **2012-16.** Be ready to adapt to **major** changes in the route, and expect **DELAYS**. Cajon Blvd will eventually connect **directly** from Kenwood Rd to Devore Rd, eliminating the need to use I-15/215.

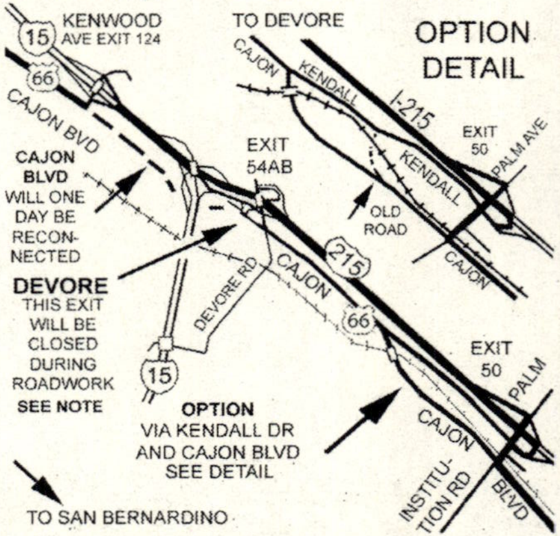

Cajon Blvd resumes in **DEVORE**. Due to pending construction, the **EZ tour** skips to **EXIT 50.**

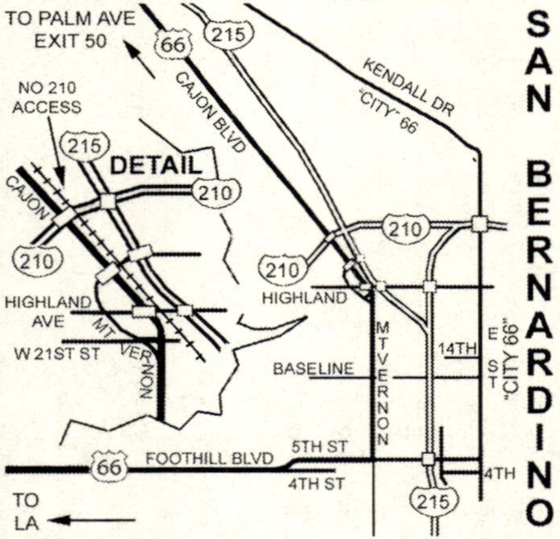

OPTION: Use the **detail map** to double back on **Kendal Drive**, a former city route, to **Cajon Blvd**. A mile south of the RR overpass on **Cajon**, look back north towards the silos. The narrow concrete slab extending out of the curve is the original 66, paved well-before 1926. This crossed the RR at grade, connecting to Kendall before continuing. This may be the only example of this era of Route 66 pavement!

In **SAN BERNARDINO**, **Mt Vernon Ave** is home to several vintage motels, bypassed long ago and catering now to "long term" trade. This urban street bears many reminders of old cafes, gas stations and garages. At 6th and Mt Vernon the **Mitla Café**, circa 1937, is a nice Mexican food place.

EB: Take **MT Vernon** for 1.8 mi (past 19th St, get in the **RIGHT** lane). Mt Vernon curves left: **Stay AHEAD (AVOID** Mt Vernon**)**, then curve with **Cajon Blvd** along the RR tracks. About 4.5 mi from the curve, at the Palm Ave/Institution Rd crossroad (first chance to cross the tracks) turn **RIGHT** on **Palm Ave**. Cross under I-215, then **LEFT** on the ramp to join **I-215 NORTH**. I-215 merges with **I-15**. Prepare to take upcoming **EXIT** 124/**Kenwood Ave**.

WB: Follow **Mt Vernon Ave** across 6th St, then get in the **RIGHT** lane, and turn **RIGHT** on **5th St/ CA HWY 66**. Follow **5th St** as it curves, straightening out to become **Foothill Blvd** westbound. Follow **Foothill Blvd** thru **RIALTO** and **FONTANA**, crossing under I-15 into **RANCHO CUCAMONGA**. Stay **AHEAD** on **Foothill Blvd**.

MILEAGE NOTE: it is about 12.5 miles via 5th St and Foothill between Mt Vernon Ave and I-15 (EXIT 112).

SIDE TRIPS: Fast food fans should investigate the **McDonalds Museum** north of downtown **SAN BERNARDINO** on E St (City 66) at 14th, once the site of the world's first McDonalds (see map CA page-17). From here, the **McDonald Brothers** branched out and created the Golden Arches, years before Ray Kroc. On display are artifacts and collectibles. (909) 885-6324 A **Route 66 Museum** is housed at **Juan Pollo** restaurant, east of Mt Vernon on 5th. www.juanpollo.com The city is famed for the "**Stater Bros. Route 66 Rendezvous**" held yearly downtown (hopefully despite city money woes). On the north side of City Hall, at Court and E St, a wall houses the plaques of inductees to their "**Cruisin' Hall of Fame**." route-66.org Also in downtown on 4th is the 1928 **California Theatre**.

Located just east of the **RIALTO** city limits are the classic concrete Tee-Pees of the wonderful **Wig Wam Motel**. The owners of this beloved icon are dedicated to its preservation. Renovated and well-maintained in a park-like setting, the Wigwams, one of two such motels on 66 and the last of the chain built, are a proud testament to the re-emergence of Route 66. **wigwammotel.com** (909) 875-3005 **Scavenger Hunt!** What is the shape of the **El Camino Real** marker on the south at Riverside and Foothill in **RIALTO**?

Foothill Blvd (AKA **CA Hwy 66**, although most signs are of the "Historic 66" variety) west from **RIALTO** is a mix of shopping centers and former tourism-related buildings. Most of the old motels have lost their neon, but some quaint names and examples of bungalow courts survive. **GIANT ALERT**! **FONTANA** (hopefully) is still home to (non-operational) "**Bono's Historic Orange**," perhaps the last remnant of the **Giant Orange Stands** that once lined the state's roads, at the now closed and threatened **Bono's Restaurant**, an icon dating from 1935, at 15395 Foothill Blvd (west of Citrus Ave near Beech Ave).

EB: Follow **Foothill Blvd** under I-15, thru **FONTANA** and **RIALTO** into **SAN BERNARDINO**. About 1 mi east of the Wigwams, follow the wide curve **LEFT (AVOID** 4th**)** onto **5th St**. Continue about 0.8 mi, turn **LEFT** on **Mt Vernon Ave**.

MILEAGE NOTE: it is about 12.5 miles on Foothill and 5th St between I-15 (EXIT 112) and Mt Vernon Ave.

WB: From I-15, continue on **Foothill Blvd** thru **RANCHO CUCAMONGA**, **UPLAND** (at Euclid Ave) & **CLAREMONT**. **MILEAGE NOTE**: The stretch from I-15 (EXIT 112) east of Rancho Cucamonga to I-210 in Laverne (next page) is about **15 miles**.

As you motor east or west on **Foothill**, keep an eye open for the many instances of the **Route 66 Shield** proudly displayed on businesses along the entire stretch. There's plenty of cool Route 66 stuff to see and eat in **RANCHO CUCAMONGA**. Down the road at 8189 Foothill is **the Magic Lamp Inn** (between Baker Ave and Grove Ave), a 1957 restaurant with ornate "Arabian Nights" décor. **GIANT ALERT!** The neon sign depicting a **Giant Aladdin's Lamp** will rub you the right way! The historic **Sycamore Inn** (dating way back to 1848) at 8318 Foothill Blvd (also between Baker Ave and Grove Ave) was originally a stagecoach stop. City INFO: (909) 987-1012.

This area was once home to orange groves and vineyards. Two of the former wineries, the 1830s era **Virginia Dare Winery** (at Haven Ave), and the 1839 **Thomas Vineyards** (at Vineyard Ave) have been adapted for use as shops. **UPLAND** has revitalized its section of '66, with landscaping and retro-décor added to spice up the strip malls. Much of Foothill Blvd is surprisingly green.

GIANT ALERT #2! At Euclid and Foothill in **UPLAND** is the **Madonna of the Trail** statue, depicting a rugged pioneer mother and children, one of 12 across the country (Albuquerque also has one) honoring those sturdy women who had to listen to months of "How much longer?" and "When will we be there?" from the backseat of the covered wagon. In a similar "go-west" vein are the Buffalo Burgers at the **Buffalo Inn** (circa 1929) at 1814 W Foothill (between Benson Ave and Central). City INFO: (909) 931-4108

The tree-lined drive thru **CLAREMONT** is green and soothing. **Wolfe's Market**, at 160 W Foothill (between N Mills and Indian Hill Rd) run for 4 generations by the Wolfe family, began in 1917, moving to its current spot, on the south side of Foothill, in 1935. City INFO: (909)624-1681.

EB: Follow **Foothill Blvd** thru **CLAREMONT**, **UPLAND** (at Euclid Ave) and **RANCHO CUCAMONGA** (avoid turn-only lanes) **MILEAGE NOTE**: The stretch from I-210 (EXIT 47) in Laverne (prior page) to I-15 (east of Rancho Cucamonga) is about **15 miles**.

WB: Take **Foothill Blvd** thru **LA VERNE**, cross I-210 and continue thru **SAN DIMAS** and **GLENDORA**. **Foothill** becomes "**Route 66**," then **Alosta**. Past Citrus, follow the curve right, then straighten out on **Foothill Blvd** again, thru **AZUSA** (passing HWY 39).
MILEAGE NOTE: about 7 miles from I-210 (EXIT 47) in **LA VERNE** to **HWY 39/San Gabriel Ave** in **AZUSA**.

Many newer places are adopting an old look along **Foothill** in **LA VERNE**, where orange groves once lined the road. An example is the sparkling stainless steel **Dennys** at 919 Foothill. **La Paloma Café**, with its long, mission style facade and classic neon sign, is no latecomer. East of Amelia Ave at 269 Foothill in **SAN DIMAS**, is **Pinnacle Peak Steakhouse**, with a old wagon out front and cut-off ties on the walls.

GLENDORA OPTION: See **detail map** for the older alignment via **Amelia Ave, Foothill Blvd, Citrus Ave** & back on **Foothill**. **Amelia** is a beautiful palm-tree lined street, while **Foothill** here passes thru lushly landscaped walled residential estates. Tall slender palms compete with short trees trimmed into rounded "gumdrop" shape. Watch for the drive-thru "**66 Drive in-Altadena Dairy**" and **Tommy's Burgers** along this 5-mile section.

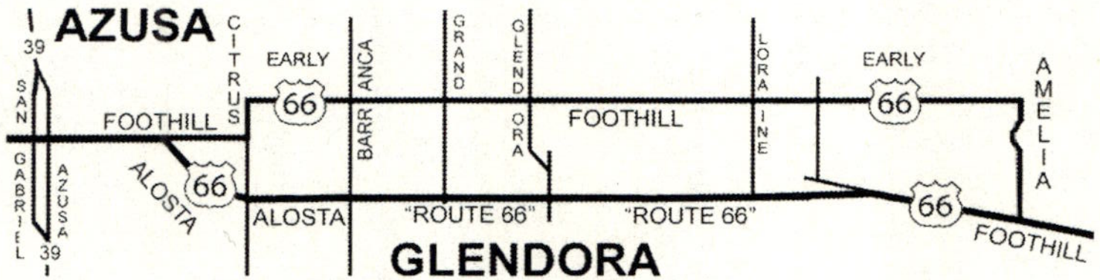

CAR GAME: The **main route** has some '66-related vibes as many ordinary businesses show their '66 pride in their names or signs. Among them are a Car Wash, Dentist and a Laptop store. How many can **YOU** spot? **Flappy Jack's Pancake House** (640 W Rte 66) is decorated in Route 66 style, while the **Golden Spur** restaurant has a "kickin" neon sign in the form of a **BIG BOOT (GIANT ALERT)**!

AZUSA boasts the photogenic tile and stucco architecture of their 1932 **City Hall and Auditorium**. At the junction of Foothill Blvd (west end of the **GLENDORA** OPTION) and "Route 66" is the preserved neon marquee of the former **Foothill Drive-In Theatre**.

EB: Take **Foothill Blvd** thru **AZUSA** (pass HWY 39). Follow the curve **RIGHT** onto **Alosta**, (becomes "**Route 66"**) into **GLENDORA**. **Foothill Blvd** resumes. Pass thru **SAN DIMAS**. Cross I-210 into **LA VERNE**. Continue on **Foothill** thru **CLAREMONT**.
MILEAGE NOTE: about 7 miles from **HWY 39/San Gabriel Ave** in **AZUSA** to I-210 (EXIT 47) in **LA VERNE**.

WB: Take **Foothill Blvd** from <u>**AZUSA**</u> (at HWY 39) for about 4 mi (thru <u>**IRWINDALE**</u>…Foothill becomes **Huntington Dr**) to <u>**DUARTE**</u> at Buena Vista St. Continue with **Huntington** for 0.8 mi, then turn **RIGHT** on **Shamrock Ave**. Go 0.8 mi, then **LEFT** on **Foothill Blvd**. Go 2.3 mi, then turn **LEFT** on **Santa Anita Ave**. Cross under I-210, then turn **RIGHT** on **Colorado <u>Blvd</u>**. Go 0.6 mi, then curve right to join **Colorado <u>Place</u>**. Follow the wide street (becomes **Colorado <u>St</u>**, then **<u>Blvd</u>)** for 6.2 mi into and thru <u>**PASADENA**</u>.

West of <u>**IRWINDALE**</u> (the San Gabriel "River" runs thru it) is <u>**DUARTE**</u>, home to the **Justice Brothers Racing Museum** at 2734 E

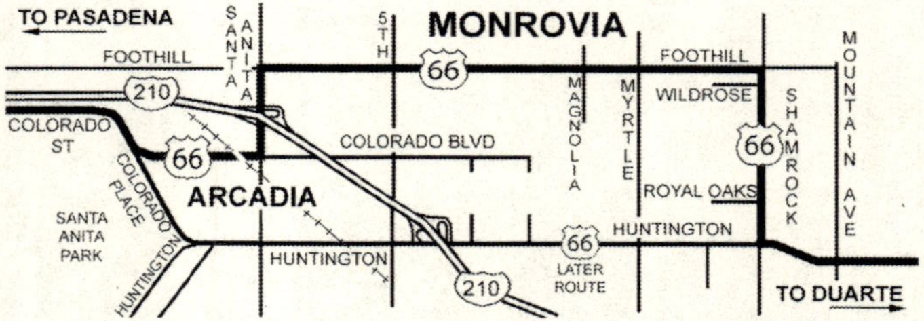

Huntington Dr, east of Las Lomas, on the south (98-5 weekdays: FREE admission). The museum features a variety of vintage racing vehicles, plus memorabilia and miscellany. The cars are so colorful the kids will love them. Hard to see (no sign), so look for the street address. (800) 835-8784. justicebrothers.com <u>**DUARTE**</u> also hosts an annual **Route 66 Parade**. Info: (626) 357-3333. **Huntington Drive** here is landscaped with "bell-shaped" trees, and the center median bears replica mission bells that serve as "City of Duarte" markers.

A jewel of an antique gas station survives in <u>**MONROVIA**</u> on **Shamrock** at Walnut, in front of **Dale's Garage**. Vintage gas pumps and classic style in an attractive setting make this a real **PHOTO OP!** Scenes from a movie about the Lindberg kidnapping were filmed here. Up on **Foothill Blvd**, that is **NOT** a lost "Aztec temple" at Magnolia Ave, but the unique **1925 Aztec Hotel**, designed in "Aztec ruins" style. <u>**OPTION:**</u> The later route along **Huntington Dr** has its share of sites. At the corner of Santa Anita and Huntington in <u>**ARCADIA**</u> is an example of California drive-in style. Now a **Denny's**, this exotic structure, with folded plate roof and **windmill tower**, was the last of the Van de Kamp's restaurant chain on '66. <u>**ARCADIA**</u> is most famous for the **Santa Anita Park and Racetrack**.

EB: Take **Colorado Blvd (**becomes **Colorado <u>St</u>**) from <u>**PASADENA**</u>. Follow the curve onto **Colorado <u>Place</u> (**for about 0.3 mi**)**. Past Harvard Dr, join left turn lane. At the light, curve **LEFT** onto **Colorado <u>Blvd</u>**. Go 0.6 mi then **LEFT** on **Santa Anita Ave**. Cross under I-210 (AVOID right lane), then turn **RIGHT** on **Foothill Blvd**. Go 2.3 mi, then **RIGHT** on **Shamrock**. Go 0.8 mi, then turn **LEFT** on **Huntington Dr**. Continue thru <u>**DUARTE**</u> and <u>**IRWINDALE**</u> (**Foothill Blvd** resumes) and thru <u>**AZUSA**</u> (past HWY 39).

(see **MAP # 4 CA page-15**)

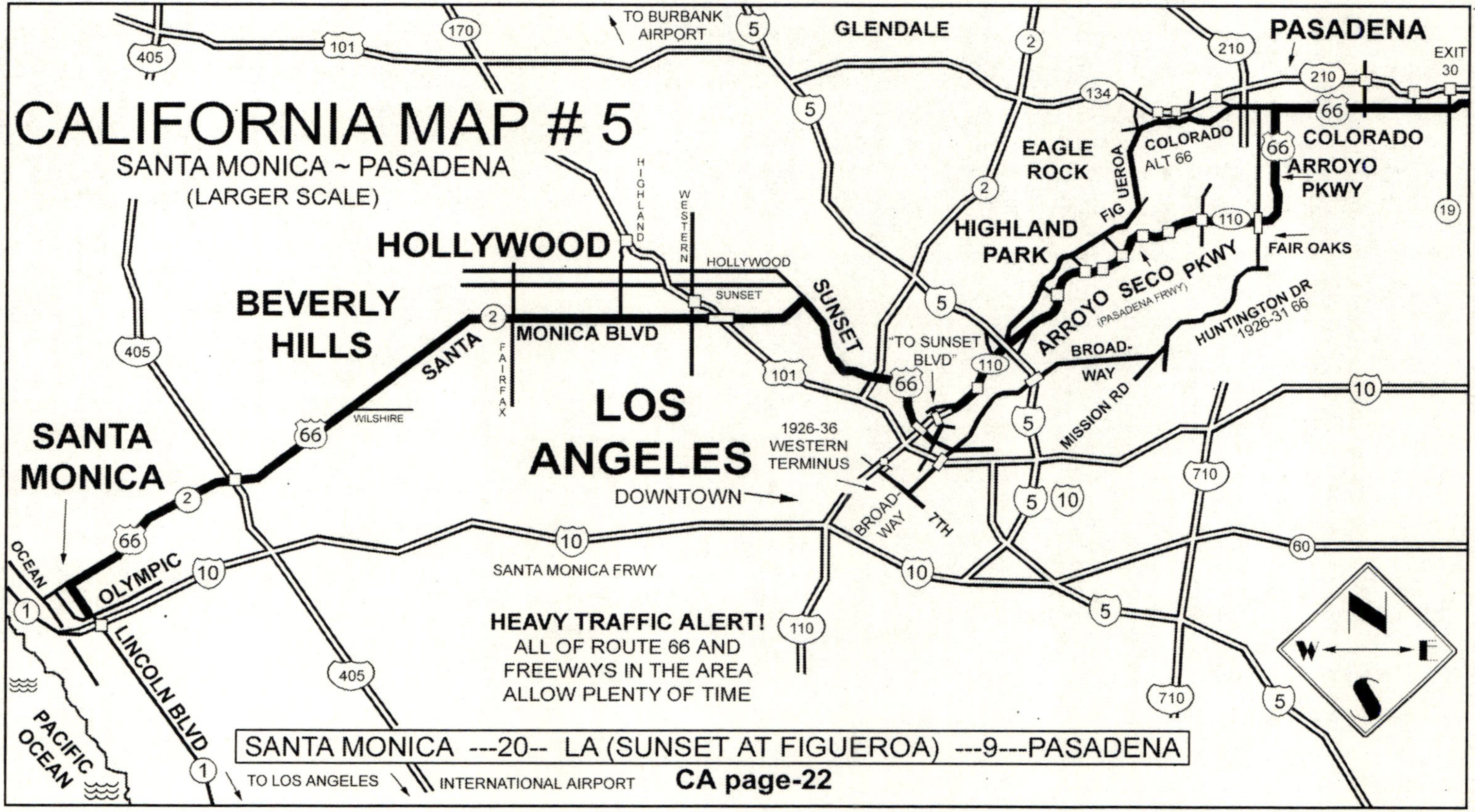
CALIFORNIA MAP # 5
SANTA MONICA ~ PASADENA
(LARGER SCALE)
TO BURBANK AIRPORT
GLENDALE
PASADENA
EXIT 30
HOLLYWOOD
BEVERLY HILLS
SANTA MONICA
LOS ANGELES
DOWNTOWN
EAGLE ROCK
HIGHLAND PARK
COLORADO
COLORADO ALT 66
ARROYO PKWY
FAIR OAKS
FIGUEROA
ARROYO SECO PKWY
(PASADENA FRWY)
HUNTINGTON DR 1926-31 66
BROAD-WAY
MISSION RD
"TO SUNSET BLVD"
1926-36 WESTERN TERMINUS
BROAD-WAY
7TH
HIGHLAND
WESTERN
HOLLYWOOD
SUNSET
SANTA MONICA BLVD
FAIRFAX
WILSHIRE
OCEAN
OLYMPIC
LINCOLN BLVD
PACIFIC OCEAN
SANTA MONICA FRWY
HEAVY TRAFFIC ALERT!
ALL OF ROUTE 66 AND
FREEWAYS IN THE AREA
ALLOW PLENTY OF TIME
TO LOS ANGELES
INTERNATIONAL AIRPORT
SANTA MONICA ---20-- LA (SUNSET AT FIGUEROA) ---9---PASADENA
N
W
E
S

WB: On downtown **PASADENA**'s west side, cross Marengo Ave, then **LEFT** on **S Arroyo Pkwy/Hwy 110**. Go 1.3 mi (past Glenarm St stoplight) then stay **AHEAD** onto **110 Fwy/Arroyo Seco Pkwy** (it's 7.7 mi to your next exit). See **CA page-24** for map & ALT routes

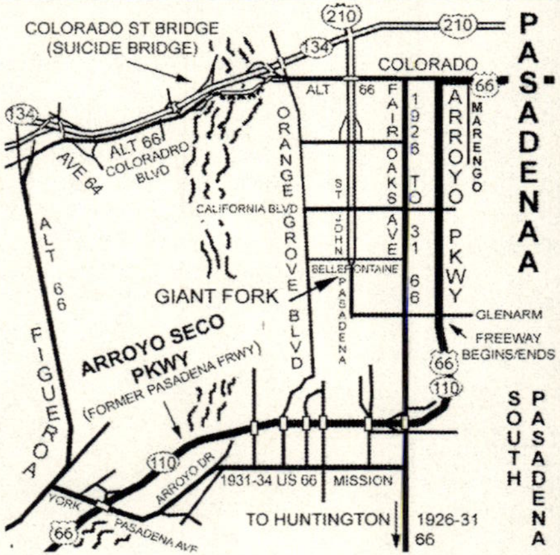

If you've watched the annual **Tournament of Roses Parade**, you've seen the flower-flocked floats "float" right down '66 along **PASADENA**'s stretch of **Colorado Blvd.** This attractive city is chock-full of preserved architectural styles and varieties of popular culture, in a typical SO-CAL mix. "National Register of Historic Places" listings abound, as do old motels, of which I heartily recommend the **Saga Motor Lodge** as a well-preserved 1950s motel (800) 793-7242.

GIANT ALERT: **"FORK** in the ROAD" From S Arroyo Pkwy turn WEST on Glenarm. Go 2 blocks to Pasadena Ave, then **RIGHT** to the **FORK** near Bellefontaine. See map.

SIDE TRIPS: **Route 66** followed many routes to reach **LA** from **PASADENA**. Scattered on these alignments are choice cultural sites. Check out the majestically curved 1913 **Colorado St Bridge** (AKA: "**Suicide Bridge**") that spans the **Arroyo Seco** (dry river). Follow **Colorado** west from the **Arroyo Parkway** intersection, across the freeway. Once thru the Orange Grove Blvd stoplight, **AVOID** the Hwy 134 W onramp by bearing **LEFT** with **Colorado Blvd** to pass between the gauntlet of ornate lamps and guardrails lining the bridge. Ahead is the "**ALT" 66** route via **Figueroa**, which later joins the **Arroyo Seco Parkway** past Ave 26 in **HIGHLAND PARK**. On this route is the 1924 **Highland Theatre**.

On **1926-'31 US 66**, along **Fair Oaks Ave** (south of Arroyo Seco Pkwy at Mission St) is the 1915-era **Fair Oaks Pharmacy**. The **1925 Rialto Theatre** is nearby. At **Fairview** and **Mission St** (on the **1931-34 Route**) is the former **El Centro Market (now Mike & Annes)**, the first **Drive-Thru** market. Original **1926-'31 66** continued south on **Fair Oaks** to **Huntington**, then joined **Mission Rd** briefly to pick up **Broadway** all the way to **7th St** in downtown **LA**: the original **Western Terminus** of **US 66** (moved to **SANTA MONICA** in 1936).

See CA page-24 for detail maps.

EB: At freeway's end, continue on **Arroyo Pkwy** 1.3 mi into **PASADENA**. Turn **RIGHT** on **Colorado Blvd** (becomes **Colorado St**)

CA page-23

WB: Stay in **CENTER** lane of **110 Fwy/Arroyo Seco Parkway** until past the I-5 JCT. Pass College St Overpass, then take **EXIT 24B** ("to Sunset Blvd"). STOP, then angle **LEFT** on **Figueroa Terrace** (follow "Sunset Blvd" signs).Turn **LEFT** onto **Alpine St** and cross the freeway, then bear **RIGHT** onto **Figueroa**. Turn **RIGHT again** (next light) onto **Sunset Blvd** in **LOS ANGELES**.

The scenic and historic 1940 **Arroyo Seco Parkway** (AKA **Pasadena Freeway** and CA Hwy 110), the first "freeway" west of the Mississippi, is infamous for traffic. Built as a landscaped parkway intended for slower speeds, the Arroyo's curves and scanty exit ramps cause back ups and wrecks at modern velocity. The Arroyo, for all its flaws, is well worth driving, and the most direct way to LA. Thanks to road warrior **Scott Piotrowski**, here's the straight scoop on surviving the Arroyo. **NOTE**: This is **LA**: there will **ALWAYS** be traffic!!! The **best** time to take the **Arroyo Seco Pkwy** to **LA** is the **afternoon.** Try to drive from **LA** to **PASADENA** from about 10 am to 1 pm. Try to keep up to 55 mph, but slow down for the big curves. The **EB lanes**, thru the four ornate **TUNNELS**, are the most scenic option. Efforts are underway to restore the Parkway to its 1930s appearance. **OPTIONS**: The map shows alternate routes of '66 via Figueroa or Huntington.

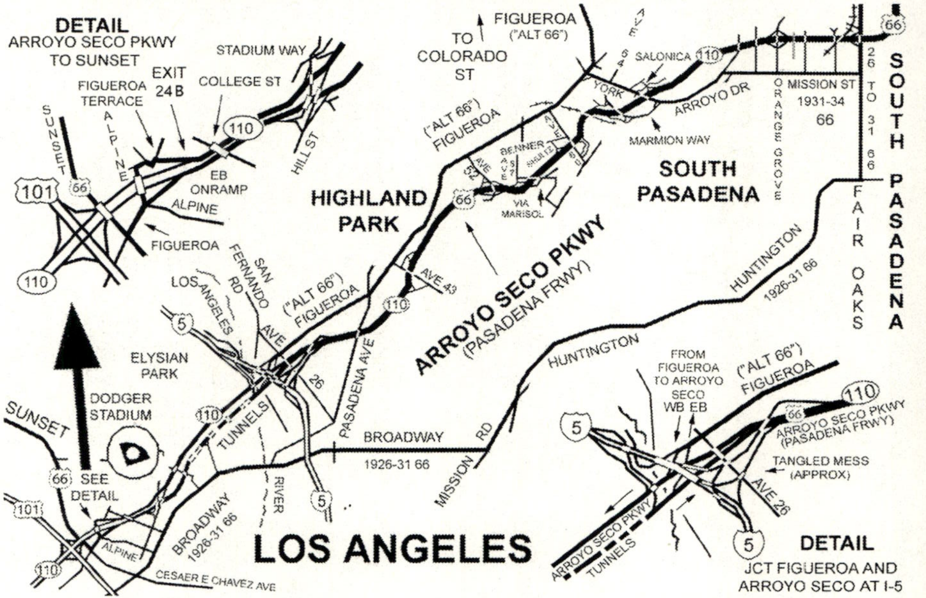

EB: Turn **LEFT** on **Figueroa**. Go thru the Alpine St light, then **KEEP RIGHT** to join the **110 Fwy/Arroyo Seco Pkwy**. Stay in the far **RIGHT** lane thru the 4 tunnels, then move to the **CENTER LANE** past the last tunnel. Stay there to the freeway's end in **PASADENA** (about 7.9 mi from Figueroa to end of Fwy).

WB: Continue about 3 mi on **Sunset Blvd**, and cross Hyperion Ave. Go one block, cross Sanborne, then get in the **left turn lane**. Quickly turn **LEFT** onto **Manzanita (NO** light…sign: "Santa Monica Blvd"**…**A difficult turn if traffic is heavy. See detail map WB note). At the STOP, turn right with **Santa Monica Blvd** (AKA: **CA Hwy 2**). Continue thru **WEST HOLLYWOOD** to **BEVERLY HILLS**.

ADVISORY: **Santa Monica Blvd** from Sunset thru **WEST HOLLYWOOD** is a congested city strip, with heavy traffic. **Drive Carefully!**

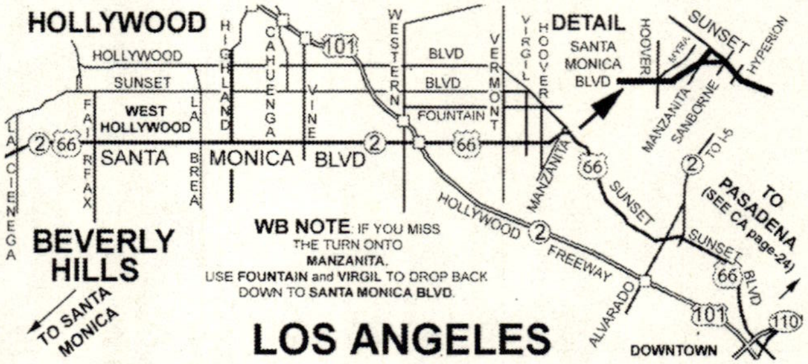

There is just TOO much to do in the **LA** area. To start mining info, check the Los Angeles Chamber at www.lachamber.org or (213)580-7500. From Sunset Blvd, sports fans can take Elysian Park Ave to visit **Dodger Stadium**. **GIANT ALERT**! Nearby, **Sunset** cruises the colorful **ECHO PARK** area, where another sport is enacted ad infinitum atop **Jensen's Recreation Center**, as the enormous animated bowler on the antique sign hurls strike after illuminated strike. For a bite, try **Millie's** "Home of Good Food" since 1926, on the south side, just east of Maltman St.

Car buffs may wish to visit the **Petersen Automotive Museum** at 6060 Wilshire Blvd (at Fairfax: take Wilshire Blvd east from 66 in Beverly Hills). Three floors of auto history are portrayed in "streetscapes." www.petersen.org

From **Santa Monica Blvd**, the famed **Hollywood Sign** is visible at times on the north. Also north of 66 runs **Hollywood Blvd** and the continuation of **Sunset**. Up here, you'll find the famous corner of **Hollywood and Vine**, plus sites like **Grauman's Chinese Theatre**, and the **Egyptian Theatre**. INFO: http://www.hollywoodchamber.net/ (323) 469-8311 for these and other movie-related locales. On old 66 in **W HOLLYWOOD** is **Barney's Beanery** (third oldest eatery in LA). Speaking of **HOLLYWOOD**, the **last route** of US 66 ('53 to '64) used the **Hollywood (101) Freeway** from the 4-level interchange (one of the first) with the Arroyo Seco Pkwy up to Santa Monica Blvd.

EB: Take **Santa Monica Blvd** thru **WEST HOLLYWOOD**. Cross US 101/Hollywood Fwy. Continue on **Santa Monica Blvd** past Hoover St, then curve **RIGHT** (past Manzanita) thru the Sanborne Ave stoplight onto **Sunset Blvd**. Continue 3.1 mi to **Figueroa St**.

WB: Continue on **Santa Monica Blvd** (Hwy 2) thru **BEVERLY HILLS** and **WEST LA**. Cross under I-405 into **SANTA MONICA**. Cross 9th St, then get in the **LEFT** lane, and turn **LEFT** on **Lincoln Blvd** ("To I-10") to **Olympic Blvd**, the "**END**" of US 66.

Check out the **BEVERLY HILLS** sign at Doheny Dr. Of architectural note are the **Art Moderne Police Station** and the domed **City Hall**. **$$$ ALERT**! The route crosses high-zoot **Rodeo Drive** along the way. At Wilshire, **Trader Vic's** has a long history of Polynesian ambiance. Approaching **SANTA MONICA**, scattered signs of past Route 66 life begin to emerge from the urbanscape.

WB Drivers: **Congratulations** on being true **Road Warriors**! After touring **SANTA MONICA**, use **I-10** to access the freeway system and begin your homeward trip. **Thanks** for driving **Route 66**! Come back again, real soon! **AIRPORTS: Los Angeles International** is south of **SANTA MONICA** (via I-405 to Century Blvd, or Lincoln Blvd/Hwy 1 to Sepulveda). Other airports are at **Burbank** (via I-5 north) or **Ontario** (off I-10 just west of I-15, near **SAN BERNARDINO**).

SIDE TRIPS: The "Official" end of 66 at Lincoln and **Olympic** is rather unsatisfying. There are better ways to finish your voyage. The **Will Rogers Hwy Marker**, in **Palisades Park**, is at the "T" intersection of **Santa Monica Blvd** and **Ocean**. The 14-block park tops a sheer bluff, lined with exotic palms and shrubs, overlooking the **Pacific Ocean**. The neon **Santa Monica Yacht Harbor Sign**, the gateway to the attractions of the **Santa Monica Pier**, is at **Colorado** and **Ocean**. On the pier, please visit **66 to Cali**, Dan Rice's great Rte 66 T-Shirt emporium and gift shop (the earliest on the pier). Dan is responsible for placing of the "**End of the Trail**" sign on the pier. The long rows of tall hotels that line the inland side of Ocean mirror the line of skyscrapers that mark the east end of 66. Some **30 minute** metered parking is available on Ocean; otherwise try the many **public lots** downtown for the long term or park on the pier. **RV ALERT**! The streets here are rather tight and crowded. Might be time to use the tow car (or park and walk). City INFO: www.smchamber.com or (310) 393-9825.

MILEAGE NOTE: about 9 miles on this page

EB: To **BEGIN** at the **Western Terminus** in **SANTA MONICA**: Take **I-10 EXIT 1B (**from **LA)** or **EXIT 1A (**from **Hwy 1/Pacific Coast Hwy)**. Turn at the light onto **HWY 2/Lincoln Blvd** (66 "began" here at the Hwy 1 and 2 JCT). The route turns **RIGHT** on **Santa Monica Blvd (**tour town first**)**, then continues across I-405 and thru **WEST LA** and **BEVERLY HILLS** to **WEST HOLLYWOOD**.

(see CA INTRO CA page-1)

(see MAP #5 CA page-22)

RECOMMENDED READING

These are books that have proven helpful to me in my research, or that will enhance your Route 66 experience. Where possible, I have included the author's website for the self-published books so that you may order directly from them. (asterisked books may be purchased from the Federation website). Look on the web for reviews and further information.

GUIDEBOOKS: IL: *Traveling the New, Historic Route 66 in Illinois** by John Weiss www.il66authority.com

MO: *Missouri US 66 Tour Book* by C.H. (Skip) Curtis www.birthplaceofroute66.com/bk2.html

OK: *Oklahoma Route 66** by Jim Ross /Ghost Town Press www.66maps.com

Official Oklahoma Route 66 Association Trip Guide www.oklahomaroute66.com

NM: *New Mexico Route 66 on Tour. Legendary Architecture from Glenrio to Gallup* by Don J. Unser Museum of New Mexico Press

AZ: *Route 66 Across Arizona: A Comprehensive Two-Way Guide for Touring Route 66* by Richard K. and Sherry G. Mangum Hexagon Press

CA: *Guide To Historic Route 66 in California* by Vivian Davies and Darin Kuna *OUT OF PRINT*

Finding the End of the Mother Road by Scott Piotrowski *OUT OF PRINT*

ENTIRE ROUTE: *Route 66 Dining & and Lodging Guide** An indispensable guide. GET ONE! National Historic Route 66 Federation www.national66.org

*Route 66 Map Series** 8 maps of the whole route, by Jim Ross and Jerry McClanahan Ghost Town Press www.66maps.com

*Route 66 Adventure Handbook** Drew Knowles Interesting places and attractions along 66 www.ExitHere.net

Route 66 for Kids A small, hand-produced booklet with good suggestions for kids by Emily Priddy www.kidson66.com

The Complete Route 66 Guidebook and Atlas by Bob Moore and Rich Cunningham. Two book set. Not for beginners.

ADDITIONAL READING: *Route 66: The Mother Road** by Michael Wallis (75th Anniversary Edition)

The Federation News Magazine of the National Historic Route 66 Federation. Jerry has written many articles for them (and will continue).

*The Mother Road ... Route 66** by David Knudson

Images of 66 Vols #1 and #2 by David Wickline. Great albums of modern photos along the Route.

Route 66 Remembered by Michael Karl Witzel

Route 66: The Empires of Amusement and Route 66: The Romance of the West by Thomas Arthur Repp Mock Turtle Press

American Road Magazine My Route 66 Kicks dept. www.americanroadmagazine.com

Route 66 Magazine www.route66magazine.com Check for back issues with Jerry's articles, from 1994 thru 1999. Some featured his ROOTIE ™ cartoon.

WEBSITES: There are many websites devoted to Route 66. Try an internet search and see what comes up (wow). The sites below are helpful:

www.mcjerry66.com Jerry McClanahan's Route 66 gallery website and home to the EZ66 GUIDE updates.

www.national66.org National Historic Route 66 Federation. Online store, links to other Route 66 websites and more.

www.route66photographs.com Shellee Graham's and Jim Ross' exceptional roadside images

www.route66egroup.info/index.html Yahoo Route 66 E- Group. Lots of timely 66 info, up to the minute news, links and chit chat.

www.route66guidebooks.com A site that lists all the Route 66 guidebooks currently in print.

ROUTE 66 ASSOCIATIONS: Great resources for info on Route 66 and events. Dedicated people, all. Consider joining one or more!

Route 66 Association of Illinois www.il66assoc.org

Route 66 Association of Missouri www.missouri66.org

Route 66 Association of Kansas (Riverton) Email: route66@kans.com

Kansas Historic Route 66 Association (Baxter Springs) www.ksrt66association.us

Oklahoma Route 66 Association oklahomaroute66.com

The Old Route 66 Association of Texas www.barbwiremuseum.com/TexasRoute66.htm

New Mexico Route 66 Association www.rt66nm.org

Historic Route 66 Association of Arizona www.azrt66.com

The California Route 66 Preservation Foundation www.cart66pf.org

California Historic Route 66 Association www.route66ca.org

ACKNOWLEDGEMENTS

Many members of the Route 66 community have shown me great hospitality and generosity in my 20 years of researching Route 66.

Jim Ross, Scott Piotrowski and David Clark were especially helpful in preparing this guide by sharing their wealth of knowledge in their areas of expertise, plus their gracious hospitality (can't forget Carol and Julie, either). Scott ushered me around the complex Pasadena to LA area (which is well documented in his excellent book *Finding the End of the Mother Road: Route 66 in Los Angeles County*) and David did the same on his end of '66, the Chicago area (covered in detail in his two exceptional books *Exploring Route 66 In Chicagoland* and *Route 66 In Chicago*). Jim is, of course, my valued collaborator on The Route 66 Map Series (which we have updated and improved) and the Bones of the Old Road video, neither of which would exist without his vision. His ability to organize and categorize Route 66 research inspired my own to greater heights.

Other fine folk that aided my research, or are great Route 66 people that offered moral support over the years include, but are not limited to (in no particular order): John Weiss. Delbert and Ruth Trew. Pat and Virgil Smith. Thomas and Becky Repp. Johnny "V" Meier. Kathy Anderson. Shellee Graham. Becky Ransom. Jon Robinson. Laurel Kane of Afton Station. Steve Rider. Frank Maloney. Akkey Takeuchi. Bob "Crocodile" Lyle. Carl Johnson. Cheryl Nowka. Dan Harlow. Bob Waldmire. David Rushing. Dawn Welch at the Rock Café. Sue Preston at Seaba Station. Debrah Hodkin. Don Holland. Emily Priddy. Eric Finley. Jeff Jensen. Mike Ward. Kathy Miller. Greg Laxton. Bob Harmon. Jim Conkle. Jim Powell. Marian Clark. Linda and Rocky Drake. Mark Potter. Bill and Linda Fernau. Michael Taylor. Ramona Lehman at the Munger Moss Motel. Michael and Suzanne Wallis. Rich Henry. Jeff Meyer. Pat and Jennifer Bremer. Ron Jones. Ken Turmel. Glenda and Tommy Pike. John Turnbull. Kathy Miller. Fran Houser at the Midpoint Café in Vega. Dale and Hilda Bakke. Guy Randall. Skip Curtis. Drew Knowles. Elaine Downing. The members of the Route 66 E-Group. (Please forgive me if I've forgotten anyone).

I cannot forget all the dedicated volunteers at the many Route 66 museums and associations, and the many business owners along the highway who work hard to keep our Route 66 icons alive. They are the backbone of the Route 66 renaissance.

And of course, David and Mary Lou Knudson, without whom this guide would not have been possible.

This book is dedicated to my mother, Reba McClanahan (for years of moral support in my Route 66 endeavors) and my father, Don McClanahan (for driving us on those Route 66 vacations while my kid brother Steve and I drove him nuts.)